ROBINSON CRUSOE

BARNES & NOBLE CLASSICS

Other Works by Daniel Defoe

MOLL FLANDERS
A JOURNAL OF THE PLAGUE YEAR
ROXANA
MEMOIRS OF A CAVALIER
CAPTAIN SINGLETON
CAPTAIN JACK

ROBINSON CRUSOE

Daniel Defoe

BARNES
&NOBLE
BOOKS
NEW YORK

1996 Barnes & Noble Books

ISBN 0-76070-402-3 *casebound*
ISBN 0-76070-401-5 *trade paperback*

Printed and bound in the United States of America

02 03 04 05 MC 20 19 18 17 16 15 14 13 12
01 02 03 04 TP 12 11 10 9 8 7 6 5 4 3 2

BVG

The stock for this book is milled acid-free for archival durability.
It is manufactured as elemental chlorine free paper in a process that avoids the
discharge of toxic by-products into the environment.

I WAS BORN in the year 1632, in the city of York, of a good family, though not of that country, my father being a foreigner of Bremen, named Kreutznaer, who settled first at Hull. He got a good estate by merchandise, and leaving off his trade, lived afterwards at York; from whence he had married my mother, whose relations were named Robinson, a very good family in that country, and after whom I was so called, that is to say, Robinson Kreutznaer; but by the usual corruption of words in England, we are now called, nay, we call ourselves, and write our name, Crusoe; and so my companions always called me.

I had two elder brothers, one of whom was lieutenant-colonel, to an English regiment of foot in Flanders, formerly commanded by the famous Colonel Lockhart, and was killed at the battle near Dunkirk against the Spaniards. What became of my second brother, I never knew, any more than my father and mother did know what was become of me.

Being the third son of the family, and not bred to any trade, my head began to be filled very early with rambling thoughts. My father, who was very aged, had given me a competent share of learning, as far as house education and a country free school generally go, and designed me for the law; but I would be satisfied with nothing but going to sea; and my inclination to this led me so strongly against the will, nay, the commands of my father, and against all the entreaties and persuasions of my mother and other friends, that there seemed to be something fatal in that propension of nature, tending directly to the life of misery which was to befall me.

My father, a wise and grave man, gave me serious and excellent counsel against what he foresaw was my design. He called me one morning into his chamber, where he was confined by the gout, and expostulated very warmly with me upon this subject: he asked me what reasons, more than a mere wandering inclination, I had for leaving his house, and my native country, where I might be well introduced, and had a prospect of raising my fortune, by application and industry, with a life of ease and pleasure. He told me it was men of desperate fortunes, on one hand, or of superior fortunes, on the other, who went abroad upon adventures, aspiring to rise by enterprise, and make themselves famous in undertakings of a nature out of the common road; that these things were all either too far above me, or too far below me; that mine was the middle state, or what might be called the upper station of low life, which he had found, by long experience, was the best state in the world, the most suited to human happiness; not exposed to the miseries and hardships, the labour and sufferings, of the mechanic part of mankind, and not embarrassed with the pride, luxury, ambition, and envy of the upper part of mankind: he told me, I might judge of the happiness of this state by one thing, viz., that this was the state of life which all other people envied; that kings have frequently lamented the miserable consequences of being born to great things, and wished they had been placed in the middle of two extremes, between the mean and the great; that the wise man gave his testimony to this as the just standard of true felicity, when he prayed to have "neither poverty nor riches."

He bade me observe it, and I should always find, that the calamities of life were shared among the upper and lower part of mankind; but that the middle station had the fewest disasters, and was not exposed to so many vicissitudes as the higher or lower part of mankind: nay, they were not subjected to so many distempers and uneasinesses, either of body or mind, as those were, who, by vicious living, luxury, and extravagancies, on one hand, or by hard labour, want of necessaries, and mean and insufficient diet, on the other hand, bring distempers upon themselves by the natural consequences of their way of living; that the middle station of life was calculated for all kind of virtues, and all kind of enjoyments; that peace and plenty were the handmaids of a middle fortune; that temperance, moderation, quietness, health, society, all agreeable diversions, and all desirable pleasures were the blessings attending the middle station of life; that this way men went silently and smoothly through the world, and comfortably out of it, not embarrassed with the labours of the hands or of the head, not sold to the life of slavery for daily bread, or harassed with perplexed circumstances, which rob the soul of peace, and the body of rest; not enraged with the passion of envy, or secret burning lust of ambition for great things; but, in easy circumstances, sliding gently through the world, and sensibly tasting the sweets of living, without the bitter; feeling that they are happy, and learning by every day's experience, to know it more sensibly.

After this he pressed me earnestly, and in the most affectionate manner, not to play the young man, nor to precipitate myself into miseries which nature and the station of life I was born in, seemed to have provided against; that I was under no necessity of seeking my bread; that he would do well for me, and endeavour to enter me fairly into the station of life which he had been just recommending to me; and that if I was not very easy and happy in the world, it must be my mere fate, or fault, that must hinder it; and that he should have nothing to answer for, having thus discharged his duty in warning me against measures which he knew would be to my hurt: in a word, that as he would do very kind things for me if I would stay and settle at home, as he directed; so he would not have so much hand in my misfortunes as to give me any encouragement to go away: and, to close all, he told me I had my elder brother for an example, to whom he had used the same earnest persuasions to keep him from going into the Low Country wars; but could not prevail, his young desires prompting him to run into the army, where he was killed; and though, he said, he would not cease to pray for me, yet he would venture to say to me, that if I did take this foolish step, God would not bless me; and I would have leisure, hereafter, to reflect upon having neglected his counsel, when there might be none to assist in my recovery.

I observed, in the last part of his discourse, which was truly prophetic, though, I suppose, my father did not know it to be so himself; I say, I observed the tears run down his face very plentifully, especially when he spoke of my brother who was killed; and that, when he spoke of my having leisure to repent, and none to assist me, he was so moved that he broke off the discourse, and told me his heart was so full, he could say no more to me.

I was sincerely affected with this discourse, as indeed who could be otherwise? and I resolved not to think of going abroad any more, but to settle at home, according to my father's desire. But, alas! a few days wore it all off; and, in short, to prevent any of my father's farther importunities, in a few weeks after, I resolved to run quite away from him. However, I did not act so hastily neither, as my first heat of resolution prompted, but I took my mother at a time when I thought her a little pleasanter than ordinary, and told her, that my thoughts were so entirely bent upon seeing the world, that I should never settle to anything with resolution enough to go through with it, and my father had better give me his consent, than force me to go without it; that I was now eighteen years old, which was too late to go apprentice to a trade, or clerk to an attorney; that I was sure, if I did I should never serve out my time, and I should certainly run away from my master before my time was out, and go to sea; and if she would speak to my father to let me make but one voyage abroad, if I came home again, and did not like it, I would go no more, and I would promise, by a double diligence, to recover the time I had lost.

This put my mother into a great passion: she told me, she knew it would be to no purpose to speak to my father upon any such a subject; that he knew too well what was my interest, to give his consent to anything so much for my hurt; and that she wondered how I could think of any such thing, after the discourse I had had with my father, and such kind and tender expressions, as she knew my father had used to me; and that, in short, if I would ruin myself, there was no help for me; but I might depend I should never have their consent to it: that, for her part, she would not have so much hand in my destruction; and I should never have it to say, that my mother was willing when my father was not.

Though my mother refused to move it to my father, yet I heard afterwards, that she reported all the discourse to him; and that my father, after showing a great concern at it, said to her, with a sigh, "That boy might be happy, if he would stay at home; but if he goes abroad, he will be the most miserable wretch that ever was born: I can give no consent to it."

It was not till almost a year after this that I broke loose, though in the mean time I continued obstinately deaf to all proposals of settling to business, and frequently expostulating with my father and mother about their being so positively determined against what they knew my inclination prompted me to. But being one day at Hull, whither I went casually, and without any purpose of making an elopement at that time, and one of my companions then going to London by sea in his father's ship, and prompting me to go with them by the common allurement of seafaring men, viz., that it should cost me nothing for my passage, I consulted neither father nor mother any more, nor so much as sent them word of it; but left them to hear of it as they might, without asking God's blessing, or my father's, without any consideration of circumstances or consequences, and in an ill hour, God knows.

O N THE 1ST of September, 1651, I went on board a ship bound for London. Never any young adventurer's misfortunes, I believe, began younger, or continued longer than mine. The ship had no sooner got out of the Humber, than the wind began to blow, and the waves to rise, in a most frightful manner; and as I had never been at sea before, I was most inexpressibly sick in body, and terrified in mind: I began now seriously to reflect upon what I had done, and how justly I was overtaken by the judgment of Heaven, for wickedly leaving my father's house. All the good counsels of my parents, my father's tears, and my mother's entreaties, came now fresh into my mind; and my conscience, which was not yet come to the pitch of hardness to which it has been since, reproached me with the contempt of advice, and the abandonment of my duty.

All this while the storm increased, and the sea, which I had never been upon before, went very high, though nothing like what I have seen many times since; no, nor what I saw a few days after; but, such as it was, enough to affect me then, who was but a young sailor, and had never known anything of the matter. I expected every wave would have swallowed us up, and that every time the ship fell down, as I thought, into the trough or hollow of the sea, we should never rise more; and in this agony of mind I made many vows and resolutions, that if it would please God to spare my life this voyage, if ever I got my foot once on dry land, I would go directly home to my father, and never set it into a ship again, while I lived; that I would take his advice, and never run myself into such miseries as these any more. Now I saw plainly the goodness of his observations about the middle station of life; how easy, how comfortable, he had lived all his days, and never had been exposed to tempests at sea or troubles on shore; and I resolved that I would, like a true repenting prodigal, go home to my father.

These wise and sober thoughts continued during the storm, and indeed some time after; but the next day, as the wind was abated, and the sea calmer, I began to be a little inured to it. However, I was very grave that day, being also a little sea-sick still: but towards night the weather cleared up, the wind was quite over, and a charming fine evening followed; the sun went down perfectly clear, and rose so the next morning; and having little or no wind, and a smooth sea, the sun shining upon it, the sight was, as I thought, the most delightful that I ever saw.

I had slept well in the night, and was now no more sea-sick, but very cheerful, looking with wonder upon the sea that was so rough and terrible the day before, and could be so calm and pleasant in a little time after.

And now, lest my good resolution should continue, my companion, who had indeed enticed me away, came to me and said, Well, Bob, clapping me on the shoulder, how do you do after it? I warrant you you were frightened, wa'n't you, last night, when it blew but a cap-full of wind?—A cap-full, do you call it? said I; 'twas a terrible storm.—A storm, you fool! replies he, do you call that a storm? Why, it was nothing at all; give us but a good ship, and sea-room, and we think nothing of such a squall of wind as that: you are but a fresh-water sailor, Bob; come, let us make a bowl of punch, and we'll forget all that. D'ye see what charming weather 'tis now? To make short this sad part of my story, we went the way of all sailors; the punch was made, and I was made drunk with it; and in that one night's wickedness I drowned all my repentance, all my reflections upon my past conduct, and all my resolutions for the future. In a word, as the sea was returned to its smoothness of surface and settled calmness by the abatement of the storm, so the hurry of my thoughts being over, my fears and apprehensions of being swallowed up by the sea forgotten, and the current of my former desires returned, I entirely forgot the vows and promises I had made in my distress. I found, indeed, some intervals of reflection; and serious thoughts did, as it were, endeavour to return again sometimes; but I shook them off and roused myself from them, as it were from a distemper, and, applying myself to drink and company, soon mastered the return of those fits—for so I called them; and had in five or six days got as complete a victory over conscience as any young sinner, that resolved not to be troubled with it, could desire. But I was to have another trial for it still; and Providence, as in such cases generally it does, resolved to leave me entirely without excuse: for if I would not take this for a deliverance, the next was to be such a one as the worst and most hardened wretch among us would confess both the danger and the mercy of. The sixth day of our being at sea we came into Yarmouth Roads; the wind having been contrary and the weather calm, we had made but little way since the storm. Here we were obliged to come to an anchor, and here we lay, the wind continuing contrary, viz., at south-west, for seven or eight days, during which time a great many ships from Newcastle came into the same roads, as the common harbour where the ships might wait for a wind for the River Thames. We had not, however, rid here so long, but we should have tided up the river, but that the wind blew too fresh; and, after we had lain four or five days, blew very hard. However, the roads being reckoned as good as a harbour, the anchorage good, and our ground tackle very strong, our men were unconcerned, and not in the least apprehensive of danger, but spent the time in rest and mirth, after the manner of the sea. But the eighth day, in the morning, the wind increased, and we had all hands at work to strike our topmasts, and make everything snug and close, that the ship might ride as easy as possible. By noon the sea went very high indeed, and our ship rode forecastle in, shipped several seas, and we thought, once or twice, our anchor had come home; upon which our master ordered out the sheet anchor; so that we rode with two anchors ahead, and the cables veered out to the better end.

By this time it blew a terrible storm indeed; and now I began to see terror and amazement in the faces of even the seamen themselves. The master was vigilant in the business of preserving the ship; but, as he went in and out of his cabin by me, I could hear him softly say to himself several times, Lord, be merciful to us! we shall be all lost; we shall be all undone! and the like. During these first hurries I was stupid, lying still in my cabin, which was in the steerage, and cannot describe my temper. I could ill reassume the first penitence, which I had so apparently trampled upon, and hardened myself against; I thought that the bitterness of death had been past, and that this would be nothing, too, like the first: but when the master himself came by me, as I said just now, and said we should be all lost, I was dreadfully frightened. I got up out of my cabin, and looked out, but such a dismal sight I never saw; the sea went mountains high, and broke upon us every three or four minutes. When I could look about, I could see nothing but distress around us; two ships, that rid near us, we found had cut their masts by the board, being deeply laden; and our men cried out that a ship, which rid about a mile ahead of us, was foundered. Two more ships being driven from their anchors, were run out of the roads to sea, at all adventures, and that with not a mast standing. The light ships fared the best, as not so much labouring in the sea; but two or three of them drove, and came close to us, running away, with only their spritsails out, before the wind. Toward evening, the mate and boatswain begged the master of our ship to let them cut away the foremast, which he was very loath to do; but the boatswain protesting to him, that if he did not, the ship would founder, he consented; and when they had cut away the foremast, the mainmast stood so loose, and shook the ship so much, they were obliged to cut it away also, and make a clear deck.

Any one may judge what a condition I must be in at all this, who was but a young sailor, and who had been in such a fright before at but a little. But if I can express, at this distance, the thoughts I had about me at that time, I was in tenfold more horror of mind upon account of my former convictions, and the having returned from them to the resolutions I had wickedly taken at first, than I was at death itself; and these, added to the terror of the storm, put me into such a condition, that I can by no words describe it; but the worst was not come yet; the storm continued with such fury, that the seamen themselves acknowledged they had never known a worse. We had a good ship, but she was deep laden, and so swallowed in the sea, that the seamen every now and then cried out she would founder. It was my advantage, in one respect, that I did not know what they meant by *founder*, till I inquired. However, the storm was so violent, that I saw what is not often seen, the master, the boatswain, and some others, more sensible than the rest, at their prayers, and expecting every moment the ship would go to the bottom. In the middle of the night, and under all the rest of our distresses, one of the men, that had been down on purpose to see, cried out, we had sprung a leak; another said there was four feet water in the hold. Then all hands were called to the pump. At that very word my heart, as I thought, died within me, and I fell backwards upon the side of my bed, where I sat in the cabin. However, the men roused me, and told me that I, who was able to do nothing before, was as well able to pump as another: at which I stirred up and went to the pump, and worked very heartily. While this was doing, the master, seeing some light colliers, who, not able to ride out the storm, were obliged to slip and run away to sea, and would not come near us, ordered us to fire a gun, as a signal of distress. I, who knew nothing what that meant, was so surprised, that I thought the ship had broke, or some dreadful thing had happened. In a word, I was so surprised, that I fell down in a swoon. As this was a time when everybody had his own life to think of, no one minded me, or what was become of me; but another man stepped up to the pump, and thrusting me aside with his foot, let me lie, thinking I had been dead; and it was a great while before I came to myself.

We worked on; but the water increasing in the hold, it was apparent that the ship would founder; and though the storm began to abate a little, yet as it was not possible she could swim till we might run into a port, so the master continued firing guns for help; and a light ship, who had rid it out just ahead of us, ventured a boat out to help us. It was with the utmost hazard that the boat came near us, but it was impossible for us to get on board, or for the boat to lie near the ship's side; till at last the men rowing very heartily, and venturing their lives to save ours, our men cast them a rope over the stern with a buoy to it, and then veered it out a great length, which they, after great labour and hazard, took hold of, and we hauled them close under our stern, and got all into their boat. It was to no purpose for them or us, after we were in the boat, to think of reaching their own ship; so all agreed to let her drive, and only to pull her towards shore as much as we could: and our master promised them, that if the boat was staved upon shore, he would make it good to their master; so partly rowing, and partly driving, our boat went away to the northward, sloping towards the shore almost as far as Winterton-Ness.

We were not much more than a quarter of an hour out of our ship when we saw her sink; and then I understood, for the first time, what was meant by a ship foundering in the sea. I must acknowledge, I had hardly eyes to look up when the seamen told me she was sinking; for, from that moment, they rather put me into the boat, than that I might be said to go in. My heart was, as it were, dead within me, partly with fright, partly with horror of mind, and the thoughts of what was yet before me.

While we were in this condition, the men yet labouring at the oar to bring the boat near the shore, we could see (when, our boat mounting the waves, we were able to see the shore) a great many people running along the strand, to assist us when we should come near; but we made slow way towards the shore; nor were we able to reach it, till, being past the lighthouse at Winterton, the shore falls off to the westward, towards Cromer, and so the land broke off a little the violence of the wind. Here we got in, and, though not without much difficulty, got all safe on shore, and walked afterwards on foot to Yarmouth; where, as unfortunate men, we were used with great humanity, as well by the magistrates of the town, who assigned us good quarters, as by the particular merchants and owners of ships: and had money given us sufficient to carry us either to London or back to Hull, as we thought fit.

Had I now had the sense to have gone back to Hull, and have gone home, I had been happy: and my father, an emblem of our blessed Saviour's parable, had even killed the fatted calf for me: for, hearing the ship I went in was cast away in Yarmouth Roads, it was a great while before he had any assurance that I was not drowned.

But my ill fate pushed me on with an obstinacy that nothing could resist; and though I had several times loud calls from my reason, and my more composed judgment, to go home, yet I had no power to do it.— I know not what to call this, nor will I urge that it is a secret, overruling decree, that hurries us on to be the instruments of our own destruction, even though it be before us, and that we rush upon it with our eyes open. Certainly, nothing but some such decreed unavoidable misery attending, and which it was impossible for me to escape, could have pushed me forward against the calm reasonings and persuasions of my most retired thoughts, and against two such visible instructions as I had met with in my first attempt.

My comrade, who had helped to harden me before, and who was the master's son, was now less forward than I: the first time he spoke to me after we were at Yarmouth, which was not till two or three days, for we were separated in the town to several quarters; I say, the first time he saw me, it appeared his tone was altered, and, looking very melancholy, and shaking his head, he asked me how I did; telling his father who I was, and how I had come this voyage only for a trial, in order to go farther abroad. His father, turning to me, with a grave and concerned tone, Young man, says he, you ought never to go to sea any more; you ought to take this for a plain and visible token, that you are not to be a seafaring man.—Why, sir? said I; will you go to sea no more?—That is another case, said he; it is my calling, and therefore my duty; but as you made this voyage for a trial, you see what a taste Heaven has given you of what you are to expect if you persist. Perhaps this has all befallen us on your account, like Jonah in the ship of the Tarshish.—Pray, continues he, what are you, and on what account did you go to sea? Upon that I told him some of my story; at the end of which he burst out with a strange kind of passion. What had I done, said he, that such an unhappy wretch should have come into my ship? I would not set my foot in the same ship with thee again for a thousand pounds. This indeed was, as I said, an excursion of his spirits, which were yet agitated by the sense of his loss, and was farther than he could have authority to go.—However, he afterwards talked very gravely to me; exhorted me to go back to my father, and not tempt Providence to my ruin; told me, I might see a visible hand of Heaven against me; and, young man, said he, depend upon it, if you do not go back, wherever you go, you will meet with nothing but disasters and disappointments, till your father's words are fulfilled upon you.

We parted soon after, for I made him little answer, and I saw him no more: which way he went, I know not: as for me, having some money in my pocket, I travelled to London by land; and there, as well as on the road, had many struggles with myself what course of life I should take, and whether I should go home or go to sea. As to going home, shame opposed the best motions that offered to my thoughts; and it immediately occurred to me how I should be laughed at among the neighbours, and should be ashamed to see, not my father and mother only, but even everybody else. From whence I have often since observed, how incongruous and irrational the common temper of mankind is, especially of youth, to that reason which ought to guide them in such cases, viz., that they are not ashamed to sin, and yet are ashamed to repent; not ashamed of the action, for which they ought justly to be esteemed fools; but are ashamed of the returning, which only can make them be esteemed wise men.

In this state of life, however, I remained some time, uncertain what measures to take, and what course of life to lead. An irresistible reluctance continued to going home; and as I stayed awhile, the remembrance of the distress I had been in wore off; and as that abated, the little motion I had in my desires to a return wore off with it, till at last I quite laid aside the thoughts of it, and looked out for a voyage. That evil influence which carried me first away from my father's house, that hurried me into the wild and indigested notion of raising my fortune, and that impressed those conceits so forcibly upon me, as to make me deaf to all good advice, and to the entreaties, and even the commands of my father; I say, the same influence, whatever it was, presented the most unfortunate of all enterprises to my view; and I went on board a vessel bound to the coast of Africa; or, as our sailors vulgarly call it, a voyage to Guinea.

It was my great misfortune, that in all these adventures I did not ship myself as a sailor; whereby, though I might indeed have worked a little harder than ordinary, yet, at the same time, I had learned the duty and office of a foremastman, and in time might have qualified myself for a mate or lieutenant, if not a master: but as it was always my fate to choose for the worse, so I did here; for having money in my pocket, and good clothes upon my back, I would always go on board in the habit of a gentleman; and so I neither had any business in the ship, nor learned to do any. It was my lot, first of all, to fall into pretty good company in London; which does not always happen to such loose and misguided young fellows as I then was; the devil, generally, not omitting to lay some snare for them very early. But it was not so with me: I first fell acquainted with the master of a ship, who had been on the coast of Guinea, and who, having had very good success there, was resolved to go again. He, taking a fancy to my conversation, which was not at all disagreeable at that time, and hearing me say I had a mind to see the world, told me, that if I would go the voyage with him, I should be at no expense; I should be his messmate and his companion; and if I could carry anything with me, I should have all the advantage of it that the trade would admit; and perhaps I might meet with some encouragement. I embraced the offer, and entering into a strict friendship with this captain, who was an honest and plain-dealing man, I went the voyage with him, and carried a small adventure with me; which, by the disinterested honesty of my friend the captain, I increased very considerably; for I carried about forty pounds in such toys and trifles as the captain directed me to buy. This forty pounds I had mustered together by the assistance of some of my relations whom I corresponded with: and who, I believe, got my father, or, at least, my mother, to contribute so much as that to my first adventure. This was the only voyage which I may say was successful in all my adventures, and which I owe to the integrity and honesty of my friend the captain; under whom I also got a competent knowledge of mathematics and the rules of navigation, learned how to keep an account of the ship's course, take an observation, and, in short, to understand some things that were needful to be understood by a sailor; for, as he took delight to instruct me, I took delight to learn; and, in a word, this voyage made me both a sailor and a merchant: for I brought home five pounds nine ounces of gold dust for my adventure, which yielded me in London, at my return, almost three hundred pounds, and this filled me with those aspiring thoughts which have since so completed my ruin. Yet even in this voyage I had my misfortunes too; particularly that I was continually sick, being thrown into a violent calenture by the excessive heat of the climate; our principal trading being upon the coast, from the latitude of fifteen degrees north, even to the Line itself.

I WAS now set up for a Guinea trader; and my friend, to my great misfortune, dying soon after his arrival, I resolved to go the same voyage again; and I embarked in the same vessel with one who was his mate in the former voyage, and had now got the command of the ship. This was the unhappiest voyage that ever man made; for though I did not carry quite a hundred pounds of my new-gained wealth, so that I had two hundred pounds left, and which I lodged with my friend's widow, who was very just to me, yet I fell into terrible misfortunes in this voyage: and the first was this, viz.—our ship, making her course towards the Canary Islands, or rather between those islands and the African shore, was surprised, in the gray of the morning, by a Turkish rover, of Sallee, who gave chase to us with all the sail she could make. We crowded also as much canvas as our yards would spread, or our masts carry, to get clear; but finding the pirate gained upon us, and would certainly come up with us in a few hours, we prepared to fight, our ship having twelve guns and the rover eighteen. About three in the afternoon he came up with us; and bringing to, by mistake, just athwart our quarter, instead of athwart our stern, as he intended, we brought eight of our guns to bear on that side, and poured in a broadside upon him, which made him sheer off again, after returning our fire and pouring in also his small shot from near two hundred men which he had on board. However, we had not a man touched, all our men keeping close. He prepared to attack us again, and we to defend ourselves; but laying us on board the next time upon our other quarter, he entered sixty men upon our decks, who immediately fell to cutting and hacking the sails and rigging. We plied them with small shot, half-pikes, powder-chests, and such like, and cleared our deck of them twice. However, to cut short this melancholy part of our story, our ship being disabled, and three of our men killed and eight wounded, we were obliged to yield, and were carried all prisoners into Sallee, a port belonging to the Moors.

The usage I had there was not so dreadful as at first I apprehended: nor was I carried up the country to the emperor's court, as the rest of our men were, but was kept by the captain of the rover as his proper prize, and made his slave, being young and nimble, and fit for his business. At this surprising change of my circumstances, from a merchant to a miserable slave, I was perfectly overwhelmed; and now looked back upon my father's prophetic discourse to me, that I should be miserable, and have none to relieve me; which I thought was now so effectually brought to pass, that it could not be worse; that now the hand of Heaven had overtaken me, and I was undone, without redemption. But, alas! this was but a taste of the misery I was to go through, as will appear in the sequel of this story.

As my new patron, or master, had taken me home to his house, so I was in hopes he would take me with him when he went to sea again, believing that it would, some time or other, be his fate to be taken by a Spanish or Portuguese man of war, and that then I should be set at liberty. But this hope of mine was soon taken away, for when he went to sea, he left me on shore to look after his little garden, and do the common drudgery of slaves about his house; and when he came home again from his cruise, he ordered me to lie in the cabin, to look after the ship.

Here I meditated nothing but my escape, and what method I might take to effect it, but found no way that had the least probability in it. Nothing presented to make the supposition of it rational; for I had nobody to communicate it to that would embark with me; no fellow-slave, no Englishman, Irishman, or Scotchman there but myself; so that for two years, though I often pleased myself with the imagination, yet I never had the least encouraging prospect of putting it in practice.

After about two years, an odd circumstance presented itself, which put the old thought of making some attempt for my liberty again in my head. My patron lying at home longer than usual, without fitting out his ship, which, as I heard, was for want of money, he used constantly, once or twice a week, sometimes oftener, if the weather was fair, to take the ship's pinnacle, and go out into the road a fishing; and as he always took me and a young Moresco with him to row the boat, we made him very merry, and I proved very dexterous in catching fish, insomuch that sometimes he would send me with a Moor, one of his kinsmen, and the youth, the Moresco, as they called him, to catch a dish of fish for him.

It happened one time, that going a fishing in a stark calm morning, a fog rose so thick, that though we were not half a league from the shore, we lost sight of it; and rowing, we knew not whither, or which way, we laboured all day, and all the next night, and when the morning came, we found we had pulled off to sea, instead of pulling in for the shore, and that we were at least two leagues from the shore: however, we got well in again, though with a great deal of labour, and some danger, for the wind began to blow pretty fresh in the morning; but particularly we were all very hungry.

But our patron, warned by this disaster, resolved to take more care of himself for the future; and having lying by him the longboat of our English ship he had taken, he resolved he would not go a fishing any more without a compass and some provision; so he ordered the carpenter of the ship, who was an English slave, to build a little state-room or cabin in the middle of the longboat, like that of a barge, with a place to stand behind it, to steer and haul home the main sheet, and room before for a hand or two to stand and work the sails. She sailed with what we call a shoulder-of-mutton sail, and the boom jibbed over the top of the cabin, which lay very snug and low, and had in it room for him to lie, with a slave or two, and a table to eat on, with some small lockers to put in some bottles of such liquor as he thought fit to drink, and particularly his bread, rice, and coffee.

We went frequently out with this boat a fishing, and as I was most dexterous to catch fish for him, he never went without me. It happened that he had appointed to go out in this boat, either for pleasure or for fish, with two or three Moors of some distinction in that place, and for whom he had provided extraordinarily, and had therefore sent on board the boat, overnight, a larger store of provisions than ordinary, and had ordered me to get ready three fusees, with powder and shot, which were on board his ship, for that they designed some sport of fowling as well as fishing.

I got all things ready as he directed, and waited the next morning with the boat washed clean, her ensign and pendants out, and everything to accommodate his guests: when, by and by, my patron came on board alone, and told me his guests had put off going, upon some business that fell out, and ordered me with a man and boy, as usual, to go out with the boat, and catch them some fish, for that his friends were to sup at his house; and commanded, that as soon as I had got some fish, I should bring it home to his house; all which I prepared to do.

This moment my former notions of deliverance darted into my thoughts, for now I found I was like to have a little ship at my command; and my master being gone, I prepared to furnish myself, not for a fishing business, but for a voyage; though I knew not, neither did I so much as consider, whither I should steer; for any where, to get out of that place, was my way.

My first contrivance was to make a pretence to speak to this Moor, to get something for our subsistence on board; for I told him we must not presume to eat of our patron's bread: he said that was true; so he brought a large basket of rusk or biscuit, of their kind, and three jars with fresh water, into the boat. I knew where my patron's case of bottles stood, which it was evident, by the make, were taken out of some English prize, and I conveyed them into the boat while the Moor was on shore, as if they had been there before for our master. I conveyed also a great lump of beeswax into the boat, which weighed above half a hundred weight, with a parcel of twine or thread, a hatchet, a saw, and a hammer, all which were of great use to us afterwards, especially the wax, to make candles. Another trick I tried upon him, which he innocently came into also: his name was Ismael, whom they call Muley, or Moley: so I called to him; Moley, said I, our patron's guns are on board the boat, can you not get a little powder and shot? it may be we may kill some alcamies (fowls like our curlews) for ourselves, for I know he keeps the gunner's stores in the ship. Yes, says he, I will bring some; and accordingly he brought a great leather pouch, which held about a pound and a half of powder, or rather more, and another of shot, that had five or six pounds, with some bullets, and put all into the boat: at the same time I found some powder of my master's in the great cabin, with which I filled one of the large bottles in the case, which was almost empty, pouring what was in it into another; and thus furnished with everything needful, we sailed out of the port to fish. The castle, which is at the entrance of the port, knew who we were, and took no notice of us; and we were not above a mile out of the port, before we hauled in our sail, and set us down to fish. The wind blew from N.N.E., which was contrary to my desire; for, had it blown southerly, I had been sure to have made the coast of Spain, and at last reached the bay of Cadiz: but my resolutions were, blow which way it would, I would be gone from the horrid place where I was, and leave the rest to fate.

After we had fished some time and catched nothing, for when I had fish on my hook I would not pull them up, that he might not see them, I said to the Moor, This will not do; our master will not be thus served; we must stand farther off. He, thinking no harm, agreed; and being at the head of the boat, set the sails; and as I had the helm, I run the boat near a league farther, and then brought to, as if I would fish. Then giving the boy the helm, I stepped forward to where the Moor was, and I took him by surprise, with my arm under his waist, and tossed him clear overboard into the sea. He rose immediately, for he swam like a cork, and called to me, begged to be taken in, and told me he would go all the world over with me. He swam so strong after the boat, that he would have reached me very quickly, there being but little wind; upon which I stepped into the cabin, and fetching one of the fowling-pieces, I presented it at him, and told him I had done him no hurt, and if he would be quiet, I would do him none: But, said I, you swim well enough to reach the shore, and the sea is calm; make the best of your way to shore, and I will do you no harm; but if you come near the boat, I will shoot you through the head; for I am resolved to have my liberty. So he turned himself about, and swam for the shore; and I make no doubt but he reached it with ease, for he was an excellent swimmer.

I could have been content to have taken this Moor with me, and have drowned the boy, but there was no venturing to trust him. When he was gone I turned to the boy, whom they called Xury, and said to him, Xury, if you will be faithful to me I will make you a great man; but if you will not stroke your face to be true to me (that is, swear by Mahomet and his father's beard), I must throw you into the sea too. The boy smiled in my face, and spoke so innocently, that I could not mistrust him; and swore to be faithful to me, and go all over the world with me.

While I was in view of the Moor that was swimming, I stood out directly to sea with the boat, rather stretching to windward, that they might think me gone towards the Strait's mouth (as indeed any one that had been in their wits must have been supposed to do); for who would have supposed we were sailing on to the southward, to the truly Barbarian coast, where whole nations of Negroes were sure to surround us with their canoes, and destroy us; where we could never once go on shore but we should be devoured by savage beasts, or more merciless savages of human kind?

But as soon as it grew dusk in the evening, I changed my course, and steered directly south and by east, bending my course a little towards the east, that I might keep in with the shore; and having a fair fresh gale of wind, and a smooth quiet sea, I made such sail, that I believe by the next day, at three o'clock in the afternoon, when I made the land, I could not be less than one hundred and fifty miles south of Sallee, quite beyond the Emperor of Morocco's dominions, or indeed of any other king thereabout; for we saw no people.

Yet such was the fright I had taken at the Moors, and the dreadful apprehensions I had of falling into their hands, that I would not stop, or go on shore, or come to an anchor, the wind continuing fair, till I had sailed in that manner five days; and then the wind shifting to the southward, I concluded also that if any of our vessels were in chase of me, they also would now give over: so I ventured to make to the coast, and came to an anchor in the mouth of a little river; I knew not what or where, neither what latitude, what country, what nation, or what river. I neither saw, nor desired to see, any people; the principal thing I wanted was fresh water. We came into this creek in the evening, resolving to swim on shore as soon as it was dark, and discover the country: but as soon as it was quite dark, we heard such dreadful noises of the barking, roaring, and howling of wild creatures, of we knew not what kinds, that the poor boy was ready to die with fear, and begged of me not to go on shore till day. Well, Xury, said I, then I will not; but it may be, we may see men by day, who will be as bad to us as those lions. Then we may give them the shoot-gun, says Xury, laughing; make them run away. Such English Xury spoke by conversing among us slaves. However, I was glad to see the boy so cheerful, and I gave him a dram out of our patron's case of bottles to cheer him up. After all, Xury's advice was good, and I took it. We dropped our little anchor, and lay still all night. I say still, for we slept none; for in two or three hours we saw vast creatures, (we knew not what to call them,) of many sorts, come down to the sea-shore, and run into the water, wallowing and washing themselves, for the pleasure of cooling themselves; and they made such hideous howlings and yellings, that I never indeed heard the like.

Xury was dreadfully frightened, and indeed so was I too; but we were both more frightened when we heard one of these mighty creatures swimming towards our boat: we could not see him, but we might hear him by his blowing, to be a monstrous, huge, and furious beast. Xury said it was a lion, and it might be so, for aught I know; but poor Xury cried to me to weigh the anchor and row away. No, says I, Xury; we can slip our cable with a buoy to it, and go off to sea; they cannot follow us far. I had no sooner said so, but I perceived the creature (whatever it was) within two oars' length, which something surprised me; however, I immediately stepped to the cabin door, and taking up my gun, fired at him; upon which he immediately turned about, and swam to the shore again.

But it is impossible to describe the horrible noises, and hideous cries and howlings that were raised, as well upon the edge of the shore as higher within the country, upon the noise or report of the gun; a thing, I believe, those creatures had never heard before. This convinced me there was no going on shore for us in the night upon that coast; and how to venture on shore in the day, was another question too; for to have fallen into the hands of any of the savages, had been as bad as to have fallen into the paws of lions and tigers; at least, we were equally apprehensive of the danger of it.

Be that as it would, we were obliged to go on shore somewhere or other for water, for we had not a pint left in the boat; when and where to get it was the point. Xury said, if I would let him go on shore with one of the jars, he would find if there was any water, and bring some to me. I asked him why he would go; why I should not go, and he stay in the boat. The boy answered with so much affection, that he made me love him ever after. Says he, if wild mans come, they eat me, you go away.—Well, Xury, said I, we will both go; and if the wild mans come, we will kill them; they shall eat neither of us. So I gave Xury a piece of rusk bread to eat, and a dram out of our patron's case of bottles, which I mentioned before; and we hauled in the boat as near the shore as we thought was proper, and so waded to shore, carrying nothing but our arms, and two jars for water.

I did not care to go out of sight of the boat, fearing the coming of canoes with savages down the river; but the boy, seeing a low place about a mile up the country, rambled to it; and, by and by, I saw him come running towards me. I thought he was pursued by some savage, or frightened by some wild beast, and I therefore ran forwards to help him; but when I came nearer to him, I saw something hanging over his shoulders, which was a creature that he had shot, like a hare, but different in colour, and longer legs: however, we were very glad of it, and it was very good meat: but the great joy that poor Xury came with, was to tell me he had found good water, and seen no wild mans.

But we found afterwards that we need not take such pains for water; for a little higher up the creek where we were, we found the water fresh when the tide was out, which flowed but a little way up; so we filled our jars, and having a fire, feasted on the hare we had killed; and prepared to go on our way, having seen no footsteps of any human creature in that part of the country.

As I had been one voyage to this coast before, I knew very well that the islands of the Canaries, and the Cape de Verd Islands also, lay not far from the coast. But as I had no instruments to take an observation, to find what latitude we were in; and did not exactly know, or at least remember, what latitude they were in, I knew not where to look for them, or when to stand off to sea towards them, otherwise I might now have easily found some of these islands. But my hope was, that if I stood along this coast till I came to the part where the English traded, I should find some of their vessels upon their usual design of trade, that would relieve and take us in.

By the best of my calculation, the place where I now was, must be that country which, lying between the Emperor of Morocco's dominions and the Negroes, lies waste, and uninhabited, except by wild beasts; the Negroes having abandoned it, and gone farther south, for fear of the Moors, and the Moors not thinking it worth inhabiting, by reason of its barrenness; and, indeed, both forsaking it because of the prodigious numbers of tigers, lions, leopards, and other furious creatures which harbour there: so that the Moors use it for their hunting only, where they go like an army, two or three thousand men at a time: and, indeed, for near a hundred miles together upon this coast, we saw nothing but a waste, uninhabited country by day, and heard nothing but howlings and roaring of wild beasts by night.

Once or twice, in the day-time, I thought I saw the Pico of Teneriffe, being the top of the mountain Teneriffe, in the Canaries, and had a great mind to venture out, in hopes of reaching thither; but having tried twice, I was forced in again by contrary winds; the sea also going too high for my little vessel; so I resolved to pursue my first design, and keep along the shore.

Several times I was obliged to land for fresh water, after we had left this place; and once, in particular, being early in the morning, we came to an anchor under a little point of land which was pretty high; and the tide beginning to flow, we lay still, to go farther in. Xury, whose eyes were more about him than, it seems, mine were, calls softly to me, and tells me, that we had best go farther off the shore; for, says he, Look, yonder lies a dreadful monster on the side of that hillock, fast asleep. I looked where he pointed, and saw a dreadful monster indeed, for it was a terrible great lion, that lay on the side of the shore, under the shade of a piece of the hill, that hung, as it were, over him. Xury, says I, you shall go on shore and kill him. Xury looked frightened, and said, Me kill! he eat me at one mouth: one mouthful he meant. However, I said no more to the boy but bade him be still; and I took our biggest gun, which was almost musket bore, and loaded it with a good charge of powder, and with two slugs, and laid it down; then I loaded another gun with two bullets: and a third, for we had three pieces, I loaded with five smaller bullets. I took the best aim I could with the first piece, to have shot him in the head; but he lay so, with his leg raised a little above his nose, that the slugs hit his leg about the knee, and broke the bone: he started up, growling at first, but finding his leg broke, fell down again and then got up upon three legs, and gave the most hideous roar that ever I heard. I was a little surprised that I had not hit him on the head; however, I took up the second piece immediately, and though he began to move off, fired again, and shot him in the head, and had the pleasure to see him drop, and make but little noise, but lie struggling for life. Then Xury took heart, and would have me let him go on shore. Well, go, said I; so the boy jumped into the water, and taking a little gun in one hand, swam to shore with the other hand, and coming close to the creature, put the muzzle of the piece to his ear, and shot him in the head again, which despatched him quite.

This was game, indeed, to us, but it was no food; and I was very sorry to loose three charges of powder and shot upon a creature that was good for nothing to us. However, Xury said he would have some of him; so he comes on board, and asked me to give him the hatchet: for what, Xury? said I. Me cut off his head, said he. However, Xury could not cut off his head; but he cut off a foot, and brought it with him, and it was a monstrous great one. I bethought myself, however, that perhaps the skin of him might, one way or other, be of some value to us; and I resolved to take off his skin, if I could. So Xury and I went to work with him: but Xury was much the better workman at it, for I knew very ill how to do it. Indeed, it took us both up the whole day; but at last we got off the hide of him, and spreading it on the top of our cabin, the sun effectually dried it in two days' time, and it afterwards served me to lie upon.

After this stop we made on to the southward continually, for ten or twelve days, living very sparingly on our provisions, which began to abate very much, and going no oftener into the shore than we were obliged to for fresh water. My design in this, was to make the river Gambia, or Senegal; that is to say, anywhere about the Cape de Verd, where I was in hopes to meet with some European ship; and if I did not, I knew not what course I had to take, but to seek for the islands or perish among the Negroes. I knew that all the ships from Europe, which sailed either to the coast of Guinea, or to Brazil, or to the East Indies, made this Cape, or those islands; and in a word I put the whole of my fortune upon this single point, either that I must meet with some ship, or must perish.

When I had pursued this resolution about ten days longer, as I have said, I began to see that the land was inhabited; and in two or three places, as we sailed by, we saw people stand upon the shore to look at us: we could also perceive they were quite black and stark naked. I was once inclined to have gone on shore to them; but Xury was my better counsellor, and said to me, No go, no go. However, I hauled in nearer the shore, that I might talk to them; and I found they ran along the shore by me a good way. I observed they had no weapons in their hands, except one, who had a long slender stick, which Xury said was a lance, and that they would throw them a great way with good aim; so I kept at a distance, but talked to them by signs, as well as I could, and particularly made signs for something to eat. They beckoned to me to stop my boat, and they would fetch me some meat: upon this I lowered the top of my sail, and lay by, and two of them ran up into the country; and in less than half an hour came back, and brought with them two pieces of dry flesh and some corn, such as the produce of their country; but we neither knew what the one or the other was; however, we were willing to accept it. But how to come at it was our next dispute, for I was not for venturing on shore to them, and they were as much afraid of us: but they took a safe way for us all, for they brought it to the shore, and laid it down, and went and stood a great way off till we fetched it on board, and then came close to us again.

We made signs of thanks to them, for we had nothing to make them amends; but an opportunity offered that very instant to oblige them wonderfully; for while we were lying by the shore, came two mighty creatures, one pursuing the other (as we took it) with great fury, from the mountains towards the sea; whether it was the male pursuing the female, or whether they were in sport or in rage, we could not tell, any more than we could tell whether it was usual or strange; but I believe it was the latter, because, in the first place, those ravenous creatures seldom appear but in the night; and, in the second place, we found the people terribly frightened, especially the women. The man that had the lance, or dart, did not fly from them, but the rest did; however, as the two creatures ran directly into the water, they did not seem to offer to fall upon any of the Negroes, but plunged themselves into the sea, and swam about, as if they had come for their diversion; at last, one of them began to come nearer our boat than I at first expected; but I lay ready for him, for I had loaded my gun with all possible expedition, and bade Xury load both the others. As soon as he came fairly within my reach, I fired, and shot him directly in the head: immediately he sunk down into the water, but rose instantly, and plunged up and down, as if he was struggling for life, and so indeed he was: he immediately made to the shore; but between the wound which was his mortal hurt, and the strangling of the water, he died just before he reached the shore.

It is impossible to express the astonishment of these poor creatures, at the noise and fire of my gun; some of them were even ready to die for fear, and fell down as dead with the very terror; but when they saw the creature dead, and sunk in the water, and that I made signs to them to come to the shore, they took heart and came to the shore, and began to search for the creature. I found him by his blood staining the water; and by the help of a rope, which I slung round him, and gave the Negroes to haul, they dragged him on shore, and found that it was a most curious leopard, spotted, and fine to an admirable degree; and the Negroes held up their hands with admiration, to think what it was I had killed him with.

The other creature, frightened with the flash of fire, and the noise of the gun, swam on shore, and ran up directly to the mountains from whence they came; nor could I, at that distance, know what it was. I found quickly the Negroes were for eating the flesh of this creature, so I was willing to have them take it as a favour from me; which, when I made signs to them that they might take him, they were very thankful for. Immediately they fell to work with him; and though they had no knife, yet with a sharpened piece of wood, they took off his skin as readily, and much more readily, than we could have done with a knife. They offered me some of the flesh, which I declined, making as if I would give it them, but made signs for the skin, which they gave me very freely, and brought me a great deal more of their provisions, which, though I did not understand, yet I accepted. I then made signs to them for some water, and held out one of my jars to them, turning it bottom upwards, to show that it was empty, and that I wanted to have it filled. They called immediately to some of their friends, and there came two women, and brought a great vessel made of earth, and burnt, as I suppose, in the sun; this they set down to me, as before, and I sent Xury on shore with my jars, and filled them all three. The women were as stark naked as the men.

I was now furnished with roots and corn, such as it was, and water; and leaving my friendly Negroes, I made forward for about eleven days more, without offering to go near the shore, till I saw the land run out a great length into the sea, at about the distance of four or five leagues before me; and the sea being very calm, I kept a large offing, to make this point. At length, doubling the point, at about two leagues from the land, I saw plainly land on the other side, to seaward: then I concluded, as it was most certain indeed, that this was the Cape de Verd, and those the islands, called, from thence, Cape de Verd Islands. However, they were at a great distance, and I could not well tell what I had best to do; for if I should be taken with a gale of wind, I might neither reach one nor the other.

In this dilemma, as I was very pensive, I stepped into the cabin, and sat me down, Xury having the helm; when, on a sudden, the boy cried out, Master, master, a ship with a sail! and the foolish boy was frightened out of his wits, thinking it must needs be some of his master's ships sent to pursue us, when I knew we were gotten far enough out of their reach. I jumped out of the cabin, and immediately saw, not only the ship, but what she was, viz., that it was a Portuguese ship, and, as I thought, was bound to the coast of Guinea, for Negroes. But, when I observed the course she steered, I was soon convinced they were bound some other way, and did not design to come any nearer to the shore; upon which, I stretched out to sea as much as I could, resolving to speak with them, if possible.

With all the sail I could make, I found I should not be able to come in their way, but that they would be gone by before I could make any signal to them; but after I had crowded to the utmost, and began to despair, they, it seems, saw me, by the help of their perspective glasses, and that it was some European boat, which, they supposed, must belong to some ship that was lost: so they shortened sail, to let me come up. I was encouraged with this, and as I had my patron's ensign on board, I made a waft of it to them, for a signal of distress, and fired a gun, both which they saw; for they told me they saw the smoke, though they did not hear the gun. Upon these signals, they very kindly brought to, and lay by for me; and in about three hours' time I came up with them.

They asked me what I was, in Portuguese, and in Spanish, and in French, but I understood none of them; but, at last, a Scotch sailor who was on board, called to me, and I answered him, and told him I was an Englishman, that I had made my escape out of slavery from the Moors, at Sallee: they then bade me come on board, and very kindly took me in, and all my goods.

It was an inexpressible joy to me, which any one will believe, that I was thus delivered, as I esteemed it, from such a miserable, and almost hopeless, condition as I was in; and I immediately offered all I had to the captain of the ship, as a return for my deliverance; but he generously told me, he would take nothing from me, but that all I had should be delivered safe to me, when I came to the Brazils. For, says he, I have saved your life on no other terms than I would be glad to be saved myself; and it may, one time or other, be my lot to be taken up in the same condition. Besides, said he, when I carry you to the Brazils, so great a way from your own country, if I should take from you what you have, you will be starved there, and then I only take away that life I had given. No, no, Senhor Ingles (Mr. Englishman), says he, I will carry you thither in charity, and these things will help to buy your subsistence there, and your passage home again.

A S HE WAS charitable in this proposal, so he was just in the performance, to a tittle: for he ordered the seamen, that none should offer to touch anything I had: then he took everything into his own possession, and gave me back an exact inventory of them, that I might have them, even so much as my three earthen jars.

As to my boat, it was a very good one; and that he saw, and told me he would buy it of me for the ship's use; and asked me what I would have for it? I told him, he had been so generous to me in everything, that I could not offer to make any price of the boat, but left it entirely to him: upon which, he told me he would give me a note of hand to pay me eighty pieces of eight for it at Brazil; and when it came there, if any one offered to give more, he would make it up. He offered me also sixty pieces of eight more for my boy Xury, which I was loath to take; not that I was not willing to let the captain have him, but I was very loath to sell the poor boy's liberty, who had assisted me so faithfully in procuring my own. However, when I let him know my reason, he owned it to be just, and offered me this medium, that he would give the boy an obligation to set him free in ten years, if he turned Christian; upon this, and Xury saying he was willing to go with him, I let the captain have him.

We had a very good voyage to the Brazils, and arrived in the Bay de Todos los Santos, or All Saints' Bay, in about twenty-two days after. And now I was once more delivered from the most miserable of all conditions of life; and what to do next with myself, I was now to consider.

The generous treatment the captain gave me, I can never enough remember: he would take nothing of me for my passage, gave me twenty ducats for the leopard's skin, and forty for the lion's skin, which I had in my boat, and caused everything I had in the ship to be punctually delivered to me; and what I was willing to sell, he bought of me; such as the case of bottles, two of my guns, and a piece of the lump of beeswax,—for I had made candles of the rest: in a word, I made about two hundred and twenty pieces of eight of all my cargo; and with this stock, I went on shore in the Brazils.

I had not been long here, before I was recommended to the house of a good honest man, like himself, who had an ingenio as they call it (that is, a plantation and a sugarhouse). I lived with him some time, and acquainted myself, by that means, with the manner of planting and of making sugar; and seeing how well the planters lived, and how they got rich suddenly, I resolved, if I could get a license to settle there, I would turn planter among them: endeavouring, in the mean time, to find out some way to get my money, which I had left in London, remitted to me. To this purpose, getting a kind of letter of naturalisation, I purchased as much land that was uncured as my money would reach, and formed a plan for my plantation and settlement; such a one as might be suitable to the stock which I proposed to myself to receive from England.

I had a neighbour, a Portuguese of Lisbon, but born of English parents, whose name was Wells, and in much such circumstances as I was. I call him my neighbour, because his plantation lay next to mine, and we went on very sociably together. My stock was but low, as well as his; and we rather planted for food than anything else, for about two years. However, we began to increase, and our land began to come in order; so that the third year we planted some tobacco, and made each of us a large piece of ground ready for planting canes in the year to come; but we both wanted help; and now I found more than before, I had done wrong in parting with my boy Xury.

But, alas! for me to do wrong, that never did right, was no great wonder. I had no remedy, but to go on: I had got into an employment quite remote to my genius, and directly contrary to the life I delighted in, and for which I forsook my father's house, and broke through all his good advice: nay, I was coming into the very middle station, or upper degree of low life, which my father advised me to before; and which, if I resolved to go on with, I might as well have stayed at home, and never have fatigued myself in the world, as I had done: and I used often to say to myself, I could have done this as well in England, among my friends, as to have gone five thousand miles off to do it among strangers and savages, in a wilderness, and at such a distance as never to hear from any part of the world that had the least knowledge of me.

In this manner, I used to look upon my condition with the utmost regret. I had nobody to converse with, but now and then this neighbour; no work to be done, but by the labour of my hands: and I used to say, I lived just like a man cast away upon some desolate island, that had nobody there but himself. But how just has it been! and how should all men reflect, that when they compare their present conditions with others that are worse, Heaven may oblige them to make the exchange, and be convinced of their former felicity by their experience: I say, how just has it been, that the truly solitary life I reflected on, in an island of mere desolation, should be my lot, who had so often unjustly compared it with the life which I then led, in which, had I continued, I had, in all probability, been exceeding prosperous and rich!

I was, in some degree, settled in my measures for carrying on the plantation, before my kind friend, the captain of the ship that took me up at sea, went back; for the ship remained there, in providing his lading, and preparing for his voyage, near three months; when telling him what little stock I had left behind me in London, he gave me this friendly and sincere advice: Senhor Ingles, says he (for so he always called me), if you will give me letters, and a procuration here in form to me, with orders to the person who has your money in London, to send your effects to Lisbon, to such persons as I shall direct, and in such goods as are proper for this country, I will bring you the produce of them, God willing, at my return: but since human affairs are all subject to changes and disasters, I would have you give orders for but one hundred pounds sterling, which, you say, is half your stock, and let the hazard be run for the first, so that if it come safe, you may order the rest the same way; and, if it miscarry, you may have the other half to have recourse to for your supply. This was so wholesome advice, and looked so friendly, that I could not but be convinced it was the best course I could take; so I accordingly prepared letters to the gentlewoman with whom I left my money, and a procuration to the Portuguese captain, as he desired me.

I wrote the English captain's widow a full account of all my adventures; my slavery, escape, and how I had met with the Portuguese captain at sea, the humanity of his behaviour, and what condition I was now in, with all other necessary directions for my supply; and when this honest captain came to Lisbon, he found means, by some of the English merchants there, to send over, not the order only, but a full account of my story to a merchant at London, who represented it effectually to her: whereupon she not only delivered the money, but, out of her own pocket, sent the Portuguese captain a very handsome present for his humanity and charity to me.

The merchant in London, vesting this hundred pounds in English goods, such as the captain had wrote for, sent them directly to him at Lisbon, and he brought them all safe to me at the Brazils: among which, without my direction (for I was too young in my business to think of them), he had taken care to have all sorts of tools, iron work, and utensils, necessary for my plantation, and which were of great use to me. When this cargo arrived, I thought my fortune made, for I was surprised with joy of it; and my good steward, the captain, had laid out the five pounds, which my friend had sent him as a present for himself, to purchase and bring me over a servant, under bond for six years' service, and would not accept of any consideration, except a little tobacco, which I would have him accept, being of my own produce. Neither was this all: but my goods being all English manufactures, such as cloths, stuffs, baize, and things particularly valuable and desirable in the country, I found means to sell them to a very great advantage; so that I might say, I had more than four times the value of my first cargo, and was now infinitely beyond my poor neighbour, I mean in the advancement of my plantation: for the first thing I did, I bought me a Negro slave, and a European servant also: I mean another besides that which the captain brought me from Lisbon.

But as abused prosperity is oftentimes made the very means of our adversity, so was it with me. I went on the next year with great success in my plantation; I raised fifty great rolls of tobacco on my own ground, more than I had disposed of for necessaries among my neighbours: and these fifty rolls, being each of above one hundred pounds' weight, were well cured, and laid by against the return of the fleet from Lisbon: and now, increasing in business and in wealth, my head began to be full of projects and undertakings beyond my reach; such as are, indeed, often the ruin of the best heads in business. Had I continued in the station I was now in, I had room for all the happy things to have yet befallen me, for which my father so earnestly recommended a quiet, retired life, and which he had so sensibly described the middle station of life to be full of: but other things attended me, and I was still to be the wilful agent of all my own miseries; and, particularly, to increase my fault, and double the reflections upon myself, which in my future sorrows I should have leisure to make, all these miscarriages were procured by my apparent obstinate adhering to my foolish inclination, of wandering about, and pursuing that inclination, in contradiction to the clearest views of doing myself good in a fair and plain pursuit of those prospects, and those measures of life, which nature and Providence concurred to present me with, and to make my duty.

As I had once done thus in breaking away from my parents, so I could not be content now, but I must go and leave the happy view I had of being a rich and thriving man in my new plantation, only to pursue a rash and immoderate desire of rising faster than the nature of the thing admitted; and thus I cast myself down again into the deepest gulf of human misery that ever man fell into, or perhaps could be consistent with life, and a state of health in the world.

To come then, by just degrees, to the particulars of this part of my story.—You may suppose, that having now lived almost four years in the Brazils, and beginning to thrive and prosper very well upon my plantation, I had not only learned the language, but had contracted an acquaintance and friendship among my fellow-planters, as well as among the merchants of St. Salvador, which was our port: and that, in my discourses among them, I had frequently given them an account of my two voyages to the coast of Guinea, the manner of trading with the Negroes there, and how easy it was to purchase on the coast for trifles—such as beads, toys, knives, scissors, hatchets, bits of glass, and the like—not only gold dust, Guinea grains, elephants' teeth, &c., but Negroes, for the service of the Brazils, in great numbers.

They listened always very attentively to my discourses on these heads, but especially to that part which related to the buying Negroes; which was a trade, at that time, not only not far entered into, but, as far as it was, had been carried on by the *assientos*, or permission of the kings of Spain and Portugal, and engrossed from the public; so that few Negroes were bought, and those excessively dear.

It happened, being in company with some merchants and planters of my acquaintance, and talking of those things very earnestly, three of them came to me the next morning, and told me they had been musing very much upon what I had discoursed with them of the last night, and they came to make a secret proposal to me: and, after enjoining me to secrecy, they told me that they had a mind to fit out a ship to go to Guinea; that they had all plantations as well as I, and were straitened for nothing so much as servants; that it was a trade that could not be carried on, because they could not publicly sell the Negroes when they came home, so they desired to make but one voyage, to bring the Negroes on shore privately, and divide them among their own plantations; and, in a word, the question was, whether I would go their supercargo in the ship, to manage the trading part upon the coast of Guinea; and they offered me that I should have an equal share of the Negroes, without providing any part of the stock.

This was a fair proposal, it must be confessed, had it been made to any one that had not a settlement and plantation of his own to look after, which was in a fair way of coming to be very considerable, and with a good stock upon it. But for me, that was thus entered and established, and had nothing to do but go on as I had begun, for three or four years more, and to have sent for the other hundred pounds from England; and who, in that time and with that little addition, could scarce have failed of being worth three or four thousand pounds sterling, and that increasing too; for me to think of such a voyage, was the most preposterous thing that ever man, in such circumstances, could be guilty of.

But I, that was born to be my own destroyer, could no more resist the offer, than I could restrain my first rambling designs, when my father's good counsel was lost upon me. In a word, I told them I would go with all my heart, if they would undertake to look after my plantation in my absence, and would dispose of it to such as I should direct, if I miscarried. This they all engaged to do, and entered into writings or covenants to do so: and I made a formal will, disposing of my plantation and effects, in case of my death; making the captain of the ship that had saved my life, as before, my universal heir; but obliging him to dispose of my effects as I had directed in my will; one-half of the produce being to himself, and the other to be shipped to England. In short, I took all possible caution to preserve my effects, and to keep up my plantation: had I used half as much prudence to have looked into my own interest, and have made a judgment of what I ought to have done, and not to have done, I had certainly never gone away from so prosperous an undertaking, leaving all the probable views of a thriving circumstance, and gone a voyage to sea, attended with all its common hazards, to say nothing of the reasons I had to expect particular misfortunes to myself.

But I was hurried on, and obeyed blindly the dictates of my fancy, rather than my reason: and accordingly, the ship, being fitted out, and the cargo furnished, and all things done as by agreement, by my partners in the voyage, I went on board in an evil hour again, the first of September, 1659, being the same day eight years that I went from my parents at Hull, in order to act the rebel to their authority, and the fool to my own interest.

Our ship was about one hundred and twenty tons' burden, carried six guns and fourteen men, besides the master, his boy, and myself; we had on board no large cargo of goods, except of such toys as were fit for our trade with the Negroes, such as beads, bits of glass, shells, and odd trifles, especially little looking-glasses, knives, scissors, hatchets, and the like.

The very same day I went on board we set sail, standing away to the northward upon our own coast, with design to stretch over for the African coast. When they came about ten or twelve degrees of northern latitude, which, it seems, was the manner of their course in those days, we had very good weather, only excessively hot all the way upon our own coast, till we came to the height of Cape St. Augustino; from whence, keeping farther off at sea, we lost sight of land, and steered as if we were bound for the isle Fernando de Noronha, holding our course N.E. by N. and leaving those isles on the east. In this course we passed the Line in about twelve days' time, and were, by our last observation, in seven degrees twenty-two minutes northern latitude, when a violent tornado, or hurricane, took us quite out of our knowledge: it began from the south-east, came about to the north-west, and then settled in the north-east; from whence it blew in such a terrible manner, that for twelve days together we could do nothing but drive, and, scudding away before it, let it carry us whithersoever fate and the fury of the winds directed; and, during these twelve days, I need not say that I expected every day to be swallowed up, nor, indeed, did any in the ship expect to save their lives.

In this distress, we had, besides the terror of the storm, one of our men died of the calenture, and one man and a boy washed overboard. About the twelfth day, the weather abating a little, the master made an observation as well as he could, and found that he was in about eleven degrees north latitude, but that he was twenty-two degrees of longitude difference, west from Cape St. Augustino; so that he found he was got upon the coast of Guiana, or the north part of Brazil, beyond the river Amazons, toward that of the river Orinoco, commonly called the Great River; and began to consult with me what course he should take, for the ship was leaky and very much disabled, and he was for going directly back to the coast of Brazil.

I was positively against that; and looking over the charts of the sea-coast of America with him, we concluded there was no inhabited country for us to have recourse to, till we came within the circle of the Carribee islands, and therefore resolved to stand away for Barbadoes; which by keeping off to sea, to avoid the indraft of the bay or gulf of Mexico, we might easily perform, as we hoped, in about fifteen days' sail; whereas we could not possibly make our voyage to the coast of Africa without some assistance, both to our ship and ourselves.

With this design, we changed our course, and steered away N.W. by W. in order to reach some of our English islands, where I hoped for relief: but our voyage was otherwise determined; for being in the latitude of twelve degrees eighteen minutes a second storm came upon us, which carried us away with the same impetuosity westward, and drove us so out of the very way of all human commerce, that had all our lives been saved, as to the sea, we were rather in danger of being devoured by savages than ever returning to our own country.

In this distress, the wind still blowing very hard, one of our men early in the morning, cried out, Land! and we had no sooner run out of the cabin to look out, in hopes of seeing whereabouts in the world we were, than the ship struck upon a sand, and in a moment, her motion being so stopped, the sea broke over her in such a manner, that we expected we should all have perished immediately; and we were immediately driven into our close quarters, to shelter us from the very foam and spray of the sea.

It is not easy for any one who has not been in the like condition to describe or conceive the consternation of men in such circumstances: we knew nothing where we were, or upon what land it was we were driven, whether an island or the main, whether inhabited or not inhabited; and as the rage of the wind was still great, though rather less than at first, we could not so much as hope to have the ship hold many minutes without breaking in pieces, unless the wind, by a kind of miracle, should immediately turn about. In a word we sat looking upon one another, and expecting death every moment, and every man acting accordingly, as preparing for another world; for there was little or nothing more for us to do in this: that which was our present comfort, and all the comfort we had, was, that, contrary to our expectation, the ship did not break yet, and that the master said the wind began to abate.

Now, though we thought that the wind did a little abate, yet the ship having thus struck upon the sand, and sticking too fast for us to expect her getting off, we were in a dreadful condition indeed, and had nothing to do, but to think of saving our lives as well as we could. We had a boat at our stern just before the storm, but she was first staved by dashing against the ship's rudder, and, in the next place, she broke away, and either sunk, or was driven off to sea; so there was no hope from her: we had another boat on board, but how to get her off into the sea was a doubtful thing; however, there was no room to debate, for we fancied the ship would break in pieces every minute, and some told us she was actually broken already.

In this distress, the mate of our vessel laid hold of the boat, and with the help of the rest of the men, they got her flung over the ship's side; and getting all into her, we let her go, and committed ourselves, being eleven in number, to God's mercy, and the wild sea: for though the storm was abated considerably, yet the sea went dreadfully high upon the shore, and might be well called *den wild zee*, as the Dutch call the sea in a storm.

And now our case was very dismal indeed; for we all saw plainly, that the sea went so high, that the boat could not live, and that we should be inevitably drowned. As to making sail, we had none; nor, if we had, could we have done anything with it; so we worked at the oar towards the land, though with heavy hearts, like men going to execution; for we all knew that when the boat came nearer to the shore, she would be dashed in a thousand pieces by the breach of the sea. However, we committed our souls to God in the most earnest manner; and the wind driving us towards the shore, we hastened our destruction with our own hands, pulling as well as we could towards land.

What the shore was—whether rock or sand, whether steep or shoal— we knew not; the only hope that could rationally give us the least shadow of expectation, was, if we might happen into some bay or gulf, or the mouth of some river, where by great chance we might have run our boat in, or got under the lee of the land, and perhaps made smooth water. But nothing of this appeared; and as we made nearer and nearer the shore, the land looked more frightful than the sea.

After we had rowed, or rather driven, about a league and a half, as we reckoned it, a raging wave, mountain-like, came rolling astern of us, and plainly bade us expect the *coup de grâce*. In a word, it took us with such fury, that it overset the boat at once; and separating us, as well from the boat as from one another, gave us not time hardly to say, "O God!" for we were all swallowed up in a moment.

Nothing can describe the confusion of thought which I felt, when I sunk into the water; for though I swam very well, yet I could not deliver myself from the waves so as to draw my breath, till that wave having driven me, or rather carried me, a vast way on towards the shore, and having spent itself, went back, and left me upon the land almost dry, but half dead with the water I took in. I had so much presence of mind, as well as breath left, that seeing myself nearer the main land than I expected, I got upon my feet, and endeavoured to make on towards the land as fast as I could, before another wave should return and take me up again; but I soon found it was impossible to avoid it; for I saw the sea come after me as high as a great hill, and as furious as an enemy which I had no means or strength to contend with: my business was to hold my breath, and raise myself upon the water, if I could; and so, by swimming, to preserve my breathing, and pilot myself towards the shore, if possible; my greatest concern now being, that the wave, as it would carry me a great way towards the shore when it came on, might not carry me back again with it when it gave back towards the sea.

The wave that came upon me again buried me at once twenty or thirty feet deep in its own body; and I could feel myself carried with mighty force and swiftness towards the shore, a very great way; but I held my breath, and assisted myself to swim still forward with all my might. I was ready to burst with holding my breath, when, as I felt myself rising up, so, to my immediate relief, I found my head and hands shoot out above the surface of the water; and though it was not two seconds of time that I could keep myself so, yet it relieved me greatly, gave me breath and new courage. I was covered again with water a good while, but not so long but I held it out; and finding the water had spent itself, and began to return, I struck forward against the return of the waves, and felt ground again with my feet. I stood still a few moments, to recover breath, and till the water went from me, and then took to my heels, and ran with what strength I had farther towards the shore. But neither would this deliver me from the fury of the sea, which came pouring in after me again; and twice more I was lifted up by the waves and carried forwards as before, the shore being very flat.

The last time of these two had well nigh been fatal to me; for the sea, having hurried me along, as before, landed me, or rather dashed me, against a piece of a rock, and that with such force, that it left me senseless, and indeed helpless, as to my own deliverance; for the blow, taking my side and breast, beat the breath, as it were, quite out of my body; and had it returned again immediately, I must have been strangled in the water: but I recovered a little before the return of the waves, and, seeing I should again be covered with the water, I resolved to hold fast by a piece of the rock, and so to hold my breath, if possible, till the wave went back. Now as the waves were not so high as the first, being nearer land, I held my hold till the wave abated, and then fetched another run, which brought me so near the shore, that the next wave, though it went over me, yet did not so swallow me up as to carry me away; and the next run I took, I got to the main land; where to my great comfort, I clambered up the cliffs of the shore, and sat me down upon the grass, free from danger, and quite out of the reach of the water.

I was now landed, and safe on shore; and began to look up and thank God that my life was saved, in a case wherein there were, some minutes before, scarcely any room to hope. I believe it is impossible to express, to the life, what the ecstasies and transports of the soul are, when it is so saved, as I may say, out of the grave: and I did not wonder now at the custom, viz., that when a malefactor, who has the halter about his neck, is tied up, and just going to be turned off, and has a reprieve brought to him; I say, I do not wonder that they bring a surgeon with it, to let him blood that very moment they tell him of it, that the surprise may not drive the animal spirits from the heart, and overwhelm him,—

For sudden joys, like griefs, confound at first.

I walked about on the shore, lifting up my hands, and my whole being, as I may say, wrapped up in the contemplation of my deliverance; making a thousand gestures and motions, which I cannot describe; reflecting upon my comrades that were drowned, and that there should not be one soul saved but myself; for, as for them, I never saw them afterwards, or any sign of them, except three of their hats, one cap, and two shoes that were not fellows.

I cast my eyes to the stranded vessel—when the breach and froth of the sea being so big I could hardly see it, it lay so far off—and considered, Lord! how was it possible I could get on shore?

After I had solaced my mind with the comfortable part of my condition, I began to look around me, to see what kind of a place I was in, and what was next to be done; and I soon found my comforts abate, and that, in a word, I had a dreadful deliverance: for I was wet, had no clothes to shift me, nor anything either to eat or drink, to comfort me; neither did I see any prospect before me, but that of perishing with hunger, or being devoured by wild beasts: and that which was particularly afflicting to me was, that I had no weapon either to hunt and kill any creature for my sustenance, or to defend myself against any other creature that might desire to kill me for theirs. In a word, I had nothing about me but a knife, a tobacco-pipe, and a little tobacco in a box. This was all my provision; and this threw me into such terrible agonies of mind, that, for a while, I ran about like a madman. Night coming upon me I began, with a heavy heart, to consider what would be my lot if there were any ravenous beasts in that country, seeing at night they always come abroad for their prey.

All the remedy that offered to my thoughts, at that time, was, to get up into a thick bushy tree, like a fir, but thorny—which grew near me, and where I resolved to sit all night—and consider the next day what death I should die, for as yet I saw no prospect of life. I walked about a furlong from the shore, to see if I could find any fresh water to drink, which I did, to my great joy; and having drank, and put a little tobacco into my mouth to prevent hunger, I went to the tree, and getting up into it, endeavoured to place myself so as that, if I should fall asleep, I might not fall; and having cut me a short stick, like a truncheon, for my defence, I took up my lodging; and having been excessively fatigued, I fell fast asleep, and slept as comfortably as, I believe, few could have done in my condition; and found myself the most refreshed with it that I think I ever was on such an occasion.

WHEN I WAKED it was broad day, the weather clear, and the storm abated, so that the sea did not rage and swell as before; but that which surprised me most was, that the ship was lifted off in the night from the sand where she lay, by the swelling of the tide, and was driven up almost as far as the rock which I at first mentioned, where I had been so bruised by the wave dashing me against it. This being within about a mile from the shore where I was, and the ship seeming to stand upright still, I wished myself on board, that at least I might save some necessary things for my use.

When I came down from my apartment in the tree, I looked about me again, and the first thing I found was the boat; which lay, as the wind and the sea had tossed her up, upon the land, about two miles on my right hand. I walked as far as I could upon the shore to have got to her; but found a neck, or inlet of water, between me and the boat, which was about half a mile broad; so I came back for the present, being more intent upon getting at the ship, where I hoped to find something for my present subsistence.

A little after noon, I found the sea very calm, and the tide ebbed so far out, that I could come within a quarter of a mile of the ship: and here I found a fresh renewing of my grief; for I saw evidently, that if we had kept on board, we had been all safe; that is to say, we had all got safe on shore, and I had not been so miserable as to be left entirely destitute of all comfort and company, as I now was. This forced tears from my eyes again; but as there was little relief in this, I resolved, if possible, to get to the ship: so I pulled off my clothes, for the weather was hot to extremity, and took to the water: but when I came to the ship, my difficulty was still greater to know how to get on board; for as she lay aground, and high out of the water, there was nothing within my reach to lay hold of. I swam round her twice, and the second time I spied a small piece of rope, which I wondered I did not see at first, hang down by the fore-chains so low, as that with great difficulty I got hold of it, and by the help of that rope got into the forecastle of the ship. Here I found that the ship was bulged, and had a great deal of water in her hold; but that she lay so on the side of a bank of hard sand, or rather earth, that her stern lay lifted up upon the bank, and her head low, almost to the water. By this means all her quarter was free, and all that was in that part was dry; for you may be sure my first work was to search and to see what was spoiled and what was free; and, first, I found that all the ship's provisions were dry and untouched by the water: and, being very well disposed to eat, I went to the bread-room, and filled my pockets with biscuit, and ate it as I went about other things, for I had no time to lose. I also found some rum in the great cabin, of which I took a large dram, and which I had indeed need enough of, to spirit me for what was before me. Now I wanted nothing but a boat, to furnish myself with many things which I foresaw would be very necessary to me.

It was in vain to sit still and wish for what was not to be had, and this extremity roused my application: we had several spare yards, and two or three large spars of wood, and a spare topmast or two in the ship; I resolved to fall to work with these, and flung as many overboard as I could manage for their weight, tying every one with a rope, that they might not drive away. When this was done, I went down to the ship's side, and pulling them to me, I tied four of them fast together at both ends, as well as I could, in the form of a raft, and laying two or three short pieces of plank upon them, crossways, I found I could walk upon it very well, but that it was not able to bear any great weight, the pieces being too light; so I went to work, and with the carpenter's saw I cut a spare topmast into three lengths, and added them to my raft, with a great deal of labour and pains. But the hope of furnishing myself with necessaries, encouraged me to go beyond what I should have been able to have done upon another occasion.

My raft was now strong enough to bear any reasonable weight. My next care was what to load it with, and how to preserve what I laid upon it from the surf of the sea; but I was not long considering this. I first laid all the planks or boards upon it that I could get, and having considered well what I most wanted, I got three of the seamen's chests, which I had broken open and emptied, and lowered them down upon my raft; these I filled with provisions, viz., bread, rice, three Dutch cheeses, five pieces of dried goat's flesh (which we lived much upon), and a little remainder of European corn, which had been laid by for some fowls which we had brought to sea with us, but the fowls were killed. There had been some barley and wheat together, but, to my great disappointment, I found afterwards that the rats had eaten or spoiled it all. As for liquors, I found several cases of bottles belonging to our skipper, in which were some cordial waters; and, in all, about five or six gallons of rack. These I stowed by themselves, there being no need to put them into the chests, nor any room for them. While I was doing this, I found the tide began to flow, though very calm; and I had the mortification to see my coat, shirt, and waistcoat, which I had left on shore, upon the sand, swim away; as for my breeches, which were only linen, and open-kneed, I swam on board in them, and my stockings. However, this put me upon rummaging for clothes, of which I found enough, but took no more than I wanted for present use, for I had other things which my eye was more upon: as, first, tools to work with on shore: and it was after long searching that I found the carpenter's chest, which was indeed a very useful prize to me, and much more valuable than a ship-lading of gold would have been at that time. I got it down to my raft, even whole as it was, without losing time to look into it, for I knew in general what it contained.

My next care was for some ammunition and arms. There were two very good fowling-pieces in the great cabin, and two pistols; these I secured first, with some powder-horns and a small bag of shot, and two old rusty swords. I knew there were three barrels of powder in the ship, but knew not where our gunner had stowed them; but with much search I found them, two of them dry and good, the third had taken water. Those two I got to my raft, with the arms. And now I thought myself pretty well freighted, and began to think how I should get to shore with them, having neither sail, oar, nor rudder; and the least cap-full of wind would have overset all my navigation.

I had three encouragements: 1st, A smooth, calm sea; 2dly, The tide rising, and setting in to the shore; 3dly, What little wind there was blew me towards the land. And thus, having found two or three broken oars belonging to the boat, and besides the tools which were in the chest, I found two saws, an axe, and a hammer; and with this cargo I put to sea. For a mile, or thereabouts, my raft went very well, only that I found it drive a little distant from the place where I had landed before; by which I perceived that there was some indraft of the water, and consequently I hoped to find some creek or river there, which I might make use of as a port to get to land with my cargo.

As I imagined, so it was: there appeared before me a little opening of the land, and I found a strong current of the tide set into it; so I guided my raft, as well as I could, to get into the middle of the stream. But here I had like to have suffered a second shipwreck, which, if I had, I think it verily would have broken my heart; for, knowing nothing of the coast, my raft ran aground at one end of it upon a shoal, and, not being aground at the other end, it wanted but a little that all my cargo had slipped off towards that end that was afloat, and so fallen into the water. I did my utmost, by setting my back against the chests, to keep them in their places, but could not thrust off the raft with all my strength; neither durst I stir from the posture I was in, but holding up the chests with all my might, I stood in that manner near half an hour, in which time the rising of the water brought me a little more upon a level; and a little after, the water still rising, my raft floated again, and I thrust her off with the oar I had into the channel, and then driving up higher, I at length found myself in the mouth of a little river, with land on both sides, and a strong current or tide running up. I looked on both sides for a proper place to get to shore, for I was not willing to be driven too high up the river; hoping, in time, to see some ship at sea, and therefore resolved to place myself as near the coast as I could.

At length I spied a little cove on the right shore of the creek, to which, with great pain and difficulty, I guided my raft, and at last got so near, as that, reaching ground with my oar, I could thrust her directly in; but here I had like to have dipped all my cargo into the sea again; for that shore lying pretty steep, that is to say, sloping, there was no place to land, but where one end of my float, if it ran on shore, would lie so high, and the other sink lower, as before, that it would endanger my cargo again. All that I could do was to wait till the tide was at the highest, keeping the raft with my oar like an anchor, to hold the side of it fast to the shore, near a flat piece of ground, which I expected the water would flow over; and so it did. As soon as I found water enough, for my raft drew about a foot of water, I thrust her upon that flat piece of ground, and there fastened or moored her, by sticking my two broken oars into the ground, one on one side, near one end, and one on the other side, near the other end: and thus I lay till the water ebbed away, and left my raft and all my cargo safe on shore.

My next work was to view the country, and seek a proper place for my habitation, and where to stow my goods, to secure them from whatever might happen. Where I was I yet knew not; whether on the continent, or on an island; whether inhabited, or not inhabited; whether in danger of wild beasts, or not. There was a hill, not above a mile from me, which rose up very steep and high, and which seemed to overtop some other hills, which lay as in a ridge from it, northward. I took out one of the fowling-pieces, and one of the pistols, and a horn of powder; and thus armed, I travelled for discovery up to the top of that hill; where after I had, with great labour and difficulty, got up to the top, I saw my fate, to my great affliction, viz., that I was on an island, environed every way with the sea, no land to be seen, except some rocks, which lay a great way off, and two small islands, less than this, which lay about three leagues to the west.

I found also that the island I was in was barren, and, as I saw good reason to believe, uninhabited, except by wild beasts, of whom, however, I saw none; yet I saw abundance of fowls, but knew not their kinds; neither, when I killed them, could I tell what was fit for food, and what not. At my coming back, I shot at a great bird, which I saw sitting upon a tree, on the side of a great wood. I believe it was the first gun that had been fired there since the creation of the world: I had no sooner fired, but from all the parts of the wood there arose an innumerable number of fowls, of many sorts, making a confused screaming, and crying, every one according to his usual note; but not one of them of any kind that I knew. As for the creature I killed, I took it to be a kind of a hawk, its colour and beak resembling it, but it had no talons or claws more than common. Its flesh was carrion and fit for nothing.

Contented with this discovery, I came back to my raft, and fell to work to bring my cargo on shore, which took me up the rest of the day: what to do with myself at night I knew not, nor indeed, where to rest: for I was afraid to lie down on the ground, not knowing but some wild beast might devour me; though, as I afterwards found, there was really no need for those fears. However, as well as I could, I barricadoed myself round with chests and boards that I had brought on shore, and made a kind of hut for that night's lodging. As for food, I yet saw not which way to supply myself, except that I had seen two or three creatures, like hares, run out of the wood where I shot the fowl.

I now began to consider that I might yet get a great many things out of the ship, which would be useful to me, and particularly some of the rigging and sails, and such other things as might come to land; and I resolved to make another voyage on board the vessel, if possible. And as I knew that the first storm that blew must necessarily break her all in pieces, I resolved to set all other things apart, till I got everything out of the ship that I could get. Then I called a council, that is to say, in my thoughts, whether I should take back the raft; but this appeared impracticable: so I resolved to go as before, when the tide was down; and I did so, only that I stripped before I went from my hut; having nothing on but a chequered shirt, a pair of linen drawers, and a pair of pumps on my feet.

I got on board the ship as before, and prepared a second raft; and having had experience of the first, I neither made this so unwieldy, nor loaded it so hard, but yet I brought away several things very useful to me: as, first, in the carpenter's stores, I found two or three bags of nails and spikes, a great screw-jack, a dozen or two of hatchets; and, above all, that most useful thing called a grindstone. All these I secured together, with several things belonging to the gunner; particularly, two or three iron crows, and two barrels of musket bullets, seven muskets, and another fowling-piece, with some small quantity of powder more; a large bag full of small shot, and a great roll of sheet lead; but this last was so heavy, I could not hoist it up to get it over the ship's side. Besides these things, I took all the men's clothes that I could find, and a spare fore-topsail, a hammock, and some bedding; and with this I loaded my second raft, and brought them all safe on shore, to my very great comfort.

I was under some apprehensions lest, during my absence from the land, my provisions might be devoured on shore: but when I came back, I found no sign of any visitor; only there sat a creature like a wild cat, upon one of the chests, which, when I came towards it, ran away a little distance and then stood still. She sat very composed and unconcerned, and looked full in my face, as if she had a mind to be acquainted with me. I presented my gun to her, but, as she did not understand it, she was perfectly unconcerned at it, nor did she offer to stir away; upon which I tossed her a bit of biscuit, though, by the way, I was not very free of it, for my store was not great; however, I spared her a bit, I say, and she went to it, smelled of it, and ate it, and looked (as pleased) for more; but I thanked her, and could spare no more: so she marched off.

Having got my second cargo on shore—though I was fain to open the barrels of powder, and bring them by parcels, for they were too heavy, being large casks—I went to work to make me a little tent, with the sail, and some poles, which I cut for that purpose; and into this tent I brought everything that I knew would spoil either with rain or sun; and I piled all the empty chests and casks up in a circle round the tent, to fortify it from any sudden attempt either from man or beast.

When I had done this, I blocked up the door of the tent with some boards within, and an empty chest set up on end without; and spreading one of the beds upon the ground, laying my two pistols just at my head, and my gun at length by me, I went to bed for the first time, and slept very quietly all night, for I was very weary and heavy; for the night before I had slept little, and had laboured very hard all day, as well to fetch all those things from the ship as to get them on shore.

I had the biggest magazine of all kinds now that ever was laid up, I believe, for one man: but I was not satisfied still; for while the ship sat upright in that posture, I thought I ought to get everything out of her that I could; so every day, at low water, I went on board, and brought away something or other; but particularly the third time I went I brought away as much of the rigging as I could, as also all the small ropes and rope-twine I could get, with a piece of spare canvas, which was to mend the sails upon occasion, and the barrel of wet gunpowder. In a word, I brought away all the sails first and last; only that I was fain to cut them in pieces, and bring as much at a time as I could; for they were no more useful to be sails, but as mere canvas only.

But that which comforted me still more was, that, last of all, after I had made five or six such voyages as these, and thought I had nothing more to expect from the ship that was worth my meddling with; I say, after all this, I found a great hogshead of bread, and three large runlets of rum or spirits, and a box of sugar, and a barrel of fine flour; this was surprising to me, because I had given over expecting any more provisions, except what was spoiled by the water. I soon emptied the hogshead of that bread, and wrapped it up, parcel by parcel, in pieces of the sails, which I cut out; and, in a word, I got all this safe on shore also.

The next day I made another voyage, and now having plundered the ship of what was portable and fit to hand out, I began with the cables, and cutting the great cable into pieces such as I could move, I got two cables and a hawser on shore, with all the iron work I could get; and having cut down the spritsail-yard, and the mizen-yard, and everything I could, to make a large raft, I loaded it with all those heavy goods, and came away; but my good luck began now to leave me; for this raft was so unwieldy, and so overladen, that after I was entered the little cove, where I had landed the rest of my goods, not being able to guide it so handily as I did the other, it overset, and threw me and all my cargo into the water; as for myself, it was no great harm, for I was near the shore; but as to my cargo, it was a great part of it lost, especially the iron, which I expect would have been of great use to me: however, when the tide was out, I got most of the pieces of cable ashore, and some of the iron, though with infinite labour; for I was fain to dip for it into the water, a work which fatigued me very much. After this I went every day on board, and brought away what I could get.

I had been now thirteen days ashore, and had been eleven times on board the ship; in which time I had brought away all that one pair of hands could well be supposed capable to bring; though I believe verily, had the calm weather held, I should have brought away the whole ship, piece by piece, but preparing, the twelfth time, to go on board, I found the wind began to rise: however, at low water, I went on board; and though I thought I had rummaged the cabin so effectually, as that nothing could be found, yet I discovered a locker with drawers in it, in one of which I found two or three razors, and one pair of large scissors, with some ten or a dozen of good knives and forks; in another I found about thirty-six pounds in money, some European coin, some Brazil, some pieces of eight, some gold, and some silver.

I smiled to myself at the sight of this money; O drug! I exclaimed, what art thou good for? Thou art not worth to me, no, not the taking off the ground; one of those knives is worth all this heap: I have no manner of use for thee; e'en remain where thou art, and go to the bottom, as a creature whose life is not worth saving. However, upon second thoughts, I took it away; and wrapping all this in a piece of canvas, I began to think of making another raft; but while I was preparing this, I found the sky overcast, and the wind began to rise, and in a quarter of an hour it blew a fresh gale from the shore. It presently occurred to me, that it was in vain to pretend to make a raft with the wind off shore; and that it was my business to be gone before the tide or flood began, or otherwise I might not be able to reach the shore at all. Accordingly I let myself down into the water, and swam across the channel which lay between the ship and the sands, and even that with difficulty enough, partly with the weight of the things I had about me, and partly the roughness of the water; for the wind rose very hastily, and before it was quite high water it blew a storm.

But I was got home to my little tent, where I lay, with all my wealth about me very secure. It blew very hard all that night, and in the morning, when I looked out, behold, no more ship was to be seen! I was a little surprised, but recovered myself with this satisfactory reflection, viz., that I had lost no time, nor abated no diligence, to get everything out of her, that could be useful to me, and that, indeed, there was little left in her that I was able to bring away, if I had more time.

I now gave over any more thoughts of the ship, or of anything out of her, except what might drive on shore, from her wreck; as indeed, divers pieces of her afterwards did; but those things were of small use to me.

My thoughts were now wholly employed about securing myself against either savages, if any should appear, or wild beasts, if any were in the island: and I had many thoughts of the method how to do this, and what kind of dwelling to make, whether I should make me a cave in the earth, or a tent upon the earth; and, in short, I resolved upon both; the manner and description of which, it may not be improper to give an account of.

I soon found the place I was in was not for my settlement, particularly because it was upon a low, moorish ground, near the sea, and I believed it would not be wholesome; and more particularly because there was no fresh water near it: so I resolved to find a more healthy and more convenient spot of ground.

I consulted several things in my situation, which I found would be proper for me; first, air and fresh water, I just now mentioned: secondly, shelter from the heat of the sun: thirdly, security from ravenous creatures, whether men or beasts: fourthly, a view to the sea, that if God sent any ship in sight, I might not lose any advantage for my deliverance, of which I was not willing to banish all my expectation yet.

In search for a place proper for this, I found a little plain on the side of a rising hill, whose front towards this little plain was steep as a house-side, so that nothing could come down upon me from the top. On the side of this rock, there was a hollow place, worn a little way in, like the entrance or door of a cave; but there was not really any cave, or way into the rock, at all.

On the flat of the green, just before this hollow place, I resolved to pitch my tent. This plain was not above a hundred yards broad, and about twice as long, and lay like a green before my door; and, at the end of it, descended irregularly every way down into the low ground by the seaside. It was on the N.N.W. side of the hill; so that it was sheltered from the heat every day, till it came to a W. and by S. sun, or thereabouts, which, in those countries, is near the setting.

Before I set up my tent, I drew a half-circle before the hollow place, which took in about ten yards in its semi-diameter from the rock, and twenty yards in its diameter, from its beginning and ending.

In this half-circle I pitched two rows of strong stakes, driving them into the ground till they stood very firm like piles, the biggest end being out of the ground, about five feet and a half, and sharpened on the top. The two rows did not stand above six inches from one another.

Then I took the pieces of cable which I cut in the ship, and laid them in rows, one upon another, within the circle, between these two rows of stakes, up to the top, placing other stakes in the inside, leaning against them, about two feet and a half high, like a spur to a post; and this fence was so strong, that neither man nor beast could get into it or over it. This cost me a great deal of time and labour, especially to cut the piles in the woods, bring them to the place, and drive them into the earth.

The entrance into this place I made to be not by a door, but by a short ladder to go over the top; which ladder, when I was in, I lifted over after me; and so I was completely fenced in and fortified, as I thought, from all the world, and consequently slept secure in the night, which otherwise I could not have done; though, as it appeared afterwards, there was no need of all this caution against the enemies that I apprehended danger from.

INTO THIS FENCE, or fortress, with infinite labour, I carried all my riches, all my provisions, ammunition, and stores, of which you have the account above; and I made a large tent, which, to preserve me from the rains, that in one part of the year are very violent there, I made double, viz., one smaller tent within, and one larger tent above it, and covered the uppermost with a large tarpaulin, which I had saved among the sails.

And now I lay no more for a while in the bed which I had brought on shore, but in a hammock which was indeed a very good one, and belonged to the mate of the ship.

Into this tent I brought all my provisions, and everything that would spoil by the wet; and having thus enclosed all my goods, I made up the entrance, which till now I had left open, and so passed and repassed, as I said, by a short ladder.

When I had done this, I began to work my way into the rock, and bringing all the earth and stones that I dug down out through my tent, I laid them up within my fence in the nature of a terrace, so that it raised the ground within about a foot and a half; and thus I made me a cave, just behind my tent, which served me like a cellar to my house. It cost me much labour and many days, before all these things were brought to perfection; and therefore I must go back to some other things which took up some of my thoughts. At the same time it happened, after I had laid my scheme for the setting up my tent, and making the cave, that a storm of rain falling from a thick, dark cloud, a sudden flash of lightning happened, and after that, a great clap of thunder, as is naturally the effect of it. I was not so much surprised with the lightning, as I was with a thought, which darted into my mind as swift as the lightning itself: O my powder! My very heart sank within me when I thought, that at one blast, all my powder might be destroyed; on which, not my defence only, but the providing me food, as I thought, entirely depended. I was nothing near so anxious about my own danger, though, had the powder taken fire, I should never have known who had hurt me.

Such impression did this make upon me, that after the storm was over, I laid aside all my works, my building and fortifying, and applied myself to make bags and boxes, to separate the powder, and to keep it a little and a little in a parcel, in hope that whatever might come, it might not all take fire at once; and to keep it so apart, that it should not be possible to make one part fire another. I finished this work in about a fortnight; and I think my powder, which in all was about two hundred and forty pounds' weight, was divided into not less than a hundred parcels. As to the barrel that had been wet, I did not apprehend any danger from that; so I placed it in my new cave, which, in my fancy, I called my kitchen, and the rest I hid up and down in holes among the rocks, so that no wet might come to it, marking very carefully where I laid it.

In the interval of time while this was doing, I went out at least once every day with my gun, as well to divert myself, as to see if I could kill anything fit for food; and, as near as I could, to acquaint myself with what the island produced. The first time I went out, I presently discovered that there were goats upon the island, which was a great satisfaction to me; but then it was attended with this misfortune to me, viz., that they were so shy, so subtle, and so swift of foot, that it was the most difficult thing in the world to come at them: but I was not discouraged at this, not doubting but I might now and then shoot one, as it soon happened; for after I had found their haunts a little, I laid wait in this manner for them; I observed, if they saw me in the valleys, though they were upon the rocks, they would run away as in a terrible fright; but if they were feeding in the valleys, and I was upon the rocks, they took no notice of me; from whence I concluded, that by the position of their optics, their sight was so directed downward, that they did not readily see objects that were above them: so afterwards, I took this method—I always climbed the rocks first, to get above them, and then had frequently a fair mark. The first shot I made among these creatures, I killed a she-goat, which had a little kid by her, which she gave suck to, which grieved me heartily; but when the old one fell, the kid stood stock still by her, till I came and took her up; and not only so, but when I carried the old one with me, upon my shoulders, the kid followed me quite to my enclosure; upon which I laid down the dam, and took the kid in my arms, and carried it over my pale, in hopes to have bred it up tame; but it would not eat; so I was forced to kill it and eat it myself. These two supplied me with flesh a great while, for I ate sparingly, and preserved my provisions (my bread especially) as much as possibly I could.

Having now fixed my habitation, I found it absolutely necessary to provide a place to make a fire in, and fuel to burn; and what I did for that, as also how I enlarged my cave, and what conveniences I made, I shall give a full account of in its proper place: but I must first give some little account of myself, and of my thoughts about living, which, it may well be supposed, were not a few.

I had a dismal prospect of my condition; for as I was not cast away upon that island without being driven, as is said, by a violent storm quite out of the course of our intended voyage; and a great way, viz., some hundreds of leagues, out of the ordinary course of the trade of mankind, I had great reason to consider it as a determination of Heaven, that in this desolate place, and in this desolate manner, I should end my life. The tears would run plentifully down my face when I made these reflections; and sometimes I would expostulate with myself why Providence should thus completely ruin its creatures, and render them so absolutely miserable; so abandoned without help, so entirely depressed, that it could hardly be rational to be thankful for such a life.

But something always returned swift upon me to check these thoughts, and to reprove me; and particularly, one day walking with my gun in my hand, by the seaside, I was very pensive upon the subject of my present condition, when reason, as it were, expostulated with me the other way, thus: Well, you are in a desolate condition it is true; but, pray remember, where are the rest of you? Did not you come eleven of you into the boat? Where are the ten? Why were not they saved, and you lost? Why were you singled out? Is it better to be here or there? And then I pointed to the sea. All evils are to be considered with the good that is in them, and with what worse attends them.

Then it occurred to me again, how well I was furnished for my subsistence, and what would have been my case if it had not happened (which was a hundred thousand to one) that the ship floated from the place where she first struck, and was driven so near to the shore, that I had time to get all these things out of her; what would have been my case, if I had been to have lived in the condition in which I at first came on shore, without necessaries of life, or necessaries to supply and procure them? Particularly, said I aloud (though to myself), what should I have done without a gun, without ammunition, without any tools to make anything, or to work with, without clothes, bedding, a tent, or any manner of covering? and that now I had all these to a sufficient quantity, and was in a fair way to provide myself in such a manner as to live without my gun, when my ammunition was spent: so that I had a tolerable view of subsisting, without any want, as long as I lived; for I considered, from the beginning, how I would provide for the accidents that might happen, and for the time that was to come, not only after my ammunition should be spent, but even after my health or strength should decay.

I confess, I had not entertained any notion of my ammunition being destroyed at one blast, I mean my powder being blown up by lightning; and this made the thoughts of it so surprising to me, when it lightninged and thundered, as I observed just now.

And now being to enter into a melancholy relation of a scene of silent life, such, perhaps, as was never heard of in the world before, I shall take it from its beginning, and continue it in its order. It was, by my account, the 30th of September, when, in the manner as above said, I first set foot

upon this horrid island; when the sun being to us in its autumnal equinox, was almost just over my head: for I reckoned myself, by observation, to be in the latitude of nine degrees twenty-two minutes north of the
Line.

AFTER I HAD BEEN there about ten
or twelve days, it came into my
thoughts that I should lose my reckoning of time for want of books, and
pen and ink, and should even forget the sabbath days from the working
days: but, to prevent this, I cut it with my knife upon a large post, in
capital letters; and making it into a great cross, I set it up on the shore
where I first landed, viz., "I came on shore here on the 30th of September, 1659." Upon the sides of this square post I cut every day a notch
with my knife, and every seventh notch was as long again as the rest, and
every first day of the month as long again as that long one: and thus I
kept my calendar, or weekly, monthly, and yearly reckoning of time.

But it happened, that among the many things which I brought out of
the ship, in the several voyages which, as above mentioned, I made to it,
I got several things of less value, but not at all less useful to me, which I
found, some time after, in rummaging the chests: as, in particular, pens,
ink, and paper; several parcels in the captain's, mate's, gunner's, and
carpenter's keeping; three or four compasses, some mathematical instruments, dials, perspectives, charts, and books of navigation; all of
which I huddled together whether I might want them or no: also I found
three very good Bibles, which came to me in my cargo from England,
and which I had packed up among my things; some Portuguese books
also, and, among them, two or three popish prayer-books, and several
other books, all which I carefully secured. And I must not forget, that
we had in the ship a dog, and two cats, of whose eminent history I may
have occasion to say something, in its place: for I carried both the cats
with me; and as for the dog, he jumped out of the ship himself, and
swam on shore to me the day after I went on shore with my first cargo,
and was a trusty servant to me for many years: I wanted nothing that
he could fetch me, nor any company that he could make up to me, I only
wanted to have him talk to me, but that would not do. As I observed before, I found pens, ink, and paper, and I husbanded them to the utmost;

and I shall show that while my ink lasted, I kept things very exact, but after that was gone, I could not; for I could not make any ink, by any means that I could devise.

And this put me in mind that I wanted many things, notwithstanding all that I had amassed together; and of these, this of ink was one; as also a spade, pickaxe, and shovel, to dig or remove the earth; needles, pins, and thread; as for linen, I soon learned to want that without much difficulty.

This want of tools made every work I did go on heavily: and it was near a whole year before I had entirely finished my little pale, or surrounded my habitation. The piles or stakes, which were as heavy as I could well lift, were a long time in cutting and preparing in the woods, and more by far, in bringing home; so that I spent sometimes two days in cutting and bringing home one of those posts, and a third day in driving it into the ground; for which purpose, I got a heavy piece of wood at first, but at last bethought myself of one of the iron crows; which, however, though I found it answer, made driving these posts or piles very laborious and tedious work. But what need I have been concerned at the tediousness of anything I had to do; seeing I had time enough to do it in? nor had I any other employment, if that had been over, at least that I could foresee, except the ranging the island to seek for food; which I did, more or less, every day.

I now began to consider seriously my condition, and the circumstance I was reduced to; and I drew up the state of my affairs in writing, not so much to leave them to any that were to come after me (for I was like to have but few heirs), as to deliver my thoughts from daily poring upon them, and afflicting my mind: and as my reason began now to master my despondency, I began to comfort myself as well as I could, and to set the good against the evil, that I might have something to distinguish my case from worse; and I stated very impartially, like debtor and creditor, the comforts I enjoyed against the miseries I suffered, thus:

EVIL	GOOD
I AM cast upon a horrible, desolate island, void of all hope of recovery.	BUT I am alive; and not drowned, as all my ship's company were.
I am singled out and separated, as it were, from all the world, to be miserable.	But I am singled out too from all the ship's crew, to be spared from death; and He that miraculously saved me from death, can deliver me from this condition.
I am divided from mankind, a solitaire; one banished from human society.	But I am not starved, and perishing in a barren place, affording no sustenance.
I have no clothes to cover me.	But I am in a hot climate, where if I had clothes, I could hardly wear them.
I am without any defence, or means to resist any violence of man or beast.	But I am cast on an island where I see no wild beasts to hurt me, as I saw on the coast of Africa: and what if I had been shipwrecked there?

I have no soul to speak to, or relieve me.

But God wonderfully sent the ship in near enough to the shore, that I have got out so many necessary things, as will either supply my wants, or enable me to supply myself, even as long as I live.

Upon the whole, here was an unbounded testimony, that there was scarce any condition in the world so miserable, but there was something negative, or something positive, to be thankful for in it; and let this stand as a direction, from the experience of the most miserable of all conditions in this world, that we may always find in it something to comfort ourselves from, and to set, in the description of good and evil, on the credit side of the account.

Having now brought my mind a little to relish my condition, and given over looking out to sea, to see if I could spy a ship; I say, given over these things, I began to apply myself to accommodate my way of living, and to make things as easy to me as I could.

I have already described my habitation, which was a tent under the side of a rock, surrounded with a strong pale of posts and cables; but I might now rather call it a wall, for I raised a kind of wall against it of turfs, about two feet thick on the outside: and after some time (I think it was a year and a half) I raised rafters from it, leaning to the rock, and thatched or covered it with boughs of trees, and such things as I could get, to keep out the rain; which I found at some times of the year, very violent.

I have already observed how I brought all my goods into this pale, and into the cave which I had made behind me. But I must observe, too, that at first this was a confused heap of goods, which, as they lay in no order, so they took up all my place; I had no room to turn myself: so I set myself to enlarge my cave, and work farther into the earth; for it was a loose sandy rock which yielded easily to the labour I bestowed on it: and when I found I was pretty safe as to the beasts of prey, I worked sideways, to the right hand, into the rock, and then turning to the right again, worked quite out, and made me a door to come out in the outside of my pale or fortification.

This gave me not only egress and regress, as it were, a back way to my tent, and to my storehouse, but gave me room to stow my goods.

And now I began to apply myself to make such necessary things as I found I most wanted, particularly a chair and a table; for without these I was not able to enjoy the few comforts I had in the world; I could not write, or eat, or do several things with so much pleasure, without a table: so I went to work. And here I must needs observe, that as reason is the substance and original of the mathematics, so by stating and squaring everything by reason, and by making the most rational judgment of things, every man may be, in time, master of every mechanic art. I had never handled a tool in my life; and yet, in time, by labour, application, and contrivance I found at last, that I wanted nothing but I could have made, especially if I had had tools. However, I made abundance of things, even without tools; and some with no more tools than an adze and a hatchet, which perhaps were never made that way before, and that with infinite labour. For example, if I wanted a board, I had no other way but to cut down a tree, set it on an edge before me, and hew it flat on either side with my axe, till I had brought it to be as thin as a plank, and then dub it smooth with my adze. It is true, by this method, I could make but one board of a whole tree; but this I had no remedy for but patience, any more than I had for a prodigious deal of time and labour which it took me up to make a plank or board: but my time or labour was little worth, and so it was as well employed one way as another.

However, I made me a table and a chair, as I observed above, in the first place; and this I did out of the short pieces of boards that I brought on my raft from the ship. But when I wrought out some boards, as above, I made large shelves, of the breadth of a foot and a half, one over another, all along one side of my cave, to lay all my tools, nails, and iron work on; and in a word, to separate everything at large in their places, that I might easily come at them. I knocked pieces into the wall of the rock, to hang my guns, and all things that would hang up: so that had my cave been seen, it looked like a general magazine of all necessary things; and I had everything so ready at my hand, that it was a great pleasure to me to see all my goods in such order, and especially to find my stock of all necessaries so great.

And now it was that I began to keep a journal of every day's employment; for, indeed, at first, I was in too much hurry, and not only as to labour, but in much discomposure of mind; and my journal would, too, have been full of many dull things: for example, I must have said thus—"*Sept.* 30th. After I had got to shore, and had escaped drowning, instead of being thankful to God for my deliverance, having first vomited, with the great quantity of salt water which was gotten into my stomach, and recovering myself a little, I ran about the shore, wringing my hands, and beating my head and face, exclaiming at my misery, and crying out I was undone, undone! till, tired and faint, I was forced to lie down on the ground to repose; but durst not sleep, for fear of being devoured."

Some days after this, and after I had been on board the ship, and got all that I could out of her, I could not forbear getting up to the top of a little mountain, and looking out to sea, in hopes of seeing a ship: then fancy that, at a vast distance, I spied a sail, please myself with the hopes of it, and, after looking steadily, till I was almost blind, lose it quite, and sit down and weep like a child, and thus increase my misery by my folly.

But, having gotten over these things in some measure, and having settled my household stuff and habitation, made me a table and a chair, and all as handsome stuff about me as I could, I began to keep my journal: of which I shall here give you the copy (though in it will be told all these particulars over again) as long as it lasted; for, having no more ink, I was forced to leave it off.

THE JOURNAL

SEPTEMBER 30TH, 1659. I, poor miserable Robinson Crusoe, being shipwrecked, during a dreadful storm, in the offing, came on shore on this dismal unfortunate island, which I called the ISLAND OF DESPAIR; all the rest of the ship's company being drowned and myself almost dead.

All the rest of that day I spent in afflicting myself at the dismal circumstances I was brought to, viz., I had neither food, house, clothes, weapon, nor place to fly to: and in despair of any relief, saw nothing but death before me: that I should either be devoured by wild beasts, murdered by savages, or starved to death for want of food. At the approach of night I slept in a tree, for fear of wild creatures; but slept soundly, though it rained all night.

OCTOBER 1. In the morning I saw, to my great surprise, the ship had floated with the high tide, and was driven on shore again much nearer the island; which, as it was some comfort on one hand (for seeing her sit upright, and not broken in pieces, I hoped, if the wind abated, I might get on board, and get some food and necessaries out of her for my relief), so, on the other hand, it renewed my grief at the loss of my comrades, who, I imagined, if we had all stayed on board, might have saved the ship, or, at least, that they would not have been all drowned, as they were: and that, had the men been saved, we might perhaps have built us a boat, out of the ruins of the ship, to have carried us to some other part of the world. I spent great part of this day in perplexing myself on these things; but, at length, seeing the ship almost dry, I went upon the sand as near as I could, and then swam on board. This day also it continued raining, though with no wind at all.

From the 1st of October to the 24th. All these days entirely spent in many several voyages to get all I could out of the ship; which I brought on shore, every tide of flood, upon rafts. Much rain also in these days, though with some intervals of fair weather; but, it seems, this was the rainy season.

OCT. 20. I overset my raft, and all the goods I had got upon it; but being in shoal water, and the things being chiefly heavy I recovered many of them when the tide was out.

OCT. 25. It rained all night and all day, with some gusts of wind; during which time the ship broke in pieces (the wind blowing a little harder than before) and was no more to be seen, except the wreck of her, and that only at low water. I spent this day in covering and securing the goods which I had saved, that the rain might not spoil them.

OCT. 26. I walked about the shore almost all day, to find out a place to fix my habitation; greatly concerned to secure myself from any attack in the night, either from wild beasts or men. Towards night I fixed upon a proper place, under a rock, and marked out a semicircle for my encampment; which I resolved to strengthen with a work, wall, or fortification, made of double piles lined within with cables, and without with turf.

From the 26th to the 30th, I worked very hard in carrying all my goods to my new habitation, though some part of the time it rained exceedingly hard.

The 31st, in the morning, I went out into the island with my gun, to seek for some food, and discover the country; when I killed a she-goat, and her kid followed me home, which I afterwards killed also, because it would not feed.

NOVEMBER 1. I set up my tent under a rock, and lay there for the first night; making it as large as I could, with stakes driven in to swing my hammock upon.

Nov. 2. I set up all my chests and boards, and the pieces of timber which made my rafts; and with them formed a fence round me, a little within the place I had marked out for my fortification.

Nov. 3. I went out with my gun, and killed two fowls like ducks, which were very good food. In the afternoon I went to work to make me a table.

Nov. 4. This morning I began to order my times of work, of going out with my gun, time of sleep, and time of diversion; viz., every morning I walked out with my gun for two or three hours, if it did not rain; then employed myself to work till about eleven o'clock; then ate what I had to live on; and from twelve to two I lay down to sleep, the weather being excessive hot; and then, in the evening, to work again. The working part of this day and the next was wholly employed in making my table, for I was yet but a very sorry workman: though time and necessity made me a complete natural mechanic soon after, as I believe they would any one else.

Nov. 5. This day went abroad with my gun and dog, and killed a wild cat; her skin pretty soft, but her flesh good for nothing: of every creature that I killed I took off the skins, and preserved them. Coming back by the seashore, I saw many sorts of sea-fowl which I did not understand: but was surprised, and almost frightened, with two or three seals; which while I was gazing at them (not well knowing what they were) got into the sea, and escaped me for that time.

Nov. 6. After my morning walk, I went to work with my table again, and finished it, though not to my liking: nor was it long before I learned to mend it.

Nov. 7. Now it began to be settled fair weather. The 7th, 8th, 9th, 10th, and part of the 12th (for the 11th was Sunday, according to my reckoning), I took wholly up to make me a chair, and with much ado brought it to a tolerable shape, but never to please me; and, even in the making, I pulled it to pieces several times.

Note. I soon neglected my keeping Sundays; for, omitting my mark for them on my post, I forgot which was which.

Nov. 13. This day it rained; which refreshed me exceedingly, and cooled the earth: but it was accompanied with terrible thunder and lightning, which frightened me dreadfully, for fear of my powder. As soon as it was over I resolved to separate my stock of powder into as many little parcels as possible, that it might not be in danger.

Nov. 14, 15, 16. These three days I spent in making little square chests or boxes, which might hold about a pound, or two pounds at most, of powder; and so, putting the powder in, I stowed it in places as secure and as remote from one another as possible. On one of these three days I killed a large bird that was good to eat; but I knew not what to call it.

Nov. 17. This day I began to dig behind my tent, into the rock, to make room for my further convenience.

Note. Three things I wanted exceedingly for this work, viz., a pickaxe, a shovel, and a wheelbarrow, or basket; so I desisted from my work, and began to consider how to supply these wants, and make me some tools. As for a pickaxe, I made use of the iron crows, which were proper enough, though heavy: but the next thing was a shovel or spade; this was so absolutely necessary, that, indeed, I could do nothing effectually without it; but what kind of one to make I knew not.

Nov. 18. The next day, in searching the woods, I found a tree of that wood, or like it, which, in the Brazils, they call the iron tree, from its exceeding hardness: of this, with great labour, and almost spoiling my axe, I cut a piece; and brought it home, too, with difficulty enough, for it was exceeding heavy. The excessive hardness of the wood, and my having no other way, made me a long while upon this machine: for I worked it effectually, by little and little, into the form of a shovel or spade; the handle exactly shaped like ours in England, only that the broad part having no iron shod upon it at bottom, it would not last me so long: however, it served well enough for the uses which I had occasion to put it to; but never was a shovel, I believe, made after that fashion, or so long in making.

I was still deficient; for I wanted a basket or a wheelbarrow. A basket I could not make by any means, having no such things as twigs that would bend to make wicker-ware; at least, none yet found out: and as to the wheelbarrow, I fancied I could make all but the wheel, but that I had no notion of; neither did I know how to get about it: besides, I had no possible way to make iron gudgeons for the spindle or axis of the wheel to run in; so I gave it over; and, for carrying away the earth which I dug out of the cave, I made me a thing like a hod, which the labourers carry mortar in for the bricklayers. This was not so difficult for me as the making the shovel: and yet this and the shovel, and the attempt which I made in vain to make a wheelbarrow, took me up no less than four days: I mean, always excepting my morning walk with my gun, which

I seldom omitted, and very seldom failed also bringing home something fit to eat.

Nov. 23. My other work having now stood still, because of my making these tools, when they were finished I went on: and working every day, as my strength and time allowed, I spent eighteen days entirely in widening and deepening my cave, that it might hold my goods commodiously.

Note. During all this time, I worked to make this room or cave spacious enough to accommodate me as a warehouse, or magazine, a kitchen, a dining-room, and a cellar. As for a lodging, I kept the tent: except that sometimes, in the wet season of the year, it rained so hard that I could not keep myself dry; which caused me afterwards to cover all my place within my pale with long poles, and in the form of rafters, leaning against the rock, and load them with flags and large leaves of trees, like a thatch.

DECEMBER 10. I began now to think my cave or vault finished; when on a sudden (it seems I had made it too large) a great quantity of earth fell down from the top and one side; so much, that, in short, it frightened me, and not without reason too; for if I had been under it, I should never have wanted a grave-digger. Upon this disaster, I had a great deal of work to do over again, for I had the loose earth to carry out; and, which was of more importance, I had the ceiling to prop up, so that I might be sure no more would come down.

DEC. 11. This day I went to work with it accordingly; and got two shores or posts pitched upright to the top, with two pieces of board across over each post: this I finished the next day; and setting more posts up with boards, in about a week more I had the roof secured; and the posts, standing in rows, served me for partitions to part off my house.

DEC. 17. From this day to the 30th, I placed shelves, and knocked up nails on the posts, to hang everything up that could be hung up: and now I began to be in some order within doors.

DEC. 20. I carried everything into the cave, and began to furnish my house, and set up some pieces of boards, like a dresser, to order my victuals upon; but boards began to be very scarce with me; also I made me another table.

DEC. 24. Much rain all night and all day: no stirring out.

DEC. 25. Rain all day.

DEC. 26. No rain; and the earth much cooler than before, and pleasanter.

DEC. 27. Killed a young goat; and lamed another, so that I catched it, and led it home in a string: when I had it home, I bound and splintered up its leg, which was broke.

N. B. I took such care of it that it lived; and the leg grew well, and as strong as ever: but, by nursing it so long, it grew tame, and fed upon the little green at my door, and would not go away. This was the first time that I entertained a thought of breeding up some tame creatures, that I might have food when my powder and shot was all spent.

DEC. 28, 29, 30, 31. Great heats, and no breeze: so that there was no stirring abroad, except in the evening, for food; this time I spent in putting all my things in order within doors.

JANUARY 1. Very hot still; but I went abroad early and late with my gun, and lay still in the middle of the day. This evening, going farther into the valleys which lay towards the centre of the island, I found there were plenty of goats, though exceeding shy, and hard to come at; however, I resolved to try if I could not bring my dog to hunt them down. Accordingly, the next day, I went out with my dog, and set him upon the goats; but I was mistaken, for they all faced about upon the dog: and he knew his danger too well, for he would not come near them.

JAN. 3. I began my fence or wall; which, being still jealous of my being attacked by somebody, I resolved to make very thick and strong.

N. B. This wall being described before, I purposely omit what was said in the journal; it is sufficient to observe that I was no less time than from the 3d of January to the 14th of April, working, finishing, and perfecting this wall; though it was no more than about twenty-five yards in length, being a half circle, from one place in the rock to another place, about twelve yards from it, the door of the cave being in the centre, behind it.

All this time I worked very hard; the rains hindering me many days, nay, sometimes weeks together: but I thought I should never be perfectly secure till this wall was finished; and it is scarce credible what inexpressible labour everything was done with, especially the bringing of piles out of the woods, and driving them into the ground; for I made them much bigger than I needed to have done.

When this wall was finished, and the outside double fenced, with a turf-wall raised up close to it, I persuaded myself that if any people were to come on shore there they would not perceive anything like a habitation: and it was very well I did so, as may be observed hereafter, upon a very remarkable occasion.

During this time, I made my rounds in the woods for game every day, when the rain permitted me, and made frequent discoveries, in these walks, of something or other to my advantage; particularly, I found a kind of wild pigeons, who build, not as wood-pigeons, in a tree, but rather as house-pigeons, in the holes of the rocks: and, taking some young ones, I endeavoured to breed them up tame, and did so; but when they grew older, they flew all away; which, perhaps, was, at first, for want of feeding them, for I had nothing to give them; however, I frequently found their nests, and got their young ones, which were very good meat. And now, in the managing my household affairs, I found myself wanting in many things, which I thought at first it was impossible for me to make; as indeed, as to some of them, it was: for instance, I could never make a cask to be hooped. I had a small runlet or two, as I observed before; but I could never arrive at the capacity of making one by them, though I spent many weeks about it; I could neither put in the heads, nor join the staves so true to one another as to make them hold water; so I gave that also over. In the next place, I was at a great loss for a candle; so that as soon as it was dark, which was generally by seven o'clock, I was obliged to go to bed. I remember the lump of beeswax with which I made candles in my African adventure; but I had none of that now; the only remedy I had was, that when I had killed the goat, I saved the tallow; and with a little dish made of clay, which I baked in the sun, to which I added a wick of some oakum, I made me a lamp; and this gave me light, though not a clear steady light like a candle. In the middle of all my labours it happened, that in rummaging my things, I found a little bag; which, as I hinted before, had been filled with corn, for the feeding of poultry, not for this voyage, but before, as I suppose, when the ship came from Lisbon. What little remainder of corn had been in the bag was all devoured by the rats, and I saw nothing in the bag but husks and dust: and being willing to have the bag for some other use (I think it was to put powder in, when I divided it for fear of the lightning, or some such use), I shook the husks of corn out of it, on one side of my fortification, under the rock.

It was a little before the great rain just now mentioned, that I threw this stuff away; taking no notice of anything, and not so much as remembering that I had thrown anything there: when, about a month after, I saw some few stalks of something green, shooting out of the ground, which I fancied might be some plant I had not seen; but I was surprised, and perfectly astonished, when, after a little longer time, I saw about ten or twelve ears come out, which were perfect green barley, of the same kind as our European, nay, as our English barley.

It is impossible to express the astonishment and confusion of my thoughts on this occasion. I had hitherto acted upon no religious foundation at all: indeed, I had very few notions of religion in my head, nor had entertained any sense of any things that had befallen me, otherwise than as chance, or, as we lightly say, what pleases God: without so much as inquiring into the end of Providence in these things, or his order in governing events in the world. But after I saw barley grow there, in a climate which I knew was not proper for corn, and especially as I knew not how it came there, it startled me strangely; and I began to suggest, that God had miraculously caused this grain to grow without any help of seed sown, and that it was so directed purely for my sustenance, on that wild miserable place.

This touched my heart a little, and brought tears out of my eyes; and I began to bless myself that such a prodigy of nature should happen upon my account: and this was the more strange to me, because I saw near it still, all along by the side of the rock, some other straggling stalks, which proved to be stalks of rice, and which I knew, because I had seen it grow in Africa, when I was ashore there.

I not only thought these the pure productions of Providence for my support, but, not doubting that there was more in the place, I went over all that part of the island where I had been before, searching in every corner, and under every rock, for more of it; but I could not find any. At last it occurred to my thoughts, that I had shook out a bag of chicken's-meat in that place, and then the wonder began to cease; and I must confess, my religious thankfulness to God's providence began to abate too, upon the discovering that all this was nothing but what was common; though I ought to have been as thankful for so strange and unforeseen a providence, as if it had been miraculous; for it was really the work of Providence, as to me, that should order or appoint that ten or twelve grains of corn should remain unspoiled, when the rats had destroyed all the rest, as if it had been dropped from heaven; as also, that I should throw it out in that particular place, where, it being in the shade of a high rock, it sprang up immediately; whereas, if I had thrown it anywhere else, at that time, it would have been burned up and destroyed.

I carefully saved the ears of this corn, you may be sure, in their season, which was about the end of June; and, laying up every corn, I resolved to sow them all again; hoping, in time, to have some quantity sufficient to supply me with bread. But it was not till the fourth year that I could allow myself the least grain of corn to eat, and even then but sparingly, as I shall show afterwards in its order; for I lost all that I sowed the first season, by not observing the proper time; as I sowed just before the dry season, so that it never came up at all, at least not as it would have done; of which in its place.

Besides this barley, there were, as above, twenty or thirty stalks of rice, which I preserved with the same care; and whose use was of the same kind, or to the same purpose, viz., to make me bread, or rather food; for I found ways to cook it up without baking, though I did that also after some time.—But to return to my Journal.

I worked excessively hard these three or four months, to get my wall done; and the 14th of April I closed it up; contriving to get into it, not by a door, but over the wall, by a ladder, that there might be no sign of my habitation.

APRIL 16. I finished the ladder; so I went up with the ladder to the top, and then pulled it up after me, and let it down in the inside: this was a complete enclosure to me; for within I had room enough, and nothing could come at me from without, unless it could first mount my wall.

The very next day after this wall was finished, I had almost all my labour overthrown at once, and myself killed; the case was thus:—As I was busy in the inside of it behind my tent, just at the entrance into my cave, I was terribly frightened with a most dreadful surprising thing indeed; for, all on a sudden, I found the earth come crumbling down from the roof of my cave, and from the edge of the hill over my head, and two of the posts I had set up in the cave cracked in a frightful manner. I was heartily scared; but thought nothing of what really was the cause, only thinking that the top of my cave was falling in, as some of it had done before; and for fear I should be buried in it, I ran forward to my ladder, and not thinking myself safe there neither, I got over my wall for fear of the pieces of the hill which I expected might roll down upon me. I had no sooner stepped down upon the firm ground, than I plainly saw it was a terrible earthquake: for the ground I stood on shook three times at about eight minutes' distance, with three such shocks as would have overturned the strongest building that could be supposed to have stood on the earth; and a great piece of the top of a rock, which stood about a half a mile from me, next the sea, fell down with such a terrible noise as I never heard in all my life. I perceived also that the very sea was put into a violent motion by it; and I believe the shocks were stronger under the water than on the island.

I was so much amazed with the thing itself (having never felt the like, nor discoursed with any one that had) that I was like one dead or stupefied; and the motion of the earth made my stomach sick, like one that was tossed at sea: but the noise of the falling of the rock awaked me, as it were; and rousing me from the stupefied condition I was in, filled me with horror, and I thought of nothing but the hill falling upon my tent and my household goods, and burying all at once; this sunk my very soul within me a second time.

After the third shock was over, and I felt no more for some time, I began to take courage; yet I had not heart enough to go over my wall again, for fear of being buried alive; but sat still upon the ground greatly cast down, and disconsolate, not knowing what to do. All this while I had not the least serious religious thought; nothing but the common *Lord, have mercy upon me!* and when it was over that went away too.

While I sat thus, I found the air overcast, and grow cloudy, as if it would rain; and soon after the wind rose by a little and little, so that in less than half an hour, it blew a most dreadful hurricane: the sea was, all on a sudden, covered with foam and froth; the shore was covered with a breach of the water; the trees were torn up by the roots; and a terrible storm it was. This held about three hours, and then began to abate; and in two hours more it was quite calm, and began to rain very hard. All this while I sat upon the ground, very much terrified and dejected: when, on a sudden, it came into my thoughts that these winds and rain being the consequence of the earthquake, the earthquake itself was spent and over, and I might venture into my cave again. With this thought my spirits began to revive; and the rain also helping to persuade me, I went in, and sat down in my tent; but the rain was so violent, that my tent was ready to be beaten down with it; and I was forced to get into my cave, though very much afraid and uneasy, for fear it should fall on my head. This violent rain forced me to a new work, viz., to cut a hole through my new fortification, like a sink, to let the water go out, which would else have drowned my cave. After I had been in my cave for some time, and found no more shocks of the earthquake follow, I began to be more composed. And now, to support my spirits, which indeed wanted it very much, I went to my little store, and took a small cup of rum; which, however, I did then, and always, very sparingly, knowing I could have no more when that was gone. It continued raining all that night and great part of the next day, so that I could not stir abroad: but my mind being more composed, I began to think of what I had best do; concluding, that if the island was subject to these earthquakes, there would be no living for me in a cave, but I must consider of building me some little hut in an open place, which I might surround with a wall, as I had done here, and so make myself secure from wild beasts or men: for if I stayed where I was, I should certainly, one time or other, be buried alive.

With these thoughts, I resolved to remove my tent from the place where it now stood, being just under the hanging precipice of the hill, and which, if it should be shaken again, would certainly fall upon my tent. I spent the two next days, being the 19th and 20th of April, in contriving where and how to remove my habitation. The fear of being swallowed alive affected me so, that I never slept in quiet; and yet the apprehension of lying abroad, without any fence, was almost equal to it: but still, when I looked about, and saw how everything was put in order, how pleasantly I was concealed, and how safe from danger, it made me very loath to remove. In the meantime, it occurred to me that it would require a vast deal of time for me to do this; and that I must be contented to run the risk where I was, till I had formed a convenient camp, and secured it so as to remove to it. With this conclusion I composed myself for a time; and resolved that I would go to work with all speed to build me a wall with piles and cables, etc., in a circle as before, and set up my tent in it when it was finished; but that I would venture to stay where I was till it was ready, and fit to remove to. This was the 21st.

APRIL 22. The next morning I began to consider of means to put this measure into execution; but I was at a great loss about the tools. I had three large axes, and abundance of hatchets (for we carried the hatchets for traffic with the Indians); but with much chopping and cutting knotty hard wood, they were all full of notches, and dull: and though I had a grindstone, I could not turn it and grind my tools too. This caused me as much thought as a statesman would have bestowed upon a grand point of politics, or a judge upon the life and death of a man. At length I contrived a wheel with a string, to turn it with my foot, that I might have both my hands at liberty.

Note. I had never seen any such thing in England, or at least not to take notice how it was done, though since I have observed it is very common there: besides that, my grindstone was very large and heavy. This machine cost me a full week's work to bring it to perfection.

APRIL 28, 29. These two whole days I took up in grinding my tools, my machine for turning my grindstone performing very well.

APRIL 30. Having perceived that my bread had been low a great while, I now took a survey of it, and reduced myself to one biscuit-cake a day, which made my heart very heavy.

MAY 1. In the morning, looking towards the seaside, the tide being low, I saw something lie on the shore bigger than ordinary, and it looked like a cask: when I came to it, I found a small barrel, and two or three pieces of the wreck of the ship, which were driven on shore by the late hurricane; and looking towards the wreck itself, I thought it seemed to lie higher out of the water than it used to do. I examined the barrel that was driven on shore, and soon found it was a barrel of gunpowder; but it had taken water, and the powder was caked as hard as a stone: however, I rolled it farther on the shore for the present, and went on upon the sands, as near as I could to the wreck of the ship, to look for more.

When I came down to the ship, I found it strangely removed. The forecastle, which lay before buried in the sand, was heaved up at least six feet; and the stern (which was broke to pieces, and parted from the rest, by the force of the sea, soon after I had left rummaging of her) was tossed, as it were, up, and cast on one side: and the sand was thrown so high on that side next her stern, that I could now walk quite up to her when the tide was out; whereas there was a great piece of water before, so that I could not come within a quarter of a mile of the wreck without swimming. I was surprised with this at first, but soon concluded it must be done by the earthquake; and as by this violence the ship was more broken open than formerly, so many things came daily on shore, which the sea had loosened, and which the winds and water rolled by degrees to the land.

This wholly diverted my thoughts from the design of removing my habitation; and I busied myself mightily, that day especially, in searching whether I could make any way into the ship: but I found nothing was to be expected of that kind, for all the inside of the ship was choked up with sand. However, as I had learned not to despair of anything, I resolved to pull everything to pieces that I could out of the ship, concluding that everything I could get from her would be of some use or other to me.

MAY 3. I began with my saw, and cut a piece of a beam through, which I thought held some of the upper part or quarter-deck together; and when I had cut it through, I cleared away the sand as well as I could from the side which lay highest; but the tide coming in, I was obliged to give over for that time.

MAY 4. I went a fishing, but caught not one fish that I durst eat of, till I was weary of my sport; when, just going to leave off, I caught a young dolphin. I had made me a long line of some rope-yarn, but I had no hooks; yet I frequently caught fish enough, as much as I cared to eat; all which I dried in the sun, and ate them dry.

MAY 5. Worked on the wreck: cut another beam asunder, and brought three great fir planks off from the decks, which I tied together, and made swim on shore when the tide of flood came on.

MAY 6. Worked on the wreck: got several iron bolts out of her, and other pieces of iron work: worked very hard, and came home very much tired, and had thoughts of giving it over.

MAY 7. Went to the wreck again, but not with an intent of work; but found the weight of the wreck had broke itself down, the beams being cut; that several pieces of the ship seemed to lie loose; and the inside of the hold lay so open that I could see into it; but almost full of water and sand.

MAY 8. Went to the wreck, and carried an iron crow, to wrench up the deck, which lay now quite clear of the water and sand. I wrenched up two planks, and brought them on shore also with the tide. I left the iron crow in the wreck for next day.

MAY 9. Went to the wreck, and with the crow made way into the body of the wreck, and felt several casks, and loosened them with the crow, but could not break them up. I felt also a roll of English lead, and could stir it; but it was too heavy to remove.

MAY 10 to 14. Went every day to the wreck, and got a great many pieces of timber, and boards, or plank, and two or three hundred weight of iron.

MAY 15. I carried two hatchets, to try if I could not cut a piece off the roll of lead, by placing the edge of one hatchet, and driving it with the other; but as it lay about a foot and a half in the water, I could not make any blow to drive the hatchet.

MAY 16. It had blown hard in the night, and the wreck appeared more broken by the force of the water; but I stayed so long in the woods, to get pigeons for food, that the tide prevented me going to the wreck that day.

MAY 17. I saw some pieces of the wreck blown on shore, at a great distance, two miles off me, but resolved to see what they were, and found it was a piece of the head, but too heavy for me to bring away.

MAY 24. Every day, to this day, I worked on the wreck; and with hard labour I loosened some things so much, with the crow, that the first blowing tide several casks floated out, and two of the seamen's chests: but the wind blowing from the shore, nothing came to land that day but pieces of timber, and a hogshead, which had some Brazil pork in it; but the salt water and the sand had spoiled it. I continued this work every day to the 15th of June, except the time necessary to get food;

which I always appointed, during this part of my employment, to be when the tide was up, that I might be ready when it was ebbed out; and by this time I had gotten timber, and plank, and iron work, enough to have built a good boat, if I had known how: and I also got, at several times, and in several places, near one hundred weight of the sheet-lead.

JUNE 16. Going down to the seaside, I found a large tortoise, or turtle. This was the first I had seen; which, it seems, was only my misfortune, not any defect of the place, or scarcity; for had I happened to be on the other side of the island, I might have had hundreds of them every day, as I found afterwards; but perhaps had paid dear enough for them.

JUNE 17 I spent in cooking the turtle. I found in her three-score eggs: and her flesh was to me, at that time, the most savoury and pleasant that I ever tasted in my life: having had no flesh, but of goats and fowls, since I landed in this horrid place.

JUNE 18. Rained all that day, and I stayed within. I thought, at this time, the rain felt cold, and I was somewhat chilly; which I knew was not unusual in that latitude.

JUNE 19. Very ill, and shivering, as if the weather had been cold.

JUNE 20. No rest all night; violent pains in my head, and feverish.

JUNE 21. Very ill; frightened almost to death with the apprehensions of my sad condition, to be sick, and no help: prayed to God, for the first time since the storm off Hull; but scarce knew what I said, or why, my thoughts being all confused.

JUNE 22. A little better: but under dreadful apprehensions of sickness.

JUNE 23. Very bad again; cold and shivering, and then a violent headache.

JUNE 24. Much better.

JUNE 25. An ague very violent: the fit held me seven hours; cold fit, and hot, with faint sweats after it.

JUNE 26. Better; and having no victuals to eat, took my gun, but found myself very weak: however, I killed a she-goat, and with much difficulty got it home, and broiled some of it, and ate. I would fain have stewed it, and made some broth, but had no pot.

JUNE 27. The ague again so violent that I lay a-bed all day, and neither ate nor drank. I was ready to perish for thirst; but so weak, I had not strength to stand up, or to get myself any water to drink. Prayed to God again, but was light-headed; and when I was not, I was so ignorant that I knew not what to say: only lay and cried, Lord, look upon me! Lord, pity me! Lord, have mercy upon me! I suppose I did nothing else for two or three hours; till the fit wearing off, I fell asleep, and did not wake till far in the night. When I awoke, I found myself much refreshed, but weak, and exceeding thirsty: however, as I had no water in my whole habitation, I was forced to lie till morning, and went to sleep again. In this second sleep I had this terrible dream: I thought that I was sitting on the ground, on the outside of my wall, where I sat when the storm blew after the earthquake, and that I saw a man descend from a great black cloud, in a bright flame of fire, and light upon the ground: he was all over as bright as a flame, so that I could but just bear to look towards him: his countenance was inexpressibly dreadful, impossible for words to describe: when he stepped upon the ground with his feet, I thought the earth trembled, just as it had done before in the earthquake; and all the air looked, to my apprehension, as if it had been filled with flashes of fire. He had no sooner landed upon the earth, but he moved forward towards me, with a long spear or weapon in his hand, to kill me; and when he came to a rising ground, at some distance, he spoke to me, or I heard a voice so terrible that it is impossible to express the terror of it; all that I can say I understood, was this! Seeing all these things have not brought thee to repentance, now thou shalt die; at which words, I thought he lifted up the spear that was in his hand, to kill me.

No one that shall ever read this account, will expect that I should be able to describe the horrors of my soul at this terrible vision; I mean, that even while it was a dream, I even dreamed of those horrors; nor is it any more possible to describe the impression that remained upon my mind when I awaked, and found it was but a dream.

I had, alas! no divine knowledge: what I had received by the good instruction of my father was then worn out, by an uninterrupted series, for eight years, of seafaring wickedness, and a constant conversation with none but such as were, like myself, wicked and profane to the last degree. I do not remember that I had, in all that time, one thought that so much as tended either to looking upward towards God, or inward towards a reflection upon my own ways; but a certain stupidity of soul, without desire of good, or consciousness of evil, had entirely overwhelmed me; and I was all that the most hardened, unthinking, wicked creature, among our common sailors, can be supposed to be; not having the least sense, either of the fear of God, in danger, or of thankfulness to him, in deliverances.

In the relating what is already part of my story, this will be the more easily believed, when I shall add, that through all the variety of miseries that had to this day befallen me, I never had so much as one thought of its being the hand of God, or that it was a just punishment for my sin; either my rebellious behaviour against my father, or my present sins, which were great; or even as punishment for the general course of my wicked life. When I was on the desperate expedition on the desert shores of Africa, I never had so much as one thought of what would become of me; or one wish to God to direct me, whither I should go, or to keep me from the danger which apparently surrounded me, as well from voracious creatures as cruel savages: but I was quite thoughtless of a God or a Providence; acted like a mere brute, from the principles of nature, and by the dictates of common sense only; and indeed hardly that. When I was delivered and taken up at sea by the Portuguese captain, well used, and dealt with justly, and honourably, as well as charitably, I had not the least thankfulness in my thoughts. When, again, I was shipwrecked, ruined, and in danger of drowning, on this island, I was as far from remorse, or looking on it as a judgment; I only said to myself often, that I was an unfortunate dog, and born to be always miserable.

It is true, when I first got on shore here, and found all my ship's crew drowned, and myself spared, I was surprised with a kind of ecstasy, and some transports of soul, which, had the grace of God assisted, might have come up to true thankfulness: but it ended where it began, in a mere common flight of joy: or, as I may say, being glad I was alive, without the least reflection upon the distinguished goodness of the hand which had preserved me, and had singled me out to be preserved when all the rest were destroyed, or any inquiry why Providence had been thus merciful to me: just the same common sort of joy which seamen generally have, after they are got safe ashore from a shipwreck; which they drown all in the next bowl of punch, and forget almost as soon as it is over: and all the rest of my life was like it. Even when I was, afterwards, on due consideration, made sensible of my condition,—how I was cast on this dreadful place, out of the reach of human kind, out of all hope of relief, or prospect of redemption,—as soon as I saw but a prospect of living, and that I should not starve and perish for hunger, all the sense of my affliction wore off, and I began to be very easy, applied myself to the works proper for my preservation and supply, and was far enough from being afflicted at my condition, as a judgment from Heaven or as the hand of God against me; these were thoughts which very seldom entered into my head.

The growing up of the corn, as is hinted in my Journal, had, at first, some little influence upon me, and began to affect me with seriousness, as long as I thought it had something miraculous in it; but as soon as that part of the thought was removed, all the impression which was raised from it wore off also, as I have noted already. Even the earthquake, though nothing could be more terrible in its nature, or more immediately directing to the invisible Power which alone directs such things, yet no sooner was the fright over, but the impression it had made went off also. I had no more sense of God, or his judgments, much less of the present affliction of my circumstances being from his hand, than if I had been in the most prosperous condition of life. But now, when I began to be sick, and a leisure view of the miseries of death came to place itself before me; when my spirits began to sink under the burden of a strong distemper, and nature was exhausted with the violence of the fever; conscience, that had slept so long, began to awake; and I reproached myself with my past life, in which I had so evidently, by uncommon wickedness, provoked the justice of God to lay me under uncommon strokes, and to deal with me in so vindictive a manner. These reflections oppressed me for the second or third day of my distemper; and, in the violence as well of the fever as of the dreadful reproaches of my conscience, extorted from me some words like praying to God: though I cannot say it was a prayer attended either with desires or with hopes; it was rather the voice of mere fright and distress. My thoughts were confused; the convictions great upon my mind; and the horror of dying in such a miserable condition, raised vapours in my head with the mere apprehension: and, in these hurries of my soul, I knew not what my tongue might express; but it was rather exclamation, such as, Lord, what a miserable creature am I! If I should be sick, I shall certainly die for want of help; and what will become of me? Then the tears burst out of my eyes, and I could say no more for a good while. In this interval, the good advice of my father came to my mind, and presently his prediction, which I mentioned at the beginning of this story, viz., that if I did take this foolish step, God would not bless me; and I should have leisure hereafter to reflect upon having neglected his counsel, when there might be none to assist in my recovery. Now, said I, aloud, my dear father's words are come to pass: God's justice has overtaken me, and I have none to help or hear me. I rejected the voice of Providence, which had mercifully put me in a station of life wherein I might have been happy and easy; but I would neither see it myself, nor learn from my parents to know the blessing of it. I left them to mourn over my folly; and now I am left to mourn under the consequences of it: I refused their help and assistance, who would have pushed me in the world, and would have made everything easy to me; and now I have difficulties to struggle with, too great for even nature itself to support; and no assistance, no comfort, no advice. Then I cried out, Lord, be my help, for I am in great distress. This was the first prayer, if I may call it so, that I had made for many years. But I return to my Journal.

JUNE 28. Having been somewhat refreshed with the sleep I had had, and the fit being entirely off, I got up; and though the fright and terror of my dream was very great, yet I considered that the fit of the ague would return again the next day, and now was my time to get something to refresh and support myself when I should be ill. The first thing I did was to fill a large square case-bottle with water, and set it upon my table, in reach of my bed: and to take off the chill or aguish disposition of the water, I put about a quarter of a pint of rum into it, and mixed them together. Then I got me a piece of the goat's flesh, and broiled it on the coals, but could eat very little. I walked about; but was very weak, and withal very sad and heavy-hearted in the sense of my miserable condition, dreading the return of my distemper the next day. At night, I made my supper of three of the turtle's eggs, which I roasted in the ashes, and ate, as we call it, in the shell: and this was the first bit of meat I had ever asked God's blessing to, as I could remember, in my whole life. After I had eaten, I tried to walk; but found myself so weak, that I could hardly carry the gun (for I never went out without that); so I went but a little way, and sat down upon the ground, looking out upon the sea, which was just before me, and very calm and smooth. As I sat here, some such thoughts as these occurred to me: What is this earth and sea, of which I have seen so much? Whence is it produced? And what am I, and all the other creatures, wild and tame, human and brutal? Whence are we? Surely, we are all made by some secret power, who formed the earth and sea, the air and sky. And who is that? Then it followed most naturally, It is God that has made all. Well, but then, it came on, if God has made all these things, he guides and governs them all, and all things that concern them; for the power that could make all things, must certainly have power to guide and direct them: if so, nothing can happen in the great circuit of his works, either without his knowledge or appointment.

And if nothing happens without his knowledge, he knows that I am here, and am in this dreadful condition: and if nothing happens without his appointment, he has appointed all this to befall me. Nothing occurred to my thought, to contradict any of these conclusions; and therefore it rested upon me with the greatest force, that it must needs be that God had appointed all this to befall me; that I was brought to this miserable circumstance by his direction, he having the sole power, not of me only, but of everything that happens in the world. Immediately it followed, Why has God done this to me? What have I done to be thus used? My conscience presently checked me in that inquiry, as if I had blasphemed: and methought it spoke to me like a voice! Wretch, dost *thou* ask what thou hast done? Look back upon a dreadful misspent life, and ask thyself what thou hast *not* done? Ask, why is it that thou wert not long ago destroyed? Why wert thou not drowned in Yarmouth Roads; killed in the fight when the ship was taken by the Sallee man-of-war; devoured by the wild beasts on the coast of Africa; or drowned *here*, when all the crew perished but thyself? Dost *thou* ask what thou hast done? I was struck dumb with these reflections, as one astonished, and had not a word to say; no, not to answer to myself; and, rising up pensive and sad, walked back to my retreat, and went over my wall, as if I had been going to bed: but my thoughts were sadly disturbed, and I had no inclination to sleep; so I sat down in the chair, and lighted my lamp, for it began to be dark. Now, as the apprehension of the return of my distemper terrified me very much, it occurred to my thought, that the Brazilians take no physic but their tobacco for almost all distempers; and I had a piece of a roll of tobacco in one of the chests, which was quite cured; and some also that was green, and not quite cured.

I went, directed by Heaven, no doubt; for in this chest I found a cure both for soul and body. I opened the chest, and found what I looked for, viz., the tobacco; and as the few books I had saved lay there too, I took out one of the Bibles which I mentioned before, and which, to this time,

I had not found leisure or so much as inclination, to look into. I say, I took it out, and brought both that and the tobacco with me to the table. What use to make of the tobacco I knew not, as to my distemper, nor whether it was good for it or not; but I tried several experiments with it, as if I was resolved it should hit one way or other. I first took a piece of the leaf, and chewed it in my mouth; which, indeed, at first, almost stupefied my brain; the tobacco being green and strong, and such as I had not been much used to. Then I took some and steeped it an hour or two in some rum, and resolved to take a dose of it when I lay down: and lastly, I burnt some upon a pan of coals, and held my nose close over the smoke of it as long as I could bear it; as well for the heat, as almost for suffocation. In the interval of this operation, I took up the Bible, and began to read; but my head was too much disturbed by the tobacco to bear reading, at least at that time; only, having opened the book casually, the first words that occurred to me were these: "Call on me in the day of trouble, and I will deliver thee, and thou shalt glorify me." These words were very apt to my case: and made some impression upon my thoughts at the time of reading them, though not so much as they did afterwards; for, as for being *delivered*, the word had no sound, as I may say, to me; the thing was so remote, so impossible in my apprehension of things, that, as the children of Israel said when they were promised flesh to eat, "Can God spread a table in the wilderness?" so I began to say, Can even God himself deliver me from this place? And as it was not for many years that any hopes appeared, this prevailed very often upon my thoughts: but, however, the words made a great impression upon me, and I mused upon them very often. It now grew late: and the tobacco had, as I said, dozed my head so much, that I inclined to sleep: so I left my lamp burning in the cave, lest I should want anything in the night, and went to bed. But before I lay down, I did what I never had done in all my life; I kneeled down, and prayed to God to fulfil the promise to me, that if I called upon him in the day of trouble, he would deliver me. After my broken and imperfect prayer was over, I drank the rum in which I had steeped the tobacco; which was so strong and rank of the tobacco, that indeed I could scarce get it down; immediately upon this I went to bed. I found presently the rum flew up into my head violently; but I fell into a sound sleep, and waked no more till, by the sun, it must necessarily be near three o'clock in the afternoon the next day; nay, to this hour, I am partly of opinion, that I slept all the next day and night, and till almost three the day after; for otherwise, I know not how I should lose a day out of my reckoning in the days of the week, as it appeared some years after I had done; for if I had lost it by crossing and recrossing the Line, I should have lost more than one day; but certainly I lost a day in my account, and never knew which way. Be that, however, one way or the other, when I awaked I found myself exceedingly refreshed, and my spirits lively and cheerful: when I got up I was stronger than I was the day before, and my stomach better, for I was hungry: and, in short, I had no fit the next day, but continued much altered for the better. This was the 29th.

The 30th was my well day, of course; and I went abroad with my gun, but did not care to travel too far. I killed a sea-fowl or two, something like a brand goose, and brought them home; but was not very forward to eat them; so I ate some more of the turtle's eggs, which were very good. This evening I renewed the medicine, which I had supposed did me good the day before, viz., the tobacco steeped in rum; only I did not take so much as before, nor did I chew any of the leaf, or hold my head over the smoke; however, I was not so well the next day, which was the 1st of July, as I hoped I should have been; for I had a little of the cold fit, but it was not much.

JULY 2. I renewed the medicine all the three ways; and dosed myself with it as at first, and doubled the quantity which I drank.

JULY 3. I missed the fit for good and all, though I did not recover my full strength for some weeks after. While I was thus gathering strength, my thoughts ran exceedingly upon this scripture, "I will deliver thee"; and the impossibility of my deliverance lay much upon my mind, in bar of my ever expecting it: but as I was discouraging myself with such thoughts, it occurred to my mind that I pored so much upon my deliverance from the main affliction, that I disregarded the deliverance I had received; and I was, as it were, made to ask myself such questions as these, viz., Have I not been delivered, and wonderfully, too, from sickness; from the most distressed condition that could be and that was so frightful to me? and what notice have I taken of it! Have I done my part? God has delivered me, but I have not glorified him; that is to say, I have not owned and been thankful for that as a deliverance: and how can I expect a greater deliverance? This touched my heart very much; and immediately I knelt down, and gave God thanks aloud for my recovery from my sickness.

JULY 4. In the morning I took the Bible: and beginning at the New Testament, I began seriously to read it; and imposed upon myself to read a while every morning and every night; not binding myself to the number of chapters, but as long as my thoughts should engage me. It was not long after I set seriously to this work, that I found my heart more deeply and sincerely affected with the wickedness of my past life. The impression of my dream revived; and the words, All these things have not brought thee to repentance, ran seriously in my thoughts. I was earnestly begging of God to give me repentance, when it happened providentially, the very same day, that, reading the scripture, I came to these words, "He is exalted a Prince and a Saviour; to give repentance and to give remission." I threw down the book; and with my heart as well as my hands lifted up to heaven, in a kind of ecstasy of joy, I cried out aloud, Jesus, thou son of David! Jesus, thou exalted Prince and Saviour!

give me repentance! This was the first time in all my life I could say, in the true sense of the words, that I prayed; for now I prayed with a sense of my condition, and with a true scripture view of hope, founded on the encouragement of the word of God: and from this time, I may say, I began to have hope that God would hear me.

Now I began to construe the words mentioned above, "Call on me, and I will deliver thee," in a different sense from what I had ever done before; for then I had no notion of anything being called deliverance, but my being delivered from the captivity I was in; for though I was indeed at large in the place, yet the island was certainly a prison to me, and that in the worst sense in the world. But now I learned to take it in another sense; now I looked back upon my past life with such horror, and my sins appeared so dreadful, that my soul sought nothing of God but deliverance from the load of guilt that bore down all my comfort. As for my solitary life, it was nothing; I did not so much as pray to be delivered from it, or think of it; it was all of no consideration, in comparison with this. And I add this part here, to hint to whoever shall read it, that whenever they come to a true sense of things, they will find deliverance from sin a much greater blessing than deliverance from affliction.

My condition began now to be, though not less miserable as to my way of living, yet much easier to my mind: and my thoughts being directed, by constantly reading the scripture and praying to God, to things of a higher nature, I had a great deal of comfort within, which, till now, I knew nothing of; also, as my health and strength returned, I bestirred me to furnish myself with everything that I wanted, and make my way of living as regular as I could.

From the 4th of July to the 14th, I was chiefly employed in walking about with my gun in my hand, a little and a little at a time, as a man that was gathering up his strength after a fit of sickness; for it is hardly to be imagined how low I was, and to what weakness I was reduced. The application which I made use of was perfectly new, and perhaps what had never cured an ague before: neither can I recommend it to any one to practise, by this experiment; and though it did carry off the fit, yet it rather contributed to weakening me; for I had frequent convulsions in my nerves and limbs for some time: I learned from it also this, in particular: that being abroad in the rainy season was the most pernicious thing to my health that could be, especially in those rains which came attended with storms and hurricanes of wind; for as the rain which came in the dry season was almost always accompanied with such storms, so I found that this rain was much more dangerous than the rain which fell in September and October.

I had now been in this unhappy island above ten months: all possibility of deliverance from this condition seemed to be entirely taken from me; and I firmly believed that no human shape had ever set foot upon that place. Having secured my habitation, as I thought, fully to my mind, I had a great desire to make a more perfect discovery of the island, and to see what other productions I might find, which I yet knew nothing of.

It was on the 15th of July that I began to take a more particular survey of the island itself. I went up the creek first, where, as I hinted, I brought my rafts on shore. I found, after I came about two miles up, that the tide did not flow any higher; and that it was no more than a little brook of running water, very fresh and good: but this being the dry season, there was hardly any water in some parts of it; at least, not any stream. On the banks of this brook I found many pleasant savannahs or meadows, plain, smooth, and covered with grass; and on the rising parts of them, next to the higher grounds (where the water, as it might be supposed, never overflowed), I found a great deal of tobacco, green, and growing to a very great and strong stalk: and there were divers other plants, which I had no knowledge of, or understanding about, and that might, perhaps, have virtues of their own, which I could not find out. I searched for the cassava root, which the Indians, in all that climate, make their bread of; but I could find none. I saw large plants of aloes, but did not understand them. I saw several sugar-canes, but wild; and, for want of cultivation, imperfect. I contented myself with these discoveries for this time; and came back, musing with myself what course I might take to know the virtue and goodness of any of the fruits or plants which I should discover; but could bring it to no conclusion; for, in short, I had made so little observation while I was in the Brazils, that I knew little of the plants in the field; at least, very little that might serve me to any purpose now in my distress.

The next day, the 16th, I went up the same way again; and after going something farther than I had gone the day before, I found the brook and the savannahs begin to cease and the country became more woody than before. In this part I found different fruits; and particularly I found melons upon the ground in great abundance, and grapes upon the trees; the vines, indeed, had spread over the trees, and the clusters of grapes were now just in their prime, very ripe and rich. This was a surprising discovery, and I was exceedingly glad of them, but I was warned by my experience to eat sparingly of them; remembering that when I was ashore in Barbary, the eating of grapes killed several of our Englishmen, who were slaves there, by throwing them into fluxes and fevers. I found, however, an excellent use for these grapes; and that was to cure or dry them in the sun, and keep them as dried grapes or raisins are kept; which I thought would be (as indeed they were) as wholesome and as agreeable to eat, when no grapes were to be had.

I spent all that evening there, and went not back to my habitation; which, by the way, was the first night, as I might say, I had lain from home. At night, I took my first contrivance, and got up into a tree, where I slept well; and the next morning proceeded on my discovery, travelling near four miles, as I might judge by the length of the valley; keeping still due north, with a ridge of hills on the south and north sides of me. At the end of this march I came to an opening, where the country seemed to descend to the west; and a little spring of fresh water, which issued out at the side of the hill by me, ran the other way, that is, due east; and the country appeared so fresh, so green, so flourishing, everything being in a constant verdure, or flourish of spring, that it looked like a planted garden. I descended a little on the side of that delicious vale, surveying it with a secret kind of pleasure (though mixed with other afflicting thoughts), to think that this was all my own; that I was king and lord of all this country indefeasibly, and had a right of possession; and, if I could convey it, I might have it in inheritance as completely as any lord of a manor in England. I saw here abundance of cocoa-trees, and orange, lemon, and citron trees, but all wild, and very few bearing any fruit; at least not then. However, the green limes that I gathered were not only pleasant to eat, but very wholesome; and I mixed their juice afterwards with water, which made it very wholesome, and very cool and refreshing. I found now I had business enough, to gather and carry home; and I resolved to lay up a store, as well of grapes as limes and lemons, to furnish myself for the wet season, which I knew was approaching. In order to this, I gathered a great heap of grapes in one place, a lesser heap in another place; and a great parcel of limes and lemons in another place; and taking a few of each with me, I travelled homeward; and resolved to come again, and bring a bag or sack, or what I could make, to carry the rest home. Accordingly, having spent three days in this journey, I came home (so I must now call my tent and my cave): but before I got thither, the grapes were spoiled; the richness of the fruits, and the weight of the juice, having broken and bruised them, they were good for little or nothing: as to the limes, they were good, but I could bring only a few.

The next day being the 19th, I went back, having made me two small bags to bring home my harvest; but I was surprised, when coming to my heap of grapes, which were so rich and fine when I gathered them, I found them all spread about, trod to pieces, and dragged about, some here, some there, and abundance eaten and devoured. By this I concluded there were some wild creatures thereabouts which had done this, but what they were I knew not. However, as I found there was no laying them up in heaps, and no carrying them away in a sack; but that one way they would be destroyed, and the other way they would be crushed with their own weight; I took another course. I then gathered a large quantity of the grapes, and hung them upon the out-branches of the trees, that they might cure and dry in the sun; and as for the limes and lemons, I carried as many back as I could well stand under.

When I came home from this journey, I contemplated with great pleasure the fruitfulness of that valley, and the pleasantness of the situation; the security from storms on that side; the water and the wood; and concluded that I had pitched upon a place to fix my abode in, which was by far the worst part of the country. Upon the whole, I began to consider of removing my habitation, and to look out for a place equally safe as where I was now situate; if possible, in that pleasant fruitful part of the island.

This thought ran long in my head; and I was exceeding fond of it for some time, the pleasantness of the place tempting me; but when I came to a nearer view of it, I considered that I was now by the seaside, where it was at least possible that something might happen to my advantage, and, by the same ill-fate that brought me hither, might bring some other unhappy wretches to the same place; and though it was scarce probable that any such thing should ever happen, yet to enclose myself among the hills and woods in the centre of the island, was to anticipate my bondage, and to render such an affair not only improbable, but impossible; and that therefore I ought not by any means to remove. However, I was so enamoured of this place, that I spent much of my time there for the whole remaining part of the month of July; and though, upon second thoughts, I resolved, as above stated, not to remove, yet I built me a little kind of a bower, and surrounded it at a distance with a strong fence, being a double hedge, as high as I could reach, well staked, and filled between with brushwood. Here I lay very secure sometimes two or three nights together: always going over it with a ladder, as before; so that I fancied now I had my country and my seacoast house. This work took me up till the beginning of August.

I had but newly finished my fence, and began to enjoy my labour, when the rains came on, and made me stick close to my first habitation: for though I had made a tent like the other, with a piece of sail, and spread it very well, yet I had not the shelter of a hill to keep me from storms, nor a cave behind me to retreat into when the rains were extraordinary.

About the beginning of August, as I said, I had finished my bower, and began to enjoy myself. The 3d of August, I found the grapes I had hung up were perfectly dried, and indeed were excellent good raisins of the sun; so I began to take them down from the trees; and it was very happy that I did so, as the rains which followed would have spoiled them, and I should have lost the best part of my winter food; for I had above two hundred large bunches of them. No sooner had I taken them all down, and carried most of them home to my cave, but it began to rain: and from hence, which was the 14th of August, it rained, more or less, every day till the middle of October: and sometimes so violently, that I could not stir out of my cave for several days.

In this season, I was much surprised with the increase of my family. I had been concerned for the loss of one of my cats, who ran away from me, or, as I thought, had been dead; and I heard no more of her, till, to my astonishment, she came home with three kittens. This was the more strange to me, because, about the end of August, though I had killed a wild cat, as I called it, with my gun, yet I thought it was quite a different kind from our European cats: yet the young cats were the same kind of house-breed as the old one; and both of my cats being females, I thought it very strange. But from these three, I afterwards came to be so pestered with cats that I was forced to kill them like vermin, or wild beasts, and to drive them from my house as much as possible.

From the 14th of August to the 26th, incessant rain; so that I could not stir, and was now very careful not to be much wet. In this confinement, I began to be straitened for food; but venturing out twice, I one day killed a goat, and the last day, which was the 24th, found a very large tortoise, which was a treat to me. My food was now regulated thus; I ate a bunch of raisins for my breakfast; a piece of the goat's flesh, or of the turtle, broiled, for my dinner (for, to my great misfortune, I had no vessel to boil or stew anything); and two or three of the turtle's eggs for my supper.

During this confinement in my cover from the rain, I worked daily two or three hours at enlarging my cave; and by degrees worked it on towards one side, till I came to the outside of the hill; and made a door, or way out, which came beyond my fence or wall; and so I came in and out this way. But I was not perfectly easy at lying so open: for as I had managed myself before, I was in a perfect enclosure; whereas now, I thought I lay exposed; and yet I could not perceive that there was any living thing to fear, the biggest creature that I had as yet seen upon the island being a goat.

SEPTEMBER 30. I was now come to the unhappy anniversary of my landing; I cast up the notches on my post, and found I had been on shore three hundred and sixty-five days. I kept this day as a solemn fast! setting it apart for religious exercise, prostrating myself on the ground with the most serious humiliation, confessing my sins to God, acknowledging his righteous judgments upon me, and praying to him to have mercy on me through Jesus Christ; and having not tasted the least refreshment for twelve hours, even till the going down of the sun, I then ate a biscuit and a bunch of grapes, and went to bed, finishing the day as I began it. I had all this time observed no sabbath-day; for as at first I had no sense of religion upon my mind, I had, after some time, omitted to distinguish the weeks, by making a longer notch than ordinary for the sabbath-day, and so did not really know what any of the days were: but now having cast up the days, as above, I found I had been there a year; so I divided it into weeks, and set apart every seventh day for a sabbath; though I found, at the end of my account, I had lost a day or two in my reckoning. A little after this, my ink beginning to fail me, I contented myself to use it more sparingly; and to write down only the most remarkable events of my life, without continuing a daily memorandum of other things.

The rainy season and the dry season began now to appear regular to me, and I learned to divide them so as to provide for them accordingly; but I bought all my experience before I had it; and what I am going to relate, was one of the most discouraging experiments that I had made at all.

I have mentioned that I had saved a few ears of barley, and rice, which I had so surprisingly found sprung up, as I thought, of themselves. I believe there were about thirty stalks of rice, and about twenty of barley; and now I thought it a proper time to sow it after the rains; the sun being in its southern position, going from me. Accordingly I dug a piece of ground, as well as I could, with my wooden spade; and dividing it into two parts, I sowed my grain; but as I was sowing, it casually occurred to my thoughts that I would not sow it all at first, because I did not know when was the proper time for it; so I sowed about two-thirds of the seed, leaving about a handful of each; and it was a great comfort for me afterwards that I did so, for not one grain of what I sowed this time came to anything; for the dry month following, and the earth having thus had no rain after the seed was sown, it had no moisture to assist its growth, and never came up at all till the wet season had come again, and then it grew as if it had been but newly sown. Finding my first seed did not grow, which I easily imagined was from the drought, I sought for a moister piece of ground to make another trial in; and I dug up a piece of ground near my new bower, and sowed the rest of my seed in February, a little before the vernal equinox. This having the rainy months of March and April to water it, sprung up very pleasantly, and yielded a very good crop; but having only part of the seed left, and not daring to sow all that I had, I got but a small quantity at last, my whole crop not amounting to above half a peck of each kind. But by this experiment I was made master of my business, and knew exactly when was the proper time to sow; and that I might expect two seed-times, and two harvests every year.

While this corn was growing, I made a little discovery, which was of use to me afterwards. As soon as the rains were over, and the weather began to settle, which was about the month of November, I made a visit up the country to my bower; where, though I had not been for some months, yet I found all things just as I had left them. The circle of double hedge that I had made was not only firm and entire, but the stakes which I had cut out of some trees that grew thereabouts, were all shot out and grown with long branches, as much as a willow-tree usually shoots the first year after lopping its head; but I could not tell what tree to call it that these stakes were cut from. I was surprised, and yet very well pleased, to see the young trees grow; and I pruned them, and led them to grow as much alike as I could; and it is scarce credible how beautiful a figure they grew into in three years; so that, though the hedge made a circle of about twenty-five yards in diameter, yet the trees, for such I might now call them, soon covered it, and it was a complete shade, sufficient to lodge under all the dry season. This made me resolve to cut some more stakes, and make me a hedge like this, in a semicircle round my wall (I mean that of my first dwelling), which I did; and placing the trees or stakes in a double row, at about eight yards' distance from my first fence, they grew presently; and were at first a fine cover to my habitation, and afterwards served for a defence also; as I shall observe in its order.

I FOUND now that the seasons of the year might generally be divided, not into summer and winter as in Europe, but into the rainy seasons and the dry seasons, which were generally thus: From the middle of February to the middle of April, rainy; the sun being then on or near the equinox. From the middle of April till the middle of August, dry; the sun being then north of the Line. From the middle of August till the middle of October, rainy; the sun being then come back to the Line. From the middle of October to the middle of February, dry; the sun being then to the south of the Line.

The rainy seasons held sometimes longer and sometimes shorter, as the winds happened to blow; but this was the general observation I made. After I had found, by experience, the ill consequences of being abroad in the rain, I took care to furnish myself with provisions beforehand, that I might not be obliged to go out; and I sat within doors as much as possible during the wet months. This time I found much employment, and very suitable also to the time; for I found great occasion for many things which I had no way to furnish myself with but by hard labour and constant application; particularly, I tried many ways to make myself a basket; but all the twigs I could get for the purpose proved so brittle that they would do nothing. It proved of excellent advantage to me now, that when I was a boy, I used to take great delight in standing at a basket-maker's in the town where my father lived, to see them make their wicker-ware; and being, as boys usually are, very officious to help, and a great observer of the manner how they worked those things, and sometimes lending a hand, I had by these means full knowledge of the methods of it, so that I wanted nothing but the materials; when it came into my mind, that the twigs of that tree from whence I cut my stakes might possibly be as tough as the sallows, willows, and osiers, that grew in England; and I resolved to try. Accordingly, the next day, I went to my country-house, as I called it; and cutting some of the smaller twigs, I found them to my purpose as much as I could desire; whereupon I came the next time prepared with a hatchet to cut down a quantity, which I soon found, for there was plenty of them. These I set up to dry within my circle or hedge; and when they were fit for use, I carried them to my cave; and here, during the next season, I employed myself in making, as well as I could, several baskets; both to carry earth, or to carry or lay up anything as I had occasion for. Though I did not finish them very handsomely, yet I made them sufficiently serviceable for my purpose: and thus, afterwards I took care never to be without them; and as my wicker-ware decayed, I made more; especially strong deep baskets, to place my corn in, instead of sacks, when I should come to have any quantity of it.

Having mastered this difficulty, and employed a world of time about it, I bestirred myself to see, if possible, how to supply two other wants. I had no vessel to hold anything that was liquid, except two runlets, which were almost full of rum; and some glass bottles, some of the common size, and others (which were case bottles) square, for the holding of waters, spirits, &c. I had not so much as a pot to boil anything; except a great kettle which I saved out of the ship, and which was too big for such use as I desired it, viz., to make broth, and stew a bit of meat by itself. The second thing I would fain have had, was a tobacco pipe; but it was impossible for me to make one; however, I found a contrivance for that too at last. I employed myself in planting my second row of stakes or piles, and also in this wicker-working all the summer or dry season; when another business took me up more time than it could be imagined I could spare.

I mentioned before that I had a great mind to see the whole island; and that I had travelled up the brook, and so on to where I had built my bower, and where I had an opening quite to the sea, on the other side of the island. I now resolved to travel quite across to the seashore, on that side: so taking my gun, a hatchet, and my dog, and a larger quantity of powder and shot than usual; with two biscuit-cakes, and a great bunch of raisins in my pouch, for my store; I began my journey. When I had passed the vale where my bower stood, as above, I came within view of the sea, to the west; and it being a very clear day, I fairly descried land, whether an island or continent I could not tell; but it lay very high, extending from W. to W.S.W. at a very great distance; by my guess, it could not be less than fifteen or twenty leagues off.

I could not tell what part of the world this might be; otherwise than that I knew it must be part of America; and as I concluded, by all my observations, must be near the Spanish dominions; and perhaps was all inhabited by savages, where, if I should have landed, I had been in a worse condition than I was now. I therefore acquiesced in the dispositions of Providence, which I began now to own and to believe ordered everything for the best; I say, I quieted my mind with this, and left off afflicting myself with fruitless wishes of being there. Besides, after some pause upon this affair, I considered that if this land was the Spanish coast, I should certainly, one time or other, see some vessel pass or repass one way or other; but if not, then it was the savage coast between the Spanish country and the Brazils, whose inhabitants are indeed the worst of savages; for they are cannibals, or men-eaters, and fail not to murder and devour all human beings that fall into their hands.

With these considerations, walking very leisurely forward, I found this side of the island, where I now was, much pleasanter than mine; the open or savannah fields sweetly adorned with flowers and grass, and full of very fine woods. I saw abundance of parrots; and fain would have caught one, if possible, to have kept it to be tame, and taught it to speak to me. I did, after taking some pains, catch a young parrot: for I knocked it down with a stick, and, having recovered it, I brought it home; but it was some years before I could make him speak; however, at last I taught him to call me by my name very familiarly. But the accident that followed, though it be a trifle, will be very diverting in its place.

I was exceedingly amused with this journey. I found in the low grounds hares, as I thought them to be, and foxes: but they differed greatly from all the other kinds I had met with; nor could I satisfy myself to eat them, though I killed several. But I had no need to be venturous; for I had no want of food, and of that which was very good too, especially these three sorts, viz., goats, pigeons, and turtle, or tortoise. With these, added to my grapes, Leadenhall-market could not have furnished a table better than I, in proportion to the company; and though my case was deplorable enough, yet I had great cause for thankfulness; as I was not driven to any extremities for food, but had rather plenty, even to dainties.

I never travelled on this journey above two miles outright in a day, or thereabout; but I took so many turns and returns to see what discoveries I could make, that I came weary enough to the place where I resolved to sit down for the night; and then I either reposed myself in a tree, or surrounded myself with a row of stakes, set upright in the ground, either from one tree to another, or so as no wild creature could come at me without waking me.

As soon as I came to the seashore, I was surprised to see that I had taken up my lot on the worst side of the island; for here indeed the shore was covered with innumerable turtles; whereas, on the other side, I had found but three in a year and a half. Here was also an infinite number of fowls of many kinds; some of which I had seen, and some of which I had not seen before, and many of them very good meat; but such as I knew not the names of, except those called penguins.

I could have shot as many as I pleased, but was very sparing of my powder and shot; and therefore had more mind to kill a she-goat, if I could, which I could better feed on. But, though there were many goats here, more than on my side of the island, yet it was with much more difficulty that I could come near them; the country being flat and even, and they saw me much sooner than when I was upon a hill.

I confess this side of the country was much pleasanter than mine; yet I had not the least inclination to remove; for as I was fixed in my habitation, it became natural to me, and I seemed all the while I was here to be as it were upon a journey, and from home. However, I travelled along the seashore towards the east, I suppose about twelve miles; and then setting up a great pole upon the shore for a mark, I concluded I would go home again; and that the next journey I took should be on the other side of the island, east from my dwelling, and so round till I came to my post again: of which in its place.

I took another way to come back than that I went, thinking I could easily keep so much of the island in my view, that I could not miss my first dwelling by viewing the country: but I found myself mistaken; for being come about two or three miles, I found myself descended into a very large valley, but so surrounded with hills, and those hills covered with wood, that I could not see which was my way by any direction but that of the sun, nor even then, unless I knew very well the position of the sun at that time of the day. And it happened to my further misfortune, that the weather proved hazy for three or four days while I was in this valley; and not being able to see the sun, I wandered about very uncomfortable, and at last was obliged to find out the seaside, look for my post, and come back the same way I went; and then by easy journeys I turned homeward, the weather being exceeding hot, and my gun, ammunition, hatchet, and other things very heavy.

IN THIS JOURNEY, my dog surprised a young kid, and seized upon it: and running to take hold of it, I caught it, and saved it alive from the dog. I had a great mind to bring it home if I could; for I had often been musing whether it might not be possible to get a kid or two, and so raise a breed of tame goats, which might supply me when my powder and shot should be all spent. I made a collar for this little creature, and with a string which I had made of some rope-yarn, which I always carried about me, I led him along, though with some difficulty, till I came to my bower, and there I enclosed him and left him; for I was very impatient to be at home, from whence I had been absent above a month.

I cannot express what a satisfaction it was to me to come into my old hutch, and lie down in my hammock bed. This little wandering journey, without a settled place of abode, had been so unpleasant to me, that my own house, as I called it to myself, was a perfect settlement to me, compared to that; and it rendered everything about me so comfortable, that I resolved I would never go a great way from it again, while it should be my lot to stay on the island.

I reposed myself here a week, to rest and regale myself after my long journey; during which, most of the time was taken up in the weighty affair of making a cage for my Poll, who began now to be more domestic, and to be mighty well acquainted with me. Then I began to think of the poor kid which I had penned within my little circle, and resolved to fetch it home, or give it some food; according I went, and found it where I left it (for indeed it could not get out), but was almost starved for want of food. I went and cut boughs of trees, and branches of such shrubs as I could find, and threw it over, and having fed it, I tied it as I did before, to lead it away; but it was so tame with being hungry, that I had no need to have tied it, for it followed me like a dog: and as I continually fed it, the creature became so loving, so gentle, and so fond, that it was from that time one of my domestics also, and would never leave me afterwards.

The rainy season of the autumnal equinox was now come, and I kept the 30th of September in the same solemn manner as before, being the anniversary of my landing on the island; having now been there two years, and no more prospect of being delivered than the first day I came there. I spent the whole day in humble and thankful acknowledgments for the many wonderful mercies which my solitary condition was attended with, and without which it might have been infinitely more miserable. I gave humble and hearty thanks to God for having been pleased to discover to me, that it was possible I might be more happy even in this solitary condition, than I should have been in the enjoyment of society, and in all the pleasures of the world; that he could fully make up to me the deficiencies of my solitary state, and the want of human society, by his presence, and the communications of his grace to my soul: supporting, comforting, and encouraging me to depend upon his providence here, and to hope for his eternal presence hereafter.

It was now that I began sensibly to feel how much more happy the life I now led was, with all its miserable circumstances, than the wicked, cursed, abominable life I led all the past part of my days: and now I changed both my sorrows and my joys: my very desires altered, my affections changed their gusts, and my delights were perfectly new from what they were at my first coming, or indeed for the two years past. Before, as I walked about, either on my hunting, or for viewing the country, the anguish of my soul at my condition would break out upon me on a sudden, and my very heart would die within me, to think of the woods, the mountains, the deserts I was in; and how I was a prisoner, locked up with the eternal bars and bolts of the ocean, in an uninhabited wilderness, without redemption. In the midst of the greatest composures of my mind, this would break out upon me like a storm, and make me wring my hands and weep like a child: sometimes it would take me in the middle of my work, and I would immediately sit down and sigh, and look upon the ground for an hour or two together: this was still worse to me; but if I could burst into tears, or give vent to my feelings by words, it would go off; and my grief being exhausted would abate.

But now I began to exercise myself with new thoughts; I daily read the word of God, and applied all the comforts of it to my present state. One morning, being very sad, I opened the Bible upon these words, "I will never leave thee, nor forsake thee": immediately it occurred that these words were to me; why else should they be directed in such a manner, just at the moment when I was mourning over my condition, as one forsaken of God and man? Well then, said I, if God does not forsake me, of what ill consequence can it be, or what matters it, though the world should forsake me; seeing on the other hand, if I had all the world, and should lose the favour and blessing of God, there would be no comparison in the loss?

From this moment I began to conclude in my mind that it was possible for me to be more happy in this forsaken, solitary condition, than it was probable I should ever have been in any other particular state of the world; and with this thought I was going to give thanks to God for bringing me to this place. I know not what it was, but something shocked my mind at that thought, and I durst not speak the words. How canst thou be such a hypocrite, said I, even audibly, to pretend to be thankful for a condition, which, however thou mayest endeavour to be contented with, thou wouldest rather pray heartily to be delivered from? Here I stopped; but though I could not say I thanked God for being here, yet I sincerely gave thanks to God for opening my eyes, by whatever afflicting providences, to see the former condition of my life, and to mourn for my wickedness, and repent. I never opened the Bible, or shut it, but my very soul within me blessed God for directing my friend in England, without any order of mine, to pack it up among my goods; and for assisting me afterwards to save it out of the wreck of the ship.

Thus, and in this disposition of mind, I began my third year; and though I have not given the reader the trouble of so particular an account of my works this year as the first, yet in general it may be observed, that I was very seldom idle; but having regularly divided my time, according to the several daily employments that were before me; such as, first, My duty to God, and the reading the Scriptures, which I constantly set apart some time for, thrice every day: secondly, Going abroad with my gun for food, which generally took me up three hours every morning, when it did not rain: thirdly, Ordering, curing, preserving, and cooking what I had killed or catched for my supply; these took up great part of the day; also it is to be considered, that in the middle of the day, when the sun was in the zenith, the violence of the heat was too great to stir out; so that about four hours in the evening was all the time I could be supposed to work in; with this exception, that sometimes I changed my hours of hunting and working, and went to work in the morning, and abroad with my gun in the afternoon.

To this short time allowed for labour, I desire may be added the exceeding laboriousness of my work; the many hours which, for want of tools, want of help, and want of skill, everything I did took up out of my time: for example, I was full two and forty days making me a board for a long shelf, which I wanted in my cave; whereas, two sawyers, with their tools and a saw-pit, would have cut six of them out of the same tree in half a day.

My case was this; it was a large tree that was to be cut down, because my board was to be a broad one. This tree I was three days cutting down, and two more in cutting off the boughs, and reducing it to a log, or piece of timber. With inexpressible hacking and hewing, I reduced both the sides of it into chips, till it was light enough to move; then I turned it, and made one side of it smooth and flat as a board, from end to end; then turning that side downward, cut the other side, till I brought the plank to be about three inches thick, and smooth on both sides. Any one may judge the labour of my hands in such a piece of work; but labour and patience carried me through that, and many other things; I only observe this in particular, to show the reason why so much of my time went away with so little work, viz., that what might be a little to be done with help and tools, was a vast labour, and required a prodigious time to do alone, and by hand. Notwithstanding this, with patience and labour I went through many things; and, indeed, everything that my circumstances made necessary for me to do, as will appear by what follows.

I was now in the months of November and December, expecting my crop of barley and rice. The ground I had manured or dug up for them was not great; for, as I observed, my seed of each was not above the quantity of half a peck, having lost one whole crop by sowing in the dry season: but now my crop promised very well; when, on a sudden, I found I was in danger of losing it all again by enemies of several sorts, which it was scarce possible to keep from it: as, first, the goats, and wild creatures which I called hares, who, tasting the sweetness of the blade, lay in it night and day, as soon as it came up, and ate it so close, that it could get no time to shoot up into stalk.

I saw no remedy for this, but by making an enclosure about it with a hedge, which I did with a great deal of toil; and the more, because it required speed. However, as my arable land was but small, suited to my crop, I got it tolerably well fenced in about three weeks' time; and shooting some of the creatures in the daytime, I set my dog to guard it in the night, tying him up to a stake at the gate, where he would stand and bark all night long; so in a little time the enemies forsook the place, and the corn grew very strong and well, and began to ripen apace.

But as the beasts ruined me before, while my corn was in the blade, so the birds were as likely to ruin me now, when it was in the ear; for going along by the place to see how it throve, I saw my little crop surrounded with fowls, I know not of how many sorts, who stood, as it were, watching till I should be gone. I immediately let fly among them (for I always had my gun with me); I had no sooner shot, but there rose up a little cloud of fowls, which I had not seen at all, from among the corn itself.

This touched me sensibly, for I foresaw that in a few days they would devour all my hopes; that I should be starved, and never be able to raise a crop at all; and what to do I could not tell: however, I resolved not to lose my corn, if possible, though I should watch it night and day. In the first place, I went among it, to see what damage was already done, and found they had spoiled a good deal of it; but that as it was yet too green for them, the loss was not so great, but that the remainder was likely to be a good crop, if it could be saved.

I stayed by it to load my gun, and then coming away I could easily see the thieves sitting upon all the trees about me, as if they only waited till I was gone away; and the event proved it to be so; for as I walked off, as if gone, I was no sooner out of their sight, than they dropped down, one by one, into the corn again. I was so provoked, that I could not have patience to stay till more came on, knowing that every grain they ate now was, as it might be said, a peck loaf to me in the consequence; so coming up to the hedge, I fired again, and killed three of them. This was what I wished for; so I took them up, and served them as we serve notorious thieves in England, viz., hanged them in chains, for terror to others. It is impossible to imagine that this should have such an effect as it had; for the fowls not only never came to the corn, but, in short, they forsook all that part of the island, and I could never see a bird near the place as long as my scarecrows hung there. This I was very glad of, you may be sure; and about the latter end of December, which was our second harvest of the year, I reaped my corn.

I was sadly put to it for a scythe or sickle to cut it down: and all I could do was to make one as well as I could, out of one of the broadswords, or cutlasses, which I saved among the arms out of the ship. However, as my first crop was but small, I had no great difficulty to cut it down: in short, I reaped it my way, for I cut nothing off but the ears, and carried it away in a great basket which I had made, and so rubbed it out with my hands; and at the end of all my harvesting, I found that out of my half peck of seed I had near two bushels of rice, and above two bushels and a half of barley; that is to say, by my guess, for I had no measure.

However, this was great encouragement to me; and I foresaw that, in time, it would please God to supply me with bread; and yet here I was perplexed again; for I neither knew how to grind, or make meal of my corn, or indeed how to clean it and part it; nor if made into meal, how to make bread of it; and if how to make it, yet I knew not how to bake it: these things being added to my desire of having a good quantity for store, and to secure a constant supply, I resolved not to taste any of this crop, but to preserve it for seed against the next season; and, in the mean time, to employ all my study and hours of working to accomplish this great work of providing myself with corn and bread.

It might be truly said, that now I worked for my bread. It is a little wonderful, and what I believe few people have thought much upon, viz., the strange multitude of little things necessary in the providing, producing, curing, dressing, making, and finishing this one article of bread. I, that was reduced to a mere state of nature, found this to my daily discouragement, and was made more sensible of it every hour, even after I had got the first handful of seed-corn, which, as I have said, came up unexpectedly, and indeed to a surprise.

First, I had no plough to turn up the earth; no spade or shovel to dig it: well, this I conquered, by making a wooden spade, as I observed before; but this did my work in but a wooden manner; and though it cost me a great many days to make it, yet, for want of iron, it not only wore out the sooner, but made my work the harder, and performed it much worse. However, this I bore with, and was content to work it out with patience, and bear with the badness of the performance. When the corn was sown, I had no harrow, but was forced to go over it myself, and drag a great heavy bough of a tree over it, to scratch it, as it may be called, rather than rake or harrow it. When it was growing and grown, I have observed already how many things I wanted to fence it, secure it, mow or reap it, cure and carry it home, thresh, part it from the chaff, and save it; then I wanted a mill to grind it, sieves to dress it: yeast and salt to make it into bread, and an oven to bake it; and yet all these things I did without, as shall be observed; and the corn was an inestimable comfort and advantage to me: all this, as I said, made everything laborious and tedious to me, but that there was no help for; neither was my time so much loss to me, because, as I had divided it, a certain part of it was every day appointed to these works; and as I resolved to use none of the corn for bread till I had a greater quantity by me, I had the next six months to apply myself wholly, by labour and invention, to furnish myself with utensils proper for the performing all the operations necessary for making corn fit for my use.

BUT now I was to prepare more land; for I had seed enough to sow above an acre of ground. Before I did this, I had a week's work at least to make me a spade; which, when it was done, was but a sorry one indeed, and very heavy, and required double labour to work with it: however, I went through that, and sowed my seed in two large flat pieces of ground, as near my house as I could find them to my mind, and fenced them in with a good hedge; the stakes of which were all cut off that wood which I had set before, and knew it would grow; so that, in one year's time, I knew I should have a quick or living hedge, that would want but little repair. This work took me up full three months; because a great part of the time was in the wet season, when I could not go abroad. Within doors, that is, when it rained, and I could not go out, I found employment on the following occasions; always observing, that while I was at work, I diverted myself with talking to my parrot, and teaching him to speak; and I quickly taught him to know his own name, and at last to speak it out pretty loud, Poll; which was the first word I ever heard spoken in the island by any mouth but my own. This, therefore, was not my work, but an assistant to my work; for now, as I said, I had a great employment upon my hands, as follows: I had long studied, by some means or other, to make myself some earthen vessels, which indeed I wanted much, but knew not where to come at them: however, considering the heat of the climate, I did not doubt but if I could find out any clay, I might botch up some such pot as might, being dried in the sun, be hard and strong enough to bear handling, and to hold anything that was dry, and required to be kept so; and as this was necessary in the preparing corn meal, etc., which was the thing I was upon, I resolved to make some as large as I could, and fit only to stand like jars, to hold what should be put into them.

It would make the reader pity me, or rather laugh at me, to tell how many awkward ways I took to raise this pastil; what odd, misshapen, ugly things I made; how many of them fell in, and how many fell out, the clay not being stiff enough to bear its own weight; how many cracked by the over violent heat of the sun, being set out too hastily; and how many fell in pieces with only removing, as well before as after they were dried; and, in a word, how, after having laboured hard to find the clay, to dig it, to temper it, to bring it home, and work it, I could not make above two large earthen ugly things (I cannot call them jars) in about two months' labour.

However, as the sun baked these two very dry and hard, I lifted them very gently up, and set them down again in two great wicker baskets, which I had made on purpose for them, that they might not break; and as between the pot and the basket there was a little room to spare, I stuffed it full of the rice and barley straw; and these two pots being to stand always dry, I thought would hold my dry corn, and perhaps the meal, when the corn was bruised.

Though I miscarried so much in my design for large pots, yet I made several smaller things with better success; such as little round pots, flat dishes, pitchers, and pipkins, and anything my hand turned to; and the heat of the sun baked them very hard.

But all this would not answer my end, which was to get an earthen pot to hold liquids, and bear the fire, which none of these could do. It happened some time after, making a pretty large fire for cooking my meat, when I went to put it out after I had done with it, I found a broken piece of one of my earthenware vessels in the fire, burnt as hard as a stone, and red as a tile. I was agreeably surprised to see it; and said to myself, that certainly they might be made to burn whole, if they would burn broken.

This set me to study how to order my fire, so as to make it burn some pots. I had no notion of a kiln, such as the potters burn in, or of glazing them with lead, though I had some lead to do it with; but I placed three large pipkins and two or three pots in a pile, one upon another, and placed my fire-wood all round it, with a great heap of embers under them. I plied the fire with fresh fuel round the outside, and upon the top, till I saw the pots in the inside red-hot quite through, and observed that they did not crack at all: when I saw them clear red, I let them stand in that heat about five or six hours, till I found one of them, though it did not crack, did melt or run; for the sand which was mixed with the clay melted by the violence of the heat, and would have run into glass, if I had gone on; so I slacked my fire gradually, till the pots began to abate of the red colour; and watching them all night, that I might not let the fire abate too fast, in the morning I had three very good, I will not say hand-some, pipkins, and two other earthen pots, as hard burnt as could be de-sired; and one of them perfectly glazed with the running of the sand.

After this experiment, I need not say that I wanted no sort of earthen-ware for my use: but I must needs say, as to the shapes of them, they were very indifferent, as any one may suppose, as I had no way of mak-ing them but as the children make dirt pies, or as a woman would make pies that never learned to raise paste. No joy at a thing of so mean a nature was ever equal to mine, when I found I had made an earthen pot that would bear the fire; and I had hardly patience to stay till they were cold, before I set one on the fire again, with some water in it, to boil me some meat, which it did admirably well; and with a piece of a kid I made some very good broth; though I wanted oatmeal, and several other ingredients requisite to make it so good as I would have had it been.

My next concern was to get a stone mortar to stamp or beat some corn in; for as to the mill, there was no thought of arriving to that perfection of art with one pair of hands. To supply this want I was at a great loss; for, of all trades in the world, I was as perfectly unqualified for a stonecutter as for any whatever; neither had I any tools to go about it with. I spent many a day to find out a great stone big enough to cut hollow, and make fit for a mortar; but could find none at all, except what was in the solid rock, and which I had no way to dig or cut out; nor, indeed, were the rocks in the island of sufficient hardness, as they were all of a sandy crumbling stone, which would neither bear the weight of a heavy pestle, nor would break the corn without filling it with sand; so, after a great deal of time lost in searching for a stone, I gave it over, and resolved to look out a great block of hard wood, which I found indeed much easier; and getting one as big as I had strength to stir, I rounded it, and formed it on the outside with my axe and hatchet; and then, with the help of the fire, and infinite labour, made a hollow place in it, as the Indians in Brazil make their canoes. After this, I made a great heavy pestle, or beater, of the wood, called ironwood: and this I prepared and laid by against I had my next crop of corn, when I proposed to myself to grind, or rather pound, my corn into meal, to make my bread.

My next difficulty was to make a sieve, or search, to dress my meal, and to part it from the bran and the husk, without which I did not see it possible I could have any bread. This was a most difficult thing, even but to think on; for I had nothing like the necessary thing to make it; I mean fine thin canvas or stuff, to search the meal through. Here I was at a full stop for many months; nor did I really know what to do: linen I had none left, but what was mere rags; I had goats' hair, but neither knew how to weave it nor spin it; and had I known how, here were no tools to work it with: all the remedy I found for this was, at last recollecting I had, among the seamen's clothes which were saved out of the ship, some neckcloths of calico or muslin, with some pieces of these I made three small sieves, proper enough for the work; and thus I made shift for some years: how I did afterwards, I shall show in its place.

The baking part was the next thing to be considered, and how I should make bread when I came to have corn: for, first, I had no yeast; as to that part, there was no supplying the want, so I did not concern myself much about it; but for an oven I was indeed puzzled. At length I found out an expedient for that also, which was this; I made some earthen vessels, very broad, but not deep, that is to say, about two feet diameter, and not above nine inches deep: these I burned in the fire, as I had done the other, and laid them by; and when I wanted to bake, I made a great fire upon my hearth, which I had paved with some square tiles, of my own making and burning also; but I should not call them square. When the firewood was burned into embers, or live coals, I drew them forward upon the hearth, so as to cover it all over, and there let them lie till the hearth was very hot; then sweeping away all the embers, I set down my loaf, or loaves, and covering them with the earthen pot, drew the embers all round the outside of the pot, to keep in and add to the heat; and thus, as well as in the best oven in the world, I baked my barley loaves, and became, in a little time, a good pastry-cook into the bargain; for I made myself several cakes and puddings of the rice; but made no pies, as I had nothing to put into them except the flesh of fowls or goats.

It need not be wondered at, if all these things took me up most part of the third year of my abode here; for, it is to be observed, in the intervals of these things, I had my new harvest and husbandry to manage: I reaped my corn in its season, and carried it home as well as I could, and laid it up in the ear, in my large baskets, till I had time to rub it out; for I had no floor to thresh it on, or instrument to thresh it with.

And now, indeed, my stock of corn increasing, I really wanted to build my barns bigger: I wanted a place to lay it up in; for the increase of the corn now yielded me so much, that I had of the barley about twenty bushels, and of rice as much, or more, insomuch that now I resolved to begin to use it freely; for my bread had been quite gone a great while: I resolved also to see what quantity would be sufficient for me a whole year, and to sow but once a year.

Upon the whole, I found that the forty bushels of barley and rice were much more than I could consume in a year; so I resolved to sow just the same quantity every year that I sowed the last, in hopes that such a quantity would fully provide me with bread, etc.

ALL THE WHILE these things were doing, you may be sure my thoughts ran many times upon the prospect of land which I had seen from the other side of the island; and I was not without some secret wishes that I was on shore there; fancying, that seeing the main land, and an inhabited country, I might find some way or other to convey myself farther, and perhaps at last find some means of escape.

But all this while I made no allowance for the dangers of such a condition, and that I might fall into the hands of savages, and perhaps such as I might have reason to think far worse than the lions and tigers of Africa; that if I once came in their power, I should run a hazard of more than a thousand to one of being killed, and perhaps of being eaten; for I had heard that the people of the Caribbean coast were cannibals, or man-eaters; and I knew, by the latitude, that I could not be far off from that shore. Then supposing they were not cannibals, yet that they might kill me, as they had many Europeans who had fallen into their hands, even when they have been ten or twenty together; much more I, who was but one, and could make little or no defence; all these things, I say, which I ought to have considered well of, and did cast up in my thoughts afterwards, took up none of my apprehensions at first; yet my head ran mightily upon the thought of getting over to the shore.

Now I wished for my boy Xury, and the long-boat with the shoulder-of-mutton sail, with which I sailed above a thousand miles on the coast of Africa: but this was in vain: then I thought I would go and look at our ship's boat, which, as I have said, was blown up upon the shore a great way, in the storm, when we were first cast away. She lay nearly where she did at first, but not quite; having turned, by the force of the waves and the winds, almost bottom upward, against a high ridge of beachy rough sand; but no water about her, as before. If I had had hands to have refitted her, and to have launched her into the water, the boat would have done very well, and I might have gone back into the Brazils with her easily enough; but I might have foreseen that I could no more turn her and set her upright upon her bottom, than I could remove the island: however, I went to the woods, and cut levers and rollers, and brought them to the boat, resolving to try what I could do; suggesting to myself, that if I could but turn her down, and repair the damage she had received, she would be a very good boat, and I might venture to sea in her.

I spared no pains, indeed, in this piece of fruitless toil, and spent, I think, three or four weeks about it: at last, finding it impossible to heave her up with my little strength, I fell to digging away the sand, to undermine her, and so as to make her fall down, setting pieces of wood to thrust and guide her right in the fall. But when I had done this, I was unable to stir her up again, or to get under her, much less to move her forward towards the water; so I was forced to give it over: and yet, though I gave over the hopes of the boat, my desire to venture over the main increased, rather than diminished, as the means for it seemed impossible.

At length, I began to think whether it was not possible to make myself a canoe, or periagua, such as the natives of these climates make, even without tools, or, as I might say, without hands, of the trunk of a great tree. This I not only thought possible, but easy, and pleased myself extremely with the idea of making it, and with my having much more convenience for it than any of the Negroes or Indians; but not at all considering the particular inconveniences which I lay under more than the Indians did, viz., the want of hands to move it into the water when it was made, a difficulty much harder for me to surmount than all the consequences of want of tools could be to them: for what could it avail me, if, after I had chosen my tree, and with much trouble cut it down, and might be able with my tools to hew and dub the outside into the proper shape of a boat, and burn or cut the inside to make it hollow, so as to make a boat of it—if, after all this, I must leave it just where I found it, and was not able to launch it into the water?

One would imagine, if I had had the least reflection upon my mind of my circumstances while I was making this boat, I should have immediately thought how I was to get it into the sea: but my thoughts were so intent upon my voyage in it, that I never once considered how I should get it off the land; and it was really, in its own nature, more easy for me to guide it over forty-five miles of sea, than the forty-five fathoms of land, where it lay, to set it afloat in the water.

I went to work upon this boat the most like a fool that ever man did, who had any of his senses awake. I pleased myself with the design, without determining whether I was able to undertake it; not but that the difficulty of launching my boat came often into my head; but I put a stop to my own inquiries into it, by this foolish answer: Let us first make it; I warrant I will find some way or other to get it along when it is done.

This was a most preposterous method; but the eagerness of my fancy prevailed, and to work I went. I felled a cedar tree, and I question much whether Solomon ever had such a one for the building of the Temple at Jerusalem; it was five feet ten inches diameter at the lower part next the stump, and four feet eleven inches diameter at the end of twenty-two feet, where it lessened and then parted into branches. It was not without infinite labour that I felled this tree; I was twenty days hacking and hewing at the bottom, and fourteen more getting the branches and limbs, and the vast spreading head of it, cut off; after this, it cost me a month to shape it and dub it to a proportion, and to something like the bottom of a boat, that it might swim upright as it ought to do. It cost me near three months more to clear the inside, and work it out so as to make an exact boat of it: this I did, indeed, without fire, by mere mallet and chisel, and by the dint of hard labour, till I had brought it to be a very handsome periagua, and big enough to have carried six-and-twenty men, and consequently big enough to have carried me and all my cargo.

When I had gone through this work, I was extremely delighted with it. The boat was really much bigger than ever I saw a canoe or a periagua that was made of one tree, in my life. Many a weary stroke it had cost, you may be sure; and there remained nothing but to get it into the water; which, had I accomplished, I make no question but I should have begun the maddest voyage, and the most unlikely to be performed, that ever was undertaken.

But all my devices to get it into the water failed me; though they cost me inexpressible labour too. It lay about one hundred yards from the water, and not more; but the first inconvenience was, it was up hill towards the creek. Well, to take away this discouragement, I resolved to dig into the surface of the earth and so make a declivity; this I began, and it cost me a prodigious deal of pains; (but who grudge pains that have their deliverance in view?) when this was worked through, and this difficulty managed, it was still much the same, for I could no more stir the canoe than I could the other boat. Then I measured the distance of ground, and resolved to cut a dock, or canal, to bring the water up to the canoe, seeing I could not bring the canoe down to the water. Well, I began this work; and when I began to enter upon it, and calculate how deep it was to be dug, how broad, how the stuff was to be thrown out, I found by the number of hands I had, having none but my own, that it must have been ten or twelve years before I could have gone through with it; for the shore lay so high, that at the upper end it must have been at least twenty feet deep; this attempt, though with great reluctancy, I was at length obliged to give over also.

This grieved me heartily; and now I saw, though too late, the folly of beginning a work before we count the cost, and before we judge rightly of our own strength to go through with it.

In the middle of this work, I finished my fourth year in this place, and kept my anniversary with the same devotion, and with as much comfort as before; for, by a constant study and serious application to the word of God, and by the assistance of his grace, I gained a different knowledge from what I had before; I entertained different notions of things; I looked upon the world as a thing remote, which I had nothing to do with, no expectation from, and, indeed, no desires about; in a word, I had nothing to do with it, nor was ever likely to have; I thought it looked, as we may perhaps look upon it hereafter, viz., as a place I had lived in, but was come out of it; and well might I say, as Father Abraham to Dives, "Between me and thee is a great gulf fixed."

In the first place, I was here removed from all the wickedness of the world; I had neither the lust of the flesh, the lust of the eye, nor the pride of life. I had nothing to covet, for I had all that I was now capable of enjoying; I was lord of the whole manor; or, if I pleased, I might call myself king or emperor over the whole country which I had possession of: there were no rivals; I had no competitor, none to dispute sovereignty or command with me; I might have raised shiploadings of corn, but I had no use for it; so I let as little grow as I thought enough for my occasion. I had tortoise or turtle enough, but now and then one was as much as I could put to any use; I had timber enough to have built a fleet of ships; and I had grapes enough to have made wine, or to have cured into raisins, to have loaded that fleet when it had been built.

But all I could make use of was all that was valuable; I had enough to eat and supply my wants, and what was the rest to me? If I killed more flesh than I could eat, the dog must eat it, or vermin; if I sowed more corn than I could eat, it must be spoiled; the trees that I cut down were lying to rot on the ground; I could make no use of them than for fuel, and that I had no other occasion for but to dress my food.

In a word, the nature and experience of things dictated to me, upon just reflection, that all the good things of this world are of no further good to us than for our use; and that whatever we may heap up to give others, we enjoy only as much as we can use, and no more. The most covetous griping miser in the world would have been cured of the vice of covetousness, if he had been in my case; for I possessed infinitely more than I knew what to do with. I had no room for desire, except it was for things which I had not, and they were comparatively but trifles, though indeed of great use to me. I had, as I hinted before, a parcel of money, as well gold as silver, about thirty-six pounds sterling. Alas! there the nasty, sorry, useless stuff lay: I had no manner of business for it: and I often thought within myself, that I would have given a handful of it for a gross of tobacco-pipes, or for a hand-mill to grind my corn; nay, I would have given it all for sixpenny worth of turnip and carrot seed from England, or for a handful of peas and beans, and a bottle of ink. As it was, I had not the least advantage by it, or benefit from it; but there it lay in a drawer, and grew mouldy with the damp of the cave in the wet seasons; and if I had had the drawer full of diamonds, it had been the same case,—they would have been of no manner of value to me because of no use.

I had now brought my state of life to be much more comfortable in itself than it was at first, and much easier to my mind, as well as to my body. I frequently sat down to meat with thankfulness, and admired the hand of God's providence, which had thus spread my table in the wilderness: I learned to look more upon the bright side of my condition, and less upon the dark side, and to consider what I enjoyed, rather than what I wanted: and this gave me sometimes such secret comforts, that I cannot express them; and which I take notice of here, to put those discontented people in mind of it, who cannot enjoy comfortably what God has given them, because they see and covet something that he has not given them. All our discontents about what we want appeared to me to spring from the want of thankfulness for what we have.

Another reflection was of great use to me, and doubtless would be so to any one that should fall into such distress as mine was; and this was, to compare my present condition with what I at first expected it would be: nay, with what it would certainly have been, if the good providence of God had not wonderfully ordered the ship to be cast up near to the shore, where I not only could come at her, but could bring what I got out of her to the shore, for my relief and comfort; without which, I had wanted for tools to work, weapons for defence, and gunpowder and shot for getting my food.

I spent whole hours, I may say whole days, in representing to myself, in the most lively colours, how I must have acted if I had got nothing out of the ship. I could not have so much as got any food, except fish and turtles; and that, as it was long before I found any of them, I must have perished; that I should have lived, if I had not perished, like a mere savage; that if I had killed a goat or a fowl, by any contrivance, I had no way to flay or open it, or part the flesh from the skin and the bowels, or to cut it up, but must gnaw it with my teeth, and pull it with my claws, like a beast.

These reflections made me very sensible of the goodness of Providence to me, and very thankful for my present condition, with all its hardships and misfortunes; and this part also I cannot but recommend to the reflection of those who are apt, in their misery, to say, Is any affliction like mine? Let them consider how much worse the cases of some people are, and their case might have been, if Providence had thought fit.

I had another reflection, which assisted me also to comfort my mind with hopes; and this was, comparing my present condition with what I had deserved, and had therefore reason to expect from the hand of Providence. I had lived a dreadful life, perfectly destitute of the knowledge and fear of God. I had been well instructed by my father and mother; neither had they been wanting to me, in their endeavours to infuse an early religious awe of God into my mind, a sense of my duty, and what the nature and end of my being required of me. But, alas! falling early into the seafaring life, which, of all lives, is the most destitute of the fear of God, though his terrors are always before them; I say, falling early into the seafaring life, and into seafaring company, all that little sense of religion which I had entertained was laughed out of me by my messmates; by a hardened despising of dangers, and the views of death, which grew habitual to me; by my long absence from all manner of opportunities to converse with anything but what was like myself, or to hear anything that was good, or tending toward it.

So void was I of everything that was good, or of the least sense of what I was, or was to be, that in the greatest deliverances I enjoyed (such as my escape from Sallee, my being taken up by the Portuguese master of a ship, my being planted so well in the Brazils, my receiving the cargo from England, and the like) I never had once the words, Thank God, so much as on my mind, or in my mouth; nor in the greatest distress had I so much as a thought to pray to him, or so much as to say, Lord, have mercy upon me! no, nor to mention the name of God, unless it was to swear by, and blaspheme it.

I had terrible reflections upon my mind for many months, as I have already observed, on account of my wicked and hardened life past; and when I looked about me, and considered what particular providences had attended me since my coming into this place, and how God had dealt bountifully with me,—had not only punished me less than my iniquity had deserved, but had so plentifully provided for me,—this gave me great hopes that my repentance was accepted, and that God had yet mercies in store for me.

With these reflections I worked my mind up, not only to a resignation to the will of God in the present disposition of my circumstances, but even to a sincere thankfulness for my condition; and that I, who was yet a living man, ought not to complain, seeing I had not the due punishment of my sins; that I enjoyed so many mercies which I had no reason to have expected in that place, that I ought never more to repine at my condition, but to rejoice, and to give daily thanks for that daily bread, which nothing but a crowd of wonders could have brought; that I ought to consider I had been fed by a miracle, even as great as that of feeding Elijah by ravens; nay, by a long series of miracles; and that I could hardly have named a place in the uninhabitable part of the world where I could have been cast more to my advantage; a place where, as I had no society, which was my affliction on one hand, so I found no ravenous beasts, no furious wolves or tigers, to threaten my life; no venomous or poisonous creatures, which I might feed on to my hurt; no savages, to murder and devour me. In a word, as my life was a life of sorrow one way, so it was a life of mercy another; and I wanted nothing to make it a life of comfort, but to make myself sensible of God's goodness to me, and care over me in this condition; and after I did make a just improvement of these things, I went away, and was no more sad.

I had now been here so long, that many things which I brought on shore for my help were either quite gone, or very much wasted, and near spent.

My ink, as I observed, had been gone for some time, all but a very little, which I eked out with water, a little and a little, till it was so pale, it scarce left any appearance of black upon the paper. As long as it lasted, I made use of it to minute down the days of the month on which any remarkable thing happened to me: and, first, by casting up times past, I remember that there was a strange concurrence of days in the various providences which befell me, and which, if I had been superstitiously inclined to observe days as fatal or fortunate, I might have had reason to have looked upon with a great deal of curiosity.

First, I had observed, that the same day that I broke away from my father and my friends, and ran away to Hull, in order to go to sea, the same day afterwards I was taken by the Sallee man-of-war, and made a slave; the same day of the year that I escaped out of the wreck of the ship in Yarmouth Roads, that same day, years afterwards, I made my escape from Sallee in the boat: and the same day of the year I was born on, viz., the 30th of September, that same day I had my life so miraculously saved twenty-six years after, when I was cast on shore in this island: so that my wicked life and my solitary life began both on one day.

The next thing to my ink being wasted, was that of my bread, I mean the biscuit which I brought out of the ship: this I had husbanded to the last degree, allowing myself but one cake of bread a day for above a year; and yet I was quite without bread for near a year before I got any corn of my own; and great reason I had to be thankful that I had any at all, the getting it being, as has been already observed, next to miraculous.

My clothes, too, began to decay mightily: as to linen, I had none for a great while, except some chequered shirts which I found in the chests of the other seamen, and which I carefully preserved, because many times I could bear no clothes on but a shirt; and it was a very great help to me that I had, among all the men's clothes of the ship, almost three dozen of shirts. There were also, indeed, several thick watchcoats of the seamen's which were left, but they were too hot to wear: and though it is true that the weather was so violently hot that there was no need of clothes, yet I could not go quite naked, no, though I had been inclined to it, which I was not, nor could I abide the thought of it, though I was all alone. The reason why I could not go quite naked was, I could not bear the heat of the sun so well when quite naked as with some clothes on; nay, the very heat frequently blistered my skin: whereas, with a shirt on, the air itself made some motion, and whistling under the shirt, was twofold cooler than without it. No more could I ever bring myself to go out in the heat of the sun without a cap or hat; the heat of the sun beating with such violence as it does in that place, would give me the headache presently, by darting so directly upon my head, without a cap or hat on, so that I could not bear it; whereas, if I put on my hat, it would presently go away.

Upon these views, I began to consider about putting the few rags I had, which I called clothes, into some order. I had worn out all the waistcoats I had, and my business was now to try if I could not make jackets out of the great watchcoats that I had by me, and with such other materials as I had; so I set to work a tailoring, or rather, indeed, a botching, for I made most piteous work of it. However, I made shift to make two or three new waistcoats, which I hoped would serve me a great while: as for breeches, or drawers, I made but a very sorry shift indeed, till afterwards.

I have mentioned that I saved the skins of all the creatures that I killed, I mean four-footed ones; and I had hung them up, stretched out with sticks, in the sun, by which means some of them were so dry and hard that they were fit for little, but others I found very useful. The first thing I made of these was a great cap for my head, with the hair on the outside, to shoot off the rain; and this I performed so well, that after this I made me a suit of clothes wholly of the skins, that is to say, a waistcoat, and breeches, open at the knees, and both loose; for they were rather wanting to keep me cool than warm. I must not omit to acknowledge that they were wretchedly made; for if I was a bad carpenter, I was a worse tailor. However, they were such as I made very good shift with; and when I was abroad, if it happened to rain, the hair of my waistcoat and cap being uppermost, I was kept very dry.

After this, I spent a great deal of time and pains to make me an umbrella: I was indeed in great want of one, and had a great mind to make one: I had seen them made in the Brazils, where they were very useful in the great heats which are there; and I felt the heat every jot as great here, and greater too, being nearer the equinox: besides, as I was obliged to be much abroad, it was a most useful thing to me, as well for the rains as the heats. I took a world of pains at it, and was a great while before I could make anything likely to hold; nay, after I thought I had hit the way, I spoiled two or three before I made one to my mind; but at last I made one that answered indifferently well; the main difficulty I found was to make it to let down: I could make it spread, but if it did not let down too, and draw in, it was not portable for me any way but just over my head, which would not do. However, at last, as I said, I made one to answer, and covered it with skins, the hair upwards, so that it cast off the rain like a pent-house, and kept off the sun so effectually, that I could walk out in the hottest of the weather with greater advantage than I could before in the coolest; and when I had no need of it, could close it and carry it under my arm.

Thus I lived mighty comfortably, my mind being entirely composed by resigning to the will of God, and throwing myself wholly upon the disposal of his providence. This made my life better than sociable, for when I began to regret the want of conversation, I would ask myself, whether thus conversing mutually with my own thoughts, and, as I hope I may say, with even God himself, by ejaculations, was not better than the utmost enjoyment of human society in the world?

I CANNOT SAY that after this, for five years, any extraordinary thing happened to me, but I lived on in the same course, in the same posture and place, just as before; the chief things I was employed in, besides my yearly labour of planting my barley and rice, and curing my raisins, of both which I always kept up just enough to have sufficient stock of one year's provision beforehand: I say, besides this yearly labour, and my daily pursuit of going out with my gun, I had one labour, to make me a canoe, which at last I finished; so that by digging a canal to it of six feet wide, and four feet deep, I brought it into the creek, almost half a mile. As for the first, which was so vastly big, as I made it without considering beforehand, as I ought to do, how I should be able to launch it, so, never being able to bring it into the water, or bring the water to it, I was obliged to let it lie where it was, as a memorandum to teach me to be wiser the next time: indeed, the next time, though I could not get a tree proper for it, and was in a place where I could not get the water to it at any less distance than, as I have said, near half a mile, yet as I saw it was practicable at last, I never gave it over; and though I was near two years about it, yet I never grudged my labour, in hopes of having a boat to go off to sea at last.

However, though my little periagua was finished, yet the size of it was not at all answerable to the design which I had in view when I made the first; I mean, of venturing over to the *terra firma*, where it was above forty miles broad; accordingly, the smallness of my boat assisted to put an end to that design, and now I thought no more of it. As I had a boat, my next design was to make a cruise round the island; for as I had been on the other side in one place, crossing, as I have already described it, over the land, so the discoveries I made in that little journey made me very eager to see other parts of the coast; and now I had a boat, I thought of nothing but sailing round the island.

For this purpose, that I might do everything with discretion and consideration, I fitted up a little mast in my boat, and made a sail to it out of some of the pieces of the ship's sails which lay in store, and of which I had a great stock by me. Having fitted my mast and sail, and tried the boat, I found she would sail very well: then I made little lockers, or boxes, at each end of my boat, to put provisions, necessaries, ammunition, etc., into, to be kept dry, either from rain or the spray of the sea; and a little long hollow place I cut in the inside of the boat, where I could lay my gun, making a flap to hang down over it, to keep it dry.

I fixed my umbrella also in a step at the stern, like a mast, to stand over my head, and keep the heat of the sun off me, like an awning; and thus every now and then took a little voyage upon the sea, but never went far out, nor far from the little creek. At last, being eager to view the circumference of my little kingdom, I resolved upon my cruise; and accordingly, I victualled my ship for the voyage, putting in two dozen of loaves (cakes I should rather call them) of barley bread, an earthen pot full of parched rice (a food I ate a great deal of), a little bottle of rum, half a goat, and powder and shot for killing more, and two large watch-coats, of those which, as I mentioned before, I had saved out of the sea-men's chests; these I took, one to lie upon, and the other to cover me in the night.

It was the sixth of November, in the sixth year of my reign, or my captivity, which you please, that I set out on this voyage, and I found it much longer than I expected; for though the island itself was not very large, yet when I came to the east side of it, I found a great ledge of rocks lie about two leagues into the sea, some above water, some under it; and beyond that a shoal of sand, lying dry half a league more, so that I was obliged to go a great way out to sea to double the point.

When first I discovered them, I was going to give over my enterprise, and come back again, not knowing how far it might oblige me to go out to sea, and above all, doubting how I should get back again; so I came to an anchor; for I had made me a kind of anchor with a piece of a broken grappling which I got out of the ship.

Having secured my boat, I took my gun and went on shore, climbing up on a hill, which seemed to overlook that point, where I saw the full extent of it, and resolved to venture.

In my viewing the sea from that hill where I stood, I perceived a strong, and indeed a most furious current, which ran to the east, and even came close to the point; and I took the more notice of it, because I saw there might be some danger that, when I came into it, I might be carried out to sea by the strength of it, and not be able to make the island again: and, indeed, had I not got first upon this hill, I believe it would have been so; for there was the same current on the other side the island, only that it set off at a farther distance, and I saw there was a strong eddy under the shore: so I had nothing to do but to get out of the first current, and I should presently be in an eddy.

I lay here, however, two days, because the wind blowing pretty fresh at E.S.E., and that being just contrary to the said current, made a great breach of the sea upon the point; so that it was not safe for me to keep too close to the shore, for the breach, nor to go too far off, because of the stream.

The third day, in the morning, the wind having abated over night, the sea was calm, and I ventured; but I am a warning-piece again to all rash and ignorant pilots: for no sooner was I come to the point, when I was not even my boat's length from the shore, but I found myself in a great depth of water, and a current like the sluice of a mill; it carried my boat along with it with such violence, that all I could do could not keep her so much as on the edge of it; but I found it hurried me farther and farther out from the eddy, which was on my left hand. There was no wind stirring to help me, and all I could do with my paddles signified nothing: and now I began to give myself over for lost; for as the current was on both sides of the island, I knew in a few leagues' distance they must join again, and then I was irrecoverably gone; nor did I see any possibility of avoiding it; so that I had no prospect before me but of perishing, not by the sea, for that was calm enough, but of starving for hunger. I had indeed found a tortoise on the shore, as big almost as I could lift, and had tossed it into the boat; and I had a great jar of fresh water, that is to say, one of my earthen pots; but what was all this to being driven into the vast ocean, where, to be sure, there was no shore, no main land or island, for a thousand leagues at least?

And now I saw how easy it was for the providence of God to make even the most miserable condition of mankind worse. Now I looked back upon my desolate, solitary island as the most pleasant place in the world; and all the happiness my heart could wish for was to be but there again. I stretched out my hands to it, with eager wishes: O happy desert! said I, I shall never see thee more. O miserable creature! whither am I going! Then I reproached myself with my unthankful temper, and how I had repined at my solitary condition; and now what would I give to be on shore there again! Thus we never see the true state of our condition till it is illustrated to us by its contraries, nor know how to value what we enjoy, but by the want of it. It is scarce possible to imagine the consternation I was now in, being driven from my beloved island (for so it appeared to me now to be) into the wide ocean, almost two leagues, and in the utmost despair of ever recovering it again. However, I worked hard, till indeed my strength was almost exhausted, and kept my boat as much to the northward, that is, towards the side of the current which the eddy lay on, as possibly I could; when about noon, as the sun passed the meridian, I thought I felt a little breeze of wind in my face, springing up from S.S.E. This cheered my heart a little, and especially when, in about half an hour more, it blew a pretty gentle gale. By this time I was got at a frightful distance from the island, and had the least cloudy or hazy weather intervened, I had been undone another way too; for I had no compass on board, and should never have known how to have steered towards the island, if I had but once lost sight of it; but the weather continuing clear, I applied myself to get up my mast again, and spread my sail, standing away to the north as much as possible, to get out of the current.

Just as I had set my mast and sail, and the boat began to stretch away,

I saw even by the clearness of the water some alteration of the current was near; for where the current was so strong, the water was foul; but perceiving the water clear, I found the current abate; and presently I found to the east, at about half a mile, a breach of the sea upon some rocks: these rocks I found caused the current to part again, and as the main stress of it ran away more southerly, leaving the rocks to the north-east, so the other returned by the repulse of the rocks, and made a strong eddy, which ran back again to the north-west, with a very sharp stream.

They who know what it is to have a reprieve brought to them upon the ladder, or to be rescued from thieves just going to murder them, or who have been in such-like extremities, may guess what my present surprise of joy was, and how gladly I put my boat into the stream of this eddy; and the wind also freshening, how gladly I spread my sail to it, running cheerfully before the wind, and with a strong tide or eddy under foot.

This eddy carried me about a league in my way back again, directly towards the island, but about two leagues more to the northward than the current which carried me away at first: so that when I came near the island, I found myself open to the northern shore of it, that is to say, the other end of the island, opposite to that which I went out from.

When I had made something more than a league of way by the help of this current or eddy, I found it was spent, and served me no farther. However, I found that being between two great currents, viz., that on the south side, which had hurried me away, and that on the north, which lay about a league on the other side; I say, between these two, in the wake of the island, I found the water at least still, and running no way; and having still a breeze of wind fair to me, I kept on steering directly for the island, though not making such fresh way as I did before.

About four o'clock in the evening, being then within a league of the island, I found the point of the rocks which occasioned this disaster stretching out, as is described before, to the southward, and casting off the current more southerly, had, of course, made another eddy to the north; and this I found very strong, but not directly setting the way my course lay, which was due west, but almost full north. However, having a fresh gale I stretched across this eddy, slanting north-west; and, in about an hour, came within about a mile of the shore, where, it being smooth, I soon got to land.

When I was on shore, I fell on my knees, and gave God thanks for my deliverance, resolving to lay aside all thoughts of my deliverance by my boat; and refreshing myself with such things as I had, I brought my boat close to the shore, in a little cove that I had spied under some trees, and laid me down to sleep, being quite spent with the labour and fatigue of the voyage.

I was now at a great loss which way to get home with my boat: I had run so much hazard, and knew too much of the case, to think of attempting it by the way I went out; and what might be at the other side (I mean the west side) I knew not, nor had I any mind to run any more ventures; so I only resolved in the morning to make my way westward along the shore, and see if there was no creek where I might lay up my frigate in safety, so as to have her again, if I wanted her. In about three miles, or thereabout, coasting the shore, I came to a very good inlet or bay, about a mile over, which narrowed till it came to a very little rivulet or brook, where I found a very convenient harbour for my boat, and where she lay as if she had been in a little dock made on purpose for her. Here I put in, and having stowed my boat very safe, I went on shore, to look about me, and see where I was.

I soon found I had but a little passed by the place where I had been before when I travelled on foot to that shore; so taking nothing out of my boat but my gun and umbrella, for it was exceeding hot, I began my march. The way was comfortable enough after such a voyage as I had been upon, and I reached my old bower in the evening, where I found everything standing as I had left it; for I always kept it in good order, being, as I said before, my country house.

I got over the fence, and laid me down in the shade to rest my limbs, for I was very weary, and fell asleep: but judge you, if you can, that read my story, what a surprise I must be in, when I was awaked out of my sleep by a voice, calling me by my name several times, Robin, Robin, Robin, Crusoe; poor Robin Crusoe! Where are you, Robin Crusoe? Where are you? Where have you been?

I was so dead asleep at first, being fatigued with rowing, or paddling as it is called, the first part of the day, and with walking the latter part, that I did not wake thoroughly; but dozing between sleeping and waking, thought I dreamed that somebody spoke to me; but as the voice continued to repeat Robin Crusoe, Robin Crusoe, at last I began to wake more perfectly, and was at first dreadfully frightened, and started up in the utmost consternation; but no sooner were my eyes open, but I saw my Poll sitting on the top of the hedge; and immediately knew it was he that spoke to me: for just in such bemoaning language I had used to talk to him, and teach him; and he had learned it so perfectly, that he would sit upon my finger, and lay his bill close to my face, and cry, Poor Robin Crusoe! Where are you? Where have you been? How came you here? and such things as I had taught him.

However, even though I knew it was the parrot, and that indeed it could be nobody else, it was a good while before I could compose myself. First, I was amazed how the creature got thither; and then how he should just keep about the place, and nowhere else; but as I was well satisfied it could be nobody but honest Poll, I got over it; and holding out my hand, and calling him by his name, Poll, the sociable creature came to me, and sat upon my thumb, as he used to do, and continued talking to me, Poor Robin Crusoe! and how did I come here? and where had I been? just as if he had been overjoyed to see me again: and so I carried him home along with me.

I now had enough of rambling to sea for some time, and had enough to do for many days to sit still, and to reflect upon the danger I had been in. I would have been very glad to have had my boat again on my side of the island; but I knew not how it was practicable to get it about. As to the east side of the island, which I had gone round, I knew well enough there was no venturing that way; my very heart would shrink, and my very blood run chill, but to think of it; and as to the other side of the island, I did not know how it might be there; but supposing the current ran with the same force against the shore at the east as it passed by it on the other, I might run the same risk of being driven down the stream, and carried by the island, as I had been before of being carried away from it; so, with these thoughts, I contented myself to be without any boat, though it had been the product of so many months' labour to make it, and of so many more to get it into the sea.

In this government of my temper I remained near a year, lived a very sedate, retired life, as you may well suppose; and my thoughts being very much composed as to my condition, and fully comforted in resigning myself to the dispositions of Providence, I thought I lived really very happily in all things except that of society.

I improved myself in this time in all the mechanic exercises which my necessities put me upon applying myself to; and I believe I could, upon occasion, have made a very good carpenter, especially considering how few tools I had.

Besides this, I arrived at an unexpected perfection in my earthen-ware, and contrived well enough to make them with a wheel, which I found infinitely easier and better; because I made things round and shapeable, which before were filthy things indeed to look upon. But I think I was never more vain of my own performance, or more joyful for anything I found out, than for my being able to make a tobacco-pipe; and though it was a very ugly clumsy thing when it was done, and only burned red, like other earthen-ware, yet as it was hard and firm, and would draw the smoke, I was exceedingly comforted with it, for I had been always used to smoke: and there were pipes in the ship, but I forgot them at first, not thinking that there was tobacco in the island; and afterwards, when I searched the ship again, I could not come at any pipes at all.

In my wicker-ware also I improved much, and made abundance of necessary baskets, as well as my invention showed me; though not very handsome, yet they were such as were very handy and convenient for my laying things up in, or fetching things home. For example, if I killed a goat abroad, I could hang it up in a tree, flay it, dress it, and cut it in pieces, and bring it home in a basket; and the like by a turtle; I could cut it up, take out the eggs, and a piece or two of the flesh, which was enough for me, and bring them home in a basket, and leave the rest behind me. Also large deep baskets for the receivers of my corn, which I always rubbed out as soon as it was dry, and cured, and kept it in great baskets.

I began now to perceive my powder abated considerably; this was a want which it was impossible for me to supply, and I began seriously to consider what I must do when I should have no more powder, that is to say, how I should do to kill any goats. I had, as is observed, in the third year of my being here, kept a young kid, and bred her up tame, and I was in hopes of getting a he-goat: but I could not by any means bring it to pass, till my kid grew an old goat; and as I could never find in my heart to kill her, she died at last of mere age.

BEING now in the eleventh year of my residence, and as I have said, my ammunition growing low, I set myself to study some art to trap and snare the goats, to see whether I could not catch some of them alive; and particularly, I wanted a she-goat great with young. For this purpose, I made snares to hamper them; and I do believe they were more than once taken in them: but my tackle was not good, for I had no wire, and I always found them broken, and my bait devoured. At length I resolved to try a pitfall: so I dug several large pits in the earth, in places where I had observed the goats used to feed, and over those pits I placed hurdles, of my own making too, with a great weight upon them; and several times I put ears of barley and dry rice, without setting the trap; and I could easily perceive that the goats had gone in and eaten up the corn, for I could see the marks of their feet. At length I set three traps in one night, and going the next morning, I found them all standing, and yet the bait eaten and gone. This was very discouraging: however, I altered my traps; and, not to trouble you with particulars, going one morning to see my traps, I found in one of them a large old he-goat, and in one of the others three kids, a male and two females.

As to the old one, I knew not what to do with him; he was so fierce, I durst not go into the pit to him; that is to say, to go about to bring him away alive, which was what I wanted: I could have killed him, but that was not my business, nor would it answer my end; so I even let him out, and he ran away, as if he had been frightened out of his wits. But I had forgot then, what I had learned afterwards, that hunger will tame a lion. If I had let him stay there three or four days without food, and then have carried him some water to drink, and then a little corn, he would have been as tame as one of the kids; for they are mighty sagacious, tractable creatures, where they are well used. However, for the present I let him go, knowing no better at that time: then I went to the three kids, and taking them one by one, I tied them with strings together, and with some difficulty brought them all home.

It was a good while before they would feed; but throwing them some sweet corn, it tempted them, and they began to be tame. And now I found that if I expected to supply myself with goat's flesh when I had no powder or shot left, breeding some up tame was my only way; when, perhaps, I might have them about my house like a flock of sheep. But then it occurred to me, that I must keep the tame from the wild, or else they would always run wild when they grew up; and the only way for this was, to have some enclosed piece of ground, well fenced, either with hedge or pale, to keep them in so effectually, that those within might not break out, or those without break in.

This was a great undertaking for one pair of hands; yet as I saw there was an absolute necessity for doing it, my first work was to find out a proper piece of ground, where there was likely to be herbage for them to eat, water for them to drink, and cover to keep them from the sun.

Those who understand such enclosures will think I had very little contrivance, when I pitched upon a place very proper for all these (being a plain open piece of meadow land, or savannah, as our people call it in the western colonies) which had two or three little drills of fresh water in it, and at one end was very woody; I say, they will smile at my forecast, when I shall tell them, I began my enclosing this piece of ground in such a manner, that my hedge or pale must have been at least two miles about. Nor was the madness of it so great as to the compass, for if it was ten miles about I was like to have time enough to do it in; but I did not consider that my goats would be as wild in so much compass as if they had had the whole island, and I should have so much room to chase them in, that I should never catch them.

My hedge was begun and carried on, I believe about fifty yards, when this thought occurred to me; so I presently stopped short, and, for the first beginning, I resolved to enclose a piece of about one hundred and fifty yards in length, and one hundred yards in breadth: which, as it would maintain as many as I should have in any reasonable time, so, as my stock increased, I could add more ground to my enclosure.

This was acting with some prudence, and I went to work with courage. I was about three months hedging in the first piece; and, till I had done it, I tethered the three kids in the best part of it, and used them to feed as near me as possible, to make them familiar; and very often I would go and carry them some ears of barley, or a handful of rice, and feed them out of my hand: so that after my enclosure was finished, and I let them loose, they would follow me up and down, bleating after me for a handful of corn.

This answered my end; and in about a year and a half I had a flock of about twelve goats, kids and all; and in two years more, I had three and forty, beside several that I took and killed for my food. After that I enclosed five several pieces of ground to feed them in, with little pens to drive them into, to take them as I wanted, and gates out of one piece of ground into another.

But this was not all; for now I not only had goat's flesh to feed on when I pleased, but milk too; a thing which, indeed, in the beginning, I did not so much as think of, and which, when it came into my thoughts, was really an agreeable surprise; for now I set up my dairy, and had sometimes a gallon or two of milk in a day. And as Nature, who gives supplies of food to every creature, dictates even naturally how to make use of it, so I, that had never milked a cow, much less a goat, or seen butter or cheese made, only when I was a boy, after a great many essays and miscarriages, made me both butter and cheese at last, and also salt (though I found it partly made to my hand by the heat of the sun upon some of the rocks of the sea), and never wanted it afterwards. How mercifully can our Creator treat his creatures, even in those conditions in which they seemed to be overwhelmed in destruction! How can he sweeten the bitterest providences, and give us cause to praise him for dungeons and prisons! What a table was here spread for me in a wilderness, where I saw nothing, at first, but to perish for hunger!

It would have made a stoic smile to have seen me and my little family sit down to dinner. There was my majesty, the prince and lord of the whole island; I had the lives of all my subjects at my absolute command; I could hang, draw, give liberty, and take it away; and no rebels among all my subjects.

Then to see how like a king I dined too, all alone, attended by my servants: Poll, as if he had been my favourite, was the only person permitted to talk to me. My dog, who was now grown very old and crazy, and had found no species to multiply his kind upon, sat always at my right hand; and two cats, one on one side of the table, and one on the other, expecting now and then a bit from my hand, as a mark of special favour.

But these were not the two cats which I brought on shore at first, for they were both of them dead, and had been interred near my habitation by my own hand; but one of them having multiplied by I know not what kind of creature, these were two which I had preserved tame; whereas the rest ran wild in the woods, and became indeed troublesome to me at last; for they would often come into my house, and plunder me too, till at last I was obliged to shoot them, and did kill a great many; at length they left me.—With this attendance, and in this plentiful manner,

I lived: neither could I be said to want anything but society; and of that, some time after this, I was like to have too much.

I was something impatient, as I have observed, to have the use of my boat, though very loath to run any more hazards; and therefore sometimes I sat contriving ways to get her about the island, and at other times I sat myself down contented enough without her. But I had a strange uneasiness in my mind to go down to the point of the island, where, as I have said, in my last ramble, I went up the hill to see how the shore lay, and how the current set, that I might see what I had to do: this inclination increased upon me every day, and at length I resolved to travel thither by land, following the edge of the shore. I did so; but had any one in England been to meet such a man as I was, it must either have frightened him, or raised a great deal of laughter; and as I frequently stood still to look at myself, I could not but smile at the notion of my travelling through Yorkshire, with such an equipage, and in such a dress. Be pleased to take a sketch of my figure, as follows.

I had a great high shapeless cap, made of a goat's skin, with a flap hanging down behind, as well to keep the sun from me as to shoot the rain off from running into my neck; nothing being so hurtful in these climates as the rain upon the flesh, under the clothes.

I had a short jacket of goat's skin, the skirts coming down to about the middle of the thighs, and a pair of open-kneed breeches of the same; the breeches were made of the skin of an old he-goat, whose hair hung down such a length on either side, that, like pantaloons, it reached to the middle of my legs; stockings and shoes I had none, but had made me a pair of somethings I scarce know what to call them, like buskins, to flap over my legs, and lace on either side like spatterdashes, but of a most barbarous shape, as indeed were all the rest of my clothes.

I had on a broad belt of goat's skin dried, which I drew together with two thongs of the same, instead of buckles; and in a kind of a frog on either side of this, instead of a sword and dagger, hung a little saw and a hatchet; one on one side, and one on the other. I had another belt, not so broad, and fastened in the same manner, which hung over my shoulder; and at the end of it, under my left arm, hung two pouches, both made of goat's skin too: in one of which hung my powder, in the other my shot. At my back I carried my basket, and on my shoulder my gun; and over my head a great clumsy ugly goat's-skin umbrella, but which, after all, was the most necessary thing I had about me, next to my gun. As for my face, the colour of it was really not so mulatto-like as one might expect from a man not at all careful of it, and living within nine or ten degrees of the equinox. My beard I had once suffered to grow till it was about a quarter of a yard long; but as I had both scissors and razors sufficient, I had cut it pretty short, except what grew on my upper lip, which I had trimmed into a large pair of Mahometan whiskers, such as

I had seen worn by some Turks at Sallee; for the Moors did not wear such, though the Turks did: of these mustachios or whiskers, I will not say they were long enough to hang my hat upon them, but they were of a length and shape monstrous enough, and such as, in England, would have passed for frightful.

But all this is by the bye; for, as to my figure, I had so few to observe me that it was of no manner of consequence; so I say no more to that part. In this kind of figure I went my new journey, and was out five or six days. I travelled first along the seashore, directly to the place where I first brought my boat to an anchor, to get upon the rocks; and having no boat now to take care of, I went over the land; a nearer way, to the same height that I was upon before; when looking forward to the point of the rocks which lay out, and which I was obliged to double with by boat, as is said above, I was surprised to see the sea all smooth and quiet; no rippling, no motion, no current, any more than in any other places. I was at a strange loss to understand this, and resolved to spend some time in the observing it, to see if nothing from the sets of the tide had occasioned it; but I was presently convinced how it was, viz., that the tide of ebb, setting from the west, and joining with the current of waters from some great river on the shore; must be the occasion of this current; and that according as the wind blew more forcibly from the west, or from the north, this current came nearer, or went farther from the shore: for waiting thereabouts till evening, I went up the rock again, and then the tide of ebb being made, I plainly saw the current again as before, only that it ran farther off, being near half a league from the shore; whereas, in my case, it set close upon the shore, and hurried me and my canoe along with it, which, at another time, it would not have done.

This observation convinced me, that I had nothing to do but to observe the ebbing and the flowing of the tide, and I might very easily bring my boat about the island again: but when I began to think of putting it into practice, I had such a terror upon my spirits at the remembrance of the danger I had been in, that I could not think of it again with any patience; but, on the contrary, I took up another resolution, which was more safe, though more laborious; and this was, that I would build, or rather make me another periagua or canoe; and so have one for one side of the island, and one for the other.

You are to understand, that now I had, as I may call it, two plantations in the island; one, my little fortification, or tent with the wall about it, under the rock, with the cave behind me, which, by this time, I had enlarged into several apartments or caves, one within another. One of these, which was the driest and largest, and had a door out beyond my wall or fortification, that is to say, beyond where my wall joined to the rock, was all filled up with large earthen pots, of which I have given an account, and with fourteen or fifteen great baskets, which would hold five or six bushels each, where I laid up my stores of provision, especially my corn, some in the ear, cut off short from the straw, and the other rubbed out with my hand.

As for my wall, made, as before, with long stakes or piles, those piles grew all like trees, and were by this time grown so big, and spread so very much, that there was not the least appearance, to any one's view, of my habitation behind them.

Near this dwelling of mine, but a little farther within the land, and upon lower ground, lay my two pieces of corn land, which I kept duly cultivated and sowed, and which duly yielded me their harvest in its season; and whenever I had occasion for more corn, I had more land adjoining as fit as that.

Besides this, I had my country seat; and I had now a tolerable plantation there also: for, first, I had my little bower, as I called it, which I kept in repair; that is to say, I kept the hedge which encircled it constantly fitted up to its usual height, the ladder standing always in the inside: I kept the trees, which at first were no more than my stakes, but were now grown very firm and tall, always cut so, that they might spread and grow thick and wild, and make the more agreeable shade, which they did effectually to my mind. In the middle of this I had my tent always standing, being a piece of a sail spread over poles, set up for that purpose, and which never wanted any repair or renewing; and under this I had made me a squab or couch, with the skins of the creatures I had killed, and with other soft things; and a blanket laid on them, such as belonged to our sea bedding, which I had saved, and a great watchcoat to cover me; and here, whenever I had occasion to be absent from my chief seat, I took up my country habitation.

Adjoining to this I had my enclosures for my cattle, that is to say, my goats; and as I had taken an inconceivable deal of pains to fence and enclose this ground, I was so anxious to see it kept entire, lest the goats should break through, that I never left off, till, with infinite labour, I had stuck the outside of the hedge so full of small stakes, and so near to one another, that it was rather a pale than a hedge, and there was scarce room to put a hand through between them; which afterwards, when those stakes grew, as they all did the next rainy season, made the enclosure strong like a wall,—indeed, stronger than any wall.

This will testify for me that I was not idle, and that I spared no pains to bring to pass whatever appeared necessary for my comfortable support; for I considered the keeping up a breed of tame creatures thus at my hand would be a living magazine of flesh, milk, butter, and cheese for me as long as I lived in the place, if it were to be forty years; and that keeping them in my reach depended entirely upon my perfecting my enclosures to such a degree, that I might be sure of keeping them together; which, by this method, indeed, I so effectually secured, that when these little stakes began to grow, I had planted them so very thick, that I was forced to pull some of them up again.

In this place also I had my grapes growing, which I principally depended on for my winter store of raisins, and which I never failed to preserve very carefully, as the best and most agreeable dainty of my whole diet: and, indeed, they were not only agreeable, but medicinal, wholesome, nourishing, and refreshing to the last degree.

As this was also about half-way between my other habitation and the place where I had laid up my boat, I generally stayed and lay here in my way thither: for I used frequently to visit my boat; and I kept all things about or belonging to her, in very good order: sometimes I went out in her to divert myself, but no more hazardous voyages would I go, nor scarce ever above a stone's cast or two from the shore, I was so apprehensive of being hurried out of my knowledge again by the currents or winds, or any other incident. But now I come to a new scene of my life.

IT HAPPENED one day, about noon, going towards my boat, I was exceedingly surprised with the print of a man's naked foot on the shore, which was very plain to be seen in the sand. I stood like one thunderstruck, or as if I had seen an apparition: I listened, I looked round me, but I could hear nothing, nor see anything; I went up to a rising ground, to look farther; I went up the shore and down the shore, but it was all one; I could see no other impression but that one. I went to it again to see if there were any more, and to observe if it might not be my fancy; but there was no room for that, for there was exactly the print of a foot, toes, heel, and every part of a foot: how it came thither, I knew not, nor could I in the least imagine; but, after innumerable fluttering thoughts, like a man perfectly confused and out of myself, I came home to my fortification, not feeling, as we say, the ground I went on, but terrified to the last degree; looking behind me at every two or three steps, mistaking every bush and tree, and fancying every stump at a distance to be a man. Nor is it possible to describe how many various shapes my affrighted imagination represented things to me in, how many wild ideas were found every moment in my fancy, and what strange unaccountable whimsies came into my thoughts by the way.

When I came to my castle (for so I think I called it ever after this), I fled into it like one pursued; whether I went over by the ladder, as first contrived, or went in at the hole in the rock, which I had called a door, I cannot remember; no, nor could I remember the next morning; for never frightened hare fled to cover, or fox to earth with more terror of mind than I to this retreat.

I slept none that night: the farther I was from the occasion of my fright, the greater my apprehensions were; which is something contrary to the nature of such things, and especially to the usual practice of all creatures in fear; but I was so embarrassed with my own frightful ideas of the thing, that I formed nothing but dismal imaginations to myself, even though I was now a great way off it. Sometimes I fancied it must be the Devil, and reason joined in with me upon this supposition; for how should any other thing in human shape come into the place? Where was the vessel that brought them? What marks were there of any other footsteps? And how was it possible a man should come there? But then to think that Satan should take human shape upon him in such a place, where there could be no manner of occasion for it, but to leave the print of his foot behind him, and that even for no purpose too, for he could not be sure I should see it,—this was an amusement the other way. I considered that the Devil might have found out abundance of other ways to have terrified me than this of the single print of a foot; that as I lived quite on the other side of the island, he would never have been so simple as to leave a mark in a place where it was ten thousand to one whether I should ever see it or not, and in the sand too, which the first surge of the sea, upon a high wind, would have defaced entirely: all this seemed inconsistent with the thing itself, and with all the notions we usually entertain of the subtlety of the Devil.

Abundance of such things as these assisted to argue me out of all apprehensions of its being the Devil; and I presently concluded, then, that it must be some more dangerous creature, viz., that it must be some of the savages of the main land over against me, who had wandered out to sea in their canoes, and, either driven by the currents or by contrary winds, had made the island, and had been on shore, but were gone away again to sea; being as loath, perhaps, to have stayed in this desolate island as I would have been to have had them.

While these reflections were rolling upon my mind, I was very thankful in my thoughts that I was so happy as not to be thereabouts at that time, or that they did not see my boat, by which they would have concluded that some inhabitants had been in the place, and perhaps have searched farther for me: then terrible thoughts racked my imagination about their having found my boat, and that there were people here; and that if so, I should certainly have them come again in greater numbers, and devour me: that if it should happen so that they should not find me, yet they would find my enclosure, destroy all my corn, and carry away all my flock of tame goats, and I should perish at last for mere want.

Thus my fear banished all my religious hope, all that former confidence in God, which was founded upon such wonderful experience as I had had of his goodness, as if he that had fed me by miracle hitherto could not preserve, by his power, the provision which he had made for me by his goodness. I reproached myself with my laziness, that would not sow any more corn one year than would just serve me till the next season, as if no accident would intervene to prevent my enjoying the crop that was upon the ground; and this I thought so just a reproof, that I resolved for the future to have two or three years' corn beforehand, so that, whatever might come, I might not perish for want of bread.

How strange a chequer-work of Providence is the life of man! and by what secret different springs are the affections hurried about, as different circumstances present! To-day we love what to-morrow we hate; to-day we seek what to-morrow we shun; to-day we desire what to-morrow we fear, nay, even tremble at the apprehensions of; this was exemplified in me, at this time, in the most lively manner imaginable; for I, whose only affliction was that I seemed banished from human society, that I was alone, circumscribed by the boundless ocean, cut off from mankind, and condemned to what I called silent life; that I was as one whom Heaven thought not worthy to be numbered among the living, or to appear among the rest of his creatures; that to have seen one of my own species would have seemed to me a raising me from death to life, and the greatest blessing that Heaven itself, next to the supreme blessing of salvation, could bestow; I say, that I should now tremble at the very apprehensions of seeing a man, and was ready to sink into the ground at but the shadow or silent appearance of a man's having set his foot in the island.

Such is the uneven state of human life; and it afforded me a great many curious speculations afterwards, when I had a little recovered my first surprise. I considered that this was the station of life the infinitely wise and good providence of God had determined for me; that as I could not foresee what the ends of divine wisdom might be in all this, so I was not to dispute his sovereignty, who, as I was his creature, had an undoubted right, by creation, to govern and dispose of me absolutely as he thought fit; and who, as I was a creature that had offended him, had likewise a judicial right to condemn me to what punishment he thought fit; and that it was my part to submit to bear his indignation, because I had sinned against him. I then reflected, that as God, who was not only righteous, but omnipotent, had thought fit thus to punish and afflict me, so he was able to deliver me; that if he did not think fit to do so, it was my unquestioned duty to resign myself absolutely and entirely to his will; and, on the other hand, it was my duty also to hope in him, pray to him, and quietly to attend the dictates and directions of his daily providence.

These thoughts took me up many hours, days, nay, I may say weeks and months; and one particular effect of my cogitations on this occasion I cannot omit. One morning early, lying in my bed, and filled with thoughts about my danger from the appearances of savages, I found it discomposed me very much; upon which these words of the Scripture came into my thoughts: "Call upon me in the day of trouble, and I will deliver thee, and thou shalt glorify me." Upon this, rising cheerfully out of my bed, my heart was not only comforted, but I was guided and encouraged to pray earnestly to God for deliverance: when I had done praying, I took up my Bible, and opening it to read, the first words that presented to me were, "Wait on the Lord, and be of good cheer, and he shall strengthen thy heart; wait, I say, on the Lord." It is impossible to express the comfort this gave me. In answer, I thankfully laid down the book, and was no more sad, at least on that occasion.

In the middle of these cogitations, apprehensions, and reflections, it came into my thoughts one day, that all this might be a mere chimera of my own, and that this foot might be the print of my own foot, when I came on shore from my boat: this cheered me up a little too, and I began to persuade myself it was all a delusion; that it was nothing else but my own foot: and why might I not come that way from the boat, as well as I was going that way to the boat? Again, I considered also, that I could by no means tell, for certain, where I had trod, and where I had not; and that if, at last, this was only the print of my own foot, I had played the part of those fools, who try to make stories of spectres and apparitions, and then are frightened at them more than anybody.

Now I began to take courage, and to peep abroad again, for I had not stirred out of my castle for three days and nights, so that I began to starve for provisions; for I had little or nothing within doors but some barley cakes and water: then I knew that my goats wanted to be milked too, which usually was my evening diversion; and the poor creatures were in great pain and inconvenience for want of it: and, indeed, it almost spoiled some of them, and almost dried up their milk. Encouraging myself, therefore, with the belief that this was nothing but the print of one of my own feet, and that I might be truly said to start at my own shadow, I began to go abroad again, and went to my country house to milk my flock: but to see with what fear I went forward, how often I looked behind me, how I was ready, every now and then, to lay down my basket, and run for my life, it would have made any one think I was haunted with an evil conscience, or that I had been lately most terribly frightened; and so, indeed, I had. However, as I went down thus two or three days, and having seen nothing, I began to be a little bolder, and to think there was really nothing in it but my own imagination; but I could not persuade myself fully of this till I should go down to the shore again,

and see this print of a foot, and measure it by my own, and see if there
was any similitude or fitness, that I might be assured it was my own foot:
but when I came to the place, first, it appeared evidently to me, that when
I laid up my boat, I could not possibly be on shore anywhere thereabout:
secondly, when I came to measure the mark with my own foot, I found
my foot not so large by a great deal. Both these things filled my head with
new imaginations, and gave me the vapours again to the highest degree,
so that I shook with cold like one in an ague; and I went home again,
filled with the belief that some man or men had been on shore there; or,
in short, that the island was inhabited, and I might be surprised before
I was aware; and what course to take for my security I knew not.

O, what ridiculous resolutions men take when possessed with fear!
It deprives them of the use of those means which reason offers for their
relief. The first thing I proposed to myself was, to throw down my enclosures, and turn all my tame cattle wild into the woods, lest the enemy
should find them, and then frequent the island in prospect of the same
or the like booty: then to the simple thing of digging up my two corn-
fields, lest they should find such a grain there, and still be prompted to
frequent the island: then to demolish my bower and tent, that they might
not see any vestiges of habitation, and be prompted to look farther, in
order to find out the persons inhabiting.

These were the subject of the first night's cogitations after I was come
home again, while the apprehensions which had so overrun my mind
were fresh upon me, and my head was full of vapours, as above. Thus
fear of danger is ten thousand times more terrifying than danger itself
when apparent to the eyes; and we find the burden of anxiety greater, by
much, than the evil which we are anxious about: and, which was worse
than all this, I had not that relief in this trouble from the resignation I
used to practise, that I hoped to have. I looked, I thought, like Saul, who
complained not only that the Philistines were upon him, but that God
had forsaken him; for I did not now take due ways to compose my
mind, by crying to God in my distress, and resting upon his providence,
as I had done before, for my defence and deliverance; which, if I had
done, I had at least been more cheerfully supported under this new surprise, and perhaps carried through it with more resolution.

This confusion of my thoughts kept me awake all night; but in the
morning I fell asleep; and having, by the amusement of my mind, been
as it were tired, and my spirits exhausted, I slept very soundly, and waked
much better composed than I had ever been before. And now I began to
think sedately; and, upon the utmost debate with myself, I concluded
that this island, which was so exceeding pleasant, fruitful, and no farther
from the main land than as I had seen, was not so entirely abandoned as
I might imagine; that although there were no stated inhabitants who
lived on the spot, yet that there might sometime come boats off from
the shore, who, either with design, or perhaps never but when they were

driven by cross winds, might come to this place; that I had lived here fifteen years now, and had not met with the least shadow or figure of any people yet; and that if at any time they should be driven here, it was probable they went away again as soon as ever they could, seeing they had never thought fit to fix here upon any occasion; that the most I could suggest any danger from, was from any casual accidental landing of straggling people from the main, who, as it was likely, if they were driven hither, were here against their wills, so they made no stay here, but went off again with all possible speed; seldom staying one night on shore, lest they should not have the help of the tides and daylight back again; and that, therefore, I had nothing to do but to consider of some safe retreat, in case I should see any savages land upon the spot.

Now I began sorely to repent that I had dug my cave so large as to bring a door through again, which door, as I said, came out beyond where my fortification joined to the rock: upon maturely considering this, therefore, I resolved to draw me a second fortification, in the same manner of a semicircle, at a distance from my wall, just where I had planted a double row of trees about twelve years before, of which I made mention: these trees having been planted so thick before, they wanted but few piles to be driven between them, that they might be thicker and stronger, and my wall would be soon finished: so that I had now a double wall: and my outer wall was thickened with pieces of timber, old cables, and everything I could think of, to make it strong, having in it seven little holes, about as big as I might put my arm out at. In the inside of this, I thickened my wall to about ten feet thick, with continually bringing earth out of my cave, and laying it at the foot of the wall, and walking upon it; and through the seven holes I contrived to plant the muskets, of which I took notice that I had got seven on shore out of the ship: these I planted like my cannon, and fitted them into frames, that held them like a carriage, so that I could fire all the seven guns in two minutes' time: this wall I was many a weary month in finishing, and yet never thought myself safe till it was done.

When this was done, I stuck all the ground without my wall, for a great length every way, as full with stakes, or sticks, of the osier-like wood, which I found so apt to grow, as they could well stand; insomuch, that I believe I might set in near twenty thousand of them, leaving a pretty large space between them and my wall, that I might have room to see an enemy, and they might have no shelter from the young trees, if they attempted to approach my outer wall.

Thus, in two years' time, I had a thick grove; and in five or six years' time I had a wood before my dwelling, growing so monstrous thick and strong, that it was indeed perfectly impassable; and no men, of what kind soever, would ever imagine that there was anything beyond it, much less a habitation. As for the way which I proposed to myself to go in and out (for I left no avenue), it was by setting two ladders, one to a part of the rock which was low, and then broke in, and left room to place another ladder upon that: so when the two ladders were taken down, no man living could come down to me without doing himself mischief; and if they had come down, they were still on the outside of my outer wall.

Thus I took all the measures human prudence could suggest for my own preservation; and it will be seen, at length, that they were not altogether without just reason, though I foresaw nothing at that time more than my mere fear suggested to me.

While this was doing, I was not altogether careless of my other affairs: for I had a great concern upon me for my little herd of goats; they were not only a ready supply to me on every occasion, and began to be sufficient for me, without the expense of powder and shot, but also without the fatigue of hunting after the wild ones; and I was loath to lose the advantage of them, and to have them all to nurse up over again.

For this purpose, after long consideration, I could think of but two ways to preserve them: one was, to find another convenient place to dig a cave under ground, and to drive them into it every night; and the other was, to enclose two or three little bits of land, remote from one another, and as much concealed as I could, where I might keep about half a dozen young goats in each place; so that if any disaster happened to the flock in general, I might be able to raise them again with little trouble and time; and this, though it would require a great deal of time and labour, I thought was the most rational design.

Accordingly, I spent some time to find out the most retired parts of the island; and I pitched upon one, which was as private, indeed, as my heart could wish for: it was a little damp piece of ground, in the middle of the hollow and thick woods, where, as is observed, I almost lost myself once before, endeavouring to come back that way from the eastern part of the island. Here I found a clear piece of land, near three acres, so surrounded with woods, that it was almost an enclosure by nature; at least, it did not want near so much labour to make it so as the other pieces of ground I had worked so hard at.

I IMMEDIATELY went to work with this piece of ground, and in less than a month's time I had so fenced it round, that my flock, or herd, call it which you please, who were not so wild now as at first they might be supposed to be, were well enough secured in it; so, without any further delay, I removed ten young she-goats and two he-goats to this piece; and when they were there, I continued to perfect the fence, till I had made it as secure as the other, which, however, I did at more leisure, and it took me up more time by a great deal. All this labour I was at the expense of purely from my apprehensions on the account of the print of a man's foot which I had seen; for, as yet, I never saw any human creature come near the island; and I had now lived two years under this uneasiness, which, indeed, made my life much less comfortable than it was before, as may be well imagined by any who knows what it is to live in the constant snare of the fear of man. And this I must observe, with grief too, that the discomposure of my mind had too great impressions also upon the religious part of my thoughts; for the dread and terror of falling into the hands of savages and cannibals lay so upon my spirits, that I seldom found myself in a due temper for application to my Maker, at least not with the sedate calmness and resignation of soul which I was wont to do: I rather prayed to God as under great affliction and pressure of mind, surrounded with danger, and in expectation every night of being murdered and devoured before morning; and I must testify from my experience, that a temper of peace, thankfulness, love and affection, is much the more proper frame for prayer than that of terror and discomposure; and that under the dread of mischief impending, a man is no more fit for a comforting performance of the duty of praying to God, than he is for a repentance on a sick bed; for these discomposures affect the mind, as the others do the body; and the discomposure of the mind must necessarily be as great a disability as that of the body, and much greater: praying to God being properly an act of the mind, not of the body.

But to go on: after I had thus secured one part of my little living stock, I went about the whole island, searching for another private place to make such another deposit; when, wandering more to the west point of the island than I had ever done yet, and looking out to sea, I thought I saw a boat upon the sea, at a great distance. I had found a perspective glass or two in one of the seamen's chests, which I saved out of our ship, but I had it not about me; and this was so remote, that I could not tell what to make of it, though I looked at it till my eyes were not able to hold to look any longer: whether it was a boat or not, I do not know, but as I descended from the hill I could see no more of it; so I gave it over; only I resolved to go no more out without a perspective glass in my pocket. When I was come down the hill to the end of the island, where, indeed, I had never been before, I was presently convinced that the seeing the print of a man's foot was not such a strange thing in the island as I imagined: and, but that it was a special providence that I was cast upon the side of the island where the savages never came, I should easily have known that nothing was more frequent than for the canoes from the main, when they happened to be a little too far out at sea, to shoot over to that side of the island for harbour; likewise, as they often met and fought in their canoes, the victors, having taken any prisoners, would bring them over to this shore, where, according to their dreadful customs, being all cannibals, they would kill and eat them; of which hereafter.

When I was come down the hill to the shore, as I said above, being the south-west point of the island, I was perfectly confounded and amazed; nor is it possible for me to express the horror of my mind, at seeing the shore spread with skulls, hands, feet, and other bones of human bodies; and, particularly, I observed a place where there had been a fire made, and a circle dug in the earth, like a cockpit, where I supposed the savage wretches had sat down to their inhuman feastings upon the bodies of their fellow-creatures.

I was so astonished with the sight of these things, that I entertained no notions of any danger to myself from it for a long while: all my apprehensions were buried in the thoughts of such a pitch of inhuman, hellish brutality, and the horror of the degeneracy of human nature, which, though I had heard of it often, yet I never had so near a view of before: in short, I turned away my face from the horrid spectacle; my stomach grew sick, and I was just at the point of fainting, when nature discharged the disorder from my stomach; and having vomited with uncommon violence, I was a little relieved, but I could not bear to stay in the place a moment; so I got me up the hill again with all the speed I could, and walked on towards my own habitation.

When I came a little out of that part of the island, I stood still awhile, as amazed, and then recovering myself, I looked up with the utmost affection of my soul, and, with a flood of tears in my eyes, gave God thanks, that had cast my first lot in a part of the world where I was distinguished from such dreadful creatures as these; and that, though I had esteemed my present condition very miserable, had yet given me so many comforts in it, that I had still more to give thanks for than to complain of; and this, above all, that I had, even in this miserable condition, been comforted with the knowledge of himself, and the hope of his blessing, which was a felicity more than sufficiently equivalent to all the misery which I had suffered or could suffer.

In this frame of thankfulness, I went home to my castle, and began to be much easier now, as to the safety of my circumstances, than ever I was before; for I observed that these wretches never came to this island in search of what they could get; perhaps not seeking, not wanting, or not expecting, anything here, and having often, no doubt, been up in the covered woody part of it, without finding anything to their purpose. I knew I had been here now almost eighteen years, and never saw the least footsteps of human creature there before; and I might be eighteen years more as entirely concealed as I was now, if I did not discover myself to them, which I had no manner of occasion to do; it being my only business to keep myself entirely concealed where I was, unless I found a better sort of creatures than cannibals to make myself known to. Yet I entertained such an abhorrence of the savage wretches that I have been speaking of, and of the wretched inhuman custom of their devouring and eating one another up, that I continued pensive and sad, and kept close within my own circle, for almost two years after this; when I say my own circle, I mean by it my three plantations, viz., my castle, my country seat, which I called my bower, and my enclosure in the woods: nor did I look after this for any other use than as an enclosure for my goats; for the aversion which nature gave me to these hellish wretches was such, that I was as fearful of seeing them as of seeing the Devil himself. I did not so much as go to look after my boat all this time, but began rather to think of making me another; for I could not think of ever making any more attempts to bring the other boat round the island to me, lest I should meet with some of these creatures at sea; in which if I had happened to have fallen into their hands, I knew what would have been my lot.

Time, however, and the satisfaction I had that I was in no danger of being discovered by these people, began to wear off my uneasiness about them; and I began to live just in the same composed manner as before, only with this difference, that I used more caution, and kept my eyes more about me, than I did before, lest I should happen to be seen by any of them; and particularly, I was more cautious of firing my gun, lest any of them being on the island should happen to hear it. It was therefore a very good providence to me that I had furnished myself with a tame breed of goats, and that I had no need to hunt any more about the woods, or shoot at them; and if I did catch any of them after this, it was by traps and snares, as I had done before: so that for two years after this, I believe I never fired my gun off, though I never went out without it; and, which was more, as I had saved three pistols out of the ship, I always carried them out with me, or at least two of them, sticking them in my goat's-skin belt. I also furbished up one of the great cutlasses that I had out of the ship, and made me a belt to hang it on also; so that I was now a most formidable fellow to look at when I went abroad, if you add to the former description of myself, the particular of two pistols, and a great broadsword hanging at my side in a belt, but without a scabbard.

Things going on thus, as I have said, for some time, I seemed, excepting these cautions, to be reduced to my former calm sedate way of living. All these things tended to show me more and more, how far my condition was from being miserable, compared to some others; nay, to many other particulars of life, which it might have pleased God to have made my lot. It put me upon reflecting how little repining there would be among mankind at any condition of life, if people would rather compare their condition with those that were worse, in order to be thankful, than be always comparing them with those which are better, to assist their murmurings and complainings.

As in my present condition there were not really many things which I wanted, so, indeed, I thought that the frights I had been in about these savage wretches, and the concern I had been in for my own preservation, had taken off the edge of my invention for my own conveniences; and I had dropped a good design, which I had once bent my thoughts too much upon, and that was, to try if I could not make some of my barley into malt, and then try to brew myself some beer. This was really a whimsical thought, and I reproved myself often for the simplicity of it; for I presently saw there would be want of several things necessary to the making my beer, that it would be impossible for me to supply; as, first, casks to preserve it in, which was a thing that, as I had observed already, I could never compass; no, though I spent not only many days, but weeks, nay, months, in attempting it, but to no purpose. In the next place, I had no hops to make it keep, no yeast to make it work, no copper or kettle to make it boil; and yet, with all these things wanting, I verily believe, had not the frights and terrors I was in about the savages intervened, I had undertaken it, and perhaps brought it to pass too; for I seldom gave anything over without accomplishing it, when once I had it in my head to begin it. But my invention now ran quite another way; for, night and day, I could think of nothing but how I might destroy some of these monsters in their cruel, bloody entertainment, and, if possible, save the victim they should bring hither to destroy. It would take up a larger volume than this whole work is intended to be, to set down all the contrivances I hatched, or rather brooded upon, in my thoughts, for the destroying these creatures, or at least frightening them so as to prevent their coming hither any more; but all this was abortive; nothing could be possible to take effect, unless I was to be there to do it myself; and what could one man do among them, when perhaps there might be twenty or thirty of them together, with their darts, or their bows and arrows, with which they could shoot as true to a mark as I could with my gun?

Sometimes I thought of digging a hole under the place where they made their fire, and putting in five or six pounds of gunpowder, which, when they kindled their fire, would consequently take fire, and blow up all that was near it; but as, in the first place, I should be unwilling to waste so much powder upon them, my store being now within the quantity of one barrel, so neither could I be sure of its going off at any certain time, when it might surprise them: and, at best, that it would do little more than just blow the fire about their ears and fright them, but not sufficient to make them forsake the place; so I laid it aside; and then proposed that I would place myself in ambush in some convenient place, with my three guns all double-loaded, and, in the middle of their bloody ceremony, let fly at them, when I should be sure to kill or wound perhaps two or three at every shot: and then falling in upon them with my three pistols, and my sword, I made no doubt but that if there were twenty I should kill them all. This fancy pleased my thoughts for some weeks; and I was so full of it, that I often dreamed of it, and sometimes that I was just going to let fly at them in my sleep. I went so far with it in my imagination, that I employed myself several days to find out proper places to put myself in ambuscade, as I said, to watch for them; and I went frequently to the place itself, which was now grown more familiar to me: but while my mind was thus filled with thoughts of revenge, and a bloody putting twenty or thirty of them to the sword, as I may call it, the horror I had at the place, and at the signals of the barbarous wretches devouring one another, abated my malice. Well, at length, I found a place in the side of the hill, where I was satisfied I might securely wait till I saw any of their boats coming; and might then, even before they would be ready to come on shore, convey myself, unseen, into some thickets of trees, in one of which there was a hollow large enough to conceal me entirely; and there I might sit and observe all their bloody doings, and take my full aim at their heads, when they were so close together, as that it would be next to impossible that I should miss my shot, or that I could fail wounding three or four of them at the first shot. In this place, then, I resolved to fix my design; and, accordingly, I prepared two muskets and my ordinary fowling-piece. The two muskets I loaded with a brace of slugs each, and four or five smaller bullets, about the size of pistol-bullets; and the fowling-piece I loaded with near a handful of swan-shot, of the largest size: I also loaded my pistols with about four bullets each; and in this posture, well provided with ammunition for a second and third charge, I prepared myself for my expedition.

After I had thus laid the scheme of my design, and, in my imagination, put it in practice, I continually made my tour every morning up to the top of the hill, which was from my castle, as I called it, about three miles, or more, to see if I could observe any boats upon the sea, coming near the island, or standing over towards it: but I began to tire of this hard duty, after I had, for two or three months, constantly kept my watch, but came always back without any discovery: there having not, in all that time, been the least appearance, not only on and near the shore, but on the whole ocean, so far as my eyes or glasses could reach every way.

As long as I kept my daily tour to the hill to look out, so long also I kept up the vigour of my design, and my spirits seemed to be all the while in a suitable form for so outrageous an execution as the killing twenty or thirty naked savages, for an offence, which I had not at all entered into a discussion of in my thoughts, any further than my passions were at first fired by the horror I conceived at the unnatural custom of the people of that country; who, it seems, had been suffered by Providence, in his wise disposition of the world, to have no other guide than that of their own abominable and vitiated passions; and, consequently, were left, and perhaps had been so for some ages, to act such horrid things and receive such dreadful customs, as nothing but nature, entirely abandoned by Heaven, and actuated by some hellish degeneracy, could have run them into. But now, when, as I have said, I began to be weary of the fruitless excursion, which I had made so long and so far every morning in vain, so my opinion of the action itself began to alter; and I began, with cooler and calmer thoughts, to consider what I was going to engage in: what authority or call I had to pretend to be judge and executioner upon these men as criminals, whom Heaven had thought fit, for so many ages, to suffer, unpunished, to go on, and to be, as it were, the executioners of his judgments one upon another. How far these people were offenders against me, and what right I had to engage in the quarrel of that blood which they shed promiscuously one upon another, I debated this very often with myself, thus: How do I know what God himself judges in this particular case? It is certain these people do not commit this as a crime; it is not against their own consciences reproving, or their light reproaching them; they do not know it to be an offence, and then commit it in defiance of divine justice, as we do in almost all the sins we commit. They think it no more a crime to kill a captive taken in war, than we do to kill an ox; nor to eat human flesh, than we do to eat mutton.

When I considered this a little, it followed necessarily that I was certainly in the wrong in it; that these people were not murderers in the sense that I had before condemned them in my thoughts, any more than those Christians were murderers who often put to death the prisoners taken in battle; or more frequently, upon many occasions put whole troops of men to the sword, without giving quarter, though they threw down their arms and submitted. In the next place, it occurred to me, that although the usage they gave one another was thus brutish and inhuman, yet it was really nothing to me; these people had done me no injury: that if they attempted me, or I saw it necessary, for my immediate preservation, to fall upon them, something might be said for it; but that I was yet out of their power, and they really had no knowledge of me, and consequently no design upon me; and therefore it could not be just for me to fall upon them: that this would justify the conduct of the Spaniards in all their barbarities practised in America, where they destroyed millions of these people: who, however they were idolaters and barbarians, and had several bloody and barbarous rites in their customs, such as sacrificing human bodies to their idols, were yet, as to the Spaniards, very innocent people; and that the rooting them out of the country is spoken of with the utmost abhorrence and detestation by even the Spaniards themselves at this time, and by all other Christian nations in Europe, as a mere butchery, a bloody and unnatural piece of cruelty, unjustifiable either to God or man, and for which the very name of a Spaniard is reckoned to be frightful and terrible to all people of humanity, or of Christian compassion,—as if the kingdom of Spain were particularly eminent for the produce of a race of men who were without principles of tenderness, or the common bowels of pity to the miserable, which is reckoned to be a mark of generous temper in the mind.

These considerations really put me to a pause, and to a kind of a full stop; and I began, by little and little, to be off my design, and to conclude I had taken wrong measures in my resolutions to attack the savages; and that it was not my business to meddle with them, unless they first attacked me; and that it was my business, if possible, to prevent; but that if I were discovered and attacked by them, I knew my duty. On the other hand, I argued with myself, that this really was the way not to deliver myself, but entirely to ruin and destroy myself; for unless I was sure to kill every one that not only should be on shore at that time, but that should ever come on shore afterwards, if but one of them escaped to tell their country-people what had happened, they would come over again by thousands to revenge the death of their fellows, and I should only bring upon myself a certain destruction, which at present, I had no manner of occasion for. Upon the whole, I concluded, that neither in principle nor in policy I ought, one way or other, to concern myself in this affair: that my business was, by all possible means, to conceal myself from them, and not to leave the least signal to them to guess by that there were any living creatures upon the island, I mean of human shape. Religion joined in with this prudential resolution, and I was convinced now, many ways, that I was perfectly out of my duty when I was laying all my bloody schemes for the destruction of innocent creatures, I mean innocent as to me. As to the crimes they were guilty of towards one another, I had nothing to do with them; they were national, and I ought to leave them to the justice of God, who is the governor of nations, and knows how, by national punishments, to make a just retribution for national offences, and to bring public judgments upon those who offend in a public manner, by such ways as best please him. This appeared so clear to me now, that nothing was a greater satisfaction to me than that I had not been suffered to do a thing which I now saw so much reason to believe would have been no less a sin than that of wilful murder, if I had committed it; and I gave most humble thanks on my knees to God, that had thus delivered me from blood-guiltiness; beseeching him to grant me the protection of his providence, that I might not fall into the hands of the barbarians, or that I might not lay my hands on them, unless I had a more clear call from Heaven to it, in defence of my own life.

IN THIS DISPOSITION I continued
for near a year after this; and so far
was I from desiring an occasion for falling upon these wretches, that in
all that time I never once went up the hill to see whether there were any
of them in sight, or to know whether any of them had been on shore
there or not, that I might not be tempted to renew any of my contrivances against them, or be provoked, by any advantage which might
present itself, to fall upon them: only this I did, I went and removed my
boat, which I had on the other side of the island, and carried it down to
the east end of the whole island, where I ran it into a little cove, which I
found under some high rocks, and where I knew, by reason of the currents, the savages durst not, at least would not, come with their boats,
upon any account whatever. With my boat I carried away everything
that I had left there belonging to her, though not necessary for the bare
going thither, viz., a mast and sail which I had made for her, and a thing
like an anchor, but which, indeed, could not be called either anchor or
grapnel; however, it was the best I could make of its kind: all these I removed, that there might not be the least shadow of any discovery, or any
appearance of any boat, or of any human habitation, upon the island.
Besides this, I kept myself, as I said, more retired than ever, and seldom
went from my cell, other than upon my constant employment, viz., to
milk my she-goats, and manage my little flock in the wood, which as it
was quite on the other part of the island, was quite out of danger; for
certain it is, that these savage people, who sometimes haunted this island,
never came with any thoughts of finding anything here, and consequently
never wandered off from the coast; and I doubt not but they might have
been several times on shore after my apprehensions of them had made
me cautious, as well as before. Indeed, I looked back with some horror
upon the thoughts of what my condition would have been if I had
popped upon them and been discovered before that, when, naked and
unarmed, except with one gun, and that loaded often only with small
shot, I walked everywhere, peeping and peering about the island to see
what I could get; what a surprise should I have been in, if, when I discovered the print of a man's foot, I had, instead of that, seen fifteen or

twenty savages, and found them pursuing me, and by the swiftness of their running no possibility of my escaping them? The thoughts of this sometimes sunk my very soul within me, and distressed my mind so much, that I could not soon recover it, to think what I should have done, and how I should not only have been unable to resist them, but even should not have had presence of mind enough to do what I might have done, much less what now, after so much consideration and preparation, I might be able to do. Indeed, after serious thinking on these things, I would be very melancholy, and sometimes it would last a great while; but I resolved it all, at last, into thankfulness to that Providence which had delivered me from so many unseen dangers, and had kept from me those mischiefs which I could have no way been the agent in delivering myself from, because I had not the least notion of any such thing depending, or the least supposition of its being possible. This renewed a contemplation which often had come to my thoughts in former time, when first I began to see the merciful dispositions of Heaven, in the dangers we run through in this life; how wonderfully we are delivered when we know nothing of it; how, when we are in a quandary (as we call it), as doubt or hesitation, whether to go this way, or that way, a secret hint shall direct us this way when we intended to go that way: nay, when sense, our own inclination, and perhaps business, has called to go the other way, yet a strange impression upon the mind, from we know not what springs, and by we know not what power, shall overrule us to go this way; and it shall afterwards appear, that had we gone that way which we should have gone, and even to our imagination ought to have gone, we should have been ruined and lost. Upon these, and many like reflections, I afterwards made it a certain rule with me, that whenever I found those secret hints or pressings of mind, to doing or not doing any thing that presented, or going this way or that way, I never failed to obey the secret dictate; though I knew no other reason for it than that such a pressure, or such a hint hung upon my mind. I could give many examples of the success of this conduct in the course of my life, but more especially in the latter part of my inhabiting this unhappy island; besides many occasions which it is very likely I might have taken notice of, if I had seen with the same eyes then that I see with now. But it is never too late to be wise; and I cannot but advise all considering men, whose lives are attended with such extraordinary incidents as mine, or even though not so extraordinary, not to slight such secret intimations of Providence, let them come from what invisible intelligence they will. That I shall not discuss, and perhaps cannot account for; but certainly they are a proof of the converse of spirits, and a secret communication between those embodied and those unembodied, and such a proof as can never be withstood; of which I shall have occasion to give some very remarkable instances in the remainder of my solitary residence in this dismal place.

I believe the reader of this will not think it strange if I confess that these anxieties, these constant dangers I lived in, and the concern that was now upon me, put an end to all invention, and to all the contrivances that I had laid for my future accommodations and conveniences. I had the care of my safety more now upon my hands than that of my food. I cared not to drive a nail, or chop a stick of wood now, for fear the noise I might make should be heard; much less would I fire a gun, for the same reason: and, above all, I was intolerably uneasy at making any fire, lest the smoke, which is visible at a great distance in the day, should betray me. For this reason I removed that part of my business which required fire, such as burning of pots and pipes, etc., into my new apartment in the woods; where, after I had been some time, I found, to my unspeakable consolation, a mere natural cave in the earth, which went in a vast way, and where, I dare say, no savage, had he been at the mouth of it, would be so hardy as to venture in: nor, indeed, would any man else, but one who, like me, wanted nothing so much as a safe retreat.

The mouth of this hollow was at the bottom of a great rock, where by mere accident (I would say, if I did not see abundant reason to ascribe all such things now to Providence) I was cutting down some thick branches of trees to make charcoal; and, before I go on, I must observe the reason of my making this charcoal, which was thus: I was afraid of making a smoke about my habitation, as I said before; and yet I could not live there without baking my bread, cooking my meat, etc.; so I contrived to burn some wood here, as I had seen done in England, under turf, till it became chark, or dry coal; and then putting the fire out, I preserved the coal to carry home, and perform the other services for which fire was wanting, without danger of smoke. But this is by the by. While I was cutting down some wood here, I perceived that behind a very thick branch of low brushwood, or underwood, there was a kind of hollow place: I was curious to look in it, and getting with difficulty into the mouth of it, I found it was pretty large: that is to say, sufficient for me to stand upright in it, and perhaps another with me: but I must confess to you that I made more haste out than I did in, when, looking farther into the place, and which was perfectly dark, I saw two broad shining eyes of some creature, whether devil or man I knew not, which twinkled like two stars, the dim light from the cave's mouth shining directly in, and making the reflection. However, after some pause, I recovered myself, and began to call myself a thousand fools, and to think, that he that was afraid to see the devil was not fit to live twenty years in an island all alone; and that I might well think there was nothing in this cave that was more frightful than myself. Upon this, plucking up my courage, I took up a firebrand, and in I rushed again, with the stick flaming in my hand: I had not gone three steps in, but I was almost as much frightened as I was before; for I heard a very loud sigh, like that of a man in some pain, and it was followed by a broken noise, as of words half expressed, and then a deep sigh again. I stepped back, and was indeed struck with such a surprise, that it put me into a cold sweat; and if I had had a hat on my head, I will not answer for it, that my hair might not have lifted it off. But still plucking up my spirits as well as I could, and encouraging myself a little with considering that the power and presence of God was everywhere, and was able to protect me, upon this I stepped forward again, and by the light of the firebrand, holding it up a little over my head, I saw lying on the ground a most monstrous, frightful, old he-goat, just making his will, as we say, and gasping for life, and dying, indeed, of mere old age. I stirred him a little to see if I could get him out, and he essayed to get up, but was not able to raise himself; and I thought with myself he might even lie there; for if he had frightened me, so he would certainly fright any of the savages, if any of them should be so hardy as to come in there while he had any life in him.

I was now recovered from my surprise, and began to look round me, when I found the cave was but very small, that is to say, it might be about twelve feet over, but in no manner of shape, neither round nor square, no hands having ever been employed in making it but those of mere Nature. I observed also that there was a place at the farther side of it that went in further, but was so low that it required me to creep upon my hands and knees to go into it, and whither it went I knew not: so having no candle, I gave it over for that time; but resolved to come again the next day, provided with candles and a tinder-box, which I had made of the lock of one of the muskets, with some wild-fire in the pan.

Accordingly, the next day I came provided with six large candles of my own making (for I made very good candles now of goat's tallow, but was hard set for candle-wick, using sometimes rags or rope-yarn, and sometimes the dried rind of a weed like nettles); and going into this low place, I was obliged to creep upon all fours, as I have said, almost ten yards; which, by the way, I thought was a venture bold enough, considering that I knew not how far it might go, nor what was beyond it. When I had got through the strait, I found the roof rose higher up, I believe near twenty feet; but never was such a glorious sight seen in the island, I dare say, as it was, to look round the sides and roof of this vault or cave; the wall reflected a hundred thousand lights to me from my two candles. What it was in the rock, whether diamonds, or any other precious stones, or gold, which I rather supposed it to be, I knew not. The place I was in was a most delightful cavity or grotto of its kind, as could be expected, though perfectly dark; the floor was dry and level, and had a sort of a small loose gravel upon it, so that there was no nauseous or venomous creature to be seen, neither was there any damp or wet on the sides or roof: the only difficulty in it was the entrance; which, however, as it was a place of security, and such a retreat as I wanted, I thought that was a convenience; so that I was really rejoiced at the discovery, and resolved, without any delay, to bring some of those things which I was most anxious about to this place; particularly, I resolved to bring hither my magazine of powder, and all my spare arms, viz., two fowling-pieces, for I had three in all, and three muskets, for of them I had eight in all; so I kept at my castle only five, which stood ready mounted like pieces of cannon, on my outmost fence, and were ready also to take out upon any expedition. Upon this occasion of removing my ammunition, I happened to open the barrel of powder which I took up out of the sea, and which had been wet; and I found that the water had penetrated about three or four inches into the powder on every side, which caking and growing hard, had preserved the inside like a kernel in the shell; so that I had near sixty pounds of very good powder in the centre of the cask: this was a very agreeable discovery to me at that time; so I carried all away thither, never keeping above two or three pounds of powder with me in my castle, for fear of a surprise of any kind: I also carried thither all the lead I had left for bullets.

I fancied myself now like one of the ancient giants, which were said to live in caves and holes in the rocks, where none could come at them: for I persuaded myself, while I was here, that if five hundred savages were to hunt me, they could never find me out; or, if they did, they would not venture to attack me here. The old goat, whom I found expiring, died in the mouth of the cave the next day after I made this discovery: and I found it much easier to dig a great hole there, and throw him in and cover him with earth, than to drag him out; so I interred him there, to prevent offence to my nose.

I was now in the twenty-third year of my residence in this island; and was so naturalized to the place, and the manner of living, that could I have but enjoyed the certainty that no savages would come to the place to disturb me, I could have been content to have capitulated for spending the rest of my time there, even to the last moment, till I had laid me down and died, like the old goat in the cave. I had also arrived to some little diversions and amusements, which made the time pass a great deal more pleasantly with me than it did before; as, first, I had taught my Poll, as I noted before, to speak; and he did it so familiarly, and talked so articulately and plain, that it was very pleasant to me: for I believe no bird ever spoke plainer; and he lived with me no less than six-and-twenty years; how long he might have lived afterwards I know not, though I know they have a notion in the Brazils that they live a hundred years. My dog was a very pleasant and loving companion to me for no less than sixteen years of my time, and then died of mere old age. As for my cats, they multiplied, as I have observed, to that degree, that I was obliged to shoot several of them at first, to keep them from devouring me and all I had; but, at length, when the two old ones I brought with me were gone, and after some time continually driving them from me, and letting them have no provision with me, they all ran wild into the woods, except two or three favourites, which I kept tame, and whose young, when they had any, I always drowned; and these were part of my family. Besides these, I always kept two or three household kids about me, whom I taught to feed out of my hand; and I had two more parrots, which talked pretty well, and would all call Robin Crusoe, but none like my first; nor, indeed, did I take the pains with any of them that I had done with him. I had also several tame sea-fowls, whose names I knew not, that I caught upon the shore, and cut their wings; and the little stakes which I had planted before my castle wall being now grown up to a good thick grove, these fowls all lived among these low trees, and bred there, which was very agreeable to me: so that, as I said above, I began to be very well contented with the life I led, if I could have been secured from the dread of the savages. But it was otherwise directed; and it may not be amiss for all people who shall meet with my story, to make this just observation from it, viz., How frequently, in the course of our lives, the evil which in itself we seek most to shun, and which, when we are fallen into, is the most dreadful to us, is oftentimes the very means or door of our deliverance, by which alone we can be raised again from the affliction we are fallen into. I could give many examples of this in the course of my unaccountable life, but in nothing was it more particularly remarkable than in the circumstances of my last years of solitary residence in this island.

I T WAS now the month of December, as I said above, in my twenty-third year; and this being the southern solstice (for winter I cannot call it), was the particular time of my harvest, and required my being pretty much abroad in the fields; when going out pretty early in the morning, even before it was thorough daylight, I was surprised with seeing a light of some fire upon the shore, at a distance from me of about two miles, towards the end of the island where I had observed some savages had been, as before; and not on the other side, but, to my great affliction, it was on my side of the island.

I was indeed terribly surprised at the sight, and stopped short within my grove, not daring to go out, lest I might be surprised; and yet I had no more peace within, from the apprehensions I had that if these savages, in rambling over the island, should find my corn standing or cut, or any of my works and improvements, they would immediately conclude that there were people in the place, and would then never give over till they had found me out. In this extremity, I went back directly to my castle, pulled up the ladder after me, and made all things without look as wild and natural as I could.

Then I prepared myself within, putting myself in a posture of defence: I loaded all my cannon, as I called them, that is to say, my muskets, which were mounted upon my new fortification, and all my pistols, and resolved to defend myself to the last gasp; not forgetting seriously to commend myself to the divine protection, and earnestly to pray to God to deliver me out of the hands of the barbarians. I continued in this posture about two hours; and began to be mighty impatient for intelligence abroad, for I had no spies to send out. After sitting awhile longer, and musing what I should do in this, I was not able to bear sitting in ignorance any longer; so setting up my ladder to the side of the hill, where there was a flat place, as I observed before, and then pulling the ladder up after me, I set it up again, and mounted to the top of the hill; and pulling out my perspective glass, which I had taken on purpose, I laid me down flat on my belly on the ground, and began to look for the place. I presently found there was no less than nine naked savages, sitting round a small fire they had made, not to warm them, for they had no need of that, the weather being extremely hot, but, as I supposed, to dress some of their barbarous diet of human flesh, which they had brought with them, whether alive or dead I could not tell.

They had two canoes with them, which they had hauled up upon the shore; and as it was then the tide of ebb, they seemed to me to wait for the return of the flood to go away again. It is not easy to imagine what confusion this sight put me into, especially seeing them come on my side of the island, and so near me too; but when I considered their coming must be always with the current of the ebb, I began, afterwards, to be more sedate in my mind, being satisfied that I might go abroad with safety all the time of the tide of flood, if they were not on shore before; and having made this observation, I went abroad about my harvest work with the more composure.

As I expected, so it proved; for as soon as the tide made to the westward, I saw them all take boat, and row (or paddle, as we call it) away. I should have observed, that for an hour or more before they went off, they went a dancing; and I could easily discern their postures and gestures by my glass. I could not perceive, by my nicest observation, but that they were stark naked, and had not the least covering upon them; but whether they were men or women, I could not distinguish.

As soon as I saw them shipped and gone, I took two guns upon my shoulders, and two pistols in my girdle, and my great sword by my side, without a scabbard, and with all the speed I was able to make, went away to the hill where I had discovered the first appearance of all; and as soon as I got thither, which was not in less than two hours (for I could not go apace, being so laden with arms as I was), I perceived there had been three canoes more of savages at that place; and looking out farther, I saw they were all at sea together, making over for the main. This was a dreadful sight to me, especially as, going down to the shore, I could see the marks of horror, which the dismal work they had been about had left behind it, viz., the blood, the bones, and part of the flesh, of human bodies, eaten and devoured by those wretches with merriment and sport. I was so filled with indignation at the sight, that I now began to premeditate the destruction of the next that I saw there, let them be whom or how many soever. It seemed evident to me that the visits which they made thus to this island were not very frequent, for it was above fifteen months before any more of them came on shore there again; that is to say, I neither saw them, nor any footsteps or signals of them, in all that time; for, as to the rainy seasons, then they are sure not to come abroad, at least not so far: yet all this while I lived uncomfortably, by reason of the constant apprehensions of their coming upon me by surprise: from whence I observe, that the expectation of evil is more bitter than the suffering, especially if there is no room to shake off that expectation, or those apprehensions.

During all this time I was in the murdering humour, and took up most of my hours, which should have been better employed, in contriving how to circumvent and fall upon them, the very next time I should see them; especially if they should be divided, as they were the last time, into two parties: nor did I consider at all, that if I killed one party, suppose ten or a dozen, I was still the next day, or week, or month, to kill another, and so another, even *ad infinitum*, till I should be at length no less a murderer than they were in being man-eaters, and perhaps much more so. I spent my days now in great perplexity and anxiety of mind, expecting that I should, one day or other, fall into the hands of these merciless creatures; and if I did at any time venture abroad, it was not without looking round me with the greatest care and caution imaginable. And now I found, to my great comfort, how happy it was that I provided for a tame flock or herd of goats: for I durst not, upon any account, fire my gun, especially near that side of the island, where they usually came, lest I should alarm the savages; and if they had fled from me now, I was sure to have them come again, with perhaps two or three hundred canoes with them, in a few days, and then I knew what to expect. However, I wore out a year and three months more before I ever saw any more of the savages, and then I found them again, as I shall soon observe. It is true, they might have been there once or twice, but either they made no stay, or at least I did not see them: but in the month of May, as near as I could calculate, and in my four-and-twentieth year, I had a very strange encounter with them; of which in its place.

The perturbation of my mind, during this fifteen or sixteen months' interval, was very great; I slept unquiet, dreamed always frightful dreams, and often started out of my sleep in the night: in the day, great troubles overwhelmed my mind; and in the night, I dreamed often of killing the savages, and of the reasons why I might justify the doing of it. But to waive all this for a while. It was in the middle of May, on the sixteenth day, I think, as well as my poor wooden calendar would reckon, for I marked all upon the post still; I say, it was on the sixteenth of May that it blew a very great storm of wind all day, with a great deal of lightning and thunder, and a very foul night it was after it. I knew not what was the particular occasion of it, but as I was reading in the Bible, and taken up with very serious thoughts about my present condition, I was surprised with the noise of a gun, as I thought, fired at sea. This was, to be sure, a surprise quite of a different nature from any I had met with before; for the notions this put into my thoughts were quite of another kind. I started up in the greatest haste imaginable, and, in a trice, clapped my ladder to the middle place of the rock, and pulled it after me; and mounting it the second time, got to the top of the hill the very moment that a flash of fire bid me listen for a second gun, which accordingly, in about half a minute, I heard; and, by the sound, knew that it was from that part of the sea where I was driven down the current in my boat. I immediately considered that this must be some ship in distress, and that they had some comrade, or some other ship in company, and fired these guns for signals of distress, and to obtain help. I had the presence of mind, at that minute, to think that though I could not help them, it might be they might help me: so I brought together all the dry wood I could get at hand, and making a good handsome pile, I set it on fire upon the hill. The wood was dry, and blazed freely; and though the wind blew very hard, yet it burnt fairly out: so that I was certain, if there was any such thing as a ship, they must needs see it; and no doubt they did; for as soon as ever my fire blazed up I heard another gun, and after that several others, all from the same quarter. I plied my fire all night long till daybreak; and when it was broad day, and the air cleared up, I saw something at a great distance at sea, full east of the island, whether a sail or a hull I could not distinguish, no, not with my glass; the distance was so great, and the weather still something hazy also; at least it was so out at sea.

I looked frequently at it all that day, and soon perceived that it did not move; so I presently concluded that it was a ship at anchor; and being eager, you may be sure, to be satisfied, I took my gun in my hand, and ran towards the south side of the island, to the rocks where I had formerly been carried away with the current; and getting up there, the weather by this time being perfectly clear, I could plainly see, to my great sorrow, the wreck of a ship, cast away in the night upon those concealed rocks which I found when I was out in my boat; and which rocks, as they checked the violence of the stream, and made a kind of counter-stream or eddy, were the occasion of my recovering from the most desperate, hopeless condition that ever I had been in, in all my life. Thus, what is one man's safety is another man's destruction; for it seems these men, whoever they were, being out of their knowledge, and the rocks being wholly under water, had been driven upon them in the night, the wind blowing hard at E.N.E. Had they seen the island, as I must necessarily suppose they did not, they must, as I thought, have endeavoured to have saved themselves on shore by the help of their boat; but their firing off guns for help, especially when they saw, as I imagined, my fire, filled me with many thoughts: First, I imagined that upon seeing my light, they might have put themselves into their boat, and endeavoured to make the shore; but that the sea going very high, they might have been cast away: other times I imagined that they might have lost their boat before, as might be the case in many ways; as particularly, by the breaking of the sea upon their ship, which many times obliges men to stave, or take in pieces, their boat, and sometimes to throw it overboard with their own hands: other times I imagined they had some other ship or ships in company, who, upon the signals of distress they had made, had taken them up and carried them off: other times I fancied they were all gone off to sea in their boat, and being hurried away by the current that I had been formerly in, were carried out into the great ocean, where there was nothing but misery and perishing; and that perhaps, they might by this time be starving, and in a condition to think of eating one another.

As all these were but conjectures at best, so, in the condition I was in, I could do no more than look on upon the misery of the poor men, and pity them; which had still this good effect on my side, that it gave me more and more cause to give thanks to God, who had so happily and comfortably provided for me in my desolate condition; and that of two ships' companies who were now cast away upon this part of the world, not one life should be spared but mine. I learned here again to observe, that it is very rare that the providence of God casts us into any condition of life so low, or any misery so great, but we may see something or other to be thankful for, and may see others in worse circumstances than our own. Such certainly was the case of these men, of whom I could not so much as see room to suppose any of them were saved; nothing could make it rational so much as to wish or expect that they did not all perish there, except the possibility only of their being taken up by another ship in company; and this was but mere possibility indeed, for I saw not the least sign or appearance of any such thing. I cannot explain, by any possible energy of words, what a strange longing or hankering of desires I felt in my soul upon this sight, breaking out sometimes thus—O that there had been but one or two, nay, or but one soul saved out of this ship, to have escaped to me, that I might but have had one companion, one fellow-creature to have spoken to me, and to have conversed with! In all the time of my solitary life, I never felt so earnest, so strong a desire after the society of my fellow-creatures, or so deep a regret at the want of it.

THERE ARE some secret moving springs in the affections, which, when they are set a going by some object in view, or, though not in view, yet rendered present to the mind by the power of imagination, that motion carries out the soul by its impetuosity, to such violent, eager embracings of the object, that the absence of it is insupportable. Such were these earnest wishings that but one man had been saved. I believe I repeated the words, "O that it had been but one!" a thousand times; and my desires were so moved by it, that when I spoke the words my hands would clinch together, and my fingers would press the palms of my hands so, that if I had had any soft thing in my hand it would have crushed it involuntarily; and the teeth in my head would strike together, and set against one another so strong, that for some time I could not part them again. Let the naturalists explain these things, and the reason and manner of them: all I can say to them is, to describe the fact, which was even surprising to me, when I found it, though I knew not from whence it proceeded: it was doubtless the effect of ardent wishes, and of strong ideas formed in my mind, realising the comfort which the conversation of one of my fellow-Christians would have been to me. But it was not to be; either their fate or mine, or both, forbade it: for till the last year of my being on this island, I never knew whether any were saved out of that ship or no; and had only the affliction, some days after, to see the corpse of a drowned boy come on shore at the end of the island which was next the shipwreck. He had no clothes on but a seaman's waistcoat, a pair of open-kneed linen drawers, and a blue linen shirt; but nothing to direct me so much as to guess what nation he was of: he had nothing in his pockets but two pieces-of-eight and a tobacco-pipe: the last was to me of ten times more value than the first.

It was now calm, and I had a great mind to venture out in my boat to this wreck, not doubting but I might find something on board that might be useful to me: but that did not altogether press me so much, as the possibility that there might be yet some living creature on board, whose life I might not only save, but might, by saving that life, comfort my own to the last degree. And this thought clung so to my heart, that I could not be quiet night or day, but I must venture out in my boat on board this wreck; and committing the rest to God's providence, I thought the impression was so strong upon my mind that it could not be resisted, that it must come from some invisible direction, and that I should be wanting to myself if I did not go.

Under the power of this impression, I hastened back to my castle, prepared everything for my voyage, took a quantity of bread, a great pot of fresh water, a compass to steer by, a bottle of rum (for I had still a great deal of that left), and a basket of raisins; and thus loading myself with everything necessary, I went down to my boat, got the water out of her, put her afloat, loaded all my cargo in her, and then went home again for more. My second cargo was a great bag of rice, the umbrella to set up over my head for a shade, another large pot of fresh water, and about two dozen of my small loaves, or barley-cakes, more than before, with a bottle of goat's milk and a cheese: all which, with great labour and sweat, I carried to my boat; and praying to God to direct my voyage, I put out; and rowing, or paddling, the canoe along the shore, came at last to the utmost point of the island on the north-east side. And now I was to launch out into the ocean, and either to venture or not to venture. I looked on the rapid currents which ran constantly on both sides of the island at a distance, and which were very terrible to me, from the remembrance of the hazard I had been in before, and my heart began to fail me; for I foresaw that if I were driven into either of those currents, I should be carried a great way out to sea, and perhaps out of my reach, or sight of the island again; and that, then, as my boat was but small, if any little gale of wind should rise, I should be inevitably lost.

These thoughts so oppressed my mind, that I began to give over my enterprise; and having hauled my boat into a little creek on the shore, I stepped out, and sat me down upon a rising bit of ground, very pensive and anxious, between fear and desire, about my voyage: when, as I was musing, I could perceive that the tide was turned, and the flood come on; upon which my going was impracticable for so many hours. Upon this, presently, it occurred to me that I should go up to the highest piece of ground I could find, and observe, if I could, how the sets of the tide, or currents, lay when the flood came in, that I might judge whether, if I was driven one way out, I might not expect to be driven another way home, with the same rapidness of the currents. This thought was no sooner in my head than I cast my eye upon a little hill, which sufficiently overlooked the sea both ways, and from whence I had a clear view of the currents, or sets of the tide, and which way I was to guide myself in my return. Here I found, that as the current of the ebb set out close by the south point of the island, so the current of flood set in close by the shore of the north side; and that I had nothing to do but to keep to the north side of the island in my return, and I should do well enough.

Encouraged with this observation, I resolved, the next morning, to set out with the first of the tide; and reposing myself for the night in my canoe, under the great watchcoat I mentioned, I launched out. I first made a little out to sea, full north, till I began to feel the benefit of the current, which set eastward, and which carried me at a great rate, and yet did not so hurry me as the current on the south side had done before, so as to take from me all government of the boat; but having a strong steerage with my paddle, I went at a great rate directly for the wreck, and in less than two hours I came up to it. It was a dismal sight to look at; the ship, which, by its building, was Spanish, stuck fast, jammed in between two rocks; all the stern and quarter of her were beaten to pieces with the sea; and as her forecastle, which stuck in the rocks, had run on with great violence, her mainmast and foremast were brought by the board, that is to say, broken short off; but her bowsprit was sound, and the head and bow appeared firm. When I came close to her, a dog appeared upon her, who, seeing me coming, yelped, and cried; and as soon as I called him, jumped into the sea to come to me. I took him into the boat, but found him almost dead with hunger and thirst. I gave him a cake of my bread, and he devoured it like a ravenous wolf that had been starving a fortnight in the snow. I then gave the poor creature some fresh water, with which, if I would have let him, he would have burst himself. After this, I went on board; but the first sight I met with was two men drowned in the cook-room, or forecastle of the ship, with their arms fast about one another. I concluded, as is indeed probable, that when the ship struck, it being in a storm, the sea broke so high, and so continually over her, that the men were not able to bear it, and were strangled with the constant rushing in of the water, as much as if they had been under water. Besides the dog, there was nothing left in the ship that had life; nor any goods, that I could see, but what was spoiled by the water. There were some casks of liquor, whether wine or brandy I knew not, which lay lower in the hold, and which, the water being ebbed out, I could see; but they were too big to meddle with. I saw several chests, which I believed belonged to some of the seamen; and I got two of them into the boat, without examining what was in them. Had the stern of the ship been fixed, and the forepart broken off, I am persuaded I might have made a good voyage: for, by what I found in these two chests, I had room to suppose the ship had a great deal of wealth on board; and, if I may guess from the course she steered, she must have been bound from Buenos Ayres, or the Rio de la Plata, in the south part of America, beyond the Brazils, to the Havana, in the Gulf of Mexico, and so perhaps to Spain. She had, no doubt, a great treasure in her, but of no use, at that time, to anybody; and what became of her crew, I then knew not.

I found, besides these chests, a little cask full of liquor, of about twenty gallons, which I got into my boat with much difficulty. There were several muskets in the cabin, and a great powder-horn, with about four pounds of powder in it: as for the muskets, I had no occasion for them, so I left them, but took the powder-horn. I took a fire-shovel and tongs, which I wanted extremely; as also two little brass kettles, a copper pot to make chocolate, and a gridiron: and with this cargo, and the dog, I came away, the tide beginning to make home again; and the same evening, about an hour within night, I reached the island again, weary and fatigued to the last degree. I reposed that night in the boat; and in the morning I resolved to harbour what I had got in my new cave, and not carry it home to my castle. After refreshing myself, I got all my cargo on shore, and began to examine the particulars. The cask of liquor I found to be a kind of rum, but not such as we had at the Brazils, and, in a word, not at all good; but when I came to open the chests, I found several things of great use to me: for example, I found in one a fine case of bottles, of an extraordinary kind, and filled with cordial waters, fine and very good; the bottles held about three pints each, and were tipped with silver. I found two pots of very good succades or sweetmeats, so fastened also on the top, that the salt water had not hurt them; and two more of the same which the water had spoiled. I found some very good shirts, which were very welcome to me; and about a dozen and a half of white linen handkerchiefs and coloured neck-cloths; the former were also very welcome, being exceeding refreshing to wipe my face in a hot day. Besides this, when I came to the till in the chest, I found there three great bags of pieces-of-eight, which held about eleven hundred pieces in all; and in one of them, wrapped up in a paper, six doubloons of gold and some small bars or wedges of gold; I suppose they might all weigh near a pound. In the other chests were some clothes, but of little value; but, by the circumstances, it must have belonged to the gunner's mate; though there was no powder in it, except two pounds of fine glazed powder, in three small flasks, kept, I suppose, for charging their fowling-pieces on occasion. Upon the whole, I got very little by this voyage that was of any use to me: for, as to the money, I had no manner of occasion for it; it was to me as the dirt under my feet; and I would have given it all for three or four pair of English shoes and stockings, which were things I greatly wanted, but had none on my feet for many years. I had indeed got two pair of shoes now, which I took off the feet of the two drowned men whom I saw in the wreck, and I found two pair more in one of the chests, which were very welcome to me; but they were not like our English shoes, either for ease or service, being rather what we call pumps than shoes. I found in this seaman's chest about fifty pieces-of-eight in rials, but no gold; I suppose this belonged to a poorer man than the other, which seemed to belong to some officer. Well, however, I lugged this money home to my cave, and laid it up, as I had done that before which I brought from our own ship: but it was a great pity, as I said, that the other part of this ship had not come to my share; for I am satisfied I might have loaded my canoe several times over with money; and, thought I, if I ever escape to England, it might lie here safe enough till I may come again and fetch it.

Having now brought all my things on shore, and secured them, I went back to my boat, and rowed or paddled her along the shore, to her old harbour, where I laid her up, and made the best of my way to my old habitation, where I found everything safe and quiet. I began now to repose myself, live after my old fashion, and take care of my family affairs; and, for a while, I lived easy enough, only that I was more vigilant than I used to be, looked out oftener, and did not go abroad so much; and if at any time I did stir with any freedom, it was always to the east part of the island, where I was pretty well satisfied the savages never came, and where I could go without so many precautions, and such a load of arms and ammunition as I always carried with me if I went the other way. I lived in this condition near two years more; but my unlucky head, that was always to let me know it was born to make my body miserable, was all these two years filled with projects and designs, how, if it were possible, I might get away from this island: for sometimes I was for making another voyage to the wreck, though my reason told me that there was nothing left there worth the hazard of my voyage; sometimes for a ramble one way, sometimes another; and I believe verily, if I had had the boat that I went from Sallee in, I should have ventured to sea, bound anywhere, I knew not whither. I have been, in all my circumstances, a memento to those who are touched with the general plague of mankind, whence, for aught I know, one-half of their miseries flow; I mean that of not being satisfied with the station wherein God and nature hath placed them: for, not to look back upon my primitive condition, and the excellent advice of my father, the opposition to which was, as I may call it, my *original sin*, my subsequent mistakes of the same kind had been the means of my coming into this miserable condition; for had that Providence, which had so happily seated me at the Brazils as a planter, blessed me with confined desires, and I could have been contented to have gone on gradually, I might have been, by this time, I mean in the time of my being in this island, one of the most considerable planters in the Brazils; nay, I am persuaded, that by the improvements I had made in that little time I lived there, and the increase I should probably have made if I remained, I might have been worth a hundred thousand moidores. And what business had I to leave a settled fortune, a well-stocked plantation, improving and increasing, to turn supercargo to Guinea to fetch Negroes, when patience and time would have so increased our stock at home, that we could have bought them at our own door from those whose business it was to fetch them; and though it had cost us something more, yet the difference of that price was by no means worth saving at so great a hazard? But as this is usually the fate of young heads, so reflection upon the folly of it is as commonly the exercise of more years, or of the dear-bought experience of time: so it was with me now; and yet so deep had the mistake taken root in my temper, that I could not satisfy myself in my station, but was continually poring upon the means and possibility of my escape from this place. And that I may, with the greater pleasure of the reader, bring on the remaining part of my story, it may not be improper to give some account of my first conceptions on the subject of this foolish scheme for my escape, and how, and upon what foundation, I acted.

I am now to be supposed retired into my castle, after my late voyage to the wreck, my frigate laid up and secured under water, as usual, and my condition restored to what it was before; I had more wealth, indeed, than I had before, but was not at all the richer: for I had no more use for it than the Indians of Peru had before the Spaniards came there.

It was one of the nights in the rainy season in March, the four-and-twentieth year of my first setting foot in this island of solitude, I was lying in my bed, or hammock, awake; very well in health, had no pain, no distemper, no uneasiness of body, nor any uneasiness of mind, more than ordinary, but could by no means close my eyes, that is, so as to sleep; no, not a wink all night long, otherwise than as follows:—It is impossible to set down the innumerable crowd of thoughts that whirled through that great thoroughfare of the brain, the memory, in this night's time: I ran over the whole history of my life in miniature, or by abridgment, as I may call it, to my coming to this island, and also of that part of my life since I came to this island. In my reflections upon the state of my case since I came on shore on this island, I was comparing the happy posture of my affairs in the first years of my habitation here, compared to the life of anxiety, fear, and care which I had lived in, ever since I had seen the print of a foot in the sand: not that I did not believe the savages had frequented the island even all the while, and might have been several hundreds of them at times on shore there; but I had never known it, and was incapable of any apprehensions about it; my satisfaction was perfect, though my danger was the same, and I was as happy in not knowing my danger, as if I had never really been exposed to it. This furnished my thoughts with many very profitable reflections, and particularly this one: How infinitely good that Providence is, which has provided, in its government of mankind, such narrow bounds to his sight and knowledge of things; and though he walks in the midst of so many thousand dangers, the sight of which, if discovered to him, would distract his mind and sink his spirits, he is kept serene and calm, by having the events of things hid from his eyes, and knowing nothing of the dangers which surround him.

After these thoughts had for some time entertained me, I came to reflect seriously upon the real danger I had been in for so many years in this very island, and how I had walked about in the greatest security, and with all possible tranquillity, even when perhaps nothing but the brow of a hill, a great tree, or the casual approach of night, had been between me and the worst kind of destruction, viz., that of falling into the hands of cannibals and savages, who would have seized on me with the same view as I would on a goat or a turtle, and have thought it no more a crime to kill and devour me, than I did a pigeon or a curlew. I would unjustly slander myself, if I should say I was not sincerely thankful to my great Preserver, to whose singular protection I acknowledged, with great humility, all these unknown deliverances were due, and without which I must inevitably have fallen into their merciless hands.

When these thoughts were over, my head was for some time taken up in considering the nature of these wretched creatures, I mean the savages, and how it came to pass in the world, that the wise Governor of all things should give up any of his creatures to such inhumanity, nay, to something so much below even brutality itself, as to devour its own kind; but as this ended in some (at that time) fruitless speculations, it occurred to me to inquire what part of the world these wretches lived in? how far off the coast was from whence they came? what they ventured over so far from home for? what kind of boats they had? and why I might not order myself and my business so that I might be as able to go over thither as they were to come to me.

I never so much as troubled myself to consider what I should do with myself when I went thither, what would become of me, if I fell into the hands of the savages; or how I should escape from them, if they attacked me: no, nor so much as how it was possible for me to reach the coast, and not be attacked by some or other of them, without any possibility of delivering myself; and if I should not fall into their hands, what I should do for provision, or whither I should bend my course: none of these thoughts, I say, so much as came in my way; but my mind was wholly bent upon the notion of my passing over in my boat to the main land. I looked upon my present condition as the most miserable that could possibly be; that I was not able to throw myself into anything, but death, that could be called worse; and if I reached the shore of the main, I might perhaps meet with relief, or I might coast along, as I did on the African shore, till I came to some inhabited country, and where I might find some relief; and after all, perhaps, I might fall in with some Christian ship that might take me in; and if the worst came to the worst, I could but die, which would put an end to all these miseries at once. Pray note, all this was the fruit of a disturbed mind, an impatient temper, made desperate, as it were, by the long continuance of my troubles, and the disappointments I had met in the wreck I had been on board of, and where I had been so near obtaining what I so earnestly longed for, viz., somebody to speak to, and to learn some knowledge from them of the place where I was, and of the probable means of my deliverance. I was agitated wholly by these thoughts: all my calm of mind, in my resignation to Providence, and waiting the issue in the dispositions of Heaven, seemed to be suspended; and I had as it were, no power to turn my thoughts to anything but to the project of a voyage to the main, which came upon me with such force, and such an impetuosity of desire, that it was not to be resisted.

When this had agitated my thoughts for two hours or more, with such violence that it set my very blood into a ferment, and my pulse beat as if I had been in a fever, merely with the extraordinary fervour of my mind about it, nature, as if I had been fatigued and exhausted with the very thought of it, threw me into a sound sleep. One would have thought I should have dreamed of it, but I did not, nor of anything relating to it: but I dreamed that as I was going out in the morning, as usual, from my castle, I saw upon the shore two canoes and eleven savages coming to land, and that they brought with them another savage, whom they were going to kill, in order to eat him; when, on a sudden, the savage that they were going to kill jumped away, and ran for his life; and I thought, in my sleep, that he came running into my little thick grove before my fortification, to hide himself; and that I, seeing him alone, and not perceiving that the others sought him that way, showed myself to him, and smiling upon him, encouraged him: that he kneeled down to me, seeming to pray me to assist him; upon which I showed him my ladder, made him go up, and carried him into my cave, and he became my servant: and that as soon as I had got this man, I said to myself, Now I may certainly venture to the main land; for this fellow will serve me as a pilot, and will tell me what to do, and whither to go for provisions, and whither not to go for fear of being devoured; what places to venture into, and what to shun. I waked with this thought; and was under such inexpressible impressions of joy at the prospect of my escape in my dream, that the disappointments which I felt upon coming to myself, and finding that it was no more than a dream, were equally extravagant the other way, and threw me into a very great dejection of spirits.

Upon this, however, I made this conclusion: that my only way to go about to attempt an escape was, if possible, to get a savage into my possession; and, if possible, it should be one of their prisoners whom they had condemned to be eaten, and should bring hither to kill. But those thoughts still were attended with this difficulty, that it was impossible to effect this without attacking a whole caravan of them, and killing them all: and this was not only a very desperate attempt, and might miscarry: but, on the other hand, I had greatly scrupled the lawfulness of it to myself, and my heart trembled at the thought of shedding so much blood, though it was for my deliverance. I need not repeat the arguments which occurred to me against this, they being the same mentioned before: but though I had other reasons to offer now, viz., that those men were enemies to my life, and would devour me if they could; that it was self-preservation, in the highest degree, to deliver myself from this death of a life, and was acting in my own defence as much as if they were actually assaulting me, and the like; I say, though these things argued for it, yet the thoughts of shedding human blood for my deliverance were very terrible to me, and such as I could by no means reconcile myself to for a great while. However, at last, after many secret disputes with myself, and after great perplexities about it (for all these arguments, one way and another, struggled in my head a long time), the eager prevailing desire of deliverance at length mastered all the rest; and I resolved, if possible, to get one of those savages into my hands, cost what it would. My next thing was to contrive how to do it, and this indeed was very difficult to resolve on: but as I could pitch upon no probable means for it, so I resolved to put myself upon the watch, to see them when they came on shore, and leave the rest to the event, taking such measures as the opportunity should present, let what would be.

With these resolutions in my thoughts, I set myself upon the scout as often as possible, and indeed so often, that I was heartily tired of it; for it was above a year and a half that I waited; and for a great part of that time went out to the west end, and to the south-west corner of the island, almost every day, to look for canoes, but none appeared. This was very discouraging, and began to trouble me much, though I cannot say that it did in this case (as it had done some time before) wear off the edge of my desire to the thing; but the longer it seemed to be delayed, the more eager I was for it: in a word, I was at first so careful to shun the sight of these savages, and avoid being seen by them, as I was now eager to be upon them. Besides, I fancied myself able to manage one, nay, two or three savages, if I had them, so as to make them entirely slaves to me, to do whatever I should direct them, and to prevent their being able at any time to do me any hurt. It was a great while that I pleased myself with this affair; but nothing still presented; all my fancies and schemes came to nothing, for no savages came near me for a great while.

ABOUT A YEAR AND A HALF after I entertained these notions (and by long musing had, as it were, resolved them all into nothing for want of an occasion to put them into execution), I was surprised, one morning early, with seeing no less than five canoes all on shore together on my side of the island, and the people who belonged to them all landed, and out of my sight. The number of them broke all my measures; for seeing so many, and knowing that they always come four or six, or sometimes more, in a boat, I could not tell what to think of it, or how to take my measures, to attack twenty or thirty men single-handed; so lay still in my castle, perplexed and discomforted: however, I put myself into all the same postures for an attack that I had formerly provided, and was just ready for action, if anything had presented. Having waited a good while, listening to hear if they made any noise, at length, being very impatient, I set my guns at the foot of my ladder, and clambered up to the top of the hill, by my two stages, as usual; standing so, however, that my head did not appear above the hill, so that they could not perceive me by any means. Here I observed, by the help of my perspective glass, that they were no less than thirty in number; that they had a fire kindled, and that they had meat dressed. How they had cooked it I knew not, or what it was; but they were all dancing, in I know not how many barbarous gestures and figures, their own way, round the fire.

While I was thus looking on them, I perceived, by my perspective, two miserable wretches dragged from the boats, where, it seems, they were laid by, and were now brought out for the slaughter. I perceived one of them immediately fall, being knocked down, I suppose, with a club or wooden sword, for that was their way, and two or three others were at work immediately, cutting him open for their cookery, while the other victim was left standing by himself, till they should be ready for him. In that very moment, this poor wretch seeing himself a little at liberty, and unbound, nature inspired him with hopes of life, and he started away from them, and ran with incredible swiftness along the sands, directly towards me, I mean towards that part of the coast where my habitation was. I was dreadfully frightened, I must acknowledge, when I perceived him run my way, and especially when, as I thought, I saw him pursued by the whole body: and now I expected that part of my dream was coming to pass, and that he would certainly take shelter in my grove; but I could not depend, by any means, upon my dream for the rest of it, viz., that the other savages would not pursue him thither, and find him there. However, I kept my station, and my spirits began to recover, when I found that there was not above three men that followed him; and still more was I encouraged when I found that he outstripped them exceedingly in running, and gained ground of them, so that if he could but hold it for half an hour, I saw easily he would fairly get away from them all.

There was between them and my castle the creek, which I mentioned often in the first part of my story, where I landed my cargoes out of the ship; and this I saw plainly he must necessarily swim over, or the poor wretch would be taken there: but when the savage escaping came thither, he made nothing of it, though the tide was then up; but plunging in, swam through in about thirty strokes, or thereabouts, landed, and ran on with exceeding strength and swiftness. When the three persons came to the creek, I found that two of them could swim, but the third could not, and that, standing on the other side, he looked at the others, but went no farther, and soon after went softly back again; which, as it happened, was very well for him in the end. I observed, that the two who swam were yet more than twice as long swimming over the creek as the fellow was that fled from them. It came now very warmly upon my thoughts, and indeed irresistibly, that now was the time to get me a servant, and perhaps a companion or assistant, and that I was called plainly by Providence to save this poor creature's life. I immediately ran down the ladders with all possible expedition, fetched my two guns, for they were both at the foot of the ladders, as I observed above, and getting up again, with the same haste, to the top of the hill, I crossed toward the sea, and having a very short cut, and all down-hill, placed myself in the way between the pursuers and the pursued, hallooing aloud to him that fled, who, looking back, was at first, perhaps, as much frightened at me as at them; but I beckoned with my hand to him to come back; and, in the meantime, I slowly advanced towards the two that followed: then rushing at once upon the foremost, I knocked him down with the stock of my piece. I was loath to fire, because I would not have the rest hear; though, at that distance, it would not have been easily heard, and being out of sight of the smoke too, they would not have easily known what to make of it. Having knocked this fellow down, the other who pursued him stopped, as if he had been frightened, and I advanced apace towards him: but as I came nearer, I perceived presently he had a bow and arrow, and was fitting it to shoot at me; so I was then necessitated to shoot at him first, which I did, and killed him at the first shot. The poor savage who fled but had stopped, though he saw both his enemies fallen and killed, as he thought, yet was so frightened with the fire and noise of my piece, that he stood stock still, and neither came forward nor went backward, though he seemed rather inclined still to fly than to come on. I hallooed again to him, and made signs to come forward, which he easily understood, and came a little way; then stopped again, and then a little farther, and stopped again; and I could then perceive that he stood trembling, as if he had been taken prisoner, and had just been to be killed, as his two enemies were. I beckoned to him again to come to me, and gave him all the signs of encouragement that I could think of; and he came nearer and nearer, kneeling down every ten or twelve steps, in token of acknowledgment for saving his life. I smiled at him, and looked pleasant, and beckoned to him to come still nearer: at length he came close to me; and then he kneeled down again, kissed the ground, and laid his head upon the ground, and taking me by the foot, set my foot upon his head: this, it seems, was in token of swearing to be my slave for ever. I took him up, and made much of him, and encouraged him all I could. But there was more work to do yet; for I perceived the savage whom I knocked down was not killed but stunned with the blow, and began to come to himself; so I pointed to him, and showed him the savage, that he was not dead: upon this he spoke some words to me, and though I could not understand them, yet I thought they were pleasant to hear; for they were the first sound of a man's voice that I had heard, my own excepted, for above twenty-five years. But there was no time for such reflections now; the savage who was knocked down recovered himself so far as to sit up upon the ground, and I perceived that my savage began to be afraid; but when I saw that, I presented my other piece at the man, as if I would shoot him: upon this my savage, for so I call him now, made a motion to me to lend him my sword which hung naked in a belt by my side, which I did. He no sooner had it, but he runs to his enemy, and, at one blow, cut off his head so cleverly, no executioner in Germany could have done it sooner or better; which I thought very strange for one who, I had reason to believe, never saw a sword in his life before, except their own wooden swords: however, it seems, as I learned afterwards, they make their wooden swords so sharp, so heavy, and the wood is so hard, that they will cut off heads even with them, aye and arms, and that at one blow too. When he had done this, he comes laughing to me, in sign of triumph, and brought me the sword again, and with abundance of gestures, which I did not understand, laid it down, with the head of the savage that he had killed, just before me. But that which astonished him most was to know how I killed the other Indian so far off: so pointing to him, he made signs to me to let him go to him; so I bade him go, as well as I could. When he came to him, he stood like one amazed, looking at him, turning him first on one side, then on the other, looked at the wound the bullet had made, which it seems, was just in his breast where it had made a hole, and no great quantity of blood had followed, but he had bled inwardly, for he was quite dead. He took up his bow and arrows, and came back; so I turned to go away, and beckoned him to follow me, making signs to him that more might come after them. Upon this, he made signs to me that he should bury them with sand, that they might not be seen by the rest, if they followed; and so I made signs to him again to do so. He fell to work; and, in an instant, he had scraped a hole in the sand with his hands, big enough to bury the first in, and then dragged him into it, and covered him; and did so by the other also; I believe he had buried them both in a quarter of an hour. Then calling him away, I carried him, not to my castle, but quite away, to my cave, on the farther part of the island; so I did not let my dream come to pass in that part, viz., that he came into my grove for shelter. Here I gave him bread and a bunch of raisins to eat, and a draught of water, which I found he was indeed in great distress for, by his running; and having refreshed him, I made signs for him to go and lie down to sleep, showing him a place where I had laid some rice-straw, and a blanket upon it, which I used to sleep upon myself sometimes; so the poor creature lay down, and went to sleep.

He was a comely, handsome fellow, perfectly well made, with straight, strong limbs, not too large, tall, and well-shaped, and, as I reckon, about twenty-six years of age. He had a very good countenance, not a fierce and surly aspect; but seemed to have something very manly in his face; and yet he had all the sweetness and softness of an European in his countenance too, especially when he smiled. His hair was long and black, not curled like wool; his forehead very high and large; and a great vivacity and sparkling sharpness in his eyes. The colour of his skin was not quite black, but very tawny; and yet not an ugly, yellow, nauseous tawny, as the Brazilians and Virginians, and other natives of America are, but of a bright kind of a dun olive-colour, that had in it something very agreeable, though not very easy to describe. His face was round and plump; his nose small, not flat like the Negroes; a very good mouth, thin lips, and his fine teeth well set, and as white as ivory.

After he had slumbered, rather than slept, about half an hour he awoke again, and came out of the cave to me, for I had been milking my goats, which I had in the enclosure just by; when he espied me, he came running to me, laying himself down again upon the ground, with all the possible signs of a humble, thankful disposition, making a great many antic gestures to show it. At last, he lay his head flat upon the ground, close to my foot, and set my foot upon his head, as he had done before; and after this made all the signs to me of subjection, servitude, and submission imaginable, to let me know he would serve me as long as he lived. I understood him in many things, and let him know I was very well pleased with him. In a little time I began to speak to him and teach him to speak to me; and, first, I let him know his name should be FRIDAY, which was the day I saved his life: I called him so for the memory of the time. I likewise taught him to say Master; and then let him know that was to be my name: I likewise taught him to say Yes and No, and to know the meaning of them. I gave him some milk in an earthen pot, and let him see me drink it before him, and sop my bread in it; and gave him a cake of bread to do the like, which he quickly complied with, and made signs that it was very good for him. I kept there with him all that night; but as soon as it was day, I beckoned to him to come with me, and let him know I would give him some clothes: at which he seemed very glad, for he was stark naked. As we went by the place where he had buried the two men, he pointed exactly to the place, and showed me the marks that he had made to find them again, making signs to me that we should dig them up again, and eat them. At this I appeared very angry, expressed my abhorrence of it, made as if I would vomit at the thoughts of it, and beckoned with my hand to him to come away, which he did immediately, with great submission. I then led him up to the top of the hill, to see if his enemies were gone; and pulling out my glass, I looked, and saw plainly the place where they had been, but no appearance of them or their canoes: so that it was plain that they were gone, and had left their two comrades behind them, without any search after them.

But I was not content with this discovery; but having now more courage, and consequently more curiosity, I took my man Friday with me, giving him the sword in his hand, with the bow and arrows at his back, which I found he could use very dexterously, making him carry one gun for me, and I two for myself; and away we marched to the place where these creatures had been, for I had a mind now to get some fuller intelligence of them. When I came to the place, my very blood ran chill in my veins, and my heart sunk within me, at the horror of the spectacle: indeed it was a dreadful sight, at least it was so to me, though Friday made nothing of it. The place was covered with human bones, the ground dyed with their blood, and great pieces of flesh, left here and there, half-eaten, mangled, and scorched; and, in short, all the tokens of the triumphant feast they had been making there, after a victory over their enemies. I saw three skulls, five hands, and the bones of three or four legs and feet, and abundance of other parts of the bodies; and Friday, by his signs, made me understand that they brought over four prisoners to feast upon; that three of them were eaten up, and that he, pointing to himself, was the fourth; that there had been a great battle between them and their next king, whose subjects, it seems, he had been one of, and that they had taken a great number of prisoners; all which were carried to several places by those who had taken them in the fight, in order to feast upon them, as was done here by these wretches upon those they brought hither.

I caused Friday to gather up all the skulls, bones, flesh, and whatever remained, and lay them together in a heap, and make a great fire upon it, and burn them all to ashes. I found Friday had still a hankering stomach after some of the flesh, and was still a cannibal in his nature; but I discovered so much abhorrence, at the very thoughts of it, and at the least appearance of it, that he durst not discover it; for I had, by some means, let him know that I would kill him if he offered it.

When he had done this, we came back to our castle; and there I fell to work for my man Friday: and, first of all, I gave him a pair of linen drawers, which I had out of the poor gunner's chest I mentioned which I found in the wreck; and which, with a little alteration, fitted him very well, and then I made him a jerkin of goat's skin, as well as my skill would allow (for I was now grown a tolerable good tailor); and I gave him a cap, which I made of hare's skin, very convenient and fashionable enough; and thus he was clothed for the present, tolerably well, and was mighty well pleased to see himself almost as well clothed as his master. It is true, he went awkwardly in those clothes at first; wearing the drawers was very awkward to him, and the sleeves of the waistcoat galled his shoulders, and the inside of his arms; but after a little easing them where he complained they hurt him, and using himself to them, he took to them at length very well.

The next day after I came home to my hutch with him, I began to consider where I should lodge him; and that I might do well for him, and yet be perfectly easy myself, made a little tent for him in the vacant place between my two fortifications, in the inside of the last and in the outside of the first. As there was a door or entrance there into my cave, I made a formal framed doorcase, and a door to it of boards, and set it up in the passage, a little within the entrance; and causing the door to open in the inside, I barred it up in the night, taking in my ladders too; so that Friday could no way come at me in the inside of my innermost wall, without making so much noise in getting over that it must needs waken me: for my first wall had now a complete roof over it of long poles, covering all my tent, and leaning up to the side of the hill; which was again laid across with smaller sticks, instead of laths, and then thatched over a great thickness with the rice-straw, which was strong, like reeds: and at the hole or place which was left to go in or out by the ladder, I had placed a kind of trap door, which, if it had been attempted on the outside, would not have opened at all, but would have fallen down, and made a great noise: as to weapons, I took them all into my side every night. But I needed none of all this precaution; for never man had a more faithful, loving, sincere servant than Friday was to me; without passions, sullenness, or designs, perfectly obliged and engaged—his very affections were tied to me, like those of a child to a father; and I dare say, he would have sacrificed his life for the saving mine upon any occasion whatsoever: the many testimonies he gave me of this put it out of doubt, and soon convinced me that I needed to use no precautions, as to my safety on his account.

This frequently gave me occasion to observe, and that with wonder, that however it had pleased God, in his providence, and in the government of the works of his hands, to take from so great a part of the world of his creatures the best uses to which their faculties and the powers of their souls are adapted, yet that he has bestowed upon them the same powers, the same reason, the same affections, the same sentiments of kindness and obligation, the same passions and resentments of wrongs, the same sense of gratitude, sincerity, fidelity, and all the capacities of doing good, and receiving good, that he has given to us; and that when he pleases to offer them occasions of exerting these, they are as ready, nay, more ready, to apply them to the right uses for which they were bestowed, than we are. This made me very melancholy sometimes, in reflecting, as the several occasions presented, how mean a use we make of all these, even though we have these powers enlightened by the great lamp of instruction, the Spirit of God, and by the knowledge of his word added to our understanding; and why it has pleased God to hide the like saving knowledge from so many millions of souls, who, if I might judge by this poor savage, would make a much better use of it than we did. From hence, I sometimes was led too far, to invade the sovereignty of Providence, and as it were arraign the justice of so arbitrary a disposition of things, that should hide that light from some, and reveal it to others, and yet expect a like duty from both; but I shut it up, and checked my thoughts with this conclusion: first, That we did not know by what light and law these should be condemned; but that as God was necessarily, and, by the nature of his being, infinitely holy and just, so it could not be, but if these creatures were all sentenced to absence from himself, it was no account of sinning against that light, which, as the Scripture says, was a law to themselves, and by such rules as their consciences would acknowledge to be just, though the foundation was not discovered to us; and, secondly, That still, as we all are the clay in the hand of the potter, no vessel could say to him, Why hast thou formed me thus?

But to return to my new companion:—I was greatly delighted with him, and made it my business to teach him everything that was proper to make him useful, handy, and helpful; but especially to make him speak, and understand me when I spoke; and he was the aptest scholar that ever was; and particularly was so merry, so constantly diligent, and so pleased when he could but understand me, or make me understand him, that it was very pleasant to me to talk to him. Now my life began to be so easy, that I began to say to myself, that could I but have been safe from more savages, I cared not if I was never to remove from the place where I lived.

AFTER I HAD BEEN two or three days returned to my castle, I thought that, in order to bring Friday off from his horrid way of feeding, and from the relish of a cannibal's stomach, I ought to let him taste other flesh; so I took him out with me one morning to the woods. I went, indeed, intending to kill a kid out of my own flock, and bring it home and dress it, but as I was going, I saw a she-goat lying down in the shade, and two young kids sitting by her. I catched hold of Friday;—Hold, said I; stand still; and made signs to him not to stir: immediately I presented my piece, shot, and killed one of the kids. The poor creature, who had, at a distance, indeed, seen me kill the savage, his enemy, but did not know, nor could imagine, how it was done, was sensibly surprised, trembled and shook, and looked so amazed, that I thought he would have sunk down. He did not see the kid I shot at, or perceive I had killed it, but ripped up his waistcoat to feel whether he was not wounded, and, as I found presently, thought I was resolved to kill him: for he came and kneeled down to me, and embracing my knees, said a great many things I did not understand; but I could easily see the meaning was, to pray me not to kill him.

I soon found a way to convince him that I would do him no harm; and taking him up by the hand, laughed at him, and pointing to the kid which I had killed, beckoned to him to run and fetch it, which he did; and while he was wondering, and looking to see how the creature was killed, I loaded my gun again. By and by, I saw a great fowl, like a hawk, sitting upon a tree, within shot; so, to let Friday understand a little what I would do, I called him to me again, pointed at the fowl, which was indeed a parrot, though I thought it had been a hawk; I say, pointing to the parrot, and to my gun, and to the ground under the parrot, to let him see I would make it fall, I made him understand that I would shoot and kill that bird: accordingly, I fired, and bade him look, and immediately he saw the parrot fall. He stood like one frightened again, notwithstanding all I had said to him; and I found he was the more amazed, because he did not see me put anything into the gun, but thought that there must be some wonderful fund of death and destruction in that thing, able to kill man, beast, or bird, or anything near or far off; and the astonishment this created in him was such, as could not wear off for a long time; and I believe, if I would have let him, he would have worshipped me and my gun. As for the gun itself, he would not so much as touch it for several days after; but he would speak to it, and talk to it, as if it had answered him, when he was by himself; which, as I afterwards learned of him, was to desire it not to kill him. Well, after his astonishment was a little over at this, I pointed to him to run and fetch the bird I had shot, which he did, but stayed some time; for the parrot, not being quite dead, had fluttered away a good distance from the place where she fell: however, he found her, took her up, and brought her to me; and as I had perceived his ignorance about the gun before, I took this advantage to charge the gun again, and not to let him see me do it, that I might be ready for any other mark that might present; but nothing more offered at that time; so I brought home the kid, and the same evening I took the skin off, and cut it out as well as I could; and having a pot fit for that purpose, I boiled or stewed some of the flesh, and made some very good broth. After I had begun to eat some, I gave some to my man, who seemed very glad of it, and liked it very well; but that which was strangest to him, was to see me eat salt with it. He made a sign to me that the salt was not good to eat; and putting a little into his mouth, it seemed to nauseate him, and he would spit and sputter at it, washing his mouth with fresh water after it; on the other hand, I took some meat into my mouth without salt, and I pretended to spit and sputter for want of salt, as fast as he had done at the salt; but it would not do; he would never care for salt with his meat or in his broth; at least, not for a great while, and then but very little.

Having thus fed him with boiled meat and broth, I was resolved to feast him the next day with roasting a piece of the kid: this I did, by hanging it before the fire on a string, as I had seen many people do in England, setting two poles up, one on each side of the fire, and one across on the top, and tying the string to the cross-stick, letting the meat turn continually. This, Friday admired very much: but when he came to taste the flesh, he took so many ways to tell me how well he liked it, that I could not but understand him; and at last he told me, as well as he could, he would never eat man's flesh any more, which I was very glad to hear.

The next day I set him to work to beating some corn out, and sifting it in the manner I used to do, as I observed before; and he soon understood how to do it as well as I, especially after he had seen what the meaning of it was, and that it was to make bread of it: for after that I let him see me make my bread, and bake it too; and in a little time Friday was able to do all the work for me, as well as I could do it myself.

I began now to consider, that having two mouths to feed instead of one, I must provide more ground for my harvest, and plant a larger quantity of corn than I used to do: so I marked out a larger piece of land, and began to fence in the same manner as before, in which Friday worked not only very willingly and very hard, but did it very cheerfully: and I told him what it was for; that it was for corn to make more bread, because he was now with me, and that I might have enough for him and myself too. He appeared very sensible of that part, and let me know that he thought I had much more labour upon me on his account than I had for myself; and that he would work the harder for me, if I would tell him what to do.

This was the pleasantest year of all the life I led in this place. Friday began to talk pretty well, and understand the names of almost everything I had occasion to call for, and of every place I had to send him to, and talked a great deal to me; so that, in short, I now began to have some use for my tongue again, which, indeed, I had very little occasion for before, that is to say, about speech. Besides the pleasure of talking to him, I had a singular satisfaction in the fellow himself: his simple, unfeigned honesty appeared to me more and more every day, and I began really to love the creature; and, on his side, I believe he loved me more than it was possible for him ever to love anything before.

I had a mind once to try if he had any hankering inclination to his own country again; and having taught him English so well that he could answer me almost any question, I asked him whether the nation that he belonged to, never conquered in battle? At which he smiled, and said, Yes, yes, we always fight the better: that is, he meant, always get the better in fight; and so we began the following discourse:—

MASTER. You always fight the better? how came you to be taken prisoner then, Friday?

FRIDAY. My nation beat much, for all that.

MASTER. How beat? If your nation beat them, how came you to be taken?

FRIDAY. They more many than my nation in the place where me was; they take one, two, three, and me; my nation overbeat them in the yonder place, where me no was; there my nation take one, two, great thousand.

MASTER. But why did not your side recover you from the hands of your enemies, then?

FRIDAY. They run one, two, three, and me, and make go in the canoe; my nation have no canoe that time.

MASTER. Well, Friday, and what does your nation do with the men they take? Do they carry them away and eat them, as these did?

FRIDAY. Yes, my nation eat mans too; eat all up.

MASTER. Where do they carry them?

FRIDAY. Go to other place, where they think.

MASTER. Do they come hither?

FRIDAY. Yes, yes, they come hither; come other else place.

MASTER. Have you been here with them?

FRIDAY. Yes, I have been here; (points to the N.W. side of the island, which, it seems, was their side).

By this I understood that my man Friday had formerly been among the savages who used to come on shore on the farther part of the island, on the same man-eating occasions he was now brought for: and some time after, when I took the courage to carry him to that side, being the same I formerly mentioned, he presently knew the place, and told me he was there once when they eat up twenty men, two women, and one child: he could not tell twenty in English, but he numbered them, by laying so many stones in a row, and pointing to me to tell them over.

I have told this passage, because it introduces what follows; that after I had this discourse with him, I asked him how far it was from our island to the shore, and whether the canoes were not often lost. He told me there was no danger, no canoes ever lost; but that, after a little way out to sea, there was a current and wind, always one way in the morning, the other in the afternoon. This I understood to be no more than the sets of the tide, as going out or coming in; but I afterwards understood it was occasioned by the great draft and reflux of the mighty river Oroonoko, in the mouth or gulf of which river, as I found afterwards, our island lay; and that this land which I perceived to the W. and N.W. was the great island of Trinidad, on the north point of the mouth of the river.

I asked Friday a thousand questions about the country, the inhabitants, the sea, the coast, and what nations were near: he told me all he knew, with the greatest openness imaginable. I asked him the names of the several nations of his sort of people, but could get no other name than Caribs: from whence I easily understood, that these were the Caribbees, which our maps place on the part of America which reaches from the mouth of the river Oroonoko to Guiana, and onwards to St. Martha. He told me that up a great way beyond the moon, that was, beyond the setting of the moon, which must be west from their country, there dwelt white bearded men, like me, and pointed to my great whiskers, which I mentioned before; and that they had killed much mans, that was his word; by all which I understood, he meant the Spaniards, whose cruelties in America had been spread over the whole country, and were remembered by all the nations, from father to son.

I inquired if he could tell me how I might go from this island and get among those white men: he told me, Yes, yes, you may go in two canoe. I could not understand what he meant, or make him describe to me what he meant by two canoe; till, at last, with great difficulty, I found he meant it must be in a large boat, as big as two canoes. This part of Friday's discourse began to relish with me very well; and from this time I entertained some hopes that, one time or other, I might find an opportunity to make my escape from this place, and that this poor savage might be a means to help me.

A FTER FRIDAY AND I became more intimately acquainted, and he could understand almost all I said to him, and speak pretty fluently, though in broken English, to me, I acquainted him with my own history, or at least so much of it as related to my coming to this place; how I had lived here, and how long: I let him into the mystery, for such it was to him, of gunpowder and bullet, and taught him how to shoot. I gave him a knife, which he was wonderfully delighted with; and I made him a belt with a frog hanging to it, such as in England we wear hangers in; and in the frog, instead of a hanger, I gave him a hatchet, which was not only as good a weapon, in some cases, but much more useful upon other occasions.

I described to him the country of Europe, particularly England, which I came from; how we lived, how we worshipped God, how we behaved to one another, and how we traded in ships to all parts of the world. I gave him an account of the wreck which I had been on board of, and showed him, as near as I could, the place where she lay; but she was all beaten in pieces before, and gone. I showed him the ruins of our boat, which we lost when we escaped, and which I could not stir with my whole strength then; but was now fallen almost to pieces. Upon seeing this boat, Friday stood musing a great while, and said nothing. I asked him what it was he studied upon? At last, says he, Me see such boat like come to place at my nation. I did not understand him a good while; but, at last, when I had examined further into it, I understood from him that a boat, such as that had been, came on shore upon the country where he lived; that is, as he explained it, was driven thither by stress of weather. I presently imagined that some European ship must have been cast away upon their coast, and the boat might get loose, and drive ashore; but was so dull, that I never once thought of men making their escape from a wreck thither, much less whence they might come: so I only inquired after a description of the boat.

Friday described the boat to me well enough; but brought me better to understand him when he added, with some warmth, We save the white mans from drown. Then I presently asked him, if there were any white mans, as he called them, in the boat? Yes, he said; the boat full of white mans. I asked him how many? He told upon his fingers seven teen. I asked him then what became of them? He told me, They live, they dwell at my nation.

This put new thoughts into my head; for I presently imagined that these might be the men belonging to the ship that was cast away in the sight of my island, as I now called it: and who, after the ship was struck on the rock, and they saw her inevitably lost, had saved themselves in their boat, and were landed upon that wild shore among the savages. Upon this, I inquired of him more critically what was become of them; he assured me they lived still there; that they had been there about four years; that the savages let them alone, and gave them victuals to live on. I asked him how it came to pass they did not kill them, and eat them? He said, No, they make brother with them; that is, as I understood him, a truce; and then he added, They no eat mans but when the war fight; that is to say, they never eat any men but such as come to fight with them, and are taken in battle.

It was after this some considerable time, that, being upon the top of the hill, at the east side of the island, from whence, as I have said, I had, in a clear day, discovered the main or continent of America, Friday, the weather being very serene, looks very earnestly towards the main land, and, in a kind of surprise, falls a jumping and dancing, and calls out to me, for I was at some distance from him. I asked him what was the matter? O joy! says he; O glad! there see my country, there my nation! I observed an extraordinary sense of pleasure appeared in his face, and his eyes sparkled, and his countenance discovered a strange eagerness, as if he had a mind to be in his own country again. This observation of mine put a great many thoughts into me, which made me at first not so easy about my new man, Friday, as I was before; and I made no doubt but that if Friday could get back to his own nation again, he would not only forget all his religion, but all his obligation to me, and would be forward enough to give his countrymen an account of me, and come back perhaps with a hundred or two of them, and make a feast upon me, at which he might be as merry as he used to be with those of his enemies, when they were taken in war. But I wronged the poor honest creature very much, for which I was very sorry afterwards. However, as my jealousy increased, and held me some weeks, I was a little more circumspect, and not so familiar and kind to him as before; in which I was certainly in the wrong too; the honest, grateful creature having no thought about it, but what consisted with the best principles, both as a religious Christian, and as a grateful friend, as appeared afterwards to my full satisfaction.

While my jealousy of him lasted, you may be sure I was every day pumping him, to see if he would discover any of the new thoughts which I suspected were in him: but I found everything he said was so honest and so innocent, that I could find nothing to nourish my suspicion; and, in spite of all my uneasiness, he made me at last entirely his own again; nor did he, in the least, perceive that I was uneasy, and therefore I could not suspect him of deceit.

One day, walking up the same hill, but the weather being hazy at sea, so that we could not see the continent, I called to him, and said, Friday, do not you wish yourself in your own country, your own nation?—Yes, he said, I be much O glad to be at my own nation.—What would you do there? said I: would you turn wild again, eat men's flesh again, and be a savage, as you were before? He looked full of concern, and shaking his head, said, No, no; Friday tell them to live good, tell them to pray God, tell them to eat corn-bread, cattle-flesh, milk; no eat man again.—Why then, said I to him, they will kill you. He looked grave at that, and then said, No, no; they no kill me, they willing love learn. He meant by this, they would be willing to learn. He added, they learned much of the bearded mans that came in the boat. Then I asked him if he would go back to them. He smiled at that, and told me he could not swim so far. I told him, I would make a canoe for him. He told me he would go, if I would go with him. I go? says I; why, they will eat me, if I come there.— No, no, says he; me make them no eat you; me make them much love you. He meant, he would tell them how I had killed his enemies, and saved his life, and so he would make them love me. Then he told me, as well as he could, how kind they were to seventeen white men, or bearded men, as he called them, who came on shore there in distress.

From this time, I confess I had a mind to venture over, and see if I could possibly join with those bearded men, who, I made no doubt, were Spaniards and Portuguese: not doubting but if I could, we might find some method to escape from thence, being upon the continent, and a good company together, better than I could from an island forty miles off the shore, and alone, without help. So, after some days, I took Friday to work again, by way of discourse; and told him I would give him a boat to go back to his own nation; and accordingly I carried him to my frigate, which lay on the other side of the island, and having cleared it of water (for I always kept it sunk in water) I brought it out, showed it him, and we both went into it. I found he was a most dexterous fellow at managing it, and would make it go almost as swift again as I could. So when he was in, I said to him, Well, now, Friday, shall we go to your nation? He looked very dull at my saying so; which, it seems, was because he thought the boat too small to go so far; I then told him I had a bigger; so the next day I went to the place where the first boat lay which I had made, but which I could not get into the water. He said that was big enough: but then, as I had taken no care of it, and it had lain two or three-and-twenty years there, the sun had split and dried it, that it was in a manner rotten. Friday told me such a boat would do very well, and would carry much enough vittle, drink, bread; that was his way of talking.

Upon the whole, I was by this time so fixed upon my design of going over with him to the continent, that I told him we would go and make one as big as that, and he should go home in it. He answered not one word, but looked very grave and sad. I asked him what was the matter with him? He asked me again, Why you angry mad with Friday? What me done? I asked him what he meant? I told him I was not angry with him at all. No angry? says he, repeating the words several times; Why send Friday home away to my nation?—Why, says I, Friday, did not you say you wished you were there?—Yes, yes, says he, wish be both there; no wish Friday there, no master there. In a word, he would not think of going there without me. I go there, Friday! says I; what shall I do there? He returned very quick upon me at this: You do great deal much good, says he; you teach wild mans be good, sober, tame mans; you tell them know God, pray God, and live new life.—Alas! Friday, says I, thou knowest not what thou sayest; I am but an ignorant man myself.—Yes, yes, says he, you teachee me good, you teachee them good. —No, no, Friday, says I, you shall go without me, leave me here to live by myself, as I did before. He looked confused again at that word; and running to one of the hatchets which he used to wear, he takes it up hastily, and gives it to me. What must I do with this? says I to him. You take kill Friday, says he. What must I kill you for? said I again. He returns very quick, What you send Friday away for? Take kill Friday, no send Friday away. This he spoke so earnestly, that I saw tears stand in his eyes: in a word, I so plainly discovered the utmost affection in him to me, and a firm resolution in him, that I told him then, and often after, that I would never send him away from me, if he was willing to stay with me.

Upon the whole, as I found, by all his discourse, a settled affection to me, and that nothing should part him from me, so I found all the foundation of his desire to go to his own country was laid in his ardent affection to the people, and his hopes of my doing them good; a thing, which, as I had no notion of myself, so I had not the least thought, or intention, or desire, of undertaking it. But still I found a strong inclination to my attempting an escape, as above; founded on the supposition gathered from the discourse, viz., that there were seventeen bearded men there; and, therefore, without any more delay, I went to work with Friday, to find out a great tree proper to fell, and make a large periagua, or canoe, to undertake the voyage. There were trees enough in the island to have built a little fleet, not of periaguas, or canoes, but even of good large vessels; but the main thing I looked at was, to get one so near the water that we might launch it when it was made, to avoid the mistake I committed at first. At last, Friday pitched upon a tree; for I found he knew much better than I what kind of wood was fittest for it; nor can I tell, to this day, what wood to call the tree we cut down, except that it was very like the tree we call fustic, or between that and the Nicaragua wood, for it was much of the same colour and smell. Friday was for burning the hollow or cavity of this tree out, to make it for a boat, but I showed him how to cut it with tools; which, after I had showed him how to use, he did very handily: and in about a month's hard labour we finished it, and made it very handsome; especially when, with our axes, which I showed him how to handle, we cut and hewed the outside into the true shape of a boat. After this, however, it cost us near a fortnight's time to get her along, as it were inch by inch, upon great rollers, into the water; but when she was in, she would have carried twenty men with great ease.

When she was in the water, and though she was so big, it amazed me to see with what dexterity, and how swift my man Friday would manage her, turn her, and paddle her along. So I asked him if he would, and if we might, venture over in her. Yes, he said; we venture over in her very well, though great blow wind. However, I had a further design, that he knew nothing of, and that was to make a mast and a sail, and to fit her with an anchor and cable. As to a mast, that was easy enough to get: so I pitched upon a straight young cedar tree, which I found near the place, and which there were great plenty of in the island; and I set Friday to work to cut it down, and gave him directions how to shape and order it. But as to the sail, that was my particular care. I knew I had old sails, or rather pieces of old sails, enough: but as I had had them now six-and-twenty years by me, and not been very careful to preserve them, not imagining that I should ever have this kind of use for them, I did not doubt but they were all rotten, and, indeed, most of them were so. However, I found two pieces, which appeared pretty good, and with these I went to work; and with a great deal of pains, and awkward stitching, you may be sure, for want of needles, I, at length, made a three-cornered ugly thing, like what we call in England a shoulder-of-mutton sail, to go with a boom at bottom, and a little short sprit at the top, such as usually our ship's long-boats sail with, and such as I best knew how to manage, as it was such a one I had to the boat in which I made my escape from Barbary, as related in the first part of my story.

I was near two months performing this last work, viz., rigging and fitting my mast and sails; for I finished them very complete, making a small stay, and a sail, or foresail, to it, to assist, if we should turn to windward; and, which was more than all, I fixed a rudder to the stern of her to steer with. I was but a bungling shipwright, yet, as I knew the usefulness, and even necessity of such a thing, I applied myself with so much pains to do it, that at last I brought it to pass; though, considering the many dull contrivances I had for it that failed, I think it cost me almost as much labour as making the boat.

After all this was done, I had my man Friday to teach as to what belonged to the navigation of my boat; for, though he knew very well how to paddle a canoe, he knew nothing what belonged to a sail and a rudder; and was the most amazed when he saw me work the boat to and again in the sea by the rudder, and how the sail gibbed, and filled this way, or that way, as the course we sailed changed; I say, when he saw this, he stood like one astonished and amazed. However, with a little use, I made all these things familiar to him, and he became an expert sailor, except that, as to the compass I could make him understand very little of that. On the other hand, as there was very little cloudy weather, and seldom or never any fogs in those parts, there was the less occasion for a compass, seeing the stars were always to be seen by night, and the shore by day, except in the rainy seasons, and then nobody cared to stir abroad, either by land or sea.

I was now entered on the seven-and-twentieth year of my captivity in this place; though the three last years that I had this creature with me ought rather to be left out of the account, my habitation being quite of another kind than in all the rest of the time. I kept the anniversary of my landing here with the same thankfulness to God for his mercies as at first; and if I had such cause of acknowledgment at first, I had much more so now, having such additional testimonies of the care of Providence over me, and the great hopes I had of being effectually and speedily delivered; for I had an invincible impression upon my thoughts that my deliverance was at hand, and that I should not be another year in this place. I went on, however, with my husbandry; digging, planting, and fencing, as usual. I gathered and cured my grapes, and did every necessary thing as before.

The rainy season was, in the mean time, upon me, when I kept more within doors than at other times. We had stowed our own vessel as secure as we could, bringing her up into the creek, where, as I said in the beginning, I landed my rafts from the ship; and hauling her up to the shore, at high-water mark, I made my man Friday dig a little dock, just big enough to hold her, and just deep enough to give her water enough to float in; and then, when the tide was out, we made a strong dam across the end of it, to keep the water out; and so she lay dry, as to the tide, from the sea: and to keep the rain off, we laid a great many boughs of trees, so thick, that she was as well thatched as a house; and thus we waited for the months of November and December, in which I designed to make my adventure.

When the settled season began to come in, as the thought of my design returned with the fair weather, I was preparing daily for the voyage, and the first thing I did was to lay by a certain quantity of provisions, being the stores for our voyage, and intended, in a week or a fortnight's time, to open the dock, and launch out our boat. I was busy one morning upon something of this kind, when I called to Friday, and bid him go to the sea-shore, and see if he could find a turtle, or tortoise, a thing which we generally got once a week, for the sake of the eggs as well as the flesh. Friday had not been long gone, when he came running back, and flew over my outer wall, or fence, like one that felt not the ground, or the steps he set his feet on; and before I had time to speak to him, he cries out to me, O master! O master! O sorrow! O bad!—What's the matter, Friday? says I. O yonder, there, says he, one, two, three, canoe; one, two, three! By this way of speaking, I concluded there were six; but, on inquiry, I found it was but three. Well, Friday, says I, do not be frightened! So I heartened him up as well as I could; however, I saw the poor fellow was most terribly scared; for nothing ran in his head but that they were come to look for him, and would cut him in pieces, and eat him; and the poor fellow trembled so, that I scarce knew what to do with him. I comforted him as well as I could, and told him I was in as much danger as he, and that they would eat me as well as him. But, says I, Friday, we must resolve to fight them. Can you fight, Friday?—Me shoot, says he; but there come many great number.—No matter for that, said I, again; our guns will fright them that we do not kill. So I asked him whether, if I resolved to defend him, he would defend me, and stand by me; and do just as I bid him. He said, Me die, when you bid die, master. So I went and fetched a good dram of rum and gave him; for I had been so good a husband of my rum, that I had a great deal left. When he drank it, I made him take the two fowling-pieces, which we always carried, and loaded them with large swan-shot, as big

as small pistol-bullets; then I took four muskets, and loaded them with
two slugs, and five small bullets each; and my two pistols I loaded with
a brace of bullets each; I hung my great sword, as usual, naked by my
side; and gave Friday his hatchet. When I had thus prepared myself, I
took my perspective glass, and went up to the side of the hill, to see what
I could discover; and found quickly, by my glass, that there was one-
and-twenty savages, three prisoners, and three canoes; and that their
whole business seemed to be the triumphant banquet upon these three
human bodies; a barbarous feast indeed! but nothing more than, as I
had observed, was usual with them. I observed also, that they were
landed, not where they had done when Friday made his escape, but
nearer to my creek; where the shore was low, and where a thick wood
came almost close down to the sea. This, with the abhorrence of the inhuman errand these wretches came about, filled me with such indignation, that I came down again to Friday, and told him I was resolved to
go down to them and kill them all; and asked him if he would stand by
me. He had now got over his fright, and his spirits being a little raised
with the dram I had given him, he was very cheerful, and told me, as before, he would die when I bid die.

In this fit of fury, I took and divided the arms which I had charged,
as before, between us; I gave Friday one pistol to stick in his girdle, and
three guns upon his shoulder; and I took one pistol, and the other three
guns myself; and in this posture we marched out. I took a small bottle
of rum in my pocket, and gave Friday a large bag with more powder and
bullets; and, as to orders, I charged him to keep close behind me, and
not to stir, or shoot, or do anything, till I told him; and, in the mean
time, not to speak a word. In this posture, I fetched a compass to my
right hand of near a mile, as well to get over the creek as to get into the
wood, so that I might come within shot of them before I should be discovered, which I had seen, by my glass, it was easy to do.

While I was making this march, my former thoughts returning, I began to abate my resolution: I do not mean that I entertained any fear of
their number; for, as they were naked, unarmed wretches, it is certain I
was superior to them; nay, though I had been alone. But it occurred to
my thoughts, what call, what occasion, much less what necessity I was in,
to go and dip my hands in blood, to attack people who had neither done
nor intended me any wrong? Who, as to me, were innocent, and whose
barbarous customs were their own disaster; being, in them, a token indeed of God's having left them, with the other nations of that part of
the world, to such stupidity, and to such inhuman courses; but did not
call me to take upon me to be a judge of their actions, much less an executioner of his justice; that, whenever he thought fit, he would take the
cause into his own hands, and, by national vengeance, punish them, as a
people, for national crimes; but that, in the mean time, it was none of
my business; that, it was true, Friday might justify it, because he was a

declared enemy, and in a state of war with those very particular people, and it was lawful for him to attack them; but I could not say the same with respect to myself. These things were so warmly pressed upon my thoughts all the way as I went, that I resolved I would only go and place myself near them, that I might observe their barbarous feast, and that I would act then as God should direct: but that, unless something offered that was more a call to me than yet I knew of, I would not meddle with them.

With this resolution I entered the wood; and, with all possible wariness and silence, Friday following close at my heels, I marched till I came to the skirt of the wood, on the side which was next to them, only that one corner of the wood lay between me and them. Here I called softly to Friday, and showing him a great tree, which was just at the corner of the wood, I bade him go to the tree, and bring me word if he could see there plainly what they were doing. He did so; and came immediately back to me, and told me they might be plainly viewed there; that they were all about their fire, eating the flesh of one of their prisoners, and that another lay bound upon the sand, a little from them, which, he said, they would kill next, and which fired all the very soul within me. He told me it was not one of their nation, but one of the bearded men he had told me of, that came to their country in the boat. I was filled with horror at the very naming the white bearded man; and, going to the tree, I saw plainly, by my glass, a white man, who lay upon the beach of the sea, with his hands and his feet tied with flags, or things like rushes, and that he was an European, and had clothes on.

There was another tree, and a little thicket beyond it about fifty yards nearer to them than the place where I was, which, by going a little way about, I saw I might come at undiscovered, and that then I should be within half a shot of them; so I withheld my passion, though I was indeed enraged to the highest degree; and going back about twenty paces, I got behind some bushes, which held all the way till I came to the other tree; and then came to a little rising ground, which gave me a full view of them, at the distance of about eighty yards.

I HAD now not a moment to lose, for nineteen of the dreadful wretches sat upon the ground, all close-huddled together, and had just sent the other two to butcher the poor Christian, and bring him, perhaps limb by limb, to their fire; and they were stooping down to untie the bands at his feet. I turned to Friday—Now, Friday, said I, do as I bid thee. Friday said he would. Then, Friday, says I, do exactly as you see me do; fail in nothing. So I set down one of the muskets and the fowling-piece upon the ground, and Friday did the like by his; and with my other musket I took my aim at the savages, bidding him to do the like: then asking him if he was ready, he said, Yes. Then fire at them, said I, and the same moment I fired also.

Friday took his aim so much better than I, that on the side that he shot, he killed two of them, and wounded three more; and on my side, I killed one, and wounded two. They were, you may be sure, in a dreadful consternation; and all of them who were not hurt jumped upon their feet, but did not immediately know which way to run, or which way to look, for they knew not from whence their destruction came. Friday kept his eyes close upon me that, as I had bid him, he might observe what I did; so, as soon as the first shot was made, I threw down the piece, and took up the fowling-piece, and Friday did the like: he saw me cock and present; he did the same again. Are you ready, Friday? said I. Yes, says he. Let fly, then, says I, in the name of God! And with that, I fired again among the amazed wretches, and so did Friday; and as our pieces were now loaded with what I called swan-shot, or small pistol-bullets, we found only two drop, but so many were wounded, that they ran about yelling and screaming like mad creatures, all bloody, and most miserably wounded, whereof three more fell quickly after, though not quite dead.

Now, Friday, says I, laying down the discharged pieces, and taking up the musket which was yet loaded, follow me; which he did, with a great deal of courage; upon which I rushed out of the wood, and showed myself, and Friday close at my foot. As soon as I perceived they saw me, I shouted as loud as I could, and bade Friday do so too; and running as fast as I could, which, by the way, was not very fast, being loaded with arms as I was, I made directly towards the poor victim, who was, as I said, lying upon the beach, or shore, between the place where they sat and the sea. The two butchers, who were just going to work with him, had left him at the surprise of our first fire, and fled in a terrible fright to the sea-side, and had jumped into a canoe, and three more of the rest made the same way. I turned to Friday, and bade him step forwards, and fire at them; he understood me immediately, and running about forty yards, to be nearer them, he shot at them, and I thought he had killed them all, for I saw them all fall of a heap into the boat, though I saw two of them up again quickly: however, he killed two of them, and wounded the third, so that he lay down in the bottom of the boat as if he had been dead.

While my man Friday fired at them, I pulled out my knife, and cut the flags that bound the poor victim; and loosing his hands and feet, I lifted him up, and asked him in the Portuguese tongue, what he was. He answered in Latin, Christianus; but was so weak and faint that he could scarce stand or speak. I took my bottle out of my pocket, and gave it him, making signs that he should drink, which he did; and I gave him a piece of bread, which he ate. Then I asked him what countryman he was: and he said, Espagniole; and being a little recovered, let me know, by all the signs he could possibly make, how much he was in my debt for his deliverance. Signor, said I, with as much Spanish as I could make up, we will talk afterwards, but we must fight now: if you have any strength left, take this pistol and sword, and lay about you. He took them very thankfully; and no sooner had he the arms in his hands, but, as if they had put new vigour into him, he flew upon his murderers like a fury, and had cut two of them in pieces in an instant; for the truth is, as the whole was a surprise to them, so the poor creatures were so much frightened with the noise of our pieces, that they fell down for mere amazement and fear, and had no more power to attempt their own escape, than their flesh had to resist our shot: and that was the case of those five that Friday shot at in the boat; for as three of them fell with the hurt they received, so the other two fell with the fright.

I kept my piece in my hand still without firing, being willing to keep my charge ready, because I had given the Spaniard my pistol and sword: so I called to Friday, and bade him run up to the tree from whence we first fired, and fetch the arms which lay there that had been discharged, which he did with great swiftness; and then giving him my musket, I sat down myself to load all the rest again, and bade them come to me when they wanted. While I was loading these pieces, there happened a fierce engagement between the Spaniard and one of the savages, who made at him with one of their great wooden swords, the same-like weapon that was to have killed him before, if I had not prevented it. The Spaniard, who was as bold and brave as could be imagined, though weak, had fought this Indian a good while, and had cut him two good wounds on his head; but the savage being a stout, lusty fellow, closing in with him, had thrown him down, being faint, and was wringing my sword out of his hand; when the Spaniard, though undermost, wisely quitting the sword, drew the pistol from his girdle, shot the savage through the body, and killed him upon the spot, before I, who was running to help him, could come near him.

Friday being now left to his liberty, pursued the flying wretches, with no weapon in his hand but his hatchet; and with that he dispatched those three, who, as I said before, were wounded at first, and fallen, and all the rest he could come up with: and the Spaniard coming to me for a gun, I gave him one of the fowling-pieces, with which he pursued two of the savages, and wounded them both; but, as he was not able to run, they both got from him into the wood, where Friday pursued them, and killed one of them, but the other was too nimble for him; and though he was wounded, yet he had plunged himself into the sea, and swam, with all his might, off to those two who were left in the canoe, which three in the canoe, with one wounded, that we knew not whether he died or no, were all that escaped our hands of one-and-twenty. The account of the whole is as follows: three killed at our first shot from the tree; two killed at the next shot; two killed by Friday in the boat; two killed by Friday of those at first wounded; one killed by Friday in the wood; three killed by the Spaniard; four killed, being found dropped here and there of their wounds, or killed by Friday in his chase of them; four escaped in the boat whereof one wounded, if not dead.—Twenty-one in all.

Those that were in their canoe worked hard to get out of gunshot, and though Friday made two or three shots at them, I did not find that he hit any of them. Friday would fain have had me take one of their canoes, and pursue them; and indeed, I was very anxious about their escape, lest, carrying the news home to their people, they should come back perhaps with two or three hundred of the canoes, and devour us by mere multitude; so I consented to pursue them by sea, and running to one of their canoes, I jumped in, and bade Friday follow me; but when I was in the canoe, I was surprised to find another poor creature lie there, bound hand and foot, as the Spaniard was, for the slaughter, and almost dead with fear, not knowing what was the matter; for he had not been able to look over the side of the boat, he was tied so hard neck and heels, and had been tied so long, that he had really but little life in him.

I immediately cut the twisted flags or rushes, which they had bound him with, and would have helped him up; but he could not stand or speak, but groaned most piteously, believing, it seems, still, that he was only unbound in order to be killed. When Friday came to him, I bade him speak to him, and tell him of his deliverance; and, pulling out my bottle, made him give the poor wretch a dram; which, with the news of his being delivered, revived him, and he sat up in the boat. But when

Friday came to hear him speak, and look in his face, it would have moved any one into tears to have seen how Friday kissed him, embraced him, hugged him, cried, laughed, hallooed, jumped about, danced, sung; then cried again, wrung his hands, beat his own face and head; and then sung and jumped about again, like a distracted creature. It was a good while before I could make him speak to me, or tell me what was the matter; but when he came a little to himself, he told me that it was his father.

It is not easy for me to express how it moved me to see what ecstasy and filial affection had worked in this poor savage at the sight of his father, and on his being delivered from death; nor, indeed, can I describe half the extravagancies of his affection after this; for he went into the boat, and out of the boat, a great many times: when he went in to him, he would sit down by him, open his breast, and hold his father's head close to his bosom for many minutes together, to nourish it; then he took his arms and ankles, which were numbed and stiff with the binding, and chafed and rubbed them with his hands; and I, perceiving what the case was, gave him some rum out of my bottle to rub them with, which did them a great deal of good.

This affair put an end to our pursuit of the canoe with the other savages, who were got now almost out of sight; and it was happy for us that we did not, for it blew so hard within two hours after, and before they could be got a quarter of their way, and continued blowing so hard all night, and that from the north-west, which was against them, that I could not suppose their boat could live, or that they ever reached their own coast.

But, to return to Friday; he was so busy about his father, that I could not find in my heart to take him off for some time: but after I thought he could leave him a little, I called him to me, and he came jumping and laughing, and pleased to the highest extreme; then I asked him if he had given his father any bread. He shook his head, and said, None; ugly dog eat all up self. I then gave him a cake of bread, out of a little pouch I carried on purpose: I also gave him a dram for himself, but he would not taste it, but carried it to his father. I had in my pocket two or three bunches of raisins, so I gave him a handful of them for his father. He had no sooner given his father these raisins, but I saw him come out of the boat, and run away, as if he had been bewitched, he ran at such a rate: for he was the swiftest fellow on his feet that ever I saw: I say, he ran at such a rate, that he was out of sight, as it were, in an instant; and though I called, and hallooed out too, after him, it was all one way, away he went; and in a quarter of an hour I saw him come back again, though not so fast as he went; and as he came nearer, I found his pace slacker, because he had something in his hand. When he came up to me, I found he had been quite home for an earthen jug, or pot, to bring his father some fresh water, and that he had two more cakes or loaves of bread; the bread he gave me, but the water he carried to his father; however, as I was very thirsty too, I took a little sup of it. The water revived his father more than all the rum or spirits I had given him, for he was just fainting with thirst.

When his father had drunk, I called to him to know if there was any water left; he said, Yes; and I bade him give it to the poor Spaniard, who was in as much want of it as his father: and I sent one of the cakes that Friday brought to the Spaniard too, who was indeed very weak, and was reposing himself upon a green place under the shade of a tree; and whose limbs were also very stiff, and very much swelled with the rude bandage he had been tied with. When I saw that, upon Friday's coming to him with the water, he sat up and drank, and took the bread, and began to eat, I went to him and gave him a handful of raisins: he looked up in my face with all the tokens of gratitude and thankfulness that could appear in any countenance; but was so weak, notwithstanding he had so exerted himself in the fight, that he could not stand upon his feet; he tried to do it two or three times, but was really not able, his ankles were so swelled and so painful to him; so I bade him sit still, and caused Friday to rub his ankles, and bathe them with rum, as he had done his father's.

I observed the poor affectionate creature, every two minutes, or perhaps less, all the while he was here, turn his head about to see if his father was in the same place and posture as he left him sitting; and at last he found he was not to be seen; at which he started up, and, without speaking a word, flew with that swiftness to him, that one could scarce perceive his feet to touch the ground as he went: but when he came, he only found he had lain himself down to ease his limbs, so Friday came back to me presently; and then I spoke to the Spaniard to let Friday help him up, if he could, and lead him to the boat, and then he should carry him to our dwelling, where I would take care of him: but Friday, a lusty strong fellow, took the Spaniard quite upon his back, and carried him away to the boat, and set him down softly upon the side or gunnel of the canoe, with his feet in the inside of it; and then, lifting him quite in, he set himself close to his father; and presently stepping out again, launched the boat off, and paddled it along the shore faster than I could walk, though the wind blew pretty hard too; so he brought them both safe into our creek, and leaving them in the boat, ran away to fetch the other canoe. As he passed me, I spoke to him, and asked him whither he went. He told me, Go fetch more boat: so away he went like the wind, for sure never man or horse ran like him; and he had the other canoe in the creek almost as soon as I got to it by land; so he wafted me over, and then went to help our new guests out of the boat, which he did; but they were neither of them able to walk, so that poor Friday knew not what to do.

To remedy this, I went to work in my thoughts, and calling to Friday to bid them sit down on the bank while he came to me, I soon made a kind of hand-barrow to lay them on, and Friday and I carried them both up together upon it, between us. But when we got them to the outside of our wall, or fortification, we were at a worse loss than before, for it was impossible to get them over, and I was resolved not to break it down; so I set to work again; and Friday and I, in about two hours' time, made a very handsome tent, covered with old sails, and above that with boughs of trees, being in the space without our outward fence, and between that and the grove of young wood which I had planted: and here we made them two beds of such things as I had, viz., of good rice-straw, with blankets laid upon it, to lie on, and another to cover them, on each bed.

My island was now peopled, and I thought myself rich in subjects: and it was a merry reflection, which I frequently made, how like a king I looked. First of all, the whole country was my own mere property, so that I had an undoubted right of dominion. Secondly, my people were perfectly subjected; I was absolutely lord and lawgiver; they all owed their lives to me, and were ready to lay down their lives, if there had been occasion for it, for me. It was remarkable, too, I had but three subjects: and they were of three different religions: my man Friday was a Protestant, and his father was a Pagan and a cannibal, and the Spaniard was a Papist: however, I allowed liberty of conscience throughout my dominions.—But this is by the way.

As soon as I had secured my two weak rescued prisoners, and given them shelter, and a place to rest them upon, I began to think of making some provision for them: and the first thing I did, I ordered Friday to take a yearling goat, betwixt a kid and a goat, out of my particular flock, to be killed; when I cut off the hinder quarter, and chopping it into small pieces, I set Friday to work to boiling and stewing, and made them a very good dish, I assure you, of flesh and broth, having put some barley and rice also into the broth; and as I cooked it without doors, for I made no fire within my inner wall, so I carried it all into the new tent, and having set a table there for them, I sat down, and ate my dinner also with them, and, as well as I could, cheered them, and encouraged them. Friday was my interpreter, especially to his father, and, indeed, to the Spaniard too; for the Spaniard spoke the language of the savages pretty well.

After we had dined, or rather supped, I ordered Friday to take one of the canoes, and go and fetch our muskets and other fire-arms, which, for want of time, we had left upon the place of battle: and, the next day, I ordered him to go and bury the dead bodies of the savages, which lay open to the sun, and would presently be offensive. I also ordered him to bury the horrid remains of their barbarous feast, which I knew were pretty much, and which I could not think of doing myself; nay, I could not bear to see them, if I went that way; all which he punctually performed, and effaced the very appearance of the savages being there; so that when I went again, I could scarce know where it was, otherwise than by the corner of the wood pointing to the place.

I then began to enter into a little conversation with my two new subjects: and, first, I set Friday to inquire of his father what he thought of the escape of the savages in that canoe, and whether we might expect a return of them, with a power too great for us to resist. His first opinion was, that the savages in the boat could never live out the storm which blew that night they went off, but must of necessity be drowned, or driven south to those other shores, where they were as sure to be devoured as they were to be drowned, if they were cast away; but, as to what they would do, if they came safe on shore, he said he knew not; but it was his opinion, that they were so dreadfully frightened with the manner of their being attacked, the noise and the fire, that he believed they would tell the people they were all killed by thunder and lightning, not by the hand of man; and that the two which appeared, viz., Friday and I, were two heavenly spirits, or furies, come down to destroy them, and not men with weapons. This, he said, he knew; because he heard them all cry out so, in their language one to another; for it was impossible for them to conceive that a man could dart fire, and speak thunder, and kill at a distance, without lifting up the hand, as was done now: and this old savage was in the right; for, as I understood since, by other hands, the savages never attempted to go over to the island afterwards, they were so terrified with the accounts given by those four men (for, it seems, they did escape the sea), that they believed whoever went to that enchanted island would be destroyed by fire from the gods. This, however, I knew not; and therefore was under continual apprehensions for a good while, and kept always upon my guard, with all my army; for, as there were now four of us, I would have ventured upon a hundred of them, fairly in the open field, at any time.

In a little time, however, no more canoes appearing, the fear of their coming wore off; and I began to take my former thoughts of a voyage to the main into consideration; but likewise assured, by Friday's father, that I might depend upon good usage from their nation, on his account, if I would go. But my thoughts were a little suspended when I had a serious discourse with the Spaniard, and when I understood that there were sixteen more of his countrymen and Portuguese, who, having been cast away, and made their escape to that side, lived there at peace, indeed, with the savages, but were very sore put to it for necessaries, and indeed for life. I asked him all the particulars of their voyage, and found they were a Spanish ship, bound from the Rio de la Plata, to the Havana, being directed to leave their loading there, which was chiefly hides and silver, and to bring back what European goods they could meet with there; that they had five Portuguese seamen on board, whom they took out of another wreck; that five of their own men were drowned, when first the ship was lost, and that these escaped through infinite dangers and hazards, and arrived, almost starved, on the cannibal coast, where they expected to have been devoured every moment. He told me they had some arms with them, but they were perfectly useless, for that they had neither powder nor ball, the washing of the sea having spoiled all their powder, but a little, which they used at their first landing, to provide themselves some food.

I asked him what he thought would become of them there, and if they had formed no design of making any escape. He said they had many consultations about it; but that having neither vessel, nor tools to build one, nor provisions of any kind, their councils always ended in tears and despair. I asked him how he thought they would receive a proposal from me, which might tend towards an escape; and whether, if they were all here, it might not be done. I told him, with freedom, I feared mostly their treachery and ill-usage of me, if I put my life in their hands, for that gratitude was no inherent virtue in the nature of man, nor did men always square their dealings by the obligations they had received, so much as they did by the advantages they expected. I told him it would be very hard that I should be the instrument of their deliverance, and that they should afterwards make me their prisoner in New Spain, where an Englishman was certain to be made a sacrifice, what necessity, or what accident soever brought him thither; and that I had rather be delivered up to savages, and be devoured alive, than fall into the merciless claws of the priests, and be carried into the Inquisition. I added, that otherwise I was persuaded, if they were all here, we might, with so many hands, build a bark large enough to carry us all away, either to the Brazils, southward, or to the islands, or Spanish coast, northward; but that if, in requital, they should, when I had put weapons into their hands, carry me by force among their own people, I might be ill-used for my kindness to them, and make my case worse than it was before.

He answered with a great deal of candour and ingenuousness, that their condition was so miserable, and they were so sensible of it, that he believed they would abhor the thought of using any man unkindly that should contribute to their deliverance; and that, if I pleased, he would go to them with the old man, and discourse with them about it, and return again, and bring me their answer; that he would make conditions with them upon their solemn oath, that they should be absolutely under my leading, as their commander and captain; and that they should swear upon the holy sacraments and gospel, to be true to me, and go to such Christian country as I should agree to, and no other, and to be directed wholly and absolutely by my orders, till they were landed safely in such country as I intended; and that he would bring a contract from them, under their hands, for that purpose. Then he told me he would first swear to me himself, that he would never stir from me as long as he lived, till I gave him orders; and that he would take my side to the last drop of his blood, if there should happen the least breach of faith among his countrymen. He told me they were all very civil, honest men, and they were under the greatest distress imaginable, having neither weapons, nor clothes, nor any food, but at the mercy and discretion of the savages; out of all hopes of ever returning to their own country; and that he was sure, if I would undertake their relief, they would live and die by me.

Upon these assurances, I resolved to venture to relieve them, if possible, and to send the old savage and this Spaniard over to them to treat. But when we got all things in readiness to go, the Spaniard himself started an objection, which had so much prudence in it, on one hand, and so much sincerity, on the other hand, that I could not but be very well satisfied in it; and, by his advice, put off the deliverance of his comrades for at least half a year. The case was thus: He had been with us now about a month, during which time, I had let him see in what manner I had provided, with the assistance of Providence, for my support; and he saw evidently what stock of corn and rice I had laid up; which, though it was more than sufficient for myself, yet it was not sufficient, without good husbandry, for my family, now it was increased to four; but much less would it be sufficient if his countrymen, who were, as he said, sixteen, still alive, should come over; and least of all would it be sufficient to victual our vessel, if we should build one, for a voyage to any of the Christian colonies of America; so he told me he thought it would be more advisable to let him and the other two dig and cultivate more land, as much as I could spare seed to sow, and that we should wait another harvest, that we should have a supply of corn for his countrymen, when they should come; for want might be a temptation to them to disagree, or not to think themselves delivered, otherwise than out of one difficulty into another. You know, says he, the children of Israel, though they rejoiced at first for their being delivered out of Egypt, yet rebelled even against God himself, that delivered them, when they came to want bread in the Wilderness.

His caution was so seasonable, and his voice so good, that I could not but be very well pleased with his proposal, as well as I was satisfied with his fidelity; so we fell to digging, all four of us, as well as the wooden tools permitted; and in about a month's time, by the end of which it was seed-time, we had got as much land cured and trimmed up as we sowed two-and-twenty bushels of barley on, and sixteen jars of rice; which was, in short, all the seed we had to spare; nor, indeed, did we leave ourselves barley sufficient for our own food, for the six months that we had to expect our crop; that is to say, reckoning from the time we set our seed aside for sowing; for it is not to be supposed it is six months in the ground in that country.

Having now society enough, and our number being sufficient to put us out of fear of the savages if they had come, unless their number had been very great, we went freely all over the island, whenever we found occasion: and as here we had our escape or deliverance upon our thoughts, it was impossible, at least for me, to have the means of it out of mine. For this purpose, I marked out several trees which I thought fit for our work, and I set Friday and his father to cutting them down; and then I caused the Spaniard, to whom I imparted my thought on that affair, to oversee and direct their work. I showed them with what indefatigable pains I had hewed a large tree into single planks, and I caused them to do the like, till they had made about a dozen large planks of good oak, near two feet broad, thirty-five feet long, and from two inches to four inches thick: what prodigious labour it took up, any one may imagine.

At the same time, I contrived to increase my little flock of tame goats as much as I could; and, for this purpose, I made Friday and the Spaniard go out one day, and myself with Friday the next day (for we took our turns), and by this means we got about twenty young kids to breed up with the rest: for whenever we shot the dam, we saved the kids, and added them to our flock. But, above all, the season for curing the grapes coming on, I caused such a prodigious quantity to be hung up in the sun, that, I believe, had we been at Alicant, where the raisins of the sun are cured, we could have filled sixty or eighty barrels; and these, with our bread, was a great part of our food, and was a very good living, too, I assure you, for it is exceedingly nourishing.

It was now harvest, and our crop in good order: it was not the most plentiful increase I had seen in the island, but, however, it was enough to answer our end; for from twenty-two bushels of barley we brought in and threshed out above two hundred and twenty bushels, and the like in proportion of the rice; which was store enough for our food to the next harvest, though all the sixteen Spaniards had been on shore with me; or if we had been ready for a voyage, it would very plentifully have victualled our ship to have carried us to any part of the world, that is to say, any part of America. When we had thus housed and secured our magazine of corn, we fell to work to make more wicker-ware, viz., great baskets, in which we kept it; and the Spaniard was very handy and dexterous at this part, and often blamed me that I did not make some things for defence of this kind of work; but I saw no need of it.

And now, having a full supply of food for all the guests I expected, I gave the Spaniard leave to go over to the main, to see what he could do with those he had left behind him there. I gave him a strict charge not to bring any man with him who would not first swear in the presence of himself and the old savage, that he would no way injure, fight with, or attack the person he should find in the island, who was so kind as to send for them in order to their deliverance; but that they would stand by him, and defend him against all such attempts, and wherever they went, would be entirely under and subjected to his command; and that this should be put in writing, and signed with their hands. How they were to have done this, when I knew they had neither pen nor ink, was a question which we never asked. Under these instructions, the Spaniard and the old savage, the father of Friday, went away in one of the canoes which they might be said to come in, or rather were brought in, when they came as prisoners to be devoured by the savages. I gave each of them a musket, with a fire-lock on it, and about eight charges of powder and ball, charging them to be very good husbands of both, and not to use either of them but upon urgent occasions.

This was a cheerful work, being the first measures used by me, in view of my deliverance, for now twenty-seven years and some days. I gave them provisions of bread, and of dried grapes, sufficient for themselves for many days, and sufficient for all the Spaniards for about eight days' time; and wishing them a good voyage, I saw them go; agreeing with them about a signal that they should hang out at their return, by which I should know them again, when they came back, at a distance, before they came on shore. They went away with a fair gale, on the day that the moon was at full, by my account in the month of October; but as for an exact reckoning of days, after I had once lost it, I could never recover it again; nor had I kept even the number of years so punctually as to be sure I was right; though, as it proved, when I afterwards examined my account, I found I had kept a true reckoning of years.

It was no less than eight days I had waited for them when a strange and unforeseen accident intervened, of which the like has not perhaps been heard of in history. I was fast asleep in my hutch, one morning, when my man Friday came running in to me, and called aloud, Master, master, they are come, they are come! I jumped up, and, regardless of danger, I went out as soon as I could get my clothes on, through my little grove, which, by the way, was by this time grown to be a very thick wood; I say, regardless of danger, I went without my arms, which it was not my custom to do; but I was surprised, when turning my eyes to the sea, I presently saw a boat about a league and a half distance, standing in for the shore, with a shoulder-of-mutton sail, as they call it, and the wind blowing pretty fair to bring them in: also I observed presently, that they did not come from that side which the shore lay on, but from the southernmost end of the island.

Upon this, I called Friday in, and bade him lie close, for these were not the people we looked for, and that we might not know yet whether they were friends or enemies. In the next place, I went in to fetch my perspective glass, to see what I could make of them; and having taken the ladder out, I climbed to the top of the hill, as I used to do when I was apprehensive of anything, and to take my view the plainer without being discovered. I had scarce set my foot upon the hill, when my eye plainly discovered a ship lying at an anchor, at about two leagues and a half distance from me, S.S.E., but not above a league and a half from the shore. By my observation, it appeared plainly to be an English ship, and the boat appeared to be an English long-boat.

I cannot express the confusion I was in; though the joy of seeing a ship, and one that I had reason to believe was manned by my own countrymen, and, consequently, friends, was such as I cannot describe; but yet I had some secret doubts hang about me—I cannot tell from whence they came, bidding me keep upon my guard. In the first place it occurred to me to consider what business an English ship could have in that part of the world, since it was not the way to or from any part of the world where the English had any traffic; and I knew there had been no storms to drive them in there, as in distress; and that if they were really English, it was most probable that they were here upon no good design; and that I had better continue as I was, than fall into the hands of thieves and murderers.

Let no man despise the secret hints and notices of danger, which sometimes are given him when he may think there is no possibility of its being real. That such hints and notices are given us, I believe few that have made any observations of things can deny; that they are certain discoveries of an invisible world, and a converse of spirits, we cannot doubt; and if the tendency of them seems to be to warn us of danger, why should we not suppose they are from some friendly agent (whether supreme or inferior and subordinate, is not the question), and that they are given for our good?

The present question abundantly confirms me in the justice of this reasoning; for had I not been made cautious by this secret admonition, come it from whence it will, I had been undone inevitably, and in a far worse condition than before, as you will see presently. I had not kept myself long in this posture, but I saw the boat draw near the shore, as if they looked for a creek to thrust in at, for the convenience of landing; however, as they did not come quite far enough, they did not see the little inlet where I formerly landed my rafts, but run their boat on shore upon the beach, at about half a mile from me, which was very happy for me; for otherwise they would have landed just at my door, as I may say, and would soon have beaten me out of my castle, and perhaps have plundered me of all I had. When they were on shore, I was fully satisfied they were Englishmen, at least most of them; one or two I thought were Dutch, but it did not prove so; there were in all eleven men, whereof three of them I found were unarmed, and, as I thought, bound; and when the first four or five of them were jumped on shore, they took those three out of the boat as prisoners; one of the three I could perceive using the most passionate gestures of entreaty, affliction, and despair, even to a kind of extravagance; the other two, I could perceive, lifted up their hands sometimes, and appeared concerned, indeed, but not to such a degree as the first. I was perfectly confounded at the sight, and knew not what the meaning of it should be. Friday called out to me in English, as well as he could, O master! you see English mans eat prisoner as well as savage mans.—Why, Friday, says I, do you think they are going to eat them then?—Yes, says Friday, they will eat them.—No, no, says I, Friday; I am afraid they will murder them indeed, but you may be sure they will not eat them.

All this while I had no thought of what the matter really was, but stood trembling with the horror of the sight, expecting every moment when the three prisoners should be killed; nay, once I saw one of the villains lift up his arm with a great cutlass, as the seamen call it, or sword, to strike one of the poor men; and I expected to see him fall every moment; at which all the blood in my body seemed to run chill in my veins. I wished heartily now for my Spaniard, and the savage that was gone with him, or that I had any way to have come undiscovered within shot of them, that I might have rescued the three men, for I saw no fire-arms they had among them; but it fell out to my mind another way. After I had observed the outrageous usage of the three men by the insolent seamen, I observed the fellows run scattering about the island, as if they wanted to see the country. I observed that the three other men had liberty to go also where they pleased; but they sat down all three upon the ground, very pensive, and looked like men in despair. This put me in mind of the first time when I came on shore, and began to look about me: how I gave myself over for lost; how wildly I looked around me; what dreadful apprehensions I had; and how I lodged in the tree all night, for fear of being devoured by wild beasts. As I knew nothing that night of the supply I was to receive by the providential driving of the ship nearer the land by the storms and tide, by which I have since been so long nourished and supported; so these three poor desolate men knew nothing how certain of deliverance and supply they were, how near it was to them, and how effectually and really they were in a condition of safety, at the same time that they thought themselves lost, and their case desperate. So little do we see before us in the world, and so much reason have we to depend cheerfully upon the great Maker of the world, that he does not leave his creatures so absolutely destitute, but that, in the worst circumstances, they have always something to be thankful for, and sometimes are nearer their deliverance than they imagine, nay, are even brought to their deliverance by the means by which they seem to be brought to their destruction.

I T WAS just at the top of high water when these people came on shore; and partly while they rambled about to see what kind of a place they were in, they had carelessly stayed till the tide was spent, and the water was ebbed considerably away, leaving their boat aground. They had left two men in the boat, who, as I found afterwards, having drunk a little too much brandy, fell asleep; however, one of them waking a little sooner than the other, and finding the boat too fast aground for him to stir it, hallooed out to the rest, who were straggling about; upon which they all soon came to the boat; but it was past all their strength to launch her, the boat being very heavy, and the shore on that side being a soft oozy sand, almost like a quicksand. In this condition, like true seamen, who are perhaps the least of all mankind given to forethought, they gave it over, and away they strolled about the country again; and I heard one of them say aloud to another, calling them off from the boat, Why, let her alone, Jack, can't you? she'll float next tide: by which I was fully confirmed in the main inquiry of what countrymen they were. All this while I kept myself very close, not once daring to stir out of my castle, any farther than to my place of observation, near the top of the hill; and very glad I was to think how well it was fortified. I knew it was no less than ten hours before the boat could float again, and by that time it would be dark, and I might be at more liberty to see their motions, and to hear their discourse, if they had any. In the mean time, I fitted myself up for a battle, as before, though with more caution, knowing I had to do with another kind of enemy than I had at first. I ordered Friday also, whom I had made an excellent marksman with his gun, to load himself with arms. I took myself two fowling-pieces, and I gave him three muskets. My figure, indeed, was very fierce; I had my formidable goat's skin coat on, with the great cap I have mentioned, a naked sword by my side, two pistols in my belt, and a gun upon each shoulder.

It was my design, as I said above, not to have made any attempt till it was dark: but about two o'clock, being the heat of the day, I found that, in short, they were all gone straggling into the woods, and as I thought, laid down to sleep. The three poor distressed men, too anxious for their condition to get any sleep, were, however, sat down under the shelter of a great tree, at about a quarter of a mile from me, and, as I thought, out of sight of any of the rest. Upon this I resolved to discover myself to them, and learn something of their condition; immediately I marched in the figure as above, my man Friday at a good distance behind me, as formidable for his arms as I, but not making quite so staring a spectre-like figure as I did. I came as near them undiscovered as I could, and then, before any of them saw me, I called aloud to them in Spanish, What are ye, gentlemen? They started up at the noise; but were ten times more confounded when they saw me, and the uncouth figure that I made. They made no answer at all, but I thought I perceived them just going to fly from me, when I spoke to them in English: Gentlemen, said I, do not be surprised at me; perhaps you may have a friend near, when you did not expect it.—He must be sent directly from Heaven then, said one of them very gravely to me, and pulling off his hat at the same time to me; for our condition is past the help of man.—All help is from Heaven, sir, said I: but can you put a stranger in the way how to help you? for you seem to be in some great distress. I saw you when you landed; and when you seemed to make supplication to the brutes that came with you, I saw one of them lift up his sword to kill you.

The poor man, with tears running down his face, and trembling, look-ing like one astonished, returned, Am I talking to God or man? Is it a real man or an angel?—Be in no fear about that, sir, said I; if God had sent an angel to relieve you, he would have come better clothed, and armed after another manner than you see me: pray lay aside your fears; I am a man, an Englishman, and disposed to assist you: you see I have one servant only; we have arms and ammunition; tell us freely, can we serve you? What is your case?—Our case, said he, sir, is too long to tell you, while our murderers are so near us, but, in short, sir, I was com-mander of that ship, my men have mutinied against me; they have been hardly prevailed upon not to murder me; and at last have set me on shore in this desolate place, with these two men with me, one my mate, the other a passenger, where we expected to perish, believing the place to be uninhabited, and know not yet what to think of it.—Where are these brutes, your enemies? said I: do you know where they are gone?—There they lie, sir, said he, pointing to a thicket of trees; my heart trem-bles for fear they have seen us, and heard you speak; if they have, they will certainly murder us all.—Have they any fire-arms? said I. He an-swered they had only two pieces, one of which they left in the boat. Well, then, said I, leave the rest to me; I see they are all asleep, it is an easy thing to kill them all: but shall we rather take them prisoners? He told me there were two desperate villains among them, that it was scarce safe to show any mercy to; but if they were secured, he believed all the rest would return to their duty. I asked him which they were. He told me he could not at that distance distinguish them, but he would obey my orders in anything I would direct. Well, says I, let us retreat out of their view or hearing, lest they awake, and we will resolve further. So they willingly went back with me, till the woods covered us from them.

Look you, sir, said I, if I venture upon your deliverance, are you willing to make two conditions with me? He anticipated my proposals, by telling me, that both he and the ship, if recovered, should be wholly directed and commanded by me in everything; and, if the ship was not recovered, he would live and die with me in what part of the world soever I would send him; and the two other men said the same. Well, says I, my conditions are but two: first, That while you stay in this island with me, you will not pretend to any authority here; and if I put arms in your hands, you will, upon all occasions, give them up to me, and do no prejudice to me or mine upon this island; and, in the mean time, be governed by my orders: secondly, That if the ship is, or may be, recovered, you will carry me and my man to England passage free.

He gave me all the assurances that the invention or faith of man could devise, that he would comply with these most reasonable demands; and, besides, would owe his life to me, and acknowledge it upon all occasions, as long as he lived. Well then, said I, here are three muskets for you, with powder and ball: tell me next what you think proper to be done. He showed me all the testimonies of his gratitude that he was able, but offered to be wholly guided by me. I told him I thought it was hard venturing anything; but the best method I could think of was to fire upon them at once, as they lay, and if any was not killed at the first volley, and offered to submit, we might save them, and so put it wholly upon God's providence to direct the shot. He said very modestly, that he was loath to kill them, if he could help it; but that those two were incorrigible villains, and had been the authors of all the mutiny in the ship, and if they escaped, we should be undone still; for they would go on board and bring the whole ship's company, and destroy us all. Well then, says I, necessity legitimates my advice, for it is the only way to save our lives. However, seeing him still cautious of shedding blood, I told him they should go themselves and manage as they found convenient.

In the middle of this discourse we heard some of them awake, and soon after we saw two of them on their feet. I asked him if either of them were the heads of the mutiny? He said no. Well, then, said I, you may let them escape; and Providence seems to have awakened them on purpose to save themselves. Now, says I, if the rest escape you, it is your fault. Animated with this, he took the musket I had given him in his hand, and a pistol in his belt, and his two comrades with him, with each a piece in his hand; the two men who were with him going first, made some noise, at which one of the seamen who was awake turned about, and seeing them coming, cried out to the rest; but it was too late then, for the moment he cried out they fired; I mean the two men, the captain wisely reserving his own piece. They had so well aimed their shot at the men they knew, that one of them was killed on the spot, and the other very much wounded; but not being dead, he started up on his feet, and called eagerly for help to the others; but the captain stepping to him, told him it was too late to cry for help, he should call upon God to forgive his villainy, and with that word knocked him down with the stock of his musket, so that he never spoke more; there were three more in the company, and one of them was also slightly wounded. By this time I was come; and when they saw their danger, and that it was in vain to resist, they begged for mercy. The captain told them he would spare their lives, if they would give him any assurance of their abhorrence of the treachery they had been guilty of, and would swear to be faithful to him in recovering the ship, and afterwards in carrying her back to Jamaica, from whence they came. They gave him all the protestations of their sincerity that could be desired, and he was willing to believe them, and spare their lives, which I was not against, only that I obliged him to keep them bound hand and foot while they were on the island.

While this was doing, I sent Friday with the captain's mate to the boat, with orders to secure her, and bring away the oars and sails, which they did: and by and by three straggling men, that were (happily for them) parted from the rest, came back upon hearing the guns fired, and seeing the captain, who before was their prisoner, now their conqueror, they submitted to be bound also; and so our victory was complete.

It now remained that the captain and I should inquire into one another's circumstances: I began first, and told him my whole history, which he heard with an attention even to amazement; and particularly at the wonderful manner of my being furnished with provisions and ammunition; and, indeed, as my story is a whole collection of wonders, it affected him deeply. But when he reflected from thence upon himself, and how I seemed to have been preserved there on purpose to save his life, the tears ran down his face, and he could not speak a word more. After this communication was at an end, I carried him and his two men into my apartment, leading them in just where I came out, viz., at the top of the house, where I refreshed them with such provisions as I had, and showed them all the contrivances I had made, during my long, long inhabiting that place.

All I showed them, all I said to them, was perfectly amazing; but, above all, the captain admired my fortification, and how perfectly I had concealed my retreat with a grove of trees, which, having now been planted near twenty years, and the trees growing much faster than in England, was become a little wood, and so thick, that it was impassable in any part of it, but at that one side where I had reserved my little winding passage into it. I told him this was my castle and my residence, but that I had a seat in the country, as most princes have, whither I could retreat upon occasion, and I would show him that too another time; but at present our business was to consider how to recover the ship. He agreed with me as to that; but told me he was perfectly at a loss what measures to take, for that there were still six-and-twenty hands on board, who having entered into a cursed conspiracy, by which they had forfeited their lives to the law, would be hardened in it now by desperation, and would carry it on, knowing that, if they were subdued, they would be brought to the gallows, as soon as they came to England, or to any of the English colonies; and that, therefore, there would be no attacking them with so small a number as we were.

I mused for some time upon what he had said, and found it was a very rational conclusion, and that, therefore, something was to be resolved on speedily, as well to draw the men on board into some snare for their surprise, as to prevent their landing upon us, and destroying us. Upon this, it presently occurred to me, that in a little while the ship's crew, wondering what was become of their comrades, and of the boat, would certainly come on shore in their other boat to look for them; and that then, perhaps, they might come armed, and be too strong for us: this he allowed to be rational. Upon this, I told him the first thing we had to do was to stave the boat, which lay upon the beach, so that they might not carry her off; and taking everything out of her, leave her so far useless as not to be fit to swim: accordingly we went on board, took the arms which were left on board out of her, and whatever else we found there, which was a bottle of brandy, and another of rum, a few biscuit-cakes, a horn of powder, and a great lump of sugar in a piece of canvas (the sugar was five or six pounds); all which was very welcome to me, especially the brandy and sugar, of which I had none left for many years.

When we had carried all these things on shore (the oars, mast, sail and rudder of the boat was carried away before, as above), we knocked a great hole in her bottom, that if they had come strong enough to master us, yet they could not carry off the boat. Indeed, it was not much in my thoughts that we could be able to recover the ship; but my view was, that if they went away without the boat, I did not much question to make her fit again to carry us to the Leeward Islands, and call upon our friends the Spaniards in my way; for I had them still in my thoughts.

While we were thus preparing our designs, and had first, by main strength, heaved the boat upon the beach so high, that the tide would not float her off at high-water mark, and besides, had broke a hole in her bottom too big to be quickly stopped, and were set down musing what we should do, we heard the ship fire a gun, and saw her make a waft with her ensign as a signal for the boat to come on board: but no boat stirred; and they fired several times, making other signals for the boat. At last, when all their signals and firing proved fruitless, and they found the boat did not stir, we saw them, by the help of my glasses, hoist another boat out, and row towards the shore; and we found, as they approached, that there were no less than ten men in her, and that they had fire-arms with them.

As the ship lay almost two leagues from the shore, we had a full view

of them as they came, and a plain sight even of their faces; because the
tide having set them a little to the east of the other boat, they rowed up
under shore, to come to the same place where the other had landed, and
where the boat lay; by this means, I say, we had a full view of them, and
the captain knew the persons and characters of all the men in the boat,
of whom, he said, there were three very honest fellows, who, he was sure,
were led into this conspiracy by the rest, being overpowered and frightened; but that as for the boatswain, who, it seems, was the chief officer
among them, and all the rest, they were as outrageous as any of the
ship's crew, and were no doubt made desperate in their new enterprise;
and terribly apprehensive he was that they would be too powerful for us.
I smiled at him, and told him that men in our circumstance were past
the operation of fear; that seeing almost every condition that could be
was better than that which we were supposed to be in, we ought to expect that the consequence, whether death or life, would be sure to be a
deliverance. I asked him what he thought of the circumstances of my life,
and whether a deliverance were not worth venturing for? And where,
sir, said I, is your belief of my being preserved here on purpose to save
your life, which elevated you a little while ago; for my part, said I, there
seems to me but one thing amiss in all the prospect of it. What is that?
says he. Why, says I, it is, that as you say there are three or four honest
fellows among them, which should be spared, had they been all of the
wicked part of the crew, I should have thought God's providence had
singled them out to deliver them into your hands; for, depend upon it,
every man that comes ashore are our own, and shall die or live as they
behave to us. As I spoke this with a raised voice and cheerful countenance, I found it greatly encouraged him; so we set vigorously to our
business.

We had, upon the first appearance of the boat's coming from the ship,
considered of separating our prisoners; and we had, indeed, secured
them effectually. Two of them, of whom the captain was less assured
than ordinary, I sent with Friday, and one of the three delivered men, to
my cave, where they were remote enough, and out of danger of being
heard or discovered, or of finding their way out of the woods if they
could have delivered themselves: here they left them bound, but gave
them provisions; and promised them if they continued there quietly, to
give them their liberty in a day or two: but that if they attempted their escape, they should be put to death without mercy. They promised faithfully to bear their confinement with patience, and were very thankful
that they had such good usage as to have provisions and light left them;
for Friday gave them candles (such as we made ourselves) for their comfort; and they did not know but that he stood sentinel over them at the
entrance.

The other prisoners had better usage: two of them were kept pinioned,
indeed, because the captain was not free to trust them; but the other two

were taken into my service, upon the captain's recommendation, and upon their solemnly engaging to live and die with us; so with them and the three honest men we were seven men well armed; and I made no doubt we should be able to deal well enough with the ten that were coming, considering that the captain had said that there were three or four honest men among them also. As soon as they got to the place where their other boat lay, they ran their boat into the beach, and came on shore, hauling the boat up after them, which I was glad to see; for I was afraid they would rather have left the boat at an anchor, some distance from the shore, with some hands in her to guard her, and so we should not be able to seize the boat. Being on shore, the first thing they did, they ran all to their other boat; and it was easy to see they were under a great surprise to find her stripped, as above, of all that was in her, and a great hole in her bottom. After they had mused awhile upon this, they set up two or three great shouts, hallooing with all their might, to try if they could make their companions hear; but all was to no purpose: then they came all close in a ring, and fired a volley of their small arms, which indeed, we heard, and the echoes made the woods ring; but it was all one: those in the cave we were sure could not hear; and those in our keeping, though they heard it well enough, yet durst give no answer to them. They were so astonished at the surprise of this, that, as they told afterwards, they resolved to go all on board again to their ship, and let them know that the men were all murdered, and the long-boat staved; accordingly, they immediately launched their boat again, and got all of them on board.

The captain was terribly amazed and even confounded at this, believing they would go on board the ship again, and set sail, giving their comrades over for lost, and so he should still lose the ship, which he was in hopes we should have recovered; but he was quickly as much frightened the other way.

They had not been long put off with the boat, but we perceived them all coming on shore again; but with this new measure in their conduct, which it seems they consulted together upon, viz., to leave three men in the boat, and the rest to go on shore, and go up into the country to look for their fellows. This was a great disappointment to us, for now we were at a loss what to do; as our seizing those seven men on shore would be of no advantage to us, if we let the boat escape; because they would then row away to the ship, and then the rest of them would be sure to weigh and set sail, and so our recovering the ship would be lost. However, we had no remedy but to wait and see what the issue of things might present. The seven men came on shore, and the three who remained in the boat put her off to a good distance from the shore, and came to an anchor to wait for them; so that it was impossible for us to come at them in the boat. Those that came on shore kept close together, marching towards the top of the little hill under which my habitation lay; and we could see them plainly, though they could not perceive us. We could have been very glad they would have come nearer to us, so that we might have fired at them, or that they would have gone farther off, that we might have come aboard. But when they were come to the brow of the hill, where they could see a great way into the valleys and woods, which lay towards the north-east part, and where the island lay lowest, they shouted and hallooed till they were weary; and not caring, it seems, to venture far from the shore, nor far from one another, they sat down together under a tree, to consider of it. Had they thought fit to have gone to sleep there, as the other part of them had done, they had done the job for us; but they were too full of apprehensions of danger to venture to go to sleep, though they could not tell what the danger was they had to fear neither.

The captain made a very just proposal to me upon this consultation of theirs, viz., that perhaps they would all fire a volley again, to endeavour to make their fellows hear, and that we should all sally upon them, just at the juncture when their pieces were all discharged, and they would certainly yield, and we should have them without bloodshed. I liked this proposal, provided it was done while we were near enough to come up with them before they could load their pieces again; but this even did not happen; and we lay still a long time, very irresolute what course to take. At length I told them that there would be nothing done, in my opinion, till night; and then, if they did not return to the boat, perhaps we might find a way to get between them and the shore, and so might use some stratagem with them in the boat to get them on shore. We waited a great while, though very impatient for their removing; and were very uneasy, when, after long consultations, we saw them all start up and march down towards the sea; it seems they had such dreadful apprehensions upon them of the danger of the place, that they resolved to go on board the ship again, give their companions over for lost, and so go on with their intended voyage with the ship.

As soon as I perceived them go towards the shore, I imagined it to be, as it really was, that they had given over their search, and were for going back again; and the captain, as soon as I told him my thoughts, was ready to sink at the apprehensions of it: but I presently thought of a stratagem to fetch them back again, and which answered my end to a tittle. I ordered Friday and the captain's mate to go over the little creek westward, towards the place where the savages came on shore when Friday was rescued, and as they came to a little rising ground, at about a half mile distance, I bade them halloo out, as loud as they could, and wait till they found the seamen heard them; that as soon as they heard the seamen answer them, they should return it again; and then keeping out of sight, take a round, always answering when the others hallooed, to draw them as far into the island, and among the woods, as possible, and then wheel about again to me, by such ways as I directed them.

They were just going into the boat when Friday and the mate hallooed: and they presently heard them, and answering, run along the shore westward, towards the voice they heard, when they were presently stopped by the creek, where the water being up, they could not get over, and called for the boat to come up and set them over; as, indeed, I expected. When they had set themselves over, I observed that the boat being gone a good way into the creek, and, as it were, in a harbour within the land, they took one of the three men out of her, to go along with them, and left only two in the boat, having fastened her to the stump of a little tree on the shore. This was what I wished for; and immediately leaving Friday and the captain's mate to their business, I took the rest with me, and crossing the creek out of their sight, we surprised the two men before they were aware; one of them lying on the shore, and the other being in the boat. The fellow on shore was between sleeping and waking, and going to start up; the captain, who was foremost, ran in upon him, and knocked him down; and then called out to him in the boat to yield, or he was a dead man. There needed very few arguments to persuade a single man to yield, when he saw five men upon him, and his comrade knocked down; besides, this was, it seems, one of the three who were not so hearty in the mutiny as the rest of the crew, and therefore, was easily persuaded not only to yield, but afterwards to join very sincerely with us. In the mean time, Friday and the captain's mate so well managed their business with the rest, that they drew them, by hallooing and answering, from one hill to another, and from one wood to another, till they not only heartily tired them, but left them where they were very sure they could not reach back to the boat before it was dark; and, indeed, they were heartily tired themselves also, by the time they came back to us.

We had nothing now to do but to watch for them in the dark, and to fall upon them, so as to make sure work with them. It was several hours after Friday came back to me before they came back to their boat; and we could hear the foremost of them, long before they came quite up, calling to those behind to come along; and could also hear them answer, and complain how lame and tired they were, and not able to come any faster, which was very welcome news to us. At length they came up to the boat; but it is impossible to express their confusion when they found the boat fast aground in the creek, the tide ebbed out, and their two men gone. We could hear them call to one another in a most lamentable manner, telling one another they were got into an enchanted island: that either there were inhabitants in it, and they should all be murdered, or else there were devils and spirits in it, and they should be all carried away and devoured. They hallooed again, and called their two comrades by their names a great many times; but no answer. After some time, we could see them, by the little light there was, run about, wringing their hands like men in despair; and that sometimes they would go and sit down in the boat, to rest themselves; then come ashore again, and walk about again, and so the same thing over again. My men would fain have had me give them leave to fall upon them at once in the dark; but I was willing to take them at some advantage, so to spare them, and kill as few of them as I could; and especially I was unwilling to hazard the killing of any of our men, knowing the others were very well armed. I resolved to wait, to see if they did not separate; and, therefore, to make sure of them, I drew my ambuscade nearer, and ordered Friday and the captain to creep upon their hands and feet, as close to the ground as they could, that they might not be discovered, and get as near them as they could possibly, before they offered to fire.

They had not been long in that posture, when the boatswain, who was the principal ringleader of the mutiny, and had now shown himself the most dejected and dispirited of all the rest, came walking towards them, with two more of the crew: the captain was so eager at having this principal rogue so much in his power, that he could hardly have patience to let him come so near as to be sure of him, for they only heard his tongue before: but when they came nearer, the captain and Friday, starting up on their feet, let fly at them. The boatswain was killed upon the spot; the next man was shot in the body, and fell just by him, though he did not die till an hour or two after; and the third ran for it. At the noise of the fire, I immediately advanced with my whole army, which was now eight men, viz., myself, generalissimo; Friday, my lieutenant-general; the captain and his two men, and the three prisoners of war, whom we had trusted with arms. We came upon them, indeed, in the dark, so that they could not see our number; and I made the man they had left in the boat, who was now one of us, to call them by name, to try if I could bring them to a parley, and so might perhaps reduce them to terms; which fell out just as we desired: for, indeed, it was easy to think as their condition then was, they would be willing to capitulate. So he calls out, as loud as he could, to one of them, Tom Smith! Tom Smith! Tom Smith answered immediately, Is that Robinson? For it seems, he knew the voice. The other answered, Ay, ay; for God's sake, Tom Smith, throw down your arms and yield, or you are all dead men this moment.—Who must we yield to? Where are they? says Smith again. Here they are, says he; here's our captain and fifty men with him, have been hunting you these two hours: the boatswain is killed, Will Fry is wounded, and I am a prisoner; and if you do not yield, you are all lost.— Will they give us quarter then? says Tom Smith, and we will yield.—I will go ask, if you promise to yield, says Robinson: so he asked the captain; and the captain himself then calls out, You, Smith, you know my voice; if you lay down your arms immediately, and submit, you shall have your lives, all but Will Atkins.

U PON THIS Will Atkins cried out, For
God's sake, captain, give me quar-
ter; what have I done? They have all been as bad as I: which, by the way,
was not true neither; for, it seems, this Will Atkins was the first man
that laid hold of the captain when they first mutinied, and used him barbarously, in tying his hands, and giving him injurious language. However, the captain told him he must lay down his arms at discretion, and
trust to the governor's mercy: by which he meant me, for they all called
me governor. In a word, they all laid down their arms, and begged their
lives; and I sent the man that had parleyed with them, and two more,
who bound them all; and then my great army of fifty men, which particularly with those three, were in all but eight, came up and seized upon
them, and upon their boat; only that I kept myself and one more out of
sight for reasons of state.

Our next work was to repair the boat, and think of seizing the ship!
and as for the captain, now he had leisure to parley with them, he expostulated with them upon the villainy of their practices with him, and at
length upon the further wickedness of their design, and how certainly it
must bring them to misery and distress in the end, and perhaps to the
gallows. They all appeared very penitent, and begged hard for their lives.
As for that, he told them they were none of his prisoners, but the commander's of the island; that they thought they had set him on shore on a
barren, uninhabited island; but it had pleased God so to direct them,
that it was inhabited, and that the governor was an Englishman; that he
might hang them all there, if he pleased; but as he had given them all
quarter, he supposed he would send them to England, to be dealt with
there as justice required, except Atkins, whom he was commanded by
the governor to advise to prepare for death, for that he would be hanged
in the morning.

Though all this was but a fiction of his own, yet it had its desired
effect: Atkins fell upon his knees, to beg the captain to intercede with
the governor for his life; and all the rest begged of him, for God's sake,
that they might not be sent to England.

It now occurred to me that the time of our deliverance was come, and
that it would be a most easy thing to bring these fellows in to be hearty

in getting possession of the ship; so I retired in the dark from them, that they might not see what kind of a governor they had, and called the captain to me; when I called, as at a good distance, one of the men was ordered to speak again, and say to the captain, Captain, the commander calls for you; and presently the captain replied, Tell his excellency I am just a-coming. This more perfectly amused them, and they all believed that the commander was just by with his fifty men. Upon the captain's coming to me, I told him my project for seizing the ship, which he liked wonderfully well, and resolved to put it in execution the next morning. But, in order to execute it with more heart, and to be secure of success, I told him we must divide the prisoners, and that he should go and take Atkins and two more of the worst of them, and send them pinioned to the cave where the others lay. This was committed to Friday and the two men who came on shore with the captain. They conveyed them to the cave as to a prison: and it was, indeed, a dismal place, especially to men in their condition. The others I ordered to my bower, as I called it, of which I have given a full description: and as it was fenced in, and they pinioned, the place was secure enough, considering they were upon their behaviour.

To these in the morning I sent the captain, who was to enter into a parley with them; in a word, to try them, and tell me whether he thought they might be trusted or no to go on board and surprise the ship. He talked to them of the injury done him, of the condition they were brought to, and that though the governor had given them quarter for their lives as to the present action, yet that if they were sent to England, they would all be hanged in chains, to be sure; but that if they would join in so just an attempt as to recover the ship, he would have the governor's engagement for their pardon.

Any one may guess how readily such a proposal would be accepted by men in their condition; they fell down on their knees to the captain, and promised, with the deepest imprecations, that they would be faithful to him to the last drop, and that they should owe their lives to him, and would go with him all over the world; that they would own him as a father as long as they lived. Well, says the captain, I must go and tell the governor what you say, and see what I can do to bring him to consent to it. So he brought me an account of the temper he found them in, and that he verily believed they would be faithful. However, that we might be very secure, I told him he should go back again and choose out those five, and tell them, that they might see he did not want men, that he would take out those five to be his assistants, and that the governor would keep the other two, and the three that were sent prisoners to the castle (my cave) as hostages for the fidelity of those five; and that if they proved unfaithful in the execution, the five hostages should be hanged in chains alive on the shore. This looked severe, and convinced them that the governor was in earnest: however, they had no way left them but to accept it; and it was now the business of the prisoners, as much as of the captain, to persuade the other five to do their duty.

Our strength was now thus ordered for the expedition: first, the captain, his mate, and passenger; second, the two prisoners of the first gang, to whom, having their character from the captain, I had given their liberty, and trusted them with arms: third, the other two that I had kept till now in my bower pinioned, but, on the captain's motion, had now released: fourth, these five released at last; so that they were twelve in all, besides five we kept prisoners in the cave for hostages.

I asked the captain if he was willing to venture with these hands on board the ship: but as for me and my man Friday, I did not think it was proper for us to stir, having seven men left behind; and it was employment enough for us to keep them asunder, and supply them with victuals. As to the five in the cave, I resolved to keep them fast, but Friday went in twice a day to them, to supply them with necessaries; and I made the other two carry provisions to a certain distance, where Friday was to take it.

When I showed myself to the two hostages, it was with the captain, who told them I was the person the governor had ordered to look after them; and that it was the governor's pleasure they should not stir anywhere but by my direction; that if they did, they would be fetched into the castle, and be laid in irons: so that as we never suffered them to see me as a governor, I now appeared as another person, and spoke of the governor, the garrison, the castle, and the like, upon all occasions.

The captain now had no difficulty before him, but to furnish his two boats, stop the breach of one, and man them. He made his passenger captain of one, with four of the men; and himself, his mate, and five more, went in the other; and they contrived their business very well, for they came up to the ship about midnight. As soon as they came within call of the ship, he made Robinson hail them, and tell them they had brought off the men and the boat, but that it was a long time before they had found them, and the like, holding them in a chat till they came to the ship's side; when the captain and the mate entering first, with their arms, immediately knocked down the second mate and carpenter with the butt-end of their muskets, being very faithfully seconded by their men; they secured all the rest that were upon the main and quarter decks, and began to fasten the hatches, to keep them down that were below; when the other boat and their men entering at the fore-chains, secured the forecastle of the ship, and the scuttle which went down into the cockroom, making three men they found there prisoners. When this was done, and all safe upon deck, the captain ordered the mate, with three men, to break into the round-house, where the new rebel captain lay, who having taken the alarm, had got up, and with two men and a boy had got fire-arms in their hands; and when the mate, with a crow, split open the door, the new captain and his men fired boldly among them, and wounded the mate with a musket ball, which broke his arm, and wounded two more of the men, but killed nobody. The mate, calling for help, rushed, however, into the round-house, wounded as he was, and with his pistol shot the new captain through the head, the bullet entering at his mouth, and came out again behind one of his ears, so that he never spoke a word more: upon which the rest yielded, and the ship was taken effectually, without any more lives lost.

As soon as the ship was thus secured, the captain ordered seven guns to be fired, which was the signal agreed upon with me to give me notice of his success, which you may be sure I was very glad to hear, having sat watching upon the shore for it till near two o'clock in the morning. Having thus heard the signal plainly, I laid me down; and it having been a day of great fatigue to me, I slept very sound, till I was something surprised at the noise of a gun; and presently starting up, I heard a man call me by the name of Governor, Governor, and presently I knew the captain's voice; when climbing up to the top of the hill, there he stood, and pointing to the ship, he embraced me in his arms. My dear friend and deliverer, says he, there's your ship, for she is all yours, and so are we, and all that belong to her. I cast my eyes to the ship, and there she rode within little more than half a mile of the shore; for they had weighed her anchor as soon as they were masters of her, and the weather being fair, had brought her to anchor just against the mouth of the little creek; and the tide being up, the captain had brought the pinnace in near the place where I at first landed my rafts, and so landed just at my door. I was at first ready to sink down with the surprise; for I saw my deliverance, indeed, visibly put into my hands, all things easy, and a large ship just ready to carry me away whither I pleased to go. At first, for some time, I was not able to answer him one word; but as he had taken me in his arms, I held fast by him, or I should have fallen to the ground. He perceived the surprise, and immediately pulls a bottle out of his pocket, and gave me a dram of cordial, which he had brought on purpose for me. After I had drank it, I sat down upon the ground; and though it brought me to myself, yet it was a good while before I could speak a word to him. All this time the poor man was in as great an ecstasy as I, only not under any surprise, as I was; and he said a thousand kind and tender things to me, to compose and bring me to myself: but such was the flood of joy in my breast, that it put all my spirits into confusion; at last it broke out into tears; and in a little while after I recovered my speech. I then took my turn, and embraced him as my deliverer, and we rejoiced together. I told him I looked upon him as a man sent from Heaven to deliver me, and that the whole transaction seemed to be a chain of wonders; that such things as these were the testimonies we had of a secret hand of Providence governing the world, and an evidence that the eye of an infinite power could search into the remotest corner of the world, and send help to the miserable whenever he pleased. I forgot not to lift up my heart in thankfulness to Heaven: and what heart could forbear to bless him, who had not only in a miraculous manner provided for me in such a wilderness, and in such a desolate condition, but from whom every deliverance must always be acknowledged to proceed?

When we had talked a while, the captain told me he had brought me some little refreshment, such as the ship afforded, and such as the wretches that had been so long his masters had not plundered him of. Upon this he called aloud to the boat, and bade his men bring the things ashore that were for the governor; and, indeed, it was a present as if I had been one that was not to be carried away with them, but as if I had been to dwell upon the island still. First, he had brought me a case of bottles full of excellent cordial waters, six large bottles of Madeira wine (the bottles held two quarts each), two pounds of excellent good tobacco, twelve good pieces of the ship's beef, and six pieces of pork, with a bag of peas, and about a hundred weight of biscuit: he also brought me a box of sugar, a box of flour, a bag full of lemons, and two bottles of lime juice, and abundance of other things. But, besides these, and what was a thousand times more useful to me, he brought me six new clean shirts, six very good neckcloths, two pair of gloves, one pair of shoes, a hat, and one pair of stockings, with a very good suit of clothes of his own, which had been worn but very little; in a word, he clothed me from head to foot. It was a very kind and agreeable present, as any one may imagine, to one in my circumstances; but never was anything in the world of that kind so unpleasant, awkward, and uneasy, as it was to me to wear such clothes at first.

After these ceremonies were past, and after all his good things were brought into my little apartment, we began to consult, what was to be done with the prisoners we had; for it was worth considering whether we might venture to take them away with us or no, especially two of them, whom we knew to be incorrigible and refractory to the last degree; and the captain said he knew they were such rogues, that there was no obliging them; and if he did carry them away, it must be in irons, as malefactors, to be delivered over to justice at the first English colony he could come at; and I found that the captain himself was very anxious about it. Upon this I told him, that if he desired it, I would undertake to bring the two men he spoke of to make it their own request that he should leave them upon the island. I should be very glad of that, says the captain, with all my heart.—Well, says I, I will send for them up, and talk with them for you. So I caused Friday and the two hostages, for they were now discharged, their comrades having performed their promise; I say, I caused them to go to the cave, and bring up the five men, pinioned as they were, to the bower, and keep them there till I came. After some time I came thither dressed in my new habit; and now I was called governor again. Being all met, and the captain with me, I caused the men to be brought before me, and I told them I had got a full account of their villainous behaviour to the captain, and how they had run away with the ship, and were preparing to commit further robberies, but that Providence had ensnared them in their own ways, and that they were fallen into the pit which they had dug for others. I let them know that by my direction the ship had been seized; that she lay now in the road; and they might see, by and by, that their new captain had received the reward of his villainy, and that they would see him hanging at the yard-arm: that as to them, I wanted to know what they had to say why I should not execute them as pirates, taken in the fact, as by my commission they could not doubt but I had authority so to do.

One of them answered in the name of the rest, that they had nothing to say but this, that when they were taken, the captain promised them their lives, and they humbly implored my mercy. But I told them I knew not what mercy to show them: for as for myself, I had resolved to quit the island with all my men, and had taken passage with the captain to go for England; and as for the captain, he could not carry them to England other than as prisoners, in irons, to be tried for mutiny, and running away with the ship; the consequence of which, they must needs know, would be the gallows; so that I could not tell what was best for them, unless they had a mind to take their fate in the island; if they desired that, as I had liberty to leave the island, I had some inclination to give them their lives, if they thought they could shift on shore. They seemed very thankful for it, and said they would much rather venture to stay there than to be carried to England to be hanged: so I left it on that issue.

However, the captain seemed to make some difficulty of it, as if he durst not leave them there. Upon this I seemed a little angry with the captain, and told him that they were my prisoners, not his; and seeing that I had offered them so much favour, I would be as good as my word: and that if he did not think fit to consent to it, I would set them at liberty, as I found them; and if he did not like it, he might take them again if he could catch them. Upon this they appeared very thankful, and I accordingly set them at liberty, and bade them retire into the woods from whence they came, and I would leave them some fire-arms, some ammunition, and some directions how they should live very well, if they thought fit. Upon this I prepared to go on board the ship; but told the captain I would stay that night to prepare my things, and desired him to go on board, in the mean time, and keep all right in the ship, and send the boat on shore next day for me; ordering him, at all events, to cause the new captain, who was killed, to be hanged at the yard-arm, that these men might see him.

When the captain was gone, I sent for the men up to me to my apartment, and entered seriously into discourse with them on their circumstances. I told them I thought they had made a right choice; that if the captain had carried them away, they would certainly be hanged. I showed them the new captain hanging at the yard-arm of the ship, and told them they had nothing less to expect.

When they had all declared their willingness to stay, I then told them I would let them into the story of my living there, and put them into the way of making it easy to them: accordingly, I gave them the whole history of the place, and of my coming to it; showed them my fortifications, the way I made my bread, planted my corn, cured my grapes; and, in a word, all that was necessary to make them easy. I told them the story also of the seventeen Spaniards that were to be expected, for whom I left a letter, and made them promise to treat them in common with themselves. Here it may be noted, that the captain had ink on board, who was greatly surprised that I never hit upon a way of making ink of charcoal and water, or of something else, as I had done things much more difficult.

I left them my fire-arms, viz., five muskets, three fowling-pieces, and three swords. I had above a barrel and a half of powder left; for after the first year or two I used but little, and wasted none. I gave them a description of the way I managed the goats, and directions to milk and fatten them, and to make both butter and cheese; in a word, I gave them every part of my own story, and told them I should prevail with the captain to leave them two barrels of gunpowder more, and some garden-seeds, which I told them I would have been very glad of: also I gave them the bag of peas which the captain had brought me to eat, and bade them be sure to sow and increase them.

Having done all this, I left them the next day, and went on board the ship. We prepared immediately to sail, but did not weigh that night. The next morning early, two of the five men came swimming to the ship's side, and making a most lamentable complaint of the other three, begged to be taken into the ship, for God's sake, for they should be murdered, and begged the captain to take them on board, though he hanged them immediately. Upon this, the captain pretended to have no power without me; but after some difficulty, and after their solemn promises of amendment, they were taken on board, and were some time after soundly whipped and pickled; after which they proved very honest and quiet fellows.

Some time after this, the boat was ordered on shore, the tide being up, with the things promised to the men; to which the captain, at my intercession, caused their chests and clothes to be added, which they took, and were very thankful for. I also encouraged them, by telling them that if it lay in my power to send any vessel to take them in, I would not forget them.

When I took leave of this island, I carried on board, for reliques, the great goat's-skin cap I had made, my umbrella, and one of my parrots; also I forgot not to take the money I formerly mentioned, which had laid by me so long useless, that it was grown rusty or tarnished, and could hardly pass for silver, till it had been a little rubbed and handled; as also the money I found in the wreck of the Spanish ship. And thus I left the island, the 19th of December, as I found by the ship's account, in the year 1686, after I had been upon it eight-and-twenty years, two months, and nineteen days; being delivered from this second captivity the same day of the month that I first made my escape in the long-boat, from among the Moors of Sallee. In this vessel, after a long voyage, I arrived in England the 11th of June, in the year 1687, having been thirty-five years absent.

WHEN I CAME to England, I was as perfect a stranger to all the world as if I had never been known there. My benefactor and faithful steward, whom I had left my money in trust with, was alive, but had had great misfortunes in the world; was become a widow the second time, and very low in the world. I made her very easy as to what she owed me, assuring her I would give her no trouble; but on the contrary, in gratitude for former care and faithfulness to me, I relieved her as my little stock would afford; which, at that time, would indeed allow me to do but little for her; but I assured her I would never forget her former kindness to me; nor did I forget her when I had sufficient to help her, as shall be observed in its proper place. I went down afterwards into Yorkshire; but my father and mother were dead, and all the family extinct, except that I found two sisters, and two of the children of one of my brothers; and as I had been long ago given over for dead, there had been no provision made for me: so that, in a word, I found nothing to relieve or assist me; and that the little money I had would not do much for me as to settling in the world.

I met with one piece of gratitude, indeed, which I did not expect; and this was, that the master of the ship whom I had so happily delivered, and by the same means saved the ship and cargo, having given a very handsome account to the owners of the manner how I had saved the lives of the men, and the ship, they invited me to meet them, and some other merchants concerned, and all together made me a very handsome compliment upon the subject, and a present of almost two hundred pounds sterling.

But after making several reflections upon the circumstances of my life, and how little way this would go towards settling me in the world, I resolved to go to Lisbon, and see if I might not come by some information of the state of my plantation in the Brazils, and of what was become of my partner, who, I had reason to suppose, had some years past given me over for dead. With this view I took shipping for Lisbon, where I arrived in April following; my man Friday accompanying me very honestly in all these ramblings, and proving a most faithful servant upon all occasions. When I came to Lisbon, I found out, by inquiry, and to my particular satisfaction, my old friend the captain of the ship who first took me up at sea off the shore of Africa. He was now grown old, and had left off going to sea, having put his son, who was far from a young man, into his ship, and who still used the Brazil trade. The old man did not know me; and, indeed, I hardly knew him; but I soon brought him to my remembrance, and as soon brought myself to his remembrance, when I told him who I was.

After some passionate expressions of the old acquaintance between us, I inquired, you may be sure, after my plantation and my partner. The old man told me he had not been in the Brazils for about nine years; but that he could assure me that when he came away my partner was living; but the trustees, whom I had joined with him to take cognizance of my part, were both dead: that, however, he believed I would have a very good account of the improvement of the plantation; for that upon the general belief of my being cast away and drowned, my trustees had given in the account of the produce of my part of the plantation to the procurator-fiscal, who had appropriated it, in case I never came to claim it, one-third to the king, and two-thirds to the monastery of St. Augustine, to be expended for the benefit of the poor, and for the conversion of the Indians to the Catholic faith; but that if I appeared, or any one for me, to claim the inheritance, it would be restored; only that the improvement, or annual production, being distributed to charitable uses, could not be restored: but he assured me that the steward of the king's revenue from lands, and the proviedore, or steward of the monastery, had taken great care all along that the incumbent, that is to say, my partner, gave every year a faithful account of the produce, of which they had duly received my moiety. I asked him if he knew to what height of improvement he had brought the plantation, and whether he thought it might be worth looking after; or whether, on my going thither, I should meet with any obstruction to my possessing my just right in the moiety. He told me he could not tell exactly to what degree the plantation was improved, but this he knew, that my partner was grown exceeding rich upon the enjoying his part of it; and that, to the best of his remembrance, he had heard that the king's third of my part, which was, it seems, granted away to some other monastery or religious house, amounted to above two hundred moidores a year: that as to my being restored to a quiet possession of it, there was no question to be made of that, my partner being alive to witness my title, and my name being also enrolled in the register of the country: also he told me, that the survivors of my two trustees were very fair honest people, and very wealthy; and he believed I would not only have their assistance for putting me in possession, but would find a very considerable sum of money in their hands for my account, being the produce of the farm while their fathers held the trust, and before it was given up, as above; which, as he remembered, was for about twelve years.

I showed myself a little concerned and uneasy at this account, and inquired of the old captain how it came to pass that the trustees should thus dispose of my effects, when he knew that I had made my will, and had made him, the Portuguese captain, my universal heir, etc.

He told me that was true; but that as there was no proof of my being dead he could not act as executor, until some certain account should come of my death; and, besides, he was not willing to intermeddle with a thing so remote: that it was true he had registered my will, and put in his claim; and could he have given any account of my being dead or alive, he would have acted by procuration, and taken possession of the ingenio (so they called the sugar-house), and have given his son, who was now at the Brazils, orders to do it. But, says the old man, I have one piece of news to tell you, which, perhaps, may not be so acceptable to you as the rest; and that is, believing you were lost, and all the world believing so also, your partner and trustees did offer to account with me, in your name, for six or eight of the first years' profits, which I received. There being at that time great disbursements for increasing the works, building an ingenio, and buying slaves, it did not amount to near so much as afterwards it produced: however, says the old man, I shall give you a true account of what I have received in all, and how I have disposed of it.

After a few days' further conference with this ancient friend, he brought me an account of the first six years' income of plantation, signed by my partner and the merchant trustees, being always delivered in goods, viz., tobacco in roll, and sugar in chests, besides rum, molasses, etc., which is the consequence of a sugar-work; and I found, by this account, that every year the income considerably increased; but, as above, the disbursements being large, the sum at first was small: however, the old man let me see that he was debtor to me four hundred and seventy moidores of gold, besides sixty chests of sugar, and fifteen double rolls of tobacco, which were lost in his ship; he having been shipwrecked coming home to Lisbon, about eleven years after my leaving the place. The good man then began to complain of his misfortunes; and how he had been obliged to make use of my money to recover his losses, and buy him a share in a new ship. However, my old friend, says he, you shall not want a supply in your necessity; and as soon as my son returns, you shall be fully satisfied. Upon this, he pulls out an old pouch and gives me one hundred and sixty Portugal moidores in gold; and giving the writings of his title to the ship, which his son was gone to the Brazils in, of which he was a quarter part owner, and his son, another, he puts them both into my hands, for security of the rest.

I was too much moved with the honesty and kindness of the poor man to be able to bear this; and remembering what he had done for me, how he had taken me up at sea, and how generously he had used me on all occasions, and particularly how sincere a friend he was now to me, I could hardly refrain weeping at what he had said to me; therefore I asked him if his circumstances admitted him to spare so much money at that time, and if it would not straiten him? He told me he could not say but it might straiten him a little; but, however, it was my money, and I might want it more than he.

Everything the good man said was full of affection, and I could hardly refrain from tears while he spoke; in short, I took one hundred of the moidores, and called for a pen and ink to give him a receipt for them: then I returned him the rest and told him if ever I had possession of the plantation, I would return the other to him also (as, indeed, I afterwards did); and that as to the bill of sale of his part in his son's ship, I would not take it by any means: but that if I wanted the money, I found he was honest enough to pay me; and if I did not, but came to receive what he gave me reason to expect, I would never have a penny more from him.

When this was past, the old man asked me if he should put me into a method to make my claim to my plantation? I told him I thought to go over to it myself. He said I might do so, if I pleased; but that if I did not, there were ways enough to secure my right, and immediately to appropriate the profits to my use: and as there were ships in the river of Lisbon just ready to go away to Brazil, he made me enter my name in a public register, with his affidavit, affirming, upon oath, that I was alive, and that I was the same person who took up the land for the planting the said plantation at first. This being regularly attested by a notary, and a procuration affixed, he directed me to send it, with a letter of his writing, to a merchant of his acquaintance at the place; and then proposed my staying with him till an account came of the return.

Never was anything more honourable than the proceedings upon this procuration; for in less than seven months I received a large packet from the survivors of my trustees, the merchants, for whose account I went to sea, in which were the following particular letters and papers enclosed.

First, There was the account-current of the produce of my farm or plantation, from the year when their fathers had balanced with my old Portugal captain, being for six years: the balance appeared to be one thousand one hundred and seventy-four moidores in my favour.

Secondly, There was the account of four years more, while they kept the effects in their hands, before the government claimed the administration, as being the effects of a person not to be found, which they called civil death; and the balance of this, the value of the plantation increasing, amounted to nineteen thousand four hundred and forty-six crusadoes, being about three thousand two hundred and forty moidores.

Thirdly, There was the prior of St. Augustine's account, who had received the profits for above fourteen years; but not being able to account for what was disposed of by the hospital, very honestly declared he had eight hundred and seventy-two moidores not distributed, which he acknowledged to my account: as to the king's part, that refunded nothing.

There was a letter of my partner's, congratulating me very affectionately upon my being alive, giving me an account how the estate was improved, and what it produced a year: with a particular of the number of squares of acres that it contained, how planted, how many slaves there were upon it, and making two and twenty crosses for blessings, told me he had said so many *Ave Marias* to thank the blessed Virgin that I was alive; inviting me very passionately to come over and take possession of my own; and, in the mean time, to give him orders to whom he should deliver my effects, if I did not come myself; concluding with a hearty tender of his friendship, and that of his family; and sent me, as a present, seven fine leopards' skins, which he had, it seems, received from Africa, by some other ship that he had sent thither, and who, it seems, had made a better voyage than I. He sent me also five chests of excellent sweetmeats, and a hundred pieces of gold uncoined, not quite so large as moidores. By the same fleet, my two merchant trustees shipped me one thousand two hundred chests of sugar, eight hundred rolls of tobacco, and the rest of the whole account in gold.

I might well say now, indeed, that the latter end of Job was better than the beginning. It is impossible to express the flutterings of my very heart, when I found all my wealth about me; for as the Brazil ships come all in fleets, the same ships which brought my letters brought my goods: and the effects were safe in the river before the letters came to my hand. In a word, I turned pale and grew sick; and had not the old man run and fetched me a cordial, I believe the sudden surprise of joy had overset nature, and I had died upon the spot: nay, after that, I continued very ill, and was so some hours, till a physician being sent for, and something of the real cause of my illness being known, he ordered me to be let blood; after which I had relief, and grew well: but I verily believe, if I had been eased by a vent given in that manner to the spirits, I should have died.

I was now master, all on a sudden, of about five thousand pounds sterling in money, and had an estate, as I might well call it, in the Brazils, of above a thousand pounds a year, as sure as an estate of lands in England; and, in a word, I was in a condition which I scarce knew how to understand, or how to compose myself for the enjoyment of it. The first thing I did was to recompense my original benefactor, my good old captain, who had been first charitable to me in my distress, kind to me in my beginning, and honest to me at the end. I showed him all that was sent to me; I told him, that next to the providence of Heaven, which disposed all things, it was owing to him; and that it now lay on me to reward him, which I would do a hundred-fold: so I first returned to him the hundred moidores I had received of him; then I sent for a notary, and caused him to draw up a general release or discharge from the four hundred and seventy moidores, which he had acknowledged he owed me, in the fullest and firmest manner possible. After which I caused a procuration to be drawn, empowering him to be my receiver of the annual profits of my plantation, and appointing my partner to account with him, and make the returns by the usual fleets to him in my name; and a clause in the end, being a grant of one hundred moidores a year to him during his life, out of the effects, and fifty moidores a year to his son after him, for his life: and thus I requited my old man.

I was now to consider which way to steer my course next, and what to do with the estate that Providence had thus put into my hands; and, indeed, I had more care upon my head now than I had in my silent state of life in the island, where I wanted nothing but what I had, and had nothing but what I wanted; whereas I had now a great charge upon me, and my business was how to secure it. I had never a cave now to hide my money in, or a place where it might lie without a lock or key, till it grew mouldy and tarnished, before any body would meddle with it; on the contrary, I knew not where to put it, or whom to trust with it. My old patron, the captain, indeed, was honest, and that was the only refuge I had. In the next place, my interest in the Brazils seemed to summon me thither; but now I could not tell how to think of going thither till I had settled my affairs, and left my effects in some safe hands behind me. At first I thought of my old friend the widow, who I knew was honest, and would be just to me; but then she was in years, and but poor, and, for aught I knew, might be in debt: so that, in a word, I had no way but to go back to England myself, and take my effects with me.

It was some months, however, before I resolved upon this; and therefore, as I had rewarded the old captain fully, and to his satisfaction, who had been my former benefactor, so I began to think of my poor widow, whose husband had been my first benefactor, and she, while it was in her power, my faithful steward and instructor. So the first thing I did, I got a merchant in Lisbon to write to his correspondent in London, not only to pay a bill, but to go find her out, and carry her in money a hundred pounds for me, and to talk with her, and comfort her in her poverty, by telling her she should, if I lived, have a further supply: at the same time I sent my two sisters in the country a hundred pounds each, they being, though not in want, yet not in very good circumstances; one having been married and left a widow; and the other having a husband not so kind to her as he should be. But among all my relations or acquaintances, I could not yet pitch upon one to whom I durst commit the gross of my stock, that I might go away to the Brazils, and leave things safe behind me; and this greatly perplexed me.

I had once a mind to have gone to the Brazils, and have settled myself there; for I was, as it were, naturalised to the place; but I had some little scruple in mind about religion, which insensibly drew me back. However, it was not religion which kept me from going there for the present; and as I had made no scruple of being openly of the religion of the country all the while I was among them, so neither did I yet; only that, now and then, having of late thought more of it than formerly, when I began to think of living and dying among them, I began to regret my having professed myself a Papist, and thought it might not be the best religion to die with.

But, as I have said, this was not the main thing that kept me from going to the Brazils, but that really I did not know with whom to leave my effects behind me; so I resolved, at last, to go to England with it, where, if I arrived, I concluded I should make some acquaintance, or find some relations that would be faithful to me; and accordingly, I prepared to go to England with all my wealth.

In order to prepare things for my going home, I first, the Brazil fleet being just going away, resolved to give answers suitable to the just and faithful account of things I had from thence; and, first, to the prior of St. Augustine I wrote a letter full of thanks for their just dealings, and the offer of the eight hundred and seventy-two moidores which were undisposed of, which I desired might be given, five hundred to the monastery, and three hundred and seventy-two to the poor, as the prior should direct; desiring the good padre's prayers for me, and the like. I wrote next a letter of thanks to my two trustees, with all the acknowledgment that so much justice and honesty called for; as for sending them any present, they were far above having any occasion for it. Lastly, I wrote to my partner, acknowledging his industry in the improving the plantation, and his integrity in increasing the stock of the works; giving him instructions for his future government of my part, according to the powers I had left with my old patron, to whom I desired him to send whatever became due to me, till he should hear from me more particularly; assuring him that it was my intention not only to come to him, but to settle myself there for the remainder of my life. To this I added a very handsome present of some Italian silks for his wife and two daughters, for such the captain's son informed me he had; with two pieces of fine English broadcloth, the best I could get in Lisbon, five pieces of black baize, and some Flanders lace of a good value.

Having thus settled my affairs, sold my cargo, and turned all my effects into good bills of exchange, my next difficulty was, which way to go to England: I had been accustomed enough to the sea, and yet I had a strange aversion to go to England by sea at that time; and though I could give no reason for it, yet the difficulty increased upon me so much, that though I had once shipped my baggage, in order to go, yet I altered my mind, and that not once, but two or three times.

It is true, I had been very unfortunate by sea, and this might be some of the reasons; but let no man slight the strong impulses of his own thoughts in cases of such moment: two of the ships which I had singled out to go in, I mean more particularly singled out than others, having put my things on board one of them, and in the other to have agreed with the captain; I say, two of these ships miscarried, viz., one was taken by the Algerines, and the other was cast away on the Start, near Torbay, and all the people drowned except three; so that in either of those vessels I had been made miserable.

Having been thus harassed in my thoughts, my old pilot, to whom I communicated everything, pressed me earnestly not to go by sea, but either to go by land to the Groyne (Corunna), and cross over the Bay of Biscay to Rochelle, from whence it was but an easy and safe journey by land to Paris, and so to Calais and Dover; or to go up to Madrid, and so all the way by land through France. In a word, I was so prepossessed against my going by sea at all, except from Calais to Dover, that I resolved to travel all the way by land; which, as I was not in haste, and did not value the charge, was by much the pleasanter way: and to make it more so, my old captain brought an English gentleman, the son of a merchant in Lisbon, who was willing to travel with me; after which we picked up two more English merchants also, and two young Portuguese gentlemen, the last going to Paris only; so that in all there were six of us, and five servants; the two merchants and the two Portuguese contenting themselves with one servant between two, to save the charge; and as for me, I got an English sailor to travel with me as a servant, besides my man Friday, who was too much a stranger to be capable of supplying the place of a servant on the road.

In this manner I set out from Lisbon; and our company being very well mounted and armed, we made a little troop, whereof they did me the honour to call me captain, as well because I was the oldest man, as because I had two servants, and, indeed, was the original of the whole journey.

As I have troubled you with none of my sea journals, so I shall trouble you now with none of my land journal; but some adventures that happened to us in this tedious and difficult journey I must not omit.

When we came to Madrid, we being all of us strangers to Spain, were willing to stay some time to see the court of Spain, and to see what was worth observing; but it being the latter part of the summer, we hastened away, and set out from Madrid about the middle of October; but when we came to the edge of Navarre, we were alarmed, at several towns on the way, with an account that so much snow was fallen on the French side of the mountains, that several travellers were obliged to come back to Pampeluna, after having attempted, at an extreme hazard, to pass on.

When we came to Pampeluna, itself, we found it so, indeed; and to me, that had been always used to a hot climate, and to countries where I could scarce bear any clothes on, the cold was insufferable; nor, indeed, was it more painful than surprising, to come but ten days before out of Old Castile, where the weather was not only warm, but very hot, and immediately to feel a wind from the Pyrenean mountains, so very keen, so severely cold, as to be intolerable, and to endanger the benumbing and perishing of our fingers and toes.

Poor Friday was really frightened when he saw the mountains all covered with snow, and felt cold weather, which he had never seen or felt before in his life. To mend the matter, when we came to Pampeluna, it continued snowing with so much violence, and so long, that the people said winter was come before its time; and the roads, which were difficult before, were now quite impassable; for, in a word, the snow lay in some places too thick for us to travel, and being not hard frozen, as is the case in the northern countries, there was no going without being in danger of being buried alive every step. We stayed no less than twenty days at Pampeluna; when seeing the winter coming on, and no likelihood of its being better, for it was the severest winter all over Europe that had been known in the memory of man, I proposed that we should all go away to Fontarabia, and there take shipping for Bordeaux, which was a very little voyage. But while I was considering this, there came in four French gentlemen, who having been stopped on the French side of the passes, as we were on the Spanish, had found out a guide, who traversing the country near the head of Languedoc, had brought them over the mountains by such ways, that they were not much incommoded with the snow; for where they met with snow in any quantity, they said it was frozen hard enough to bear them and their horses. We sent for this guide, who told us he would undertake to carry us the same way with no hazard from the snow, provided we were armed sufficiently to protect ourselves from wild beasts; for, he said, upon these great snows it was frequent for some wolves to show themselves at the foot of the mountains, being made ravenous for want of food, the ground being covered with snow. We told him we were well enough prepared for such creatures as they were, if he would insure us from a kind of two-legged wolves, which, we were told, we were in most danger from, especially on the French side of the mountains. He satisfied us that there was no danger of that kind in the way that we were to go; so we readily agreed to follow him, as did also twelve other gentlemen, with their servants, some French, some Spanish, who, as I said, had attempted to go, and were obliged to come back again.

Accordingly, we set out from Pampeluna, with our guide, on the 15th of November; and, indeed, I was surprised, when, instead of going forward, he came directly back with us on the same road that we came from

Madrid, about twenty miles; when having passed two rivers, and come into the plain country, we found ourselves in a warm climate again, where the country was pleasant, and no snow to be seen; but on a sudden turning to his left, he approached the mountains another way; and though it is true the hills and precipices looked dreadful, yet he made so many tours, such meanders, and led us by such winding ways, that we insensibly passed the height of the mountains without being much encumbered with the snow; and, all on a sudden, he showed us the pleasant fruitful provinces of Languedoc and Gascony, all green and flourishing, though, indeed, at a great distance, and we had some rough way to pass still.

We were a little uneasy, however, when we found it snowed one whole day and a night so fast, that we could not travel; but he bid us be easy; we should soon be past it all: we found, indeed, that we began to descend every day, and to come more north than before; and so, depending upon our guide, we went on.

I T WAS about two hours before night, when our guide being something before us, and not just in sight, out rushed three monstrous wolves, and after them a bear, out of a hollow way, adjoining to a thick wood; two of the wolves made at the guide, and had he been far before us, he would have been devoured before we could have helped him; one of them fastened upon his horse, and the other attacked the man with that violence, that he had not time, or presence of mind enough, to draw his pistol, but hallooed and cried out to me most lustily. My man Friday being next to me, I bade him ride up, and see what was the matter. As soon as Friday came in sight of the man, he hallooed out as loud as the other, O master! O master! but, like a bold fellow, rode directly up to the poor man, and with his pistol shot the wolf, that attacked him, in the head.

It was happy for the poor man that it was my man Friday; for he having been used to such creatures in his country, he had no fear respecting them, but went close up to him and shot him, as above; whereas any other of us would have fired at a greater distance, and have perhaps either missed the wolf, or endangered shooting the man.

But it was enough to have terrified a bolder man than I; and, indeed, it alarmed all our company, when, with the noise of Friday's pistol, we heard on both sides the most dismal howling of wolves; and the noise, redoubled by the echo of the mountains, appeared to us as if there had been a prodigious number of them; and, perhaps, there was not such a few as that we had no cause of apprehensions: however, as Friday had killed this wolf, the other that had fastened upon the horse left him inmediately, and fled, without doing him any damage, having happily fastened upon his head, where the bosses of the bridle had stuck in his teeth. But the man was most hurt; for the raging creature had bit him twice, once in the arm, and the other time a little above his knee; and though he had made some defence, he was just as it were tumbling down by the disorder of his horse, when Friday came up and shot the wolf.

It is easy to suppose that at the noise of Friday's pistol we all mended our pace, and rode up as fast as the way, which was very difficult, would give us leave, to see what was the matter. As soon as we came clear of the trees, which blinded us before, we saw clearly what had been the case, and how Friday had disengaged the poor guide, though we did not presently discern what kind of creature it was he had killed.

But never was a fight managed so hardily, and in such a surprising manner, as that which followed, between Friday and the bear, which gave us all, though at first we were surprised and afraid for him, the greatest diversion imaginable. As the bear is a heavy, clumsy creature, and does not gallop as the wolf does, who is swift and light, so he has two particular qualities, which generally are the rule of his actions: first, as to men, who are not his proper prey (he does not usually attempt them, except they first attack him, unless he be excessively hungry, which it is probable might now be the case, the ground being covered with snow), if you do not meddle with him, he will not meddle with you: but then you must take care to be very civil to him, and give him the road, for he is a very nice gentleman; he will not go a step out of his way for a prince; nay, if you are really afraid, your best way is to look another way, and keep going on; for sometimes if you stop, and stand still, and look steadfastly at him, he takes it for an affront; but if you throw or toss anything at him, and it hits him, though it were but a bit of stick as big as your finger, he thinks himself abused, and sets all other business aside to pursue his revenge, and will have satisfaction in point of honour;— this is his first quality: the next is, if he be once affronted, he will never leave you, night nor day, till he has his revenge, but follows, at a good round rate, till he overtakes you.

My man Friday had delivered our guide, and when we came up to him, he was helping him off from his horse, for the man was both hurt and frightened, when, on a sudden, we espied the bear come out of the wood, and a vast, monstrous one it was, the biggest by far that ever I saw. We were all a little surprised when we saw him; but when Friday saw him, it was easy to see joy and courage in the fellow's countenance; O,

O, O! says Friday, three times, pointing to him; O master, you give me te leave, me shakee te hand with him; me makee you good laugh.

I was surprised to see the fellow so well pleased: You fool, says I, he will eat you up.—Eatee me up! eatee me up! says Friday, twice over again; me eatee him up; me makee you good laugh: you all stay here, me show you good laugh. So down he sits, and gets off his boots in a moment, and puts on a pair of pumps (as we call the flat shoes they wear, and which he had in his pocket), gives my other servant his horse, and with his gun away he flew, swift like the wind.

The bear was walking softly on, and offered to meddle with nobody, till Friday coming pretty near, calls to him as if the bear could understand him, Hark ye, hark ye, says Friday, me speakee with you. We followed at distance; for now being come down on the Gascony side of the mountains, we were entered a vast great forest, where the country was plain and pretty open, though it had many trees in it scattered here and there. Friday, who had, as we say, the heels of the bear, came up with him quickly, and takes up a great stone and throws it at him, and hit him just on the head, but did him no more harm than if he had thrown it against a wall; but it answered Friday's end, for the rogue was so void of fear that he did it purely to make the bear follow him, and show us some laugh as he called it. As soon as the bear felt the blow, and saw him, he turns about, and comes after him, taking devilish long strides, and shuffling on at a strange rate, such as would have put a horse to a middling gallop; away runs Friday, and takes his course as if he ran towards us for help; so we all resolved to fire at once upon the bear, and deliver my man; though I was angry at him heartily for bringing the bear back upon us, when he was going about his own business another way; and especially I was angry that he had turned the bear upon us, and then run away; and I called out, You dog, is this your making us laugh? Come away, and take your horse, that we may shoot the creature. He heard me, and cried out, No shoot, no shoot; stand still, and you get much laugh; and as the nimble creature ran two feet for the bear's one, he turned on a sudden, on one side of us, and seeing a great oak tree fit for his purpose, he beckoned to us to follow; and doubling his pace, he gets nimbly up the tree, laying his gun down upon the ground, at about five or six yards from the bottom of the tree. The bear soon came to the tree, and we followed at a distance; the first thing he did, he stopped at the gun, smelt to it, but let it lie, and up he scrambles into the tree, climbing like a cat, though so monstrous heavy. I was amazed, at the folly, as I thought it, of my man, and could not for my life see anything to laugh at yet, till seeing the bear get up the tree, we all rode near to him.

When we came to the tree, there was Friday got out to the small end of a large branch, and the bear got about half way to him. As soon as the bear got out to that part where the limb of the tree was weaker,—Ha! says he to us, now you see me teachee the bear dance: so he falls a jumping and shaking the bough, at which the bear began to totter, but stood still, and began to look behind him, to see how he should get back; then, indeed, we did laugh heartily. But Friday had not done with him by a great deal; when seeing him stand still, he calls out to him again, as if he had supposed the bear could speak English, What, you come no farther? pray you come farther: so he left jumping and shaking the tree; and the bear, just as if he understood what he said, did come a little farther; then he fell a jumping again, and the bear stopped again. We thought now was a good time to knock him on the head, and called to Friday to stand still, and we would shoot the bear: but he cried out earnestly, O pray! O pray! no shoot, me shoot by and then; he would have said by and by. However, to shorten the story, Friday danced so much, and the bear stood so ticklish, that we had laughing enough, but still could not imagine what the fellow would do: for first we thought he depended upon shaking the bear off; and we found the bear was too cunning for that too; for he would not go out far enough to be thrown down, but clings fast with his great broad claws and feet, so that we could not imagine what would be the end of it, and what the jest would be at last. But Friday puts us out of doubt quickly: for seeing the bear cling fast to the bough, and that he would not be persuaded to come any farther, Well, well, says Friday, you no come farther, me go; you no come to me, me come to you: and upon this, he goes out to the smaller end of the bough, where it would bend with his weight, and gently lets himself down by it, sliding down the bough, till he came near enough to jump down on his feet, and away he runs to his gun, takes it up, and stands still. Well, said I to him, Friday, what will you do now? Why don't you shoot him?—No shoot, says Friday, no yet: me no shoot now, me no kill; me stay, give you one more laugh; and, indeed, so he did, as you will see presently: for when the bear saw his enemy gone, he comes back from the bough where he stood, but did it mighty cautiously, looking behind him every step, and coming backward till he got into the body of the tree; then with the same hinder-end foremost, he came down the tree, grasping it with his claws, and moving one foot at a time, very leisurely. At this juncture, and just before he could set his hind-foot on the ground, Friday stepped up close to him, clapped the muzzle of his piece into his ear, and shot him dead. Then the rogue turned about, to see if we did not laugh; and when he saw we were pleased, by our looks, he falls a laughing himself very loud. So we kill bear in my country, says Friday. So you kill them? says I: why, you have no guns.—No, says he, no gun, but shoot great much long arrow. This was a good diversion to us; but we were still in a wild place, and our guide very much hurt, and what to do we hardly knew: the howling of wolves ran much in my head; and, indeed, except the noise I once heard on the shore of Africa, of which I have said something already, I never heard anything that filled me with so much horror.

These things, and the approach of night, called us off, or else, as Friday would have had us, we should certainly have taken the skin of this monstrous creature off, which was worth saving; but we had near three leagues to go, and our guide hastened us, so we left him, and went forward on our journey.

The ground was still covered with snow, though not so deep and dangerous as on the mountains; and the ravenous creatures, as we heard afterwards, were come down into the forest and plain country, pressed by hunger, to seek for food, and had done a great deal of mischief in the villages, where they surprised the country people, killed a great many of their sheep and horses, and some people too. We had one dangerous place to pass, of which our guide told us, if there were more wolves in the country we should find them there; and this was a small plain, surrounded with woods on every side, and a long narrow defile, or lane, which we were to pass to get through the wood, and then we should come to the village where we were to lodge. It was within a half an hour of sunset when we entered the first wood, and a little after sunset when we came into the plain. We met with nothing in the first wood, except that, in a little plain within the wood, which was not above two furlongs over, we saw five great wolves cross the road, full speed one after another, as if they had been in chase of some prey, and had it in view; they took no notice of us, and were gone out of sight in a few moments. Upon this our guide, who, by the way, was but a faint-hearted fellow, bid us keep in a ready posture, for he believed there were more wolves a-coming. We kept our arms ready, and our eyes about us; but we saw no more wolves till we came through that wood, which was near half a league, and entered the plain. As soon as we came into the plain, we had occasion enough to look about us: the first object we met with was a dead horse, that is to say, a poor horse which the wolves had killed, and at least a dozen of them at work, we could not say eating of him, but picking of his bones rather: for they had eaten up all the flesh before. We did not think fit to disturb them at their feast; neither did they take much notice of us. Friday would have let fly at them, but I would not suffer him by any means; for I found we were like to have more business upon our hands than we were aware of. We were not gone half over the plain, when we began to hear the wolves howl in the wood on our left in a frightful manner, and presently after we saw about a hundred coming on directly towards us, all in a body, and most of them in a line, as regularly as an army drawn up by an experienced officer. I scarce knew in what manner to receive them, but found to draw ourselves in a close line was the only way: so we formed in a moment: but that we might not have too much interval, I ordered that only every other man should fire, and that the others who had not fired should stand ready to give them a second volley immediately, if they continued to advance upon us; and then that those who had fired at first should not pretend to load their fusees again, but stand ready every one with a pistol, for we were all armed with a fusee and a pair of pistols each man; so we were, by this method, able to fire six volleys, half of us at a time. However, at present we had no necessity; for upon firing the first volley, the enemy made a full stop, being terrified as well with the noise as with the fire; four of them being shot in the head, dropped; several others were wounded, and went bleeding off, as we could see by the snow. I found they stopped, but did not immediately retreat; whereupon, remembering that I had been told that the fiercest creatures were terrified at the voice of a man, I caused all the company to halloo as loud as we could; and I found the notion not altogether mistaken; for upon our shout, they began to retire and turn about. I then ordered a second volley to be fired in their rear, which put them to the gallop, and away they went to the woods. This gave us leisure to charge our pieces again; and that we might lose no time, we kept going; but we had little but more than loaded our fusees, and put ourselves in readiness, when we heard a terrible noise in the same wood, on our left, only that it was farther onward, the same way we were to go.

The night was coming on, and the light began to be dusky, which made it worse on our side; but the noise increasing, we could easily perceive that it was the howling and yelling of those hellish creatures; and on a sudden we perceived two or three troops of wolves, one on our left, one behind us, and one in our front, so that we seemed to be surrounded with them: however, as they did not fall upon us, we kept our way forward, as fast as we could make our horses go, which, the way being very rough, was only a good hard trot. In this manner we came in view of the entrance of the wood, through which we were to pass, at the farther side of the plain; but we were greatly surprised, when, coming nearer the lane or pass, we saw a confused number of wolves standing just at the entrance. On a sudden, at another opening of a wood, we heard the noise of a gun, and looking that way out rushed a horse, with a saddle and bridle on him, flying like the wind, and sixteen or seventeen wolves after him, full speed; indeed, the horse had the heels of them, but as we supposed that he could not hold it at that rate, we doubted not but they would get up with him at last; no question but they did.

But here we had a most horrible sight; for riding up to the entrance where the horse came out, we found the carcasses of another horse and of two men, devoured by the ravenous creatures; and one of the men was no doubt the same whom we heard fire the gun, for there lay a gun just by him fired off; but as to the man, his head and the upper part of his body were eaten up. This filled us with horror, and we knew not what course to take; but the creatures resolved us soon, for they gathered about us presently, in hopes of prey; and I verily believe there were three hundred of them. It happened very much to our advantage, that at the entrance into the wood, but a little way from it, there lay some large timber trees, which had been cut down the summer before, and I suppose lay there for carriage. I drew my little troop in among those trees, and placing ourselves in a line behind one long tree, I advised them all to alight, and keeping that tree before us for a breastwork, to stand in a triangle or three fronts enclosing our horses in the centre. We did so, and it was well we did; for never was a more furious charge than the creatures made upon us in this place. They came on with a growling kind of noise, and mounted the piece of timber, which, as I said, was our breastwork, as if they were only rushing upon their prey: and this fury of theirs, it seems, was principally occasioned by their seeing our horses behind us. I ordered our men to fire as before, every other man: and they took their aims so sure, that they killed several of the wolves at the first volley: but there was a necessity to keep a continual firing, for they came on like devils, those behind pushing on those before.

When we had fired a second volley of our fusees, we thought they stopped a little, and I hoped they would have gone off; but it was but a moment, for others came forward again: so we fired two volleys of our pistols; and I believe in these four firings we had killed seventeen or eighteen of them, and lamed twice as many, yet they came on again. I was loath to spend our shot too hastily; so I called my servant, not my man Friday, for he was better employed, for, with the greatest dexterity imaginable, he had charged my fusee and his own while we were engaged; but as I said, I called my other man, and giving him a horn of powder, I bade him lay a train all along the piece of timber, and let it be a large train. He did so: and had but just time to get away, when the wolves came up to it, and some got upon it, when I, snapping an uncharged pistol close to the powder, set it on fire: those that were upon the timber were scorched with it; and six or seven of them fell or rather jumped in among us, with the force and fright of the fire: we despatched these in an instant, and the rest were so frightened with the light, which the night, for it was now very dark, made more terrible, that they drew back a little; upon which I ordered our last pistols to be fired off in one volley, and after that we gave a shout: upon this the wolves turned tail, and we sallied immediately upon near twenty lame ones, that we found struggling on the ground, and fell a cutting them with our swords, which answered our expectation: for the crying and howling they made was better understood by their fellows; so that they all fled and left us.

We had, first and last, killed about threescore of them; and had it been daylight, we had killed many more. The field of battle being thus cleared, we made forward again, for we had still near a league to go. We heard the ravenous creatures howl and yell in the woods as we went, several times, and sometimes we fancied we saw some of them, but the snow dazzling our eyes, we were not certain: in about an hour more we came to the town where we were to lodge, which we found in a terrible fright, and all in arms; for, it seems, the night before, the wolves and some bears had broke into the village, and put them in such terror, that they were obliged to keep guard night and day, but especially in the night, to preserve their cattle, and, indeed, their people.

The next morning our guide was so ill, and his limbs swelled so much with the rankling of his two wounds, that he could go no farther; so we were obliged to take a new guide here, and go to Thoulouse, where we found a warm climate, a fruitful, pleasant country, and no snow, no wolves, nor anything like them; but when we told our story at Thoulouse, they told us it was nothing but what was ordinary in the great forest at the foot of the mountains, especially when the snow lay on the ground; but they inquired much what kind of a guide we had got, who would venture to bring us that way in such a severe season; and told us it was surprising we were not all devoured. When we told them how we placed ourselves, and the horses in the middle, they blamed us exceedingly, and told us it was fifty to one but we had been all destroyed; for it was the sight of the horses which made the wolves so furious, seeing their prey: and that, at other times, they are really afraid of a gun; but being excessive hungry, and raging on that account, the eagerness to come at the horses had made them senseless of danger; and that if we had not, by the continued fire, and at last by the stratagem of the train of powder, mastered them, it had been great odds but that we had been torn to pieces: that whereas, had we been content to have sat still on horseback, and fired as horsemen, they would not have taken the horses so much for their own, when men were on their backs, as otherwise; and withal they told us, that, at last, if we had stood all together, and left our horses, that they would have been so eager to have devoured them, that we might have come off safe, especially having our fire-arms in our hands, and being so many in number. For my part, I was never so sensible of danger in my life; for seeing above three hundred devils come roaring and open-mouthed to devour us, and having nothing to shelter us, or retreat to, I gave myself over for lost; and, as it was, I believe I shall never care to cross those mountains again: I think I would much rather go a thousand leagues by sea, though I was sure to meet with a storm once a week.

I have nothing uncommon to take notice of in my passage through France, nothing but what other travellers have given an account of, with much more advantage than I can. I travelled from Thoulouse to Paris, and without any considerable stay came to Calais, and landed safe at Dover, the 14th of January, after having a severe cold season to travel in.

I was now come to the centre of my travels, and had in a little time all my new discovered estate safe about me; the bills of exchange which I brought with me having been very currently paid.

My principal guide and privy counsellor was my good ancient widow; who, in gratitude for the money I had sent her, thought no pains too much, nor care too great, to employ for me; and I trusted her so entirely with everything, that I was perfectly easy as to the security of my effects:

and, indeed, I was very happy from the beginning, and now to the end, in the unspotted integrity of this good gentlewoman.

I now resolved to dispose of my plantation in the Brazils, if I could find means. For this purpose, I wrote to my old friend at Lisbon, who having offered it to the two merchants, the survivors of my trustees, who lived in the Brazils, they accepted the offer, and remitted thirty-three thousand pieces-of-eight to a correspondent of theirs at Lisbon, to pay for it. Having signed the instrument of sale, and sent it to my old friend, he remitted me bills of exchange for thirty-two thousand eight hundred pieces-of-eight for the estate, reserving the payment of a hundred moidores a year to himself during his life, and fifty moidores afterwards to his son for life, which I had promised them.

Though I had sold my estate in the Brazils, yet I could not keep the country out of my head; nor could I resist the strong inclination I had to see my island. My true friend, the widow, earnestly dissuaded me from it, and so far prevailed with me, that for almost seven years, she prevented my running abroad; during which time I took my two nephews, the children of one of my brothers, into my care: the eldest having something of his own, I bred up as a gentleman, and gave him a settlement of some addition to his estate, after my decease. The other I put out to a captain of a ship; and after five years, finding him a sensible, bold, enterprising young fellow, I put him into a good ship, and sent him to sea; and this young fellow afterwards drew me in, old as I was, to further adventures myself.

In the mean time, I in part settled myself here; for, first of all, I married, and that not either to my disadvantage or dissatisfaction, and had three children, two sons and one daughter; but my wife dying, and my nephew coming home with good success from a voyage to Spain, my inclination to go abroad, and his importunity prevailed, and engaged me to go in his ship as a private trader to the East Indies: this was in the year 1694.

But these things, with some very surprising incidents in some new adventures of my own, for ten years more, I shall give a further account of.

That homely proverb used on so many occasions in England, viz., "That what is bred in the bone will not go out of the flesh," was never more verified than in the story of my life. Any one would think that, after five years' affliction, and a variety of unhappy circumstances, which few men, if any, ever went through before, and after near seven years of peace and enjoyment in the fulness of all things, grown old, and when, if ever, it might be allowed me to have had experience of every state of middle life, and to know which was most adapted to make a man completely happy; I say, after all this, any one would have thought that the native propensity to rambling, which I gave an account of in my first setting out in the world to have been so predominant in my thoughts, should be worn out, the volatile part be fully evacuated, or at least condensed, and I might, at sixty-one years of age, have been a little inclined to stay at home, and have done venturing life and fortune any more.

Nay, further, the common motive of foreign adventures was taken away in me; for I had no fortune to make; I had nothing to seek: if I had gained ten thousand pounds, I had been no richer; for I had already sufficient for me, and for those I had to leave it to; and that I had was visibly increasing; for having no great family, I could not spend the income of what I had, unless I would set up for an expensive way of living, such as a great family, servants, equipage, gaiety, and the like, which were things I had no notion of, or inclination to; so that I had nothing indeed to do but to sit still, and fully enjoy what I had got, and see it increase daily upon my hands. Yet all these things had no effect upon me, or at least not enough to resist the strong inclination I had to go abroad again, which hung about me like a chronical distemper. In particular, the desire of seeing my new plantation in the island, and the colony I left there, ran in my head continually. I dreamed of it all night, and my imagination ran upon it all day; it was uppermost in all my thoughts; and my fancy worked so steadily and strongly upon it, that I talked of it in my sleep: in short, nothing could remove it out of my mind: it even broke so violently into all my discourses, that it made my conversation tiresome, for I could talk of nothing else: all my discourse ran into it, even to impertinence; and I saw it in myself.

I HAVE OFTEN HEARD persons of good judgment say, that all the stir people make in the world about ghosts and apparitions is owing to the strength of imagination, and the powerful operation of fancy in their minds; that there is no such thing as a spirit appearing, or a ghost walking, and the like: that people's poring affectionately upon the past conversation of their deceased friends, so realises it to them, that they are capable of fancying, upon some extraordinary circumstances, that they see them, talk to them, and are answered by them, when, in truth, there is nothing but shadow and vapour in the thing, and they really know nothing of the matter.

For my part, I know not to this hour whether there are any such things as real apparitions, spectres, or walking of people after they are dead : or whether there is anything in the stories they tell us of that kind, more than the product of vapours, sick minds, and wandering fancies; but this I know, that my imagination worked up to such a height, and brought me into such excess of vapours, or what else I may call it, that I actually supposed myself often upon the spot, at my old castle, behind the trees; saw my old Spaniard, Friday's father, and the reprobate sailors I left upon the island; nay, I fancied I talked with them, and looked at them steadily, though I was broad awake, as at persons just before me; and this I did till I often frightened myself with the images my fancy represented to me. One time, in my sleep, I had the villainy of the three pirate sailors so lively related to me by the first Spaniard and Friday's father, that it was surprising; they told me how they barbarously attempted to murder all the Spaniards, and that they set fire to the provisions they had laid up, on purpose to distress and starve them; things that I had never heard of, and that indeed were never all of them true in fact; but it was so warm in my imagination, and so realised to me, that, to the hour I saw them, I could not be persuaded but that it was, or would be true: also how I resented it, when the Spaniard complained to me; and how I brought them to justice, tried them before me, and ordered them all three to be hanged. What there was really in this shall be seen in its place: for however I came to form such things in my dream, and what secret converse of spirits injected it, yet there was, I say, much of it true. I own that this dream had nothing in it literally and specifically true; but the general part was so true, the base, villainous behaviour of these three hardened rogues was such, and had been so much worse than all I can describe, that the dream had too much similitude of the fact; and as I would afterwards have punished them severely, so, if I had hanged them all, I had been much in the right, and even should have been justified both by the laws of God and man. But to return to my story. In this kind of temper I lived some years; I had no enjoyment of my life, no pleasant hours, no agreeable diversion, but what had something or other of this in it; so that my wife, who saw my mind wholly bent upon it, told me very seriously one night, that she believed there was some secret powerful impulse of Providence upon me, which had determined me to go thither again; and that she found nothing hindered my going, but my being engaged to a wife and children. She told me, that it was true she could not think of parting with me; but as she was assured, that if she was dead it would be the first thing I would do, so, as it seemed to her that the thing was determined above, she would not be the only obstruction; for, if I thought fit, and resolved to go —— Here she found me very intent upon her words, and that I looked very earnestly at her, so that it a little disordered her, and she stopped. I asked her why she did not go on, and say out what she was going to say? But I perceived that her heart was too full, and some tears stood in her eyes. Speak out, my dear, said

I; are you willing I should go? No, says she, very affectionately, I am far from willing; but if you are resolved to go, says she, and rather than I would be the only hindrance, I will go with you: for though I think it a most preposterous thing for one of your years, and in your condition, yet if it must be, said she, again weeping, I would not leave you; for if it be of Heaven, you must do it; there is no resisting it: and if Heaven made it your duty to go, he will also make it mine to go with you, or otherwise dispose of me, that I may not obstruct it.

This affectionate behaviour of my wife's brought me a little out of the vapours, and I began to consider what I was doing: I corrected my wandering fancy, and I began to argue with myself sedately, what business I had, after three-score years, and after such a life of tedious sufferings and disasters, and closed in so happy and easy a manner; I say, what business had I to rush into new hazards, and put myself upon adventures fit only for youth and poverty to run into?

With those thoughts I considered my new engagements; that I had a wife, one child born, and my wife then great with child of another; that I had all the world could give me, and had no need to seek hazard for gain; that I was declining in years, and ought to think rather of leaving what I had gained, than of seeking to increase it; that as to what my wife had said of its being an impulse from Heaven, and that it should be my duty to go, I had no notion of that; so, after many of these cogitations, I struggled with the power of my imagination, reasoned myself out of it, as I believe people may always do in like cases if they will; and in a word, I conquered it; composed myself with such arguments as occurred to my thoughts, and which my present condition furnished me plentifully with; and particularly, as the most effectual method, I resolved to divert myself with other things, and to engage in some business that might effectually tie me up from any more excursions of this kind; for I found that thing returned upon me chiefly when I was idle, and had nothing to do, nor anything of moment immediately before me. To this purpose I bought a little farm in the county of Bedford, and resolved to remove myself thither. I had a little convenient house upon it; and the land about it, I found was capable of great improvement; and it was many ways suited to my inclination, which delighted in cultivating, managing, planting, and improving of land; and particularly, being an inland country, I was removed from conversing among sailors, and things relating to remote parts of the world.

In a word, I went down to my farm, settled my family, bought me ploughs, harrows, a cart, waggon, horses, cows, and sheep, and setting seriously to work, became, in one half year, a mere country gentleman; my thoughts were entirely taken up in managing my servants, cultivating the ground, enclosing, planting, etc.; and I lived, as I thought, the most agreeable life that nature was capable of directing, or that a man always bred to misfortunes was capable of retreating to.

I farmed upon my own land; I had no rent to pay, was limited by no articles: I could pull up or cut down as I pleased; what I planted was for myself, and what I improved was for my family; and having thus left off the thoughts of wandering, I had not the least discomfort in any part of life as to this world. Now I thought indeed that I enjoyed the middle state of life which my father so earnestly recommended to me, and lived a kind of heavenly life, something like what is described by the poet, upon the subject of a country life—

"——Free from vices, free from care,
Age has no pain, and youth no snare."

But, in the middle of all this felicity, one blow from unseen Providence unhinged me at once; and not only made a breach upon me inevitable and incurable, but drove me, by its consequences, into a deep relapse of the wandering disposition, which, as I may say, being born in my very blood, soon recovered its hold of me, and, like the returns of a violent distemper, came on with an irresistible force upon me. This blow was the loss of my wife. It is not my business here to write an elegy upon my wife, give a character of her particular virtues, and make my court to the sex by the flattery of a funeral sermon. She was, in a few words, the stay of all my affairs, the centre of all my enterprises, the engine that, by her prudence, reduced me to that happy compass I was in, from the most extravagant and ruinous project that fluttered in my head, as above, and did more to guide my rambling genius than a mother's tears, a father's instructions, a friend's counsel, or all my own reasoning powers could do. I was happy in listening to her tears, and in being moved by her entreaties; and to the last degree desolate and dislocated in the world by the loss of her.

When she was gone, the world looked awkward round me. I was as much a stranger in it, in my thoughts, as I was in the Brazils, when I first went on shore there; and as much alone, except as to the assistance of servants, as I was in my island. I knew neither what to think nor what to do. I saw the world busy around me: one part labouring for bread, another squandering in vile excesses or empty pleasures, equally miserable, because the end they proposed still fled from them: for the men of pleasure every day surfeited of their vice, and heaped up work for sorrow and repentance; and the men of labour spent their strength in daily struggling for bread to maintain the vital strength they laboured with: so living in a daily circulation on sorrow, living but to work, and working but to live, as if daily bread were the only end of wearisome life, and a wearisome life the only occasion of daily bread.

This put me in mind of the life I lived in my kingdom, the island; where I suffered no more corn to grow, because I did not want it, and bred no more goats, because I had no more use for them; where the money lay in the drawer till it grew mouldy, and had scarce the favour to be looked upon in twenty years.

All these things, had I improved them as I ought to have done, and as reason and religion had dictated to me, would have taught me to search further than human enjoyments for a full felicity; and that there was something which certainly was the reason and end of life, superior to all these things, and which was either to be possessed, or at least hoped for, on this side the grave.

But my sage counsellor was gone; I was like a ship without a pilot, that could only run afore the wind: my thoughts ran all away again into the old affair; my head was quite turned with the whimsies of foreign adventures; and all the pleasant, innocent amusements of my farm, my garden, my cattle, and my family, which before entirely possessed me, were nothing to me, had no relish, and were like music to one that has no ear, or food to one that has no taste: in a word, I resolved to leave off housekeeping, let my farm, and return to London; and in a few months after I did so.

When I came to London, I was still as uneasy as I was before; I had no relish for the place, no employment in it, nothing to do but to saunter about like an idle person, of whom it may be said he is perfectly useless in God's creation, and it is not one farthing's matter to the rest of his kind whether he be dead or alive. This also was the first thing which, of all other circumstances of life, was the most my diversion, who had been all my days used to an active life; and I would often say to myself: A state of idleness is the very dregs of life; and indeed I thought I was much more suitably employed when I was twenty-six days making me a deal board.

It was now the beginning of the year 1693, when my nephew, whom, as I have observed before, I had brought up to the sea, and had made him commander of a ship, was come home from a short voyage to Bilboa, being the first he had made. He came to me, and told me that some merchants of his acquaintance had been proposing to him to go a voyage for them to the East Indies and to China, as private traders.— And now, uncle, says he, if you will go to sea with me, I will engage to land you upon your old habitation in the island; for we are to touch at the Brazils.

Nothing can be a greater demonstration of a future state, and of the existence of an invisible world, than the concurrence of second causes with the ideas of things which we form in our minds, perfectly reserved, and not communicated to any in the world.

My nephew knew nothing how far my distemper of wandering was returned upon me, and I knew nothing of what he had in his thoughts to say, when the very morning, before he came to me, I had, in a greal deal of confusion of thought, and revolving every part of my circumstances in my mind, come to this resolution, viz., that I would go to Lisbon, and consult with my old sea-captain; and so, if it was rational and practicable, I would go and see the island again, and see what was become of my people there. I had pleased myself with the thoughts of peopling the place, and carrying inhabitants from hence, getting a patent for the possession, and I knew not what; when, in the middle of all this, in comes my nephew, as I have said, with his project of carrying me thither in his way to the East Indies.

I paused awhile at his words, and, looking steadily at him, What devil, said I, sent you on this unlucky errand? My nephew stared, as if he had been frightened, at first; but perceiving that I was not so much displeased with the proposal, he recovered himself. I hope it may not be an unlucky proposal, sir, says he; I dare say you would be pleased to see your new colony there, where you once reigned with more felicity than most of your brother-monarchs in the world.

In a word, the scheme hit so exactly with my temper, that is to say, the prepossession I was under, and of which I have said so much, that I told him, in a few words, if he agreed with the merchants I would go with him; but I told him I would not promise to go any farther than my own island. Why, sir, says he, you don't want to be left there again, I hope? Why, said I, can you not take me up again on your return? He told me it would not be possible to do so; that the merchants would never allow him to come that way with a laden ship of such value, it being a month's sail out of his way, and might be three or four. Besides, sir, if I should miscarry, said he, and not return at all, then you would be just reduced to the condition you were in before.

This was very rational; but we both found out a remedy for it; which was to carry a framed sloop on board the ship, which being taken in pieces, and shipped on board the ship, might by the help of some carpenters, whom we agreed to carry with us, be set up again in the island, and finished, fit to go to sea, in a few days.

I was not long resolving; for indeed the importunities of my nephew joined so effectually with my inclination, that nothing could oppose me: on the other hand, my wife being dead, I had nobody concerning themselves so much for me as to persuade me to one way or the other, except my ancient good friend the widow, who earnestly struggled with me to consider my years, my easy circumstances, and the needless hazards of a long voyage; and, above all, my young children. But it was all to no purpose;—I had an irresistible desire to the voyage; and I told her I thought there was something so uncommon in the impression I had upon my mind for the voyage, that it would be a kind of resisting Providence if I should attempt to stay at home: after which she ceased her expostulations, and joined with me, not only in making provision for my voyage, but also in settling my family affairs for my absence, and providing for the education of my children.

In order to this, I made my will, and settled the estate I had in such a manner for my children, and placed in such hands, that I was perfectly easy and satisfied they would have justice done them, whatever might befall me; and for their education, I left it wholly to the widow, with a sufficient maintenance to herself for her care: all which she richly deserved, for no mother could have taken more care in their education, or understood it better; and as she lived till I came home, I also lived to thank her for it.

My nephew was ready to sail about the beginning of January 1694–5; and I, with my man Friday, went on board in the Downs the 8th; having, besides that sloop which I mentioned above, a very considerable cargo of all kinds of necessary things for my colony; which, if I did not find in good condition, I resolved to leave so.

First, I carried with me some servants, whom I proposed to place there as inhabitants, or at least to set on work there, upon my account, while I stayed, and either to leave them there, or carry them forward, as they would appear willing: particularly, I carried two carpenters, a smith, and a very handy, ingenious fellow, who was a cooper by trade, and was also a general mechanic; for he was dexterous at making wheels, and hand-mills to grind corn, was a good turner, and a good pot-maker; he also made anything that was proper to make of earth, or of wood; in a word, we called him our Jack of all trades. With these I carried a tailor, who had offered himself to go a passenger to the East Indies with my nephew, but afterwards consented to stay on our new plantation; and proved a most necessary, handy fellow as could be desired, in many other businesses besides that of his trade: for, as I observed formerly, necessity arms us for all employments.

My cargo, as near as I can recollect, for I had not kept account of the particulars, consisted of a sufficient quantity of linen, and some English thin stuffs, for clothing the Spaniards that I expected to find there; and enough of them, as, by my calculation, might comfortably supply them for seven years: if I remember right, the materials I carried for clothing them, with gloves, hats, shoes, stockings, and all such things as they could want for wearing, amounted to above two hundred pounds, including some beds, bedding, and household stuff, particularly kitchen utensils, with pots, kettles, pewter, brass, etc., and near a hundred pounds more in iron work, nails, tools of every kind, staples, hooks, hinges, and every necessary thing I could think of.

I carried also a hundred spare arms, muskets, and fusees; besides some pistols, a considerable quantity of shot of all sizes, three or four tons of lead, and two pieces of brass cannon: and because I knew not what time and what extremities I was providing for, I carried a hundred barrels of powder, besides swords, cutlasses, and the iron part of some pikes and halberds: so that, in short, we had a large magazine of all sorts of stores: and I made my nephew carry two small quarter-deck guns more than he wanted for his ship, to leave behind if there was occasion; that, when we came there, we might build a fort, and man it against all sorts of enemies; and, indeed, I at first thought there would be need enough for all, and much more, if we hoped to maintain our possession of the island; as shall be seen in the course of that story.

I had not such bad luck in this voyage as I had been used to meet with; and therefore shall have the less occasion to interrupt the reader, who perhaps may be impatient to hear how matters went with my colony: yet some old accidents, cross winds, and bad weather, happened on this first setting out, which made the voyage longer than I expected it at first: and I, who had never made but one voyage, viz., my first voyage to Guinea, in which I might be said to come back again as the voyage was at first designed, began to think the same ill fate attended me; and that I was born to be never contented with being on shore, and yet to be always unfortunate at sea.

Contrary winds first put us to the northward, and we were obliged to put in at Galway in Ireland, where we lay windbound two-and-twenty days; but we had this satisfaction with the disaster, that provisions were here exceeding cheap, and in the utmost plenty; so that while we lay here, we never touched the ship's stores, but rather added to them. Here, also, I took in several live hogs, and two cows, with their calves; which I resolved, if I had a good passage, to put on shore in my island; but we found occasion to dispose otherwise of them.

WE SET OUT on the 5th of February from Ireland, and had a very fair gale of wind for some days. As I remember, it might be about the 20th of February, in the evening late, when the mate, having the watch, came into the round-house, and told us he saw a flash of fire, and heard a gun fired; and while he was telling us of it, a boy came in, and told us the boatswain heard another. This made us all run out upon the quarter-deck, where, for a while, we heard nothing; but in a few minutes we saw a very great light, and found that there was some very terrible fire at a distance; immediately we had recourse to our reckonings, in which we all agreed that there could be no land that way in which the fire showed itself, no, not for five hundred leagues, for it appeared at W.N.W. Upon this we concluded it must be some ship on fire at sea; and as, by our hearing the noise of guns just before, we concluded that it could not be far off, we stood directly towards it, and were presently satisfied we should discover it, because, the farther we sailed, the greater the light appeared; though, the weather being hazy, we could not perceive anything but the light for a while. In about half an hour's sailing, the wind being fair for us, though not much of it, and the weather clearing up a little, we could plainly discern that it was a great ship on fire, in the middle of the sea.

I was most sensibly touched with this disaster, though not at all acquainted with the persons engaged in it: I presently recollected my former circumstances, and in what condition I was in, when taken up by the Portuguese captain; and how much more deplorable the circumstances of the poor creatures belonging to that ship must be, if they had no other ship in company with them. Upon this, I immediately ordered that five guns should be fired, one soon after another; that, if possible, we might give notice to them that there was help for them at hand, and that they might endeavour to save themselves in their boat; for though we could see the flames of the ship, yet they, it being night, could see nothing of us.

We lay by for some time upon this, only driving as the burning ship drove, waiting for daylight; when, on a sudden, to our great terror, though we had reason to expect it, the ship blew up in the air; and immediately, that is to say, in a few minutes, all the fire was out, that is to say, the rest of the ship sunk. This was a terrible and indeed an afflicting sight, for the sake of the poor men; who I concluded, must be either all destroyed in the ship, or be in the utmost distress in their boat, in the middle of the ocean; which, at present, by reason it was dark, I could not see. However, to direct them as well as I could, I caused lights to be hung out in all parts of the ship where we could, and which we had lanterns for, and kept firing guns all the night long; letting them know, by this, that there was a ship not far off.

About eight o'clock in the morning we discovered the ship's boats by aid of our perspective glasses; found there were two of them, both thronged with people, and deep in the water. We perceived they rowed, the wind being against them; that they saw our ship, and did their utmost to let us see them.

We immediately spread our *ancient*, to let them know we saw them, and hung a waft out, as a signal for them to come on board; and then made more sail, standing directly to them. In little more than half an hour we came up with them; and, in a word, took them all in, being no less than sixty-four men, women, and children; for there were a great many passengers.

Upon the whole, we found it was a French merchant-ship of three hundred tons, home-bound from Quebec, in the river of Canada. The master gave us a long account of the distress of his ship; how the fire began in the steerage, by the negligence of the steersman; but on his crying out for help, was as every body thought, entirely put out; but they soon found that some sparks of the first fire had gotten into some part of the ship so difficult to come at, that they could not effectually quench it; and afterwards getting in between the timbers, and within the ceiling of the ship, it proceeded into the hold, and mastered all the skill and all the application they were able to exert.

They had no more to do then, but to get into their boats, which, to their great comfort, were pretty large; being their long-boat, and their great shallop, besides a small skiff, which was of no great service to them, other than to get some fresh water and provisions into her, after they had secured their lives from the fire. They had, indeed, small hope of their lives by getting into these boats, at that distance from any land; only, as they said well, that they were escaped from the fire, and a possibility that some ship might happen to be at sea, and might take them in. They had sails, oars, and a compass; and were preparing to make the best of their way back to Newfoundland, the wind blowing pretty fair, for it blew an easy gale at S.E. by E. They had as much provision and water as, with sparing it so as to be next door to starving, might support them about twelve days; in which, if they had no bad weather, and no contrary winds, the captain said he hoped he might get to the Banks of Newfoundland, and might perhaps take some fish, to sustain them till they might go on shore. But there were so many chances against them in all these cases, such as storms, to overset and founder them; rains and cold, to benumb and perish their limbs; contrary winds, to keep them out and starve them; that it must have been next to miraculous if they had escaped.

In the midst of their consternation, every one being hopeless and ready to despair, the captain, with tears in his eyes, told me they were on a sudden surprised with the joy of hearing a gun fire, and after that four more; these were the five guns which I caused to be fired at first seeing the light. This revived their hearts, and gave them the notice, which, as above, I desired it should, viz., that there was a ship at hand for their help. It was upon the hearing of these guns that they took down their masts and sails: the sound coming from the windward, they resolved to lie by till morning. Some time after this, hearing no more guns, they fired three muskets, one a considerable while after another; but these, the wind being contrary, we never heard.

Some time after that again, they were still more agreeably surprised with seeing our lights, and hearing the guns which, as I have said, I caused to be fired all the rest of the night: this set them to work with their oars, to keep their boats ahead, at least, that we might the sooner come up with them; and, at last, to their inexpressible joy, they found we saw them.

It is impossible for me to express the several gestures, the strange ecstasies, the variety of postures, which these poor delivered people ran into, to express the joy of their souls at so unexpected a deliverance. Grief and fear are easily described; sighs, tears, groans, and very few motions of the head and hands, make up the sum of its variety; but an excess of joy, a surprise of joy, has a thousand extravagancies in it: there were some in tears; some raging and tearing themselves, as if they had been in the greatest agonies of sorrow; some stark raving, and downright lunatic; some ran about the ship stamping with their feet, others wringing their hands; some were dancing, some singing, some laughing, more crying; many quite dumb, not able to speak a word; others sick and vomiting; several swooning, and ready to faint; and a few were crossing themselves, and giving God thanks.

I would not wrong them neither; there might be many that were thankful afterwards, but the passion was too strong for them at first, and they were not able to master it: they were thrown into ecstasies, and a kind of frenzy; and it was but a very few that were composed and serious in their joy.

Perhaps, also, the case may have some addition to it from the particular circumstance of that nation they belonged to: I mean the French, whose temper is allowed to be more volatile, more passionate, and more sprightly, and their spirits more fluid, than in other nations. I am not philosopher enough to determine the cause; but nothing I had ever seen before came up to it. The ecstasies poor Friday, my trusty savage, was in, when he found his father in the boat, came the nearest to it; and the surprise of the master and his two companions, whom I delivered from the villains that set them on shore in the island, came a little way towards it; but nothing was to compare to this, either that I saw in Friday, or anywhere else in my life.

It is further observable, that these extravagancies did not show themselves, in that different manner I have mentioned, in different persons only; but all the variety would appear, in a short succession of moments, in one and the same person. A man that we saw this minute dumb, and as it were stupid and confounded, would the next minute be dancing and hallooing like an antic; and the next moment be tearing his hair or pulling his clothes to pieces, and stamping them under his feet, like a madman; in a few moments after that, we would have him all in tears, then sick, swooning, and, had not immediate help been had, he would in a few moments have been dead; and thus it was, not with one or two, or ten or twenty, but with the greatest part of them: and if I remember right, our surgeon was obliged to let blood of about thirty of them.

There were two priests among them, one an old man, and the other a young man; and that which was strangest was, the oldest man was the worst. As soon as he set his foot on board our ship, and saw himself safe, he dropped down stone-dead, to all appearance; not the least sign of life could be perceived in him: our surgeon immediately applied proper remedies to recover him, and was the only man in the ship that believed he was not dead. At length he opened a vein in his arm, having first chafed and rubbed the part, so as to warm it as much as possible: upon this blood, which only dropped at first, flowing freely, in three minutes after the man opened his eyes; and a quarter of an hour after that he spoke, grew better, and in a little time quite well. After the blood was stopped, he walked about; told us he was perfectly well; took a dram of cordial which the surgeon gave him, and was what we called come to himself. About a quarter of an hour after this, they came running into the cabin to the surgeon, who was bleeding a French woman that had fainted, and told him the priest was gone stark mad. It seems he had begun to revolve the change of his circumstances in his mind, and again this put him into an ecstasy of joy; his spirits whirled about faster than the vessels could convey them, the blood grew hot and feverish, and the man was as fit for Bedlam as creature that ever was in it: the surgeon would not bleed him again in that condition, but gave him something to doze and put him to sleep, which, after some time, operated upon him, and he awoke next morning perfectly composed and well.

The younger priest behaved with great command of his passions, and was really an example of a serious, well-governed mind: at his first coming on board the ship, he threw himself flat on his face, prostrating himself in thankfulness for his deliverance, in which I unhappily and unseasonably disturbed him, really thinking he had been in a swoon, but he spoke calmly, thanked me, told me he was giving God thanks for his deliverance; begged me to leave him a few moments, and that, next to his Maker, he would give me thanks also.

I was heartily sorry that I disturbed him, and not only left him, but kept others from interrupting him also. He continued in that posture about three minutes, or little more, after I left him; then came to me, as he had said he would, and, with a great deal of seriousness and affection, but with tears in his eyes, thanked me, that had, under God, given him, and so many miserable creatures, their lives. I told him I had no room to move him to thank God for it, rather than me, for I had seen that he had done that already; but, I added, that it was nothing but what reason and humanity dictated to all men; and that we had as much reason as he to give thanks to God, who had blessed us so far, as to make us the instruments of his mercy to so many of his creatures.

After this, the young priest applied himself to his country-folks; laboured to compose them; persuaded, entreated, argued, reasoned with them; and did his utmost to keep them within the exercise of their reason; and with some he had success, though others were for a time out of all government of themselves.

I cannot help committing this to writing, as perhaps it may be useful to those into whose hands it may fall, for the guiding themselves in all the extravagancies of their passions; for if an excess of joy can carry men out to such a length beyond the reach of their reason, what will not the extravagancies of anger, rage, and a provoked mind, carry us to? And, indeed, here I saw reason for keeping an exceeding watch over our passions of every kind, as well those of joy and satisfaction, as those of sorrow and anger.

We were something disordered, by these extravagancies among our new guests, for the first day; but when they had been retired, lodgings provided for them as well as our ship would allow, and they had slept heartily—as most of them did, being fatigued and frightened—they were quite another sort of people the next day.

Nothing of good manners, or civil acknowledgments for the kindness shown them, was wanting; the French, it is known, are naturally apt enough to exceed that way. The captain and one of the priests, came to me the next day, and desired to speak with me and my nephew: the commander began to consult with us what should be done with them; and first, they told us that we had saved their lives, so all they had was little enough for a return to us for that kindness received. The captain said they had saved some money, and some things of value, in their boats, catched hastily out of the flames, and if we would accept it, they were ordered to make an offer of it all to us: they only desired to be set on shore somewhere in our way, where, if possible, they might get a passage to France. My nephew was for accepting their money at first word, and to consider what to do with them afterwards; but I overruled him in that part, for I knew what it was to be set on shore in a strange country; and if the Portuguese captain that took me up at sea had served me so, and took all I had for my deliverance, I must have starved, or have been as much a slave at the Brazils as I had been at Barbary, the mere being sold to a Mahometan excepted; and perhaps a Portuguese is not a much better master than a Turk, if not, in some cases, much worse.

I therefore told the French captain that we had taken them up in their distress, it was true, but that it was our duty to do so, as we were fellow-creatures; and we would desire to be so delivered, if we were in the like, or any other extremity; that we had done nothing for them but what we believed they would have done for us, if we had been in their case, and they in ours; but that we took them up to save them, not to plunder them; and it would be a most barbarous thing to take that little from them which they had saved out of the fire, and then set them on shore and leave them; that this would be first to save them from death, and then kill them ourselves; save them from drowning, and abandon them to starving; and therefore I would not let the least thing be taken from them. As to setting them on shore, I told them, indeed, that was an exceeding difficulty to us, for that the ship was bound to the East Indies; and though we were driven out of our course to the westward a very great way, and perhaps were directed by Heaven on purpose for their deliverance, yet it was impossible for us wilfully to change our voyage on their particular account; nor could my nephew, the captain, answer it to the freighters, with whom he was under charter-party to pursue his voyage by the way of Brazil: and all I knew we could do for them, was to put ourselves in the way of meeting with other ships homeward bound from the West Indies, and get them a passage, if possible, to England or France.

The first part of the proposal was so generous and kind, they could not but be very thankful for it; but they were in a very great consternation, especially the passengers, at the notion of being carried away to the East Indies: they then entreated me, that seeing I was driven so far to the westward before I met them, I would at least keep on the same course to the banks of Newfoundland, where it was probable I might meet with some ship or sloop that they might hire to carry them back to Canada, from whence they came.

I thought this was but a reasonable request on their part, and therefore I inclined to agree to it; for, indeed, I considered, that to carry this whole company to the East Indies would not only be an intolerable severity upon the poor people, but would be ruining our whole voyage, by devouring all our provisions; so I thought it no breach of charter-party, but what an unforeseen accident made absolutely necessary to us, and in which no one could say we were to blame: for the laws of God and nature would have forbid that we would refuse to take up two boats full of people in such a distressed condition; and the nature of the thing, as well respecting ourselves as the poor people, obliged us to set them on shore somewhere or other for their deliverance: so I consented that we would carry them to Newfoundland, if wind and weather would permit; and if not, that I would carry them to Martinico, in the West Indies.

THE WIND continued fresh easterly, but the weather pretty good; and as the winds had continued in the points between N.E. and S.E. a long time, we missed several opportunities of sending them to France; for we met several ships bound to Europe, whereof two were French, from St. Christopher's; but they had been so long beating up against the wind, that they durst take no passengers, for fear of wanting provisions for the voyage, as well for themselves as for those they should take in; so we were obliged to go on. It was about a week after this that we made the Banks of Newfoundland; where, to shorten my story, we put all our French people on board a bark, which they hired at sea there, to put them on shore, and afterwards to carry them to France, if they could get provisions to victual themselves with. When I say all the French went on shore, I should remember, that the young priest I spoke of, hearing we were bound to the East Indies, desired to go the voyage with us, and to be set on shore on the coast of Coromandel; which I readily agreed to, for I wonderfully liked the man, and had very good reason, as will appear afterwards: also four of the seamen entered themselves on our ship, and proved very useful fellows.

From hence we directed our course to the West Indies, steering away S. and S. by E. for about twenty days together, sometimes little or no wind at all; when we met with another subject for our humanity to work upon, almost as deplorable as that before.

It was in the latitude of twenty-seven degrees five minutes north, on the 19th day of March, 1694-5, when we spied a sail, our course S.E. and by S.: we soon perceived it was a large vessel, and that she bore up to us, but could not at first know what to make of her, till, after coming a little nearer, we found she had lost her main topmast, foremast, and bow-sprit; and presently she fired a gun, as a signal of distress: the weather was pretty good, wind at N.N.W., a fresh gale, and we soon came to speak with her.

We found her a ship of Bristol, bound home from Barbadoes, but had been blown out of the road at Barbadoes a few days before she was ready to sail, by a terrible hurricane, while the captain and chief mate were both gone on shore; so that, besides the terror of the storm, they were in an indifferent case for good artists to bring the ship home. They had been already nine weeks at sea, and had met with another terrible storm, after the hurricane was over, which had blown them quite out of their knowledge to the westward, and in which they lost their masts, as above. They told us they expected to have seen the Bahama islands, but were then driven away again to the south-east, by a strong gale of wind at N.N.W., the same that blew now: and having no sails to work the ship with but a maincourse, and a kind of square sail upon a jury foremast, which they had set up, they could not lie near the wind, but were endeavouring to stand away for the Canaries.

But that which was worst of all was, that they were almost starved for want of provisions, besides the fatigues they had undergone: their bread and flesh were quite gone: they had not one ounce left in the ship, and had none for eleven days. The only relief they had was, their water was not all spent, and they had about half a barrel of flour left: they had sugar enough: some succades, or sweetmeats, they had at first, but they were devoured; and they had seven casks of rum.

There were a youth and his mother, and a maid-servant, on board, who were going passengers, and thinking the ship was ready to sail, unhappily came on board the evening before the hurricane began; and having no provisions of their own left, they were in a more deplorable condition than the rest: for the seamen, being reduced to such an extreme necessity themselves, had no compassion, we may be sure, for the poor passengers; and they were, indeed, in a condition, that their misery is very hard to describe.

I had perhaps not known this part, if my curiosity had not led me (the weather being fair, and the wind abated) to go on board the ship. The second mate, who, upon this occasion, commanded the ship, had been on board our ship, and he told me, indeed, they had three passengers in the great cabin, that were in a deplorable condition: Nay, says he, I believe they are dead, for I have heard nothing of them for above two days; and I was afraid to inquire after them, said he, for I had nothing to relieve them with.

We immediately applied ourselves to give them what relief we could spare; and, indeed, I had so far overruled things with my nephew, that I would have victualled them, though we had gone away to Virginia, or any other part of the coast of America, to have supplied ourselves; but there was no necessity for that.

But now they were in a new danger; for they were afraid of eating too much, even of that little we gave them. The mate or commander brought six men with him in his boat; but these poor wretches looked like skeletons, and were so weak, that they could hardly sit to their oars. The mate himself was very ill, and half-starved; for he declared he had reserved nothing from the men, and went share and share alike with them in every bit they ate.

I cautioned him to eat sparingly, but set meat before him immediately; and he had not eaten three mouthfuls before he began to be sick, and out of order; so he stopped awhile, and our surgeon mixed him up something with some broth, which he said would be to him both food and physic; and after he had taken it, he grew better. In the mean time, I forgot not the men; I ordered victuals to be given them; and the poor creatures rather devoured than ate it: they were so exceedingly hungry, that they were in a kind ravenous, and had no command of themselves; and two of them ate with so much greediness, that they were in danger of their lives the next morning.

The sight of these people's distress was very moving to me, and brought to mind what I had a terrible prospect of at my first coming on shore in my island, where I had never the least mouthful of food, or any prospect of procuring any; besides the hourly apprehensions I had of being made the food of other creatures. But all the while the mate was thus relating to me the miserable condition of the ship's company, I could not put out of my thought the story he had told me of the three poor creatures in the great cabin, viz., the mother, her son, and the maid-servant, whom he had heard nothing of for two or three days, and whom, he seemed to confess, they had wholly neglected, their own extremities being so great: by which I understood that they had really given them no food at all, and that therefore they must be perished, and be all lying dead, perhaps, on the floor or deck of the cabin.

As I therefore kept the mate, whom we then called captain, on board with his men to refresh them, so I also forgot not the starving crew that were left on board; but ordered my own boat to go on board the ship, and with my mate and twelve men, to carry them a sack of bread, and four or five pieces of beef to boil. Our surgeon charged the men to cause the meat to be boiled while they stayed, and to keep guard in the cook-room to prevent the men taking it to eat raw, or taking it out of the pot before it was well boiled, and then to give every man but a very little at a time: and by this caution he preserved the men, who would otherwise have killed themselves with that very food that was given them on purpose to save their lives.

At the same time, I ordered the mate to go into the great cabin, and see what condition the poor passengers were in; and if they were alive, to comfort them, and give them what refreshment was proper: and the surgeon gave him a large pitcher, with some of the prepared broth which he had given the mate that was on board, and which he did not question would restore them gradually.

I was not satisfied with this; but, as I said above, having a great mind to see the scene of misery which I knew the ship itself would present me with, in a more lively manner than I could have it by report, I took the captain of the ship, as we now called him, with me, and went myself, a little after, in their boat.

I found the poor men on board almost in a tumult, to get the victuals out of the boiler before it was ready; but my mate observed his orders, and kept a good guard at the cook-room door; and the man he placed there, after using all possible persuasion to have patience, kept them off by force: however he caused some biscuit-cakes to be dipped in the pot, and softened with the liquor of the meat, which they called brewis, and gave them every one some, to stay their stomachs, and told them it was for their own safety that he was obliged to give them but little at a time. But it was all in vain; and had I not come on board, and their own commander and officers with me, and with good words, and some threats also of giving them no more, I believe they would have broken into the cook-room by force, and torn the meat out of the furnace; for words are indeed of very small force to a hungry belly: however, we pacified them, and fed them gradually and cautiously for the first, and the next time gave them more, and at last we filled their bellies, and the men did well enough.

But the misery of the poor passengers in the cabin was of another nature, and far beyond the rest; for as the ship's company had so little for themselves, it was but too true that they had at first kept them very low, and at last totally neglected them; so that for six or seven days it might be said they had really no food at all, and for several days before very little. The poor mother, who, as the men reported, was a woman of sense and good breeding, had spared all she could so affectionately for her son, that at last she entirely sunk under it; and when the mate of our ship went in, she sat upon the floor or deck, with her back up against the sides, between two chairs, which were lashed fast, and her head sunk between her shoulders, like a corpse, though not quite dead. My mate said all he could to revive and encourage her, and with a spoon put some broth into her mouth. She opened her lips, and lifted up one hand, but could not speak; yet she understood what he said, and made signs to him, intimating that it was too late for her, but pointed to her child, as if she would have said they should take care of him. However, the mate, who was exceedingly moved with the sight, endeavoured to get some of the broth into her mouth, and, as he said got two or three spoonfuls down; though I question whether he could be sure of it or not: but it was too late, and she died the same night.

The youth, who was preserved at the price of his most affectionate mother's life, was not so far gone; yet he lay in a cabin-bed, as one stretched out, with hardly any life left in him. He had a piece of an old glove in his mouth, having eaten up the rest of it: however, being young, and having more strength than his mother, the mate got something down his throat, and he began sensibly to revive; though by giving him, some time after, but two or three spoonfuls extraordinary, he was very sick, and brought it up again.

But the next care was the poor maid: she lay all along upon the deck, hard by her mistress, and just like one that had fallen down with an apoplexy, and struggled for life. Her limbs were distorted; one of her hands was clasped round the frame of a chair, and she gripped it so hard, that we could not easily make her let it go: her other arm lay over her head, and her feet lay both together, set fast against the frame of the cabin-table: in short, she lay just like one in the agonies of death, and yet she was alive too.

The poor creature was not only starved with hunger, and terrified with the thoughts of death, but, as the men told us afterwards, was broken-hearted for her mistress, whom she saw dying for two or three days before, and whom she loved most tenderly.

We knew not what to do with this poor girl; for when our surgeon, who was a man of very great knowledge and experience, had with great application recovered her as to life, he had her upon his hands as to her senses; for she was little less than distracted for a considerable time after, as shall appear presently.

Whoever shall read these memorandums must be desired to consider, that visits at sea are not like a journey into the country, where sometimes people stay a week or a fortnight at a place: our business was to relieve this distressed ship's crew, but not lie by for them; and though they were willing to steer the same course with us for some days, yet we could carry no sail, to keep pace with a ship that had no masts: however, as their captain begged of us to help him to set up a main topmast, and a kind of topmast to his jury foremast, we did, as it were, lie by him for three or four days; and then having given him five barrels of beef, a barrel of pork, two hogsheads of biscuit, and a proportion of peas, flour, and what other things we could spare; and taking three casks of sugar, some rum, and some pieces-of-eight from them for satisfaction, we left them; taking on board with us, at their own earnest request, the youth and the maid, and all their goods.

The young lad was about seventeen years of age; a pretty, well-bred, modest, and sensible youth, greatly dejected with the loss of his mother, and, as it seems, had lost his father but a few months before, at Barbadoes: he begged of the surgeon to speak to me to take him out of the ship; for he said the cruel fellows had murdered his mother: and, indeed, so they had, that is to say passively; for they might have spared a small sustenance to the poor helpless widow that might have preserved her life, though it had been but just enough to keep her alive: but hunger knows no friend, no relation, no justice, no right; and therefore is remorseless, and capable of no compassion.

The surgeon told him how far we were going, and that it would carry him away from all his friends, and put him perhaps in as bad circumstances almost as those we found him in, that is to say, starving in the world. He said it mattered not whither he went, if he was but delivered from the terrible crew that he was among; that the captain (by which he meant me, for he could know nothing of my nephew) had saved his life, and he was sure would not hurt him; and as for the maid, he was sure, if she came to herself, she would be very thankful for it, let us carry them where we would. The surgeon represented the case so affectionately to me, that I yielded, and we took them both on board, with all their goods, except eleven hogsheads of sugar, which could not be removed or come at; and as the youth had a bill of lading for them, I made his commander sign a writing, obliging himself to go, as soon as he came to Bristol, to one Mr. Rogers, a merchant there, to whom the youth said he was related, and to deliver a letter which I wrote to him, and all the goods he had belonging to the deceased widow; which I suppose was not done, for I could never learn that the ship came to Bristol, but was, as it is most probable, lost at sea; being in so disabled a condition, and so far from any land, that I am of opinion the first storm she met with afterwards she might founder in the sea; for she was leaky and had damage in her hold, when we met with her.

I was now in the latitude of nineteen degrees thirty-two minutes, and had hitherto a tolerable voyage as to weather, though, at first, the winds had been contrary. I shall trouble nobody with the little incidents of wind, weather, currents, etc., on the rest of our voyage; but to shorten my story, for the sake of what is to follow, shall observe, that I came to my old habitation, the island, on the 10th of April, 1695. It was with no small difficulty that I found the place; for as I came to it, and went from it, before, on the south and east side of the island, as coming from the Brazils, so now, coming in between the main and the island, and having no chart for the coast, nor any landmark, I did not know it when I saw it, or know whether I saw it or not.

We beat about a great while, and went on shore on several islands in the mouth of the great river Oronoco, but none for my purpose; only this I learned by my coasting the shore, that I was under one great mistake before, viz., that the continent which I thought I saw from the island I lived in, was really not a continent, but a long island, or rather a ridge of islands, reaching from one to the other side of the extended mouth of that great river; and that the savages who came to my island were not properly those which we call Caribbees, but islanders, and other barbarians of the same kind, who inhabited something nearer to our side than the rest.

In short, I visited several of these islands to no purpose; some I found were inhabited, and some were not: on one of them I found some Spaniards, and thought they had lived there; but speaking with them, found they had a sloop lay in a small creek hard by, and came thither to make salt and to catch some pearl muscles, if they could; but that they belonged to the Isle de Trinidad, which lay farther north, in the latitude of ten and eleven degrees.

Thus coasting from one island to another, sometimes with the ship, sometimes with the Frenchmen's shallop, which we had found a convenient boat, and therefore kept her with their very good will, at length I came fair on the south side of my island, and presently knew the very countenance of the place: so I brought the ship safe to an anchor, broadside with the little creek where my old habitation was.

AS SOON AS I saw the place, I called for Friday, and asked him if he knew where he was; he looked about a little, and presently clapping his hands, cried, O yes, O there, O yes, O there, pointing to our old habitation, and fell dancing and capering like a mad fellow; and I had much ado to keep him from jumping into the sea, to swim ashore to the place.

Well, Friday, says I, do you think we shall find anybody here or no? and do you think we shall see your father? The fellow stood mute as a stock a good while, but when I named his father, the poor affectionate creature looked dejected, and I could see the tears run down his face very plentifully. What is the matter, Friday? says I; are you troubled because you may see your father? No, no, says he, shaking his head, no see him more: no, never more see him again. Why so, said I, Friday? how do you know that? O no, O no, says Friday; he long ago die, long ago; he much old man. Well, well, says I, Friday, you don't know; but shall we see any one else, then? The fellow, it seems, had better eyes than I, and he points to the hill just above my old house; and though we lay half a league off, he cries out, We see, we see, yes, yes, we see much man there, and there, and there. I looked, but I saw nobody, no, not with a perspective glass, which was, I suppose, because I could not hit the place; for the fellow was right, as I found upon inquiry the next day; and there were five or six men all together, who stood to look at the ship, not knowing what to think of us.

As soon as Friday told us he saw people, I caused the English *ancient* to be spread, and fired three guns, to give them notice we were friends; and in about half a quarter of an hour after, we perceived a smoke arise from the side of the creek; so I immediately ordered the boat out, taking Friday with me; and hanging out a white flag, or a flag of truce, I went directly on shore, taking with me the young friar I mentioned, to whom I had told the story of my living there, and the manner of it, and every particular both of myself and those I left there; and who was, on that account, extremely desirous to go with me. We had besides about sixteen men well armed, if we had found any new guests there which we did not know of; but we had no need of weapons.

As we went on shore upon the tide of flood, near high water, we rowed directly into the creek; and the first man I fixed my eye upon was the Spaniard whose life I had saved, and whom I knew by his face perfectly well: as to his habit, I shall describe it afterwards. I ordered nobody to go on shore at first but myself; but there was no keeping Friday in the boat, for the affectionate creature had spied his father at a distance, a good way off the Spaniards, where indeed I saw nothing of him; and if they had not let him go ashore, he would have jumped into the sea. He was no sooner on shore, but he flew away to his father, like an arrow out of a bow. It would have made any man shed tears, in spite of the firmest resolution, to have seen the first transports of this poor fellow's joy when he came to his father: how he embraced him, kissed him, stroked his face, took him up in his arms, set him down upon a tree, and lay down by him; then stood and looked at him, as any one would look at a strange picture, for a quarter of an hour together; then lay down on the ground, and stroked his legs, and kissed them, and then got up again, and stared at him; one would have thought the fellow bewitched. But it would have made a dog laugh the next day to see how his passion ran out another way; in the morning he walked along the shore, to and again, with his father several hours, always leading him by the hand, as if he had been a lady; and every now and then he would come to the boat to fetch something or other for him, either a lump of sugar, a dram, a biscuit-cake, or something or other that was good. In the afternoon his frolics ran another way; for then he would set the old man down upon the ground and dance about him, and make a thousand antic postures and gestures; and all the while he did this, he would be talking to him, and telling him one story or other of his travels, and of what had happened to him abroad, to divert him. In short, if the same filial affection was to be found in Christians to their parents in our part of the world, one would be tempted to say, there would hardly have been any need of the fifth commandment.

But this is a digression: I return to my landing. It would be needless to take notice of all the ceremonies and civilities that the Spaniards received me with. The first Spaniard, who, as I said, I knew very well, was he whose life I had saved: he came towards the boat, attended by one more, carrying a flag of truce also; and he not only did not know me at first, but he had no thoughts, no notion of its being me that was come, till I spoke to him. Senhor, said I, in Portuguese, do you not know me? At which he spoke not a word, but giving his musket to the man that was with him, threw his arms abroad, saying something in Spanish that I did not perfectly hear, came forward and embraced me; telling me he was inexcusable not to know that face again, that he had once seen as if an angel from heaven sent to save his life: he said abundance of very handsome things, as a well-bred Spaniard always knows how; and then beckoning to the person that attended him, bade him go and call out his comrades. He then asked me if I would walk to my old habitation, where he would give me possession of my own house again, and where I should see they had made but mean improvements: so I walked along with him; but, alas! I could no more find the place again than if I had never been there; for they had planted so many trees, and placed them in such a posture, so thick and close to one another, and in ten years' time they were grown so big, that, in short, the place was inaccessible, except by such windings and blind ways as they themselves only, who made them, could find.

I asked them what put them upon all these fortifications: he told me I would say there was need enough of it, when they had given me an account how they had passed their time since their arriving in the island, especially after they had the misfortune to find that I was gone. He told me he could not but have some satisfaction in my good fortune, when he heard that I was gone in a good ship, and to my satisfaction; and that he had oftentimes a strong persuasion that, one time or other, he should see me again; but nothing that ever befell him in his life, he said, was so surprising and afflicting to him at first, as the disappointment he was under when he came back to the island and found I was not there.

As to the three barbarians (so he called them) that were left behind, and of whom, he said, he had a long story to tell me, the Spaniards all thought themselves much better among the savages, only that their number was so small; and, says he, had they been strong enough, we had been long ago in purgatory; and with that he crossed himself on the breast. But, sir, says he, I hope you will not be displeased when I shall tell you how, forced by necessity, we were obliged, for our own preservation, to disarm them, and make them our subjects, who would not be content with being moderately our masters, but would be our murderers. I answered I was heartily afraid of it when I left them there, and nothing troubled me at my parting from the island but that they were not come back, that I might have put them in possession of everything first, and left the others in a state of subjection, as they deserved; but if they had reduced them to it, I was very glad, and should be very far from finding any fault with it; for I knew they were a parcel of refractory, ungoverned villains, and were fit for any manner of mischief.

While I was thus saying this, the man came whom he had sent back, and with him eleven men more. In the dress they were in, it was impossible to guess what nation they were of; but he made all clear, both to them and me. First he turned to me, and pointing to them, said, These, sir, are some of the gentlemen who owe their lives to you; and then turning to them, and pointing to me, he let them know who I was; upon which they all came up, one by one, not as if they had been sailors and ordinary fellows, and the like, but really as if they had been ambassadors of noblemen, and I a monarch or great conqueror: their behaviour was to the last degree obliging and courteous, and yet mixed with a manly, majestic gravity, which very well became them; and, in short, they had so much more manners than I, that I scarce knew how to receive their civilities, much less how to return them in kind.

The history of their coming to, and conduct in, the island, after my going away, is so very remarkable, and has so many incidents, which the former part of my relation will help to understand, and which will, in most of the particulars, refer to the account I have already given, that I cannot but commit them, with great delight, to the reading of those that come after me.

I shall no longer trouble the story with a relation in the first person, which will put me to the expense of ten thousand *said I's*, and *said he's*, and *he told me's*, and *I told him's*, and the like; but I shall collect the facts historically, as near as I can gather them out of my memory, from what they related to me, and from what I met with in my conversing with them and with the place.

In order to do this succinctly, and as intelligibly as I can, I must go back to the circumstances in which I left the island, and in which the persons were of whom I am to speak. And first, it is necessary to repeat, that I had sent away Friday's father and the Spaniard (the two whose lives I had rescued from the savages) in a large canoe, to the main, as I then thought it, to fetch over the Spaniard's companions that he left behind him, in order to save them from the like calamity that he had been in, and in order to succour them for the present; and that, if possible, we might together find some way for our deliverance afterwards.

When I sent them away, I had no visible appearance of, or the least room to hope for, my own deliverance, any more than I had twenty years before; much less had I any foreknowledge of what afterwards happened, I mean, of an English ship coming on shore there to fetch me off; and it could not but be a very great surprise to them, when they came back, not only to find that I was gone, but to find three strangers left on the spot, possessed of all that I had left behind me, which would otherwise have been their own.

The first thing, however, that I inquired into, that I might begin where I left off, was of their own part; and I desired he would give me a particular account of his voyage back to his countrymen with the boat, when I sent him to fetch them over. He told me there was little variety in that part, for nothing remarkable happened to them on the way, having had very calm weather and a smooth sea. As for his countrymen, it could not be doubted, he said, but that they were overjoyed to see him (it seems he was the principal man among them, the captain of the vessel they had been shipwrecked in having been dead some time); they were, he said, the more surprised to see him, because they knew that he was fallen into the hands of the savages, who, they were satisfied, would devour him, as they did all the rest of their prisoners; that when he told them the story of his deliverance, and in what manner he was furnished for carrying them away, it was like a dream to them, and their astonishment, he said, was somewhat like that of Joseph's brethren, when he told them who he was, and told them the story of his exaltation in Pharaoh's court; but when he showed them the arms, the powder, the ball, and provisions, that he brought them for their journey or voyage, they were restored to themselves, took a just share of the joy of their deliverance, and immediately prepared to come away with him.

Their first business was to get canoes: and in this they were obliged not to stick so much upon the honest part of it, but to trespass upon their friendly savages, and to borrow two large canoes, or periaguas, on pretence of going out a fishing, or for pleasure. In these they came away the next morning. It seems they wanted no time to get themselves ready; for they had no baggage, neither clothes, nor provisions, nor anything in the world but what they had on them, and a few roots to eat, of which they used to make their bread.

They were in all three weeks absent; and in that time, unluckily for them, I had the occasion offered for my escape, as I mentioned in my other part, and to get off from the island, leaving three of the most impudent, hardened, ungoverned, disagreeable villains behind me, that any man could desire to meet with; to the poor Spaniards' great grief and disappointment, you may be sure.

The only just thing the rogues did was, that when the Spaniards came ashore, they gave my letter to them, and gave them provisions, and other relief, as I had ordered them to do; also they gave them the long paper of directions which I had left with them, containing the particular methods which I took for managing every part of my life there; the way how I baked my bread, bred up my tame goats, and planted my corn; how I cured my grapes, made my pots, and in a word, everything I did; all this being written down, they gave to the Spaniards (two of them understood English well enough); nor did they refuse to accommodate the Spaniards with anything else, for they agreed very well for some time. They gave them an equal admission into the house, or cave, and they began to live very sociably; and the head Spaniard, who had seen pretty much of my methods, and Friday's father together, managed all their affairs: but as for the Englishmen, they did nothing but ramble about the island, shoot parrots, and catch tortoises; and when they came home at night, the Spaniards provided their suppers for them.

The Spaniards would have been satisfied with this, had the others but let them alone; which, however, they could not find in their hearts to do long, but, like the dog in the manger, they would not eat themselves, neither would they let the others eat. The differences, nevertheless, were at first but trivial, and such as are not worth relating, but at last it broke out into open war; and it began with all the rudeness and insolence that can be imagined, without reason, without provocation, contrary to nature, and, indeed, to common sense; and though, it is true, the first relation of it came from the Spaniards themselves, whom I may call the accusers, yet when I came to examine the fellows, they could not deny a word of it.

But before I come to the particulars of this part, I must supply a defect in my former relation; and this was, I forgot to set down, among the rest, that just as we were weighing the anchor to set sail, there happened a little quarrel on board of our ship, which I was once afraid would have turned to a second mutiny; nor was it appeased till the captain, rousing up his courage, and taking us all to his assistance, parted them by force, and making two of the most refractory fellows prisoners, he laid them in irons; and as they had been active in the former disorders, and let fall some ugly, dangerous words, the second time he threatened to carry them in irons to England, and have them hanged there for mutiny, and running away with the ship. This, it seems, though the captain did not intend to do it, frightened some other men in the ship; and some of them had put it into the heads of the rest that the captain only gave them good words for the present, till they should come to some English port, and that then they should be all put into gaol, and tried for their lives. The mate got intelligence of this, and acquainted us with it; upon which it was desired that I, who still passed for a great man among them, should go down with the mate, and satisfy the men, and tell them that they might be assured, if they behaved well the rest of the voyage, all they had done for the time past should be pardoned. So I went, and after passing my honour's word to them, they appeared easy, and the more so when I caused the two men that were in irons to be released and forgiven.

But this mutiny had brought us to an anchor for that night; the wind also falling calm next morning, we found that our two men who had been laid in irons had stole each of them a musket, and some other weapons (what powder or shot they had we knew not), and had taken the ship's pinnace, which was not yet hauled up, and run away with her to their companions in roguery on shore. As soon as we found this, I ordered the long-boat on shore, with twelve men and the mate, and away they went to seek the rogues; but they could neither find them or any of the rest, for they all fled into the woods when they saw the boat coming on shore. The mate was once resolved, in justice to their roguery, to have destroyed their plantations, burned all their household stuff and furniture, and left them to shift without it; but having no orders, he let it all alone, left everything as he found it, and bringing the pinnace away, came on board without them. These two men made their number five; but the other three villains were so much more wicked than they, that after they had been two or three days together, they turned the two new comers out of doors to shift for themselves, and would have nothing to do with them; nor could they, for a good while, be persuaded to give them any food: as for the Spaniards, they are not yet come.

When the Spaniards came first on shore, the business began to go forward: the Spaniards would have persuaded the three English brutes to have taken in their two countrymen again, that, as they said, they might be all one family; but they would not hear of it; so the two poor fellows lived by themselves; and finding nothing but industry and application would make them live comfortably, they pitched their tents on the north shore of the island, but a little more to the west, to be out of danger of the savages, who always landed on the east parts of the island.

Here they built them two huts, one to lodge in, and the other to lay up their magazines and stores in; and the Spaniards having given them some corn for seed, and especially some of the peas which I had left them, they dug, planted, and enclosed, after the pattern I had set for them all, and began to live pretty well. Their first crop of corn was on the ground; and though it was but a little bit of land which they had dug up at first, having had but a little time, yet it was enough to relieve them, and find them with bread and other eatables; and one of the fellows, being the cook's mate of the ship, was very ready at making soup, puddings, and such other preparations as the rice and the milk, and such little flesh as they got, furnished him to do.

THEY WERE GOING ON in this little thriving posture, when the three unnatural rogues, their own countrymen too, in mere humour, and to insult them, came and bullied them, and told them the island was theirs; that the governor, meaning me, had given them the possession of it, and nobody else had any right to it; and that they should build no houses upon their ground, unless they would pay rent for them.

The two men, thinking they were jesting at first, asked them to come in and sit down, and see what fine houses they were that they had built, and to tell them what rent they demanded; and one of them merrily said, if they were the ground-landlords, he hoped, if they built tenements upon their land, and made improvements, they would, according to the customs of landlords, grant a long lease; and desired they would get a scrivener to draw the writings. One of the three, cursing and raging, told them they should see they were not in jest; and going to a little place at a distance, where the honest men had made a fire to dress their victuals, he takes a fire-brand, and claps it to the outside of their hut, and very fairly set it on fire; and it would have been burned all down in a few minutes, if one of the two had not run to the fellow, thrust him away, and trod the fire out with his feet, and that not without some difficulty too.

The fellow was in such a rage at the honest man's thrusting him away, that he returned upon him, with a pole he had in his hand, and had not the man avoided the blow very nimbly, and run into the hut, he had ended his days at once. His comrade, seeing the danger they were both in, ran in after him, and immediately they came both out with their muskets, and the man that was first struck at with the pole knocked the fellow down that had begun the quarrel with the stock of his musket, and that before the other two could come to help him; and then seeing the rest come at them, they stood together, and presenting the other ends of their pieces to them, bade them stand off.

The others had fire-arms with them too; but one of the two honest men, bolder than his comrade, and made desperate by his danger, told them, if they offered to move hand or foot they were dead men, and boldly commanded them to lay down their arms. They did not, indeed, lay down their arms, but seeing him so resolute, it brought them to a parley, and they consented to take their wounded man with them and be gone; and, indeed, it seems the fellow was wounded sufficiently with the blow. However, they were much in the wrong, since they had the advantage, that they did not disarm them effectually, as they might have done, and have gone immediately to the Spaniards, and given them an account how the rogues had treated them; for the three villains studied nothing but revenge, and every day gave them some intimation that they did so.

But not to crowd this part with an account of the lesser part of the rogueries, such as treading down their corn, shooting three young kids and a she-goat, which the poor men had got to breed up tame for their store; and, in a word, plaguing them night and day in this manner; it forced the two men to such a desperation, that they resolved to fight them all three, the first time they had a fair opportunity. In order to this, they resolved to go to the castle, as they called it (that was my old dwelling), where the three rogues and the Spaniards all lived together at that time, intending to have a fair battle, and the Spaniards should stand by to see fair play: so they got up in the morning before day, and came to the place, and called the Englishmen by their names, telling a Spaniard that answered that they wanted to speak with them.

It happened that the day before, two of the Spaniards, having been in the woods, had seen one of the two Englishmen, whom for distinction, I called the honest men, and he had made a sad complaint to the Spaniards of the barbarous usage they had met with from their three countrymen, and how they had ruined their plantation, and destroyed their corn that they had laboured so hard to bring forward, and killed the milch goat and their three kids, which was all they had provided for their sustenance; and that if he and his friends, meaning the Spaniards, did not assist them again, they should be starved. When the Spaniards came home at night, and they were all at supper, one of them took the freedom to reprove the three Englishmen, though in very gentle and mannerly terms, and asked them how they could be so cruel, they being harmless, inoffensive fellows; that they were putting themselves in a way to subsist by their labour, and that it had cost them a great deal of pains to bring things to such perfection as they were then in.

One of the Englishmen returned very briskly, what had they to do there? that they came on shore without leave; and that they should not plant or build upon the island; it was none of their ground. Why, says the Spaniard, very calmly, Senhor Inglese, they must not starve. The Englishman replied, like a rough-hewn tarpauling, they might starve and be d—d; they should not plant nor build in that place. But what must they do then, senhor? said the Spaniard. Another of the brutes returned, Do? d—n them, they should be servants, and work for them. But how can you expect that of them? says the Spaniard; they are not bought with your money: you have no right to make them servants. The Englishman answered, the island was theirs; the governor had given it to them, and no man had anything to do there but themselves; and with that swore by his Maker that they would go and burn all their new huts; they should build none upon their land. Why, senhor, says the Spaniard, by the same rule, we must be your servants too.—Ay, says the bold dog, and so you shall too, before we have done with you; (mixing two or three G— d— me's in the proper intervals of his speech). The Spaniard only smiled at that, and made him no answer. However, this little discourse had heated them; and, starting up, one says to the other, I think it was he they called Will Atkins, Come, Jack, let's go, and have t'other brush with 'em; we'll demolish their castle, I'll warrant you; they shall plant no colony in our dominions.

Upon this they went all trooping away, with every man a gun, a pistol, and a sword, and muttered some insolent things among themselves, of what they would do to the Spaniards too, when opportunity offered; but the Spaniards, it seems, did not so perfectly understand them as to know all the particulars, only that, in general, they threatened them hard for taking the two Englishmen's part.

Whither they went, or how they bestowed their time that evening, the Spaniards said they did not know; but it seems they wandered about the country part of the night, and then lying down in the place which I used to call my bower, they were weary, and overslept themselves. The case was this; they had resolved to stay till midnight, and so take the poor men when they were asleep, and, as they acknowledged afterwards, intended to set fire to their huts while they were in them, and either burn them there, or murder them as they came out; as malice seldom sleeps very sound, it was very strange they should not have been kept awake.

However, as the two men had also a design upon them, as I have said, though a much fairer one than that of burning and murdering, it happened, and very luckily for them all, that they were up, and gone abroad, before the bloody-minded rogues came to their huts.

When they came there, and found the men gone, Atkins, who, it seems, was the forwardest man, called out to his comrade, Ha, Jack, here's the nest, but, d—n them, the birds are flown. They mused awhile, to think what should be the occasion of their being gone abroad so soon, and suggested presently that the Spaniards had given them notice of it; and with that they shook hands, and swore to one another that they would be revenged of the Spaniards. As soon as they had made this bloody bargain, they fell to work with the poor men's habitation: they did not set fire, indeed, to anything, but they pulled down both their houses, and pulled them so limb from limb, that they left not the least stick standing, or scarce any sign on the ground where they stood; they tore all their little collected household-stuff in pieces, and threw everything about in such a manner, that the poor men afterwards found some of their things a mile off their habitation. When they had done this, they pulled up all the young trees which the poor men had planted; pulled up an enclosure they had made to secure their cattle and their corn; and, in a word, sacked and plundered everything as completely as a horde of Tartars would have done.

The two men were, at this juncture, gone to find them out, and had resolved to fight them wherever they had been, though they were but two to three; so, that, had they met, there certainly would have been bloodshed among them; for they were all very stout, resolute fellows, to give them their due.

But Providence took more care to keep them asunder than they themselves could do to meet: for as if they had dogged one another, when the three were gone thither, the two were here; and afterwards, when the two went back to find them, the three were come to the old habitation again: we shall see their different conduct presently. When the three came back like furious creatures, flushed with the rage which the work they had been about had put them into, they came up to the Spaniards, and told them what they had done, by way of scoff and bravado; and one of them, stepping up to one of the Spaniards, as if they had been a couple of boys at play, takes hold of his hat as it was upon his head, and giving it a twirl about, fleering in his face, says to him, and you, Senhor Jack Spaniard, shall have the same sauce, if you do not mend your manners. The Spaniard, who, though a quiet, civil man, was as brave a man as could be, and withal a strong, well-made man, looked at him for a good while, and then, having no weapon in his hand, stepped gravely up to him, and with one blow of his fist knocked him down, as an ox is felled with a pole-axe; at which one of the rogues, as insolent as the first, fired his pistol at the Spaniard immediately; he missed his body, indeed, for the bullets went through his hair, but one of them touched the tip of his ear, and he bled pretty much. The blood made the

Spaniard believe he was more hurt than he really was, and that put him into some heat, for before he acted all in a perfect calm; but now resolving to go through with his work, he stooped, and took the fellow's musket whom he had knocked down, and was just going to shoot the man who had fired at him, when the rest of the Spaniards, being in the cave, came out, and calling to him not to shoot, they stepped in, secured the other two, and took their arms from them.

When they were thus disarmed, and found they had made all the Spaniards their enemies, as well as their own countrymen, they began to cool, and, giving the Spaniards better words, would have their arms again; but the Spaniards, considering the feud that was between them and the other two Englishmen, and that it would be the best method they could take to keep them from killing one another, told them they would do them no harm, and if they would live peaceably, they would be very willing to assist and associate with them as they did before; but that they could not think of giving them their arms again, while they appeared so resolved to do mischief with them to their own countrymen, and had even threatened them all to make them their servants.

The rogues were now no more capable to hear reason than to act with reason; but being refused their arms, they went raving away, and raging like madmen, threatening what they would do, though they had no firearms. But the Spaniards, despising their threatening, told them they should take care how they offered any injury to their plantation or cattle, for if they did, they would shoot them as they would ravenous beasts, wherever they found them; and if they fell into their hands alive, they should certainly be hanged. However, this was far from cooling them, but away they went, raging and swearing like furies of hell. As soon as they were gone, the two men came back, in passion and rage enough also, though of another kind; for having been at their plantation, and finding it all demolished and destroyed, as above, it will easily be supposed that they had provocation enough. They could scarce have room to tell their tale, the Spaniards were so eager to tell theirs; and it was strange enough to find that three men should thus bully nineteen, and receive no punishment at all.

The Spaniards, indeed, despised them, and especially, having thus disarmed them, made light of their threatenings; but the two Englishmen resolved to have their remedy against them, what pains soever it cost to find them out. But the Spaniards interposed here too, and told them, that as they had disarmed them, they could not consent that they (the two) should pursue them with fire-arms, and perhaps kill them. But, said the grave Spaniard, who was their governor, we will endeavour to make them do you justice, if you will leave it to us; for there is no doubt but they will come to us again, when their passion is over, being not able to subsist without our assistance: we promise you to make no peace with them, without having a full satisfaction for you; and upon this condition we hope you will promise to use no violence with them, other than in your own defence. The two Englishmen yielded to this very awkwardly, and with great reluctance; but the Spaniards protested that they did it only to keep them from bloodshed, and to make all easy at last. For, said they, we are not so many of us; here is room enough for us all; and it is a great pity we should not be all good friends. At length they did consent, and waited for the issue of the thing, living for some days with the Spaniards; for their own habitation was destroyed.

In about five days' time the three vagrants, tired with wandering, and almost starved with hunger, having chiefly lived on turtles' eggs all that while, came back to the grove; and finding my Spaniard, who, as I have said, was the governor, and two more with him walking by the side of the creek, they came up in a very submissive, humble manner, and begged to be received again into the family. The Spaniards used them civilly, but told them they had acted so unnaturally by their countrymen, and so very grossly by them (the Spaniards), that they could not come to any conclusion without consulting the two Englishmen and the rest; but, however, they would go to them, and discourse about it, and they should know in half an hour. It may be guessed that they were very hard put to it: for, it seems, as they were to wait this half-hour for an answer, they begged they would send them out some bread in the mean time, which they did; sending, at the same time, a large piece of goat's flesh, and a boiled parrot, which they ate very heartily, for they were hungry enough.

After half an hour's consultation, they were called in, and a long debate ensued; their two countrymen charging them with the ruin of all their labour, and a design to murder them; all which they owned before, and therefore could not deny now. Upon the whole, the Spaniards acted the moderator between them; and as they had obliged the two Englishmen not to hurt the three while they were naked and unarmed, so they now obliged the three to go and rebuild their fellows' two huts, one to be of the same, and the other of larger dimensions, than they were before; to fence their ground again where they had pulled up their fences, plant trees in the room of those pulled up, dig up the land again for planting corn where they had spoiled it, and, in a word, to restore everything in the same state as they found it, as near as they could; for entirely it could not be, the season for the corn, and the growth of the trees and hedges, not being possible to be recovered.

Well, they submitted to all this; and as they had plenty of provisions given them all the while, they grew very orderly, and the whole society began to live pleasantly and agreeably together again; only, that these three fellows could never be persuaded to work, I mean for themselves, except now and then a little, just as they pleased: however, the Spaniards told them plainly, that if they would but live sociably and friendly together, and study the good of the whole plantation, they would be content to work for them, and let them walk about and be as idle as they pleased: and thus having lived pretty well together for about a month or two, the Spaniards gave them arms again, and gave them liberty to go abroad with them as before.

It was not above a week after they had these arms, and went abroad, but the ungrateful creatures began to be as insolent and troublesome as before: but, however, an accident happened presently upon this, which endangered the safety of them all; and they were obliged to lay by all private resentments, and look to the preservation of their lives.

It happened one night that the Spanish governor, as I call him, that is to say, the Spaniard whose life I had saved, who was now the captain, or leader, or governor of the rest, found himself very uneasy in the night, and could by no means get any sleep: he was perfectly well in body, as he told me the story, only found his thoughts tumultuous; his mind ran upon men fighting and killing of one another, but he was broad awake, and could not by any means get any sleep: in short, he lay a great while; but growing more and more uneasy, he resolved to rise. As they lay, being so many of them, upon goats' skins laid thick upon such couches and pads as they had made for themselves, and not in hammocks and ship beds, as I did, who was but one, so they had little to do, when they were willing to rise, but to get up upon their feet, and perhaps put on a coat, such as it was, and their pumps, and they were ready for going any way that their thoughts guided them. Being thus got up, he looked out: but, being dark, he could see little or nothing; and besides, the trees which I had planted, as in my former account is described, and which were now grown tall, intercepted his sight, so that he could only look up, and see that it was a clear starlight night, and hearing no noise, he returned and laid him down again: but it was all one; he could not sleep, nor could he compose himself to anything like rest; but his thoughts were to the last degree uneasy, and he knew not for what.

Having made some noise with rising and walking about, going out and coming in, another of them waked, and calling, asked who it was that was up. The governor told him how it had been with him. Say you so? says the other Spaniard; such things are not to be slighted, I assure you; there is certainly some mischief working near us; and presently he asked him, Where are the Englishmen?—They are all in their huts, says he, safe enough. It seems the Spaniards had kept possession of the main apartment, and had made a place for the three Englishmen, who, since their last mutiny, were always quartered by themselves, and could not come at the rest. Well, says the Spaniard, there is something in it, I am persuaded, from my own experience. I am satisfied our spirits embodied have a converse with, and receive intelligence from, the spirits unembodied, and inhabiting the invisible world; and this friendly notice is given for our advantage, if we knew how to make use of it. Come, says he, let us go and look abroad; and if we find nothing at all in it to justify the trouble, I'll tell you a story to the purpose, that shall convince you of the justice of my proposing it.

In a word, they went out, to go up to the top of the hill where I used to go; but they being strong, and a good company, not alone, as I was, used none of my cautions, to go up by the ladder, and pulling it up after them, to go up a second stage to the top, but were going round through the grove, unconcerned and unwary, when they were surprised with seeing a light as of fire, a very little way off from them, and hearing the voices of men, not one or two, but of a great number.

In all the discoveries I had made of the savages landing on the island, it was my constant care to prevent them making the least discovery of there being any inhabitant upon the place; and when by any occasion they came to know it, they felt it so effectually, that they that got away were scarce able to give any account of it; for we disappeared as soon as possible; nor did ever any that had seen me, escape to tell any one else, except it was the three savages in our last encounter, who jumped into the boat, of whom I mentioned, I was afraid they should go home and bring more help. Whether it was the consequence of the escape of those men that so great a number came now together, or whether they came ignorantly, and by accident, on their usual bloody errand, the Spaniards could not, it seems, understand; but whatever it was, it had been their business either to have concealed themselves, or not to have seen them at all, much less to have let the savages have seen that there were any inhabitants in the place; or to have fallen upon them so effectually, as that not a man of them should have escaped, which could only have been by getting in between them and their boats; but this presence of mind was wanting to them, which was the ruin of their tranquillity for a great while.

We need not doubt but that the governor and the man with him, surprised with this sight, ran back immediately, and raised their fellows, giving them an account of the imminent danger they were all in, and they again as readily took the alarm; but it was impossible to persuade them to stay close within, where they were, but they must all run out to see how things stood.

While it was dark, indeed, they were well enough, and they had opportunity enough for some hours, to view them by the light of three fires they had made at a distance from one another; what they were doing they knew not, and what to do themselves they knew not. For, first, the enemy were too many; and, secondly, they did not keep together, but were divided into several parties, and were on shore in several places.

The Spaniards were in no small consternation at this sight; and when they found that the fellows ran straggling all over the shore, they made no doubt but, first or last, some of them would chop in upon their habitation, or upon some other place where they would see the token of inhabitants; and they were in great perplexity also for fear of their flock of goats, which would have been little less than starving them, if they should have been destroyed: so the first thing they resolved upon was to despatch three men away before it was light, two Spaniards and one Englishman to drive all the goats away to the great valley where the cave was, and, if need were, to drive them into the very cave itself. Could they have seen the savages all together in one body, and at a distance from their canoes, they resolved, if there had been a hundred of them, to have attacked them; but that could not be obtained; for they were some of them two miles off from the other; and, as it appeared afterwards, were of two different nations.

After having mused a great while on the course they should take, and beating their brains in considering their present circumstances, they resolved, at last, while it was still dark, to send the old savage, Friday's father, out as a spy, to learn, if possible, something concerning them; as what they came for, what they intended to do, and the like. The old man readily undertook it; and stripping himself quite naked, as most of the savages were, away he went. After he had been gone an hour or two, he brings word that he had been among them undiscovered; that he found they were two parties, and of two several nations, who had war with one another, and had a great battle in their own country; and that both sides having had several prisoners taken in the fight, they were, by mere chance, landed all on the same island, for the devouring their prisoners and making merry, but their coming so by chance to the same place had spoiled all their mirth; that they were in great rage at one another, and were so near, that he believed they would fight again as soon as daylight began to appear: but he did not perceive that they had any notion of anybody being on the island but themselves. He had hardly made an end of telling his story, when they could perceive, by the unusual noise they made, that the two little armies were engaged in a bloody fight.

Friday's father used all the arguments he could to persuade our people to lie close, and not be seen: he told them their safety consisted in it, and that they had nothing to do but lie still, and the savages would kill one another to their hands, and then the rest would go away; and it was so to a tittle. But it was impossible to prevail, especially upon the Englishmen; their curiosity was so importunate upon their prudentials, that they must run out and see the battle: however, they used some caution too, viz., they did not go openly, just by their own dwelling, but went farther into the woods, and placed themselves to advantage, where they might securely see them manage the fight, and, as they thought, not be seen by them; but it seems the savages did see them, as we shall find hereafter.

The battle was very fierce; and, if I might believe the Englishmen, one of them said he could perceive that some of them were men of great bravery, of invincible spirits, and of great policy in guiding the fight.

The battle, they said, held two hours before they could guess which party would be beaten; but then, that party which was nearest our people's habitation began to appear weakest, and, after some time more, some of them began to fly; and this put our men again into a great consternation, lest any one of those that fled should run into the grove before their dwelling for shelter, and thereby involuntarily discover the place; and that, by consequence, the pursuers would do the like in search of them. Upon this they resolved that they would stand armed within the wall, and whoever came into the grove, they resolved to sally out over the wall and kill them: so that, if possible, not one should return to give an account of it, they ordered also that it should be done with their swords, or by knocking them down with the stocks of their muskets, but not by shooting them, for fear of raising an alarm by the noise.

As they expected, it fell out: three of the routed army fled for life, and crossing the creek, ran directly into the place, not in the least knowing whither they went, but running as into a thick wood for shelter. The scout they kept to look abroad gave notice of this within, with this addition, to our men's great satisfaction, viz., that the conquerors had not pursued them, or seen which way they were gone; upon this, the Spanish governor, a man of humanity, would not suffer them to kill the three fugitives, but sending three men out by the top of the hill, ordered them to go round, come in behind them, and surprise and take them prisoners; which was done. The residue of the conquered people fled to their canoes, and got off to sea; the victors retired, made no pursuit, or very little, but drawing themselves into a body together, gave two screaming shouts, which they supposed was by way of triumph, and so the fight ended: and the same day, about three o'clock in the afternoon, they also marched to their canoes. And thus the Spaniards had their island again free to themselves, their fight was over, and they saw no more savages in several years after.

After they were all gone, the Spaniards came out of their den, and viewing the field of battle, they found about two-and-thirty men dead on the spot: some were killed with great long arrows, some of which were found sticking in their bodies; but most of them were killed with great wooden swords, sixteen or seventeen of which they found on the field of battle, and as many bows, with a great many arrows. These swords were strange, great, unwieldy things, and they must be very strong men that used them: most of those men that were killed with them had their heads mashed to pieces, as we may say, or, as we call it in English, their brains knocked out, and several their arms and legs broken; so that it is evident they fight with inexpressible rage and fury. They found not one man that was not stone dead, for either they stay by their enemy till they have quite killed him, or they carry all the wounded men that are not quite dead away with them.

This deliverance tamed our Englishmen for a great while; the sight had filled them with horror, and the consequences appeared terrible to the last degree, especially upon supposing that some time or other they should fall into the hands of those creatures, who would not only kill them as enemies, but kill them for food, as we kill our cattle; and they professed to me, that the thoughts of being eaten up like beef or mutton, though it was supposed it was not to be till they were dead, had something in it so horrible, that it nauseated their very stomachs, made them sick when they thought of it, and filled their minds with such unusual terror, they were not themselves for some weeks after. This, as I said, tamed even the three English brutes I have been speaking of, and, for a great while after, they were tractable, and went about the common business of the whole society well enough; planted, sowed, reaped, and began to be all naturalised to the country. But some time after this, they fell into such simple measures again, as brought them into a great deal of trouble.

They had taken three prisoners, as I observed; and these three being lusty, stout young fellows, they made them servants, and taught them to work for them; and, as slaves, they did well enough; but they did not take their measures with them as I did by my man Friday, viz., to begin with them upon the principle of having saved their lives, and then instruct them upon the rational principles of life; much less of religion, civilising, and reducing them by kind usage and affectionate arguings; but as they gave them their food every day, so they gave them their work too, and kept them fully employed in drudgery enough; but they failed in this by it, that they never had them to assist them, and fight for them, as I had my man Friday, who was as true to me as the very flesh upon my bones.

But to come to the family part. Being all now good friends, for common danger, as I said above, had effectually reconciled them, they began to consider their general circumstances; and the first thing that came under their consideration, was, whether, seeing the savages particularly haunted that side of the island, and that there were more remote and retired parts of it equally adapted to their way of living and manifestly to their advantage, they should not rather move their habitation, and plant in some proper place for their safety, and especially for the security of their cattle and corn.

Upon this, after long debate, it was concluded that they would not remove their habitation; because that, some time or other, they thought they might hear from their governor again, meaning me; and if I should send any one to seek them, I should be sure to direct them to that side; where, if they should find the place demolished, they would conclude the savages had killed us all, and we were gone; and so our supply would go too. But as to their corn and cattle, they agreed to remove them into the valley where my cave was, where the land was as proper for both, and where indeed, there was land enough: however, upon second thoughts, they altered one part of their resolution too, and resolved only to remove part of their cattle thither, and plant part of their corn there; and so if one part was destroyed, the other might be saved. And one part of prudence they used, which it was very well they did, viz., that they never trusted those three savages, which they had prisoners, with knowing anything of the plantation they had made in that valley, or of any cattle they had there, much less of the cave there, which they kept, in case of necessity, as a safe retreat; and thither they carried also the two barrels of powder which I had sent them at my coming away. But however they resolved not to change their habitation, yet they agreed, that as I had carefully covered it first with a wall or fortification, and then with a grove of trees, so seeing their safety consisted entirely in their being concealed, of which they were now fully convinced, they set to work to cover and conceal the place yet more effectually than before. For this purpose, as I planted trees, or rather thrust in stakes, which in time all grew up to be trees, for some good distance before the entrance into my apartments, they went on in the same manner, and filled up the rest of that whole space of ground, from the trees I had set, quite down to the side of the creek, where, as I said, I landed my floats, and even into the very ooze where the tide flowed, not so much as leaving any place to land, or any sign that there had been any landing thereabout: these stakes also being of a wood very forward to grow, as I have noted formerly, they took care to have them generally much larger and taller than those which I had planted; and as they grew apace, so they planted them so very thick and close together, that when they had been three or four years grown, there was no piercing with the eye any considerable way into the plantation: and, as for that part which I had planted, the trees were grown as thick as a man's thigh, and among them they placed so many other short ones, and so thick, that, in a word, it stood like a palisade a quarter of a mile thick, and it was next to impossible to penetrate it, but with a little army to cut it all down; for a little dog could hardly get between the trees, they stood so close.

But this was not all; for they did the same by all the ground to the right hand and to the left, and round even to the top of the hill, leaving no way, not so much as for themselves to come out, but by the ladder placed up to the side of the hill, and then lifted up, and placed again from the first stage up to the top, and when the ladder was taken down, nothing but what had wings or witchcraft to assist it, could come at them. This was excellently well contrived; nor was it less than what they afterwards found occasion for; which served to convince me, that as human prudence has the authority of Providence to justify it, so it has doubtless the direction of Providence to set it to work; and if we listened carefully to the voice of it, I am persuaded we might prevent many of the disasters which our lives are now, by our own negligence, subjected to: but this by the way.

I return to the story.—They lived two years after this in perfect retirement, and had no more visits from the savages. They had indeed an alarm given them one morning, which put them into a great consternation; for some of the Spaniards being out early one morning on the west side, or rather end, of the island (which was that end where I never went, for fear of being discovered), they were surprised with seeing above twenty canoes of Indians just coming on shore. They made the best of their way home, in hurry enough; and giving the alarm to their comrades, they kept close all that day and the next, going out only at night to make their observation: but they had the good luck to be mistaken; for wherever the savages went, they did not land that time on the island, but pursued some other design.

And now they had another broil with the three Englishmen, one of whom, a most turbulent fellow, being in a rage at one of the three slaves, which I mentioned they had taken, because the fellow had not done something which he bid him do, and seemed a little untractable in his showing him, drew a hatchet out of a frog-belt, in which he wore it by his side, and fell upon the poor savage, not to correct him, but to kill him. One of the Spaniards, who was by, seeing him give the fellow a barbarous cut with the hatchet, which he aimed at his head, but struck into his shoulders, so that he thought he had cut the poor creature's arm off, ran to him, and entreating him not to murder the poor man, placed himself between him and the savage, to prevent the mischief. The fellow being enraged the more at this, struck at the Spaniard with his hatchet, and swore he would serve him as he intended to serve the savage; which the Spaniard perceiving, avoided the blow, and, with a shovel which he had in his hand (for they were all working in the field above their corn-land) knocked the brute down. Another of the Englishmen running at the same time to help his comrade, knocked the Spaniard down; and then two Spaniards more came in to help their man, and a third Englishman fell in upon them. They had none of them any fire-arms, or any other weapons but hatchets and other tools, except this third Englishman; he had one of my rusty cutlasses, with which he made at the two last Spaniards, and wounded them both. This fray set the whole family in an uproar, and more help coming in, they took the three Englishmen prisoners. The next question was, what should be done with them? They had been so often mutinous, and were so very furious, so very desperate, and so idle withal, they knew not what course to take with them, for they were mischievous to the highest degree, and valued not what hurt they did to any man; so that, in short, it was not safe to live with them.

The Spaniard who was governor told them, in so many words, that if they had been of his country, he would have hanged them; for all laws and all governors were to preserve society, and those who were dangerous to the society ought to be expelled out of it; but as they were Englishmen, and that it was to the generous kindness of an Englishman that they all owed their preservation and deliverance, he would use them with all possible lenity, and would leave them to the judgment of the other two Englishmen, who were their countrymen.

One of the two honest Englishmen stood up, and said they desired it might not be left to them; For, says he, I am sure we ought to sentence them to the gallows: and with that he gives an account how Will Atkins, one of the three, had proposed to have all the five Englishmen join together, and murder all the Spaniards when they were in their sleep.

When the Spanish governor heard this, he calls to Will Atkins, How, Senhor Atkins, would you murder us all? What have you to say to that? The hardened villain was so far from denying it, that he said it was true; and, G—d d—n him, they would do it still, before they had done with them. Well, but Senhor Atkins, says the Spaniard, what have we done to you, that you will kill us? And what would you get by killing us? And what must we do to prevent your killing us? Must we kill you, or you kill us? Why will you put us to the necessity of this, Senhor Atkins? says the Spaniard very calmly and smiling. Senhor Atkins was in such a rage at the Spaniard's making a jest of it, that, had he not been held by three men, and withal had no weapon near him, it was thought he would have attempted to have killed the Spaniard in the middle of all the company. This hairbrain carriage obliged them to consider seriously what was to be done: the two Englishmen, and the Spaniard who saved the poor savage, were of the opinion that they should hang one of the three, for an example to the rest; and that particularly it should be he that had twice attempted to commit murder with his hatchet; and, indeed, there was some reason to believe he had done it, for the poor savage was in such a miserable condition with the wound he had received, that it was thought he could not live. But the governor Spaniard still said no; it was an Englishman that had saved all their lives, and he would never consent to put an Englishman to death, though he had murdered half of them; nay, he said, if he had been killed himself by an Englishman, and had time left to speak, it should be that they should pardon him.

This was so positively insisted on by the governor Spaniard, that there was no gainsaying it; and as merciful counsels are most apt to prevail, where they are so earnestly pressed, so they all came into it: but then it was to be considered what should be done to keep them from doing the mischief they designed; for all agreed, governor and all, that means were to be used for preserving the society from danger. After a long debate, it was agreed, first, that they should be disarmed, and not permitted to have either gun, powder, shot, sword, or any weapon; and should be turned out of the society, and left to live where they would, and how they would, by themselves; but that none of the rest, either Spaniards or English, should converse with them, speak with them, or have anything to do with them: that they should be forbid to come within a certain distance of the place where the rest dwelt; and if they offered to commit any disorder, so as to spoil, burn, kill, or destroy any of the corn, plantings, buildings, fences, or cattle belonging to the society, they should die without mercy, and they would shoot them wherever they could find them.

The governor, a man of great humanity, musing upon the sentence, considered a little upon it; and turning to the two honest Englishmen, said, Hold; you must reflect that it will be long ere they can raise corn and cattle of their own, and they must not starve; we must therefore allow them provisions: so he caused to be added, that they should have a proportion of corn given them to last them eight months, and for seed to sow, by which they might be supposed to raise some of their own; that they should have six milch-goats, four he-goats, and six kids given them, as well for present subsistence as for a store; and that they should have tools given them for their work in the fields, such as six hatchets, an adze, a saw, and the like; but they should have none of these tools or provisions, unless they would swear solemnly that they would not hurt or injure any of the Spaniards with them, or of their fellow Englishmen.

Thus they dismissed them the society, and turned them out to shift for themselves. They went away sullen and refractory, as neither content to go away nor to stay; but as there was no remedy, they went, pretending to go and choose a place where they would settle themselves, and some provisions were given them, but no weapons.

About four or five days after, they came again for some victuals, and gave the governor an account where they had pitched their tents, and marked themselves out a habitation and plantation; and it was a very convenient place, indeed, on the remotest part of the island, N.E., much about the place where I providentially landed in my first voyage, when I was driven out to sea, the Lord alone knows whither, in my foolish attempt to sail round the island.

Here they built themselves two handsome huts, and contrived them in a manner like my first habitation, being close under the side of a hill, having some trees growing already on three sides of it, so that by planting others, it would be very easily covered from the sight, unless narrowly searched for. They desired some dried goats' skins, for beds and covering, which were given them; and upon giving their words that they would not disturb the rest, or injure any of their plantations, they gave them hatchets, and what other tools they could spare; some peas, barley, and rice, for sowing; and, in a word, anything they wanted, except arms and ammunition.

They lived in this separate condition about six months, and had got in their first harvest, though the quantity was but small, the parcel of land they had planted being but little; for, indeed, having all their plantation to form, they had a great deal of work upon their hands; and when they came to make boards and pots, and such things, they were quite out of their element, and could make nothing of it: and when the rainy season came on, for want of a cave in the earth, they could not keep their grain dry, and it was in great danger of spoiling; and this humbled them much; so they came and begged the Spaniards to help them, which they very readily did; and in four days worked a great hole in the side of the hill for them, big enough to secure their corn and other things from the rain: but it was but a poor place, at best, compared to mine, and especially as mine was then, for the Spaniards had greatly enlarged it, and made several new apartments in it.

About three-quarters of a year after this separation, a new frolic took these rogues, which, together with the former villainy they had committed, brought mischief enough upon them, and had very near been the ruin of the whole colony. The three new associates began, it seems, to be weary of the laborious life they led, and that without hope of bettering their circumstances: and a whim took them, that they would make a voyage to the continent, from whence the savages came, and would try if they could seize upon some prisoners among the natives there, and bring them home, so to make them do the laborious part of their work for them.

The project was not so preposterous, if they had gone no further; but they did nothing, and proposed nothing, but had either mischief in the design, or mischief in the event; and, if I may give my opinion, they seemed to be under a blast from Heaven; for if we will not allow a visible curse to pursue visible crimes, how shall we reconcile the events of things with the divine justice? It was certainly an apparent vengeance on their crime of mutiny and piracy that brought them to the state they were in; and they showed not the least remorse for the crime, but added new villainies to it, such as the piece of monstrous cruelty of wounding a poor slave, because he did not, or perhaps could not, understand to do what he was directed, and to wound him in such a manner as made him a cripple all his life, and in a place where no surgeon or medicine could be had for his cure; and what was still worse, the murderous intent, or, to do justice to the crime, the intentional murder, for such to be sure it was, as was afterwards the formed design they all laid, to murder the Spaniards in cold blood, and in their sleep.

BUT I leave observing, and return to the story.—The three fellows came down to the Spaniards one morning, and in very humble terms desired to be admitted to speak with them; the Spaniards very readily heard what they had to say, which was this:—That they were tired of living in the manner they did; and that they were not handy enough to make the necessaries they wanted, and that having no help, they found they should be starved; but if the Spaniards would give them leave to take one of the canoes which they came over in, and give them arms and ammunition proportioned to their defence, they would go over to the main and seek their fortunes, and so deliver them from the trouble of supplying them with any other provisions.

The Spaniards were glad enough to get rid of them, but very honestly represented to them the certain destruction they were running into; told them they had suffered such hardships upon that very spot, that they could, without any spirit of prophecy, tell them they would be starved, or murdered, and bade them consider of it.

The men replied audaciously, they should be starved if they stayed here, for they could not work, and would not work, and they could but be starved abroad; and if they were murdered, there was an end of them; they had no wives or children to cry after them: and, in short, insisted importunately upon their demand; declaring they would go, whether they would give them any arms or no.

The Spaniards told them, with great kindness, that if they were resolved to go, they should not go like naked men, and be in no condition to defend themselves: and that though they could ill spare their firearms, having not enough for themselves, yet they would let them have two muskets, a pistol, and a cutlass, and each man a hatchet, which they thought was sufficient for them. In a word, they accepted the offer; and having baked them bread enough to serve them a month, and given them as much goat's flesh as they could eat while it was sweet, and a great basket of dried grapes, and a pot of fresh water, and a young kid alive, they boldly set out in the canoe for a voyage over the sea, where it was at least forty miles broad.

The boat, indeed, was a large one, and would very well have carried fifteen or twenty men, and therefore was rather too big for them to manage; but as they had a fair breeze, and flood tide with them, they did well enough. They had made a mast of a long pole, and a sail of four large goats' skins dried, which they had sewed or laced together; and away they went merrily enough: the Spaniards called after them, *Buen viage;* and no man ever thought of seeing them any more.

The Spaniards were often saying to one another, and to the two honest Englishmen who remained behind, how quietly and comfortably they had lived, now these three turbulent fellows were gone: as for their coming again, that was the remotest thing from their thoughts that could be imagined; when, behold, after two-and-twenty days' absence, one of the Englishmen, being abroad upon his planting work, sees three strange men coming towards him at a distance, with guns upon their shoulders.

Away runs the Englishman, as if he was bewitched, comes frightened and amazed to the governor Spaniard, and tells him they were all undone, for there were strangers landed upon the island, but could not tell who. The Spaniard, pausing a while, says to him, How do you mean, you cannot tell who? They are the savages, to be sure.—No, no, says the Englishman; they are men in clothes, with arms.—Nay, then, says the Spaniard, why are you concerned? If they are not savages, they must be friends; for there is no Christian nation upon earth but will do us good rather than harm.

While they were debating thus, came the three Englishmen, and standing without the wood, which was new planted, hallooed to them: they presently knew their voices, and so all the wonder of that kind ceased. But now the admiration was turned upon another question, viz., What could be the matter, and what made them come back again?

It was not long before they brought the men in, and inquiring where they had been, and what they had been doing, they gave them a full account of their voyage in a few words, viz., That they reached the land in two days, or something less; but finding the people alarmed at their coming, and preparing with bows and arrows to fight them, they durst not go on shore, but sailed on to the northward six or seven hours, till they came to a great opening, by which they perceived that the land they saw from our island was not the main, but an island; upon entering that opening of the sea, they saw another island on the right hand, north, and several more west; and being resolved to land somewhere, they put over to one of the islands which lay west, and went boldly on shore: that they found the people very courteous and friendly to them; and that they gave them several roots and some dried fish, and appeared very sociable; and the women as well as the men were very forward to supply them with anything they could get for them to eat, and brought it to them a great way upon their heads.

They continued here four days; and inquired, as well as they could of them, by signs, what nations were this way, and that way; and were told of several fierce and terrible people that lived almost every way, who, as they made known by signs to them, used to eat men; but as for themselves, they said they never ate men or women, except only such as they took in the wars; and then, they owned, they made a great feast, and ate their prisoners.

The Englishmen inquired when they had had a feast of that kind; and they told them about two moons ago, pointing to the moon, and to two fingers; and that their great king had two hundred prisoners now, which he had taken in his war, and they were feeding them to make them fat for the next feast. The Englishmen seemed mighty desirous of seeing those prisoners; but the others mistaking them, thought they were desirous to have some of them to carry away for their own eating: so they beckoned to them, pointing to the setting of the sun, and then to the rising; which was to signify that the next morning at sun-rising they would bring some for them; and, accordingly, the next morning, they brought down five women, and eleven men, and gave them to the Englishmen, to carry with them on their voyage, just as we would bring so many cows and oxen down to a seaport town to victual a ship.

As brutish and barbarous as these fellows were at home, their stomachs turned at this sight, and they did not know what to do. To refuse the prisoners would have been the highest affront to the savage gentry that could be offered them, and what to do with them they knew not. However, after some debate, they resolved to accept of them; and, in return, they gave the savages that brought them one of their hatchets, an old key, a knife, and six or seven of their bullets; which, though they did not understand their use, they seemed particularly pleased with; and then tying the poor creatures' hands behind them, they dragged the prisoners into the boat for our men.

The Englishmen were obliged to come away as soon as they had them, or else they that gave them this noble present would certainly have expected that they should have gone to work with them, have killed two or three of them the next morning, and perhaps have invited the donors to dinner. But having taken their leave, with all the respect and thanks that could well pass between people, where, on either side, they understood not one word they could say, they put off with their boat, and came back towards the first island; where, when they arrived, they set eight of their prisoners at liberty, there being too many of them for their occasion.

In their voyage, they endeavoured to have some communication with their prisoners; but it was impossible to make them understand anything; nothing they could say to them, or give them, or do for them, but was looked upon as going to murder them. They first of all unbound them; but the poor creatures screamed at that, especially the women, as if they had just felt the knife at their throats; for they immediately concluded they were unbound on purpose to be killed. If they gave them anything to eat, it was the same thing; they then concluded it was for fear they should sink in flesh, and so not be fat enough to kill. If they looked at one of them more particularly, the party presently concluded it was to see whether he or she was fattest, and fittest to kill first; nay, after they had brought them quite over, and begun to use them kindly, and treat them well, still they expected every day to make a dinner or supper for their new masters.

When the three wanderers had given this unaccountable history or journal of their voyage, the Spaniard asked them where their new family was; and being told that they had brought them on shore, and put them into one of their huts, and were come up to beg some victuals for them, they (the Spaniards) and the other two Englishmen, that is to say, the whole colony, resolved to go all down to the place and see them; and did so, and Friday's father with them.

When they came into the hut, there they sat all bound: for when they had brought them on shore, they bound their hands that they might not take the boat and make their escape; there, I say, they sat, all of them stark naked. First, there were three men, lusty, comely fellows, well-shaped, straight and fair limbs, about thirty to thirty-five years of age; and five women, whereof two might be from thirty to forty; two more not above four or five-and-twenty; and the fifth, a tall comely maiden, about sixteen or seventeen. The women were well-favoured, agreeable persons, both in shape and features, only tawny; and two of them, had they been perfect white, would have passed for very handsome women, even in London itself, having pleasant agreeable countenances, and of a very modest behaviour: especially when they came afterwards to be clothed and dressed, as they called it, though that dress was very indifferent, it must be confessed; of which hereafter.

The sight, you may be sure, was something uncouth to our Spaniards, who were, to give them a just character, men of the best behaviour, of the most calm, sedate tempers, and perfect good humour, that ever I met with; and, in particular, of the most modest, as will presently appear: I say, the sight was very uncouth, to see three naked men and five naked women, all together bound, and in the most miserable circumstances that human nature could be supposed to be, viz., to be expecting every moment to be dragged out, and have their brains knocked out, and then to be eaten up like a calf that is killed for a dainty.

The first thing they did was to cause the old Indian, Friday's father, to go in, and see, first, if he knew any of them, and then if he understood any of their speech. As soon as the old man came in, he looked seriously at them, but knew none of them, neither could any of them understand a word he said, or a sign he could make, except one of the women. However, this was enough to answer the end, which was to satisfy them that the men into whose hands they were fallen were Christians; that they abhorred eating men or women; and that they might be sure they would not be killed. As soon as they were assured of this, they discovered such a joy, and by such awkward gestures, several ways, as is hard to describe; for, it seems, they were of several nations.

The woman who was their interpreter was bid, in the next place, to ask them if they were willing to be servants and to work for the men who had brought them away, to save their lives; at which they all fell a dancing; and presently one fell to taking up this, and another that, anything that lay next, to carry on their shoulders, to intimate that they were willing to work.

The governor, who found that the having women among them would presently be attended with some inconvenience and might occasion some strife, and perhaps blood, asked the three men what they intended to do with these women, and how they intended to use them, whether as servants or as women? One of the Englishmen answered very boldly and readily, that they would use them as both; to which the governor said, I am not going to restrain you from it; you are your own masters as to that; but this I think is but just, for avoiding disorders and quarrels among you, and I desire it of you for that reason only, viz., that you will all engage, that if any of you take any of these women, as a woman or wife, that he shall take but one: and that having taken one, none else shall touch her; for though we cannot marry any one of you, yet it is but reasonable that while you stay here, the woman any of you takes should be maintained by the man that takes her, and should be his wife; I mean, says he, while he continues here, and that none else shall have anything to do with her. All this appeared so just, that every one agreed to it without any difficulty.

Then the Englishmen asked the Spaniards if they designed to take any of them? But every one of them answered no: some of them said they had wives in Spain, and the others did not like women that were not Christians: and all together declared that they would not touch one of them: which was an instance of such virtue as I have not met with in all my travels. On the other hand, to be short, the five Englishmen took them every one a wife, that is to say, a temporary wife; and so they set up a new form of living; for the Spaniards and Friday's father lived in my old habitation, which they had enlarged exceedingly within. The three servants which were taken in the late battle of the savages lived with them; and these carried on the main part of the colony, supplied all the rest with food, and assisted them in anything as they could, or as they found necessity required.

But the wonder of the story was, how five such refractory, ill-matched fellows should agree about these women, and that two of them should not pitch upon the same woman, especially seeing two or three of them were, without comparison, more agreeable than the others: but they took a good way enough to prevent quarrelling among themselves: for they set the five women by themselves in one of their huts, and they went all into the other hut, and drew lots among them who should choose first.

He that drew to choose first went away by himself to the hut where the poor naked creatures were, and fetched out her he chose; and it was worth observing, that he that chose first took her that was reckoned the homeliest and oldest of the five, which made mirth enough among the rest; and even the Spaniards laughed at it: but the fellow considered better than any of them, that it was application and business they were to expect assistance in, as much as in anything else; and she proved the best wife of all the parcel.

When the poor women saw themselves set in a row thus, and fetched out one by one, the terrors of their condition returned upon them again, and they firmly believed they were now going to be devoured. Accordingly, when the English sailor came in and fetched out one of them, the rest set up a most lamentable cry, and hung about her, and took their leave of her with such agonies and affection, as would have grieved the hardest heart in the world; nor was it possible for the Englishman to satisfy them that they were not to be immediately murdered, till they fetched the old man, Friday's father, who immediately let them know that the five men, who had fetched them out one by one, had chosen them for their wives.

When they had done, and the fright the women were in was a little over, the men went to work, and the Spaniards came and helped them; and in a few hours they had built them every one a new hut or tent for their lodging apart; for those they had already were crowded with their tools, household stuff, and provisions. The three wicked ones had pitched farthest off, and the two honest ones nearer, but both on the north shore of the island, so that they continued separated as before; and thus my island was peopled in three places; and, as I might say, three towns were begun to be built.

And here it is very well worth observing, that, as it often happens in the world (what the wise ends of God's providence are, in such a disposition of things, I cannot say), the two honest fellows had the two worst wives; and the three reprobates, that were scarce worth hanging, that were fit for nothing, and neither seemed born to do themselves good, nor any one else, had three clever, diligent, careful, and ingenious wives: not that the first two were bad wives, as to their temper and humour, for all the five were most willing, quiet, passive, and subjected creatures, rather like slaves than wives; but my meaning is, they were not alike, capable, ingenious, or industrious, or alike cleanly and neat.

Another observation I must make, to the honour of a diligent application, on one hand, and to the disgrace of a slothful, negligent, idle temper, on the other, that when I came to the place, and viewed the several improvements, plantings, and management of the several little colonies, the two men had so far outgone the three, that there was no comparison. They had, indeed, both of them as much ground laid out for corn as they wanted, and the reason was, because, according to my rule, nature dictated that it was to no purpose to sow more corn than they wanted; but the difference of the cultivation, of the planting, of the fences, and, indeed, of everything else, was easy to be seen at first view.

The two men had innumerable young trees planted about their huts, so that when you came to the place, nothing was to be seen but wood: and though they had twice had their plantation demolished, once by their own countrymen, and once by the enemy, as shall be shown in its place, yet they had restored all again, and everything was thriving and flourishing about them: they had grapes planted in order, and managed like a vineyard, though they had themselves never seen anything of that kind; and by their good ordering their vines, their grapes were as good again as any of the others. They had also found themselves out a retreat in the thickest part of the woods; where, though there was not a natural cave, as I had found, yet they made one with incessant labour of their hands, and where, when the mischief which followed happened, they secured their wives and children, so as they could never be found; they having, by sticking innumerable stakes and poles of the wood which, as I said, grew so readily, made the grove unpassable, except in some places where they climbed up to get over the outside part, and then went on by ways of their own leaving.

As to the three reprobates, as I justly call them, though they were much civilised by their settlement, compared to what they were before, and were not so quarrelsome, having not the same opportunity; yet one of the certain companions of a profligate mind never left them, and that was their idleness. It is true, they planted corn, and made fences; but Solomon's words were never better verified than in them, "I went by the vineyard of the slothful, and it was all overgrown with thorns"; for when the Spaniards came to view their crop, they could not see it in some places for weeds, the hedge had several gaps in it, where the wild goats had got in and eaten up the corn; perhaps here and there a dead bush was crammed in, to stop them out for the present, but it was only shutting the stable-door after the steed was stolen: whereas, when they looked on the colony of the other two, there was the very face of industry and success upon all they did: there was not a weed to be seen in all their corn, or a gap in any of their hedges; and they, on the other hand, verified Solomon's words in another place, "that the diligent hand maketh rich"; for everything grew and thrived, and they had plenty within and without; they had more tame cattle than the others, more utensils and necessaries within doors, and yet more pleasure and diversion too.

It is true, the wives of the three were very handy and cleanly within doors, and having learned the English ways of dressing and cooking from one of the other Englishmen, who, as I said, was a cook's mate on board the ship, they dressed their husbands' victuals very nicely and well; whereas the others could not be brought to understand it: but then the husband, who, as I say, had been cook's mate, did it himself. But as for the husbands of the three wives, they loitered about, fetched turtles' eggs, and caught fish and birds; in a word, anything but labour, and they fared accordingly. The diligent lived well and comfortably; and the slothful lived hard and beggarly; and so, I believe, generally speaking it is all over the world.

But I now come to a scene different from all that had happened before, either to them or to me; and the original of the story was this: Early one morning, there came on shore five or six canoes of Indians or savages, call them which you please, and there is no room to doubt they came upon the old errand of feeding upon their slaves; but that part was now so familiar to the Spaniards, and to our men too, that they did not concern themselves about it, as I did; but having been made sensible by their experience, that their only business was to lie concealed, and that if they were not seen by any of the savages, they would go off again quietly, when their business was done, having, as yet, not the least notion of there being any inhabitants in the island; I say, having been made sensible of this, they had nothing to do but give notice to all the three plantations to keep within doors, and not show themselves, only placing a scout in a proper place, to give notice when the boats went to sea again.

This was, without doubt, very right; but a disaster spoiled all these measures, and made it known among the savages that there were inhabitants there; which was, in the end, the desolation of almost the whole colony. After the canoes with the savages were gone off, the Spaniards peeped abroad again; and some of them had the curiosity to go to the place where they had been, to see what they had been doing. Here, to their great surprise, they found three savages left behind, and lying fast asleep upon the ground. It was supposed they had either been so gorged with their inhuman feast, that, like beasts, they were fallen asleep, and would not stir when the others went, or they had wandered into the woods, and did not come back in time to be taken in.

The Spaniards were greatly surprised at this sight, and perfectly at a loss what to do. The Spanish governor, as it happened, was with them, and his advice was asked, but he professed he knew not what to do. As for slaves, they had enough already; and as to killing them, they were none of them inclined to that: the Spanish governor told me, they could not think of shedding innocent blood: for as to them, the poor creatures had done them no wrong, invaded none of their property, and they thought they had no just quarrel against them, to take away their lives. And here I must, in justice to these Spaniards, observe, that let the accounts of Spanish cruelty in Mexico and Peru be what they will, I never met with seventeen men of any nation whatsoever, in any foreign country, who were so universally modest, temperate, virtuous, so very good-humoured, and so courteous, as these Spaniards; and as to cruelty, they had nothing of it in their very nature: no inhumanity, no barbarity, no outrageous passions; and yet all of them men of great courage and spirit. Their temper and calmness had appeared in their bearing the insufferable usage of the three Englishmen; and their justice and humanity appeared now in the case of the savages, as above. After some consultation, they resolved upon this: that they would lie still a while longer, till, if possible, these three men might be gone. But then the governor Spaniard recollected, that the three savages had no boat; and if they were left to rove about the island, they would certainly discover that there were inhabitants on it; and so they should be undone that way. Upon this they went back again, and there lay the fellows fast asleep still, and so they resolved to waken them, and take them prisoners; and they did so. The poor fellows were strangely frightened when they were seized upon and bound; and afraid, like the women, that they should be murdered and eaten: for it seems those people think all the world does as they do, eating men's flesh; but they were soon made easy as to that, and away they carried them.

It was very happy for them that they did not carry them home to their castle, I mean to my palace under the hill; but they carried them first to the bower, where was the chief of their country work, such as the keeping the goats, the planting the corn, etc.; and afterwards they carried them to the habitation of the two Englishmen.

Here they were set to work, though it was not much they had for them to do; and whether it was by negligence in guarding them, or that they thought the fellows could not mend themselves, I know not, but one of them ran away, and taking to the woods, they could never hear of him any more.

They had good reason to believe he got home again soon after, in some other boats or canoes of savages who came on shore three or four weeks afterwards; and who, carrying on their revels as usual, went off in two days' time. This thought terrified them exceedingly; for they concluded, and that not without good cause indeed, that if this fellow came home safe among his comrades, he would certainly give them an account that there were people on the island, and also how few and weak they were: for this savage, as I observed before, had never been told, and it was very happy he had not, how many there were, or where they lived; nor had he ever seen or heard the fire of any of their guns, much less had they shown him any of their other retired places; such as the cave in the valley, or the new retreat which the two Englishmen had made, and the like.

The first testimony they had that this fellow had given intelligence of them was, that, about two months after this, six canoes of savages, with about seven, eight, or ten men in a canoe, came rowing along the north side of the island, where they never used to come before, and landed, about an hour after sunrise, at a convenient place, about a mile from the habitation of the two Englishmen, where this escaped man had been kept. As the Spanish governor said, had they been all there, the damage would not have been so much, for not a man of them would have escaped: but the case differed now very much, for two men to fifty was too much odds. The two men had the happiness to discover them about a league off, so that it was above an hour before they landed; and as they landed a mile from their huts, it was some time before they could come at them. Now, having great reason to believe that they were betrayed, the first thing they did was to bind the two slaves which were left, and caused two of the three men whom they brought with the women (who, it seems, proved very faithful to them) to lead them, with their two wives, and whatever they could carry away with them, to their retired places in the woods, which I have spoken of above, and there to bind the two fellows hand and foot, till they heard further.

In the next place, seeing the savages were all come on shore, and that they had bent their course directly that way, they opened the fences where the milch goats were kept, and drove them all out; leaving their goats to straggle in the woods, whither they pleased, that the savages might think they were all bred wild; but the rogue who came with them was too cunning for that, and gave them an account of it all, for they went directly to the place.

When the two poor frightened men had secured their wives and goods, they sent the other slave they had of the three who came with the women, and who was at their place by accident, away to the Spaniards with all speed, to give them the alarm, and desire speedy help; and, in the mean time, they took their arms and what ammunition they had, and retreated towards the place in the wood where their wives were sent; keeping at a distance, yet so that they might see, if possible, which way the savages took.

They had not gone far, but that from a rising ground they could see the little army of their enemies come on directly to their habitation, and, in a moment more, could see all their huts and household stuff flaming up together, to their great grief and mortification; for they had a very great loss, to them irretrievable, at least for some time. They kept their station for a while, till they found the savages, like wild beasts, spread themselves all over the place, rummaging every way and every place they could think of, in search of prey; and in particular for the people, of whom, now, it plainly appeared they had intelligence.

The two Englishmen seeing this, thinking themselves not secure where they stood, because it was likely some of the wild people might come that way, and they might come too many together, thought it proper to make another retreat about half a mile farther; believing, as it afterwards happened, that the farther they strolled the fewer would be together.

THEIR NEXT HALT was at the entrance into a very thick-grown part of the woods, and where an old trunk of a tree stood, which was hollow and vastly large; and in this tree they both took their standing, resolving to see there what might offer. They had not stood there long, before two of the savages appeared running directly that way, as if they already had notice where they stood, and were coming up to attack them; and a little way farther they espied three more coming after them, and five more beyond them, all coming the same way; besides which, they saw seven or eight more at a distance, running another way; for, in a word, they ran every way, like sportsmen beating for their game.

The poor men were now in great perplexity whether they should stand and keep their posture, or fly; but, after a very short debate with themselves, they considered, that if the savages ranged the country thus before help came, they might perhaps find out their retreat in the woods, and then all would be lost: so they resolved to stand them there; and if they were too many to deal with, then they would get up to the top of the tree, from whence they doubted not to defend themselves, fire excepted, as long as their ammunition lasted, though all the savages that were landed, which was near fifty, were to attack them.

Having resolved upon this, they next considered whether they should fire at the first two, or wait for the three, and so take the middle party, by which the two and the five that followed would be separated: at length they resolved to let the first two pass by, unless they should spy them in the tree, and come to attack them. The first two savages confirmed them also in this resolution, by turning a little from them towards another part of the wood; but the three, and the five after them, came forward directly to the tree, as if they had known the Englishmen were there. Seeing them come so straight toward them, they resolved to take them in a line as they came: and as they resolved to fire but one at a time, perhaps the first shot might hit them all three; for which purpose, the man who was to fire put three or four small bullets into his piece; and having a fair loophole, as it were, from a broken hole in the tree, he took a sure aim, without being seen, waiting till they were within about thirty yards of the tree, so that he could not miss.

While they were thus waiting, and the savages came on, they plainly saw that one of the three was the runaway savage that had escaped from them; and they both knew him distinctly, and resolved that, if possible, he should not escape, though they should both fire; so the other stood ready with his piece, that if he did not drop at the first shot, he should be sure to have a second. But the first was too good a marksman to miss his aim; for as the savages kept near one another, a little behind, in a line, he fired, and hit two of them directly: the foremost was killed outright, being shot in the head; the second, which was the runaway Indian, was shot through the body, and fell, but was not quite dead; and the third had a little scratch in the shoulder, perhaps by the same ball that went through the body of the second; and being dreadfully frightened, though not so much hurt, sat down upon the ground, screaming and yelling in a hideous manner.

The five that were behind, more frightened with the noise than sensible of the danger, stood still at first; for the woods made the sound a thousand times bigger than it really was, the echoes rattling from one side to another, and the fowls rising from all parts, screaming, and every sort making a different noise, according to their kind; just as it was when I fired the first gun that perhaps was ever shot off in the island.

However, all being silent again, and they not knowing what the matter was, came on unconcerned, till they came to the place where their companions lay, in a condition miserable enough; and here the poor ignorant creatures, not sensible that they were within reach of the same mischief, stood all of a huddle over the wounded man, talking, and, as may be supposed, inquiring of him how he came to be hurt; and who, it is very rational to believe, told them, that a flash of fire first, and immediately after that thunder from their gods, had killed those two and wounded him; this, I say, is rational; for nothing is more certain than that, as they saw no man near them, so they had never heard a gun in all their lives, nor so much as heard of a gun; neither knew they anything of killing and wounding at a distance with fire and bullets: if they had, one might reasonably believe they would not have stood so unconcerned in viewing the fate of their fellows, without some apprehensions of their own.

Our two men, though, as they confessed to me, it grieved them to be obliged to kill so many poor creatures, who, at the same time, had no notion of their danger; yet, having them all thus in their power, and the first having loaded his piece again, resolved to let fly both together among them; and singling out, by agreement, which to aim at, they shot together, and killed, or very much wounded, four of them; the fifth, frightened even to death, though not hurt, fell with the rest; so that our men, seeing them all fall together, thought they had killed them all.

The belief that the savages were all killed, made our two men come boldly out from the tree before they had charged their guns, which was a wrong step; and they were under some surprise when they came to the place, and found no less than four of them alive, and of them two very little hurt, and one not at all: this obliged them to fall upon them with the stocks of their muskets: and first they made sure of the runaway savage, that had been the cause of all the mischief, and of another that was hurt in the knee, and put them out of their pain: then the man that was hurt not at all came and kneeled down to them, with his two hands held up, and made piteous moans to them, by gestures and signs for his life, but could not say one word to them that they could understand. However, they made signs to him to sit down at the foot of a tree hard by; and one of the Englishmen, with a piece of rope twined, which he had by great chance in his pocket, tied his two hands behind him, and there they left him: and with what speed they could made after the other two, which were gone before, fearing they, or any more of them, should find the way to their covered place in the woods, where their wives, and the few goods they had left, lay. They came once in sight of the two men, but it was at a great distance; however, they had the satisfaction to see them cross over a valley towards the sea, quite the contrary way from that which led to their retreat, which they were afraid of; and being satisfied of that, they went back to the tree where they left their prisoner, who, as they supposed, was delivered by his comrades, for he was gone, and the two pieces of rope-yarn, with which they had bound him, lay just at the foot of the tree.

They were now in as great concern as before, not knowing what course to take, or how near the enemy might be, or in what numbers: so they resolved to go away to the place where their wives were, to see if all was well there, and to make them easy, who were in fright enough, to be sure; for though the savages were their own countryfolk, yet they were most terribly afraid of them, and perhaps the more for the knowledge they had of them.

When they came there, they found the savages had been in the wood, and very near that place, but had not found it: for it was indeed inaccessible, by the trees standing so thick, as before, unless the persons seeking it had been directed by those that knew it, which these did not: they found, therefore, everything very safe, only the women in a terrible fright. While they were here, they had the comfort to have seven of the Spaniards come to their assistance: the other ten, with their servants, and old Friday, I mean Friday's father, were gone in a body to defend their bower, and the corn and cattle that was kept there, in case the savages should have roved over to that side of the country; but they did not spread so far. With the seven Spaniards came one of the three savages who, as I said, were their prisoners formerly; and with them also came the savage whom the Englishmen had left bound hand and foot at the tree: for it seems, they came that way, saw the slaughter of the seven men, and unbound the eighth, and brought him along with them; where, however, they were obliged to bind him again, as they had the two others who were left when the third ran away.

The prisoners now began to be a burthen to them; and they were so afraid of their escaping, that they were once resolving to kill them all, believing they were under an absolute necessity to do so for their own preservation. However, the Spanish governor would not consent to it; but ordered, for the present, that they should be sent out of the way, to my old cave in the valley, and be kept there, with two Spaniards to guard them, and give them food for their subsistence, which was done; and they were bound there hand and foot for that night.

When the Spaniards came, the two Englishmen were so encouraged, that they could not satisfy themselves to stay any longer there; but taking five of the Spaniards and themselves, with four muskets and a pistol among them, and two stout quarter-staves, away they went in quest of the savages. And first they came to the tree where the men lay that had been killed; but it was easy to see that some more of the savages had been there, for they had attempted to carry their dead men away, and had dragged two of them a good way, but had given it over. From thence they advanced to the first rising ground, where they had stood and seen their camp destroyed, and where they had the mortification still to see some of the smoke: but neither could they here see any of the savages. They then resolved, though with all possible caution, to go forward, towards their ruined plantation; but a little before they came thither, coming in sight of the sea-shore, they saw plainly the savages all embarked again in their canoes, in order to be gone. They seemed sorry, at first, that there was no way to come at them, to give them a parting blow; but, upon the whole, they were very well satisfied to be rid of them.

The poor Englishmen being now twice ruined, and all their improvements destroyed, the rest all agreed to come and help them to rebuild, and to assist them with needful supplies. Their three countrymen, who were not yet noted for having the least inclination to do any good, yet as soon as they heard of it (for they living remote eastward, knew nothing of the matter till all was over), came and offered their help and assistance, and did, very friendly, work for several days, to restore their habitation, and make necessaries for them. And thus, in a little time, they were set upon their legs again.

About two days after this, they had the further satisfaction of seeing three of the savages' canoes come driving on shore, and, at some distance from them, two drowned men; by which they had reason to believe that they had met with a storm at sea, which had overset some of them; for it had blown very hard the night after they went off.

However, as some might miscarry, so, on the other hand, enough of them escaped to inform the rest, as well of what they had done as of what had happened to them, and to whet them on to another enterprise of the same nature; which they, it seems, resolved to attempt, with sufficient force to carry all before them; for except what the first man had told them of inhabitants, they could say little of it of their own knowledge, for they never saw one man; and the fellow being killed that had affirmed it, they had no other witness to confirm it to them.

It was five or six months after this, before they heard any more of the savages, in which time our men were in hopes they had either forgot their former bad luck, or given over hopes of better; when, on a sudden, they were invaded with a most formidable fleet of no less than eight-and-twenty canoes, full of savages, armed with bows and arrows, great clubs, wooden swords, and such-like engines of war; and they brought such numbers with them, that, in short, it put all our people into the utmost consternation.

As they came on shore in the evening, and at the easternmost side of the island, our men had that night to consult and consider what to do; and, in the first place, knowing that their being entirely concealed was their only safety before, and would be much more so now, while the number of their enemies was so great, they therefore resolved, first of all, to take down the huts which were built for the two Englishmen, and drive away their goats to the old cave; because they supposed the savages would go directly thither, as soon as it was day, to play the old game over again, though they did not now land within two leagues of it. In the next place, they drove away all the flocks of goats they had at the old bower, as I called it, which belonged to the Spaniards; and, in short, left as little appearance of inhabitants anywhere as was possible; and the next morning early they posted themselves, with all their force, at the plantation of the two men, to wait their coming. As they guessed, so it happened; these new invaders leaving their canoes at the east end of the island, came ranging along the shore, directly towards the place, to the number of two hundred and fifty, as near as our men could judge. Our army was but small, indeed; but that which was worse, they had not arms for all their number neither. The whole account, it seems, stood thus: first, as to men, seventeen Spaniards, five Englishmen, old Friday, or Friday's father, the three slaves taken with the women, who proved very faithful, and three other slaves, who lived with the Spaniards. To arm these, they had eleven muskets, five pistols, three fowling-pieces, five muskets or fowling-pieces which were taken by me from the mutinous seamen whom I reduced, two swords, and three old halberds.

To their slaves they did not give either musket or fusee, but they had every one a halberd, or a long staff, like a quarter-staff, with a great spike of iron fastened into each end of it, and by his side a hatchet; also every one of our men had a hatchet. Two of the women could not be prevailed upon but they would come into the fight, and they had bows and arrows, which the Spaniard had taken from the savages when the first action happened, which I have spoken of, where the Indians fought with one another; and the women had hatchets too.

The Spanish governor, whom I described so often, commanded the whole: and Will Atkins, who, though a dreadful fellow for wickedness, was a most daring, bold fellow, commanded under him. The savages came forward like lions; and our men, which was the worst of their fate, had no advantage in their situation; only that Will Atkins, who now proved a most useful fellow, with six men, was planted just behind a small thicket of bushes, as an advanced guard, with orders to let the first of them pass by, and then fire into the middle of them, and as soon as he had fired, to make his retreat as nimble as he could round a part of the wood, and so come in behind the Spaniards, where they stood, having a thicket of trees before them.

When the savages came on, they ran straggling about every way in heaps, out of all manner of order, and Will Atkins let about fifty of them pass by him; then seeing the rest come in a very thick throng, he orders three of his men to fire, having loaded their muskets with six or seven bullets a piece, about as big as large pistol-bullets. How many they killed or wounded they knew not, but the consternation and surprise was inexpressible among the savages; they were frightened to the last degree to hear such a dreadful noise, and see their men killed, and others hurt, but see nobody that did it: when, in the middle of their fright, Will Atkins and his other three let fly again among the thickest of them; and in less than a minute the first three being loaded again, gave them a third volley.

Had Will Atkins and his men retired immediately, as soon as they had fired, as they were ordered to do, or had the rest of the body been at hand, to have poured in their shot continually, the savages had been effectually routed; for the terror that was among them came principally from this, viz., that they were killed by the gods with thunder and lightning, and could see nobody that hurt them; but Will Atkins, staying to load again, discovered the cheat; some of the savages who were at a distance spying them, came upon them behind; and though Atkins and his men fired at them also, two or three times, and killed above twenty, retiring as fast as they could, yet they wounded Atkins himself, and killed one of his fellow-Englishmen, with their arrows, as they did afterwards one Spaniard, and one of the Indian slaves who came with the women. This slave was a most gallant fellow, and fought most desperately, killing five of them with his own hand, having no weapon but one of the armed staves and a hatchet.

Our men being thus hard laid at, Atkins wounded, and two other men killed, retreated to a rising ground in the wood: and the Spaniards, after firing three volleys upon them, retreated also; for their number was so great, and they were so desperate, that though above fifty of them were killed, and more than as many wounded, yet they came on in the teeth of our men, fearless of danger, and shot their arrows like a cloud; and it was observed that their wounded men, who were not quite disabled, were made outrageous by their wounds, and fought like mad-men.

When our men retreated, they left the Spaniard and the Englishman that were killed behind them; and the savages, when they came up to them, killed them over again in a wretched manner, breaking their arms, legs, and heads, with their clubs and wooden swords, like true savages; but finding our men were gone, they did not seem to pursue them, but drew themselves up in a ring, which is, it seems, their custom, and shouted twice, in token of their victory; after which, they had the morti-fication to see several of their wounded men fall, dying with the mere loss of blood.

The Spanish governor having drawn his little body up together upon a rising ground, Atkins, though he was wounded, would have had them march and charge again all together at once: but the Spaniard replied, Senhor Atkins, you see how their wounded men fight; let them alone till morning; all the wounded men will be stiff and sore with their wounds, and faint with the loss of blood; and so we shall have the fewer to en-gage. This advice was good; but Will Atkins replied merrily, That is true, senhor, and so shall I too; and that is the reason I would go on while I am warm.—Well, Senhor Atkins, says the Spaniard, you have behaved gallantly, and done your part: we will fight for you, if you can-not come on; but I think it best to stay till morning; so they waited.

But as it was a clear moonlight night, and they found the savages in great disorder about their dead and wounded men, and a great noise and hurry among them where they lay, they afterwards resolved to fall upon them in the night; especially if they could come to give them but one volley before they were discovered, which they had a fair opportunity to do; for one of the Englishmen, in whose quarter it was where the fight began, led them around between the woods and the sea-side westward, and then turning short south, they came so near where the thickest of them lay, that, before they were seen or heard, eight of them fired in among them, and did dreadful execution upon them; in half a minute more, eight others fired after them, pouring in their small shot in such quantity, that abundance were killed and wounded; and all this while they were not able to see who hurt them, or which way to fly.

The Spaniards charged again with the utmost expedition, and then divided themselves in three bodies, and resolved to fall in among them all together. They had in each body eight persons, that is to say, twenty-two and the two women, who, by the way, fought desperately. They divided the fire-arms equally in each party, and so the halberds and staves. They would have had the women kept back, but they said they were resolved to die with their husbands. Having thus formed their little army, they marched out from among the trees, and came up to the teeth of the enemy, shouting and hallooing as loud as they could: the savages stood all together, but were in the utmost confusion, hearing the noise of our men shouting from three quarters together: they would have fought if they had seen us; for as soon as we came near enough to be seen, some arrows were shot, and poor old Friday was wounded, though not dangerously; but our men gave them no time, but, running up to them, fired among them three ways, and then fell in with the butt-ends of their muskets, their swords, armed staves, and hatchets, and laid them about them so well, that in a word, they set up a dismal screaming and howling, flying to save their lives which way soever they could.

Our men were tired with the execution, and killed or mortally wounded in the two fights about one hundred and eighty of them; the rest being frightened out of their wits, scoured through the woods and over the hills, with all the speed fear and nimble feet could help them to: and as we did not trouble ourselves much to pursue them, they got all together to the sea-side where they landed, and where their canoes lay. But their disasters were not at an end yet; for it blew a terrible storm of wind that evening from the sea, so that it was impossible for them to go off; nay, the storm continuing all night, when the tide came up, their canoes were most of them driven by the surge of the sea so high upon the shore, that it required infinite toil to get them off; and some of them were even dashed to pieces against the beach, or against one another.

Our men, though glad of their victory, yet got little rest that night; but having refreshed themselves as well as they could, they resolved to march to that part of the island, where the savages were fled, and see what posture they were in. This necessarily led them over the place where the fight had been, and where they found several of the poor creatures not quite dead, and yet past recovering life; a sight disagreeable enough to generous minds; for a truly great man, though obliged by the law of battle to destroy his enemy, takes no delight in his misery. However, there was no need to give any orders in this case; for their own savages, who were their servants, despatched these poor creatures with their hatchets.

At length, they came in view of the place where the more miserable remains of the savages' army lay, where there appeared about a hundred still: their posture was generally sitting upon the ground, with their knees up towards their mouth, and the head put between the two hands, leaning down upon the knees.

When our men came within two musket-shots of them, the Spanish governor ordered two muskets to be fired, without ball, to alarm them: this he did, that by their countenance he might know what to expect, viz., whether they were still in heart to fight, or were so heartily beaten as to be dispirited and discouraged, and so he might manage accordingly. This stratagem took; for as soon as the savages heard the first gun and saw the flash of the second, they started up upon their feet in the greatest consternation imaginable: and as our men advanced swiftly towards them, they all ran screaming and yelling away, with a kind of howling noise, which our men did not understand, and had never heard before: and thus they ran up the hills into the country.

At first our men had much rather the weather had been calm, and they had all gone away to sea; but they did not then consider that this might probably have been the occasion of their coming again in such multitudes as not to be resisted, or, at least, to come so many, and so often, as would quite desolate the island, and starve them. Will Atkins, therefore, who, notwithstanding his wound, kept always with them, proved the best counsellor in this case: his advice was, to take the advantage that offered, and clap in between them and their boats, and so deprive them of the capacity of ever returning any more to plague the island.

They consulted long about this; and some were against it, for fear of making the wretches fly to the woods and live there desperate, and so they should have them to hunt like wild beasts, be afraid to stir out about their business, and have their plantation continually rifled, all their tame goats destroyed, and, in short, be reduced to a life of continual distress.

Will Atkins told them they had better have to do with a hundred men than with a hundred nations: that as they must destroy their boats, so they must destroy the men, or be all of them destroyed themselves. In a word, he showed them the necessity of it so plainly, that they all came into it: so they went to work immediately with the boats, and getting some dry wood together from a dead tree, they tried to set some of them on fire, but they were so wet that they would not burn; however, the fire so burned the upper part, that it soon made them unfit for swimming in the sea as boats. When the Indians saw what they were about, some of them came running out of the woods, and coming as near as they could to our men, kneeled down and cried, "Oa, Oa, Waramokoa," and some other words of their language, which none of the others understood anything of; but as they made pitiful gestures and strange noises, it was easy to understand they begged to have their boats spared, and that they would be gone, and never come there again. But our men were now satisfied that they had no way to preserve themselves, or to save their colony, but effectually to prevent any of these people from ever going home again: depending upon this, that if even so much as one of them got back into their country to tell the story, the colony was undone: so that, letting them know that they should not have any mercy, they fell to work with their canoes, and destroyed them every one that the storm had not destroyed before; at the sight of which the savages raised a hideous cry in the woods, which our people heard plain enough, after which they ran about the island like distracted men: so that, in a word, our men did not really know at first what to do with them. Nor did the Spaniards, with all their prudence, consider, that while they made those people thus desperate, they ought to have kept a good guard at the same time upon their plantations; for though, it is true, they had driven away their cattle, and the Indians did not find out their main retreat, I mean my old castle at the hill, nor the cave in the valley, yet they found out my plantation at the bower, and pulled it all to pieces, and all the fences and planting about it; trod all the corn under foot, tore up the vines and grapes, being just then almost ripe, and did our men an inestimable damage, though to themselves not one farthing's worth of service.

Though our men were able to fight them upon all occasions, yet they were in no condition to pursue them, or hunt them up and down; for as they were too nimble of foot for our men, when they found them single, so our men durst not go abroad single for fear of being surrounded with their numbers. The best was, they had no weapons; for though they had bows, they had no arrows left, nor any materials to make any; nor had they any edge tool or weapon among them.

The extremity and distress they were reduced to was great and indeed deplorable; but, at the same time, our men were also brought to very bad circumstances by them: for though their retreats were preserved, yet their provision was destroyed, and their harvest spoiled; and what to do, or which way to turn themselves, they knew not. The only refuge they had now was, the stock of cattle they had in the valley by the cave, and some little corn which grew there, and the plantation of the three Englishmen, Will Atkins and his comrades, who were now reduced to two; one of them being killed by an arrow, which struck him on the side of his head, just under the temple, so that he never spoke more: and it was very remarkable, that this was the same barbarous fellow that cut the poor savage slave with his hatchet, and who afterwards intended to have murdered the Spaniards.

I looked upon their case to have been worse at this time than mine was at any time, after I first discovered the grains of barley and rice, and got into the manner of planting and raising my corn, and my tame cattle: for now they had, as I may say, a hundred wolves upon the island, which would devour everything they could come at, yet could be hardly come at themselves.

When they saw what their circumstances were, the first thing they concluded was, that they would if possible, drive them up to the farther part of the island, south-west, that if any more savages came on shore they might not find one another: then they would daily hunt and harass them, and kill as many of them as they could come at, till they had reduced their number; and if they could at last tame them, and bring them to anything, they would give them corn, and teach them how to plant, and live upon their daily labour.

In order to do this, they so followed them, and so terrified them with their guns, that in a few days, if any of them fired a gun at an Indian, if he did not hit him, yet he would fall down for fear; and so dreadfully frightened they were, that they kept out of sight farther and farther; till, at last, our men following them, and almost every day killing or wounding some of them, they kept up in the woods or hollow places so much, that it reduced them to the utmost misery for want of food; and many were afterwards found dead in the woods, without any hurt, absolutely starved to death.

When our men found this, it made their hearts relent, and pity moved them, especially the Spanish governor, who was the most gentleman-like, generous-minded man that I ever met with in my life; and he proposed, if possible, to take one of them alive, and bring him to understand what they meant, so far as to be able to act as interpreter, and go among them, and see if they might be brought to some conditions that might be depended upon, to save their lives and do us no harm.

It was some while before any of them could be taken; but being weak and half-starved, one of them was at last surprised and made a prisoner. He was sullen at first, and would neither eat nor drink; but finding himself kindly used, and victuals given him, and no violence offered him, he at last grew tractable, and came to himself. They brought old Friday to him, who talked often with him, and told him how kind the others would be to them all: that they would not only save their lives, but would give them part of the island to live in, provided they would give satisfaction that they would keep in their own bounds and not come beyond it to injure or prejudice others; and that they should have corn given them to plant and make it grow for their bread, and some bread given them for their present subsistence; and old Friday bade the fellow go and talk with the rest of his country, and see what they said to it; assuring them, that if they did not agree immediately, they should be all destroyed.

The poor wretches thoroughly humbled, and reduced in number to about thirty-seven, closed with the proposal at the first offer, and begged to have some food given them; upon which, twelve Spaniards and two Englishmen, well armed, with three Indian slaves and old Friday, marched to the place where they were. The three Indian slaves carried them a large quantity of bread, some rice boiled up to cakes and dried in the sun, and three live goats; and they were ordered to go to the side of a hill, where they sat down, ate their provisions very thankfully, and were the most faithful fellows to their words that could be thought of: for, except when they came to beg victuals and directions, they never came out of their bounds: and there they lived when I came to the island, and I went to see them.

They had taught them both to plant corn, make bread, breed tame goats, and milk them: they wanted nothing but wives, and they soon would have been a nation. They were confined to a neck of land, surrounded with high rocks behind them, and lying plain towards the sea before them, on the south-east corner of the island. They had land enough, and it was very good and fruitful; about a mile and a half broad, and three or four miles in length.

Our men taught them to make wooden spades, such as I made for myself, and gave among them twelve hatchets and three or four knives; and there they lived, the most subjected innocent creatures that ever were heard of.

After this, the colony enjoyed a perfect tranquillity with respect to the savages till I came to revisit them, which was about two years after; not but that, now and then, some canoes of savages came on shore for their triumphal, unnatural feasts; but as they were of several nations, and perhaps had never heard of those that came before, or the reason of it, they did not make any search or inquiry after their countrymen; and if they had, it would have been very hard to have found them out.

Thus, I think, I have given a full account of all that happened to them till my return, at least, that was worth notice. The Indians or savages were wonderfully civilised by them, and they frequently went among them; but forbade, on pain of death, any one of the Indians coming to them, because they would not have their settlement betrayed again. One thing was very remarkable, viz., that they taught the savages to make wicker-work, or baskets, but they soon outdid their masters; for they made abundance of most ingenious things in wicker-work, particularly all sorts of baskets, sieves, bird-cages, cupboards, etc.; as also chairs to sit on, stools, beds, couches, and abundance of other things, being very ingenious at such work, when they were once put in the way of it.

My coming was a particular relief to these people, because we furnished them with knives, scissors, spades, shovels, pick-axes, and all things of that kind which they could want. With the help of those tools they were so very handy, that they came at last to build up their huts, or houses, very handsomely, raddling or working it up like basket-work all the way round: which was a very extraordinary piece of ingenuity, and looked very odd, but was an exceeding good fence, as well against heat as against all sorts of vermin; and our men were so taken with it, that they got the wild savages to come and do the like for them: so that when I came to see the two Englishmen's colonies, they looked, at a distance, as if they all lived like bees in a hive. As for Will Atkins, who was now become a very industrious, useful, and sober fellow, he had made himself such a tent of basket-work as, I believe, was never seen: it was one hundred and twenty paces round on the outside, as I measured by my steps; the walls were as close worked as a basket, in panels or squares of thirty-two in number, and very strong, standing about seven feet high; in the middle was another not above twenty-two paces round, but built stronger, being octagon in its form, and in the eight corners stood eight very strong posts; round the top of which he laid strong pieces, pinned together with wooden pins, from which he raised a pyramid for a roof of eight rafters, very handsome, I assure you, and joined together very well, though he had no nails, and only a few iron spikes, which he made himself too, out of the old iron that I left there; and, indeed, this fellow showed abundance of ingenuity in several things which he had no knowledge of: he made him a forge, with a pair of wooden bellows to blow the fire; he made himself charcoal for his work; and he formed out of the iron crows a middling good anvil to hammer upon: in this manner he made many things, but especially hooks, staples and spikes, bolts and hinges.—But, to return to the house. After he had pitched the roof of his innermost tent, he worked it up between the rafters with basket-work, so firm, and thatched that over again so ingeniously with rice-straw, and over that a large leaf of a tree, which covered the top, that his house was as dry as if it had been entiled or slated. Indeed, he owned that the savages had made the basket-work for him. The outer circuit was covered as a lean-to, all round this inner apartment, and long rafters lay from the thirty-two angles to the top posts of the inner house, being about twenty feet distant; so that there was a space like a walk within the outer wicker wall and without the inner, near twenty feet wide.

The inner place he partitioned off with the same wicker-work, but much fairer, and divided into six apartments, so that he had six rooms on a floor, and out of every one of these there was a door; first into the entry, or coming into the main tent, another door into the main tent, and another door into the space or walk that was round it; so that walk was also divided into six equal parts, which served not only for a retreat, but to store up any necessaries which the family had occasion for. These six spaces not taking up the whole circumference, what other apartments the outer circle had were thus ordered:—As soon as you were in at the door of the outer circle, you had a short passage straight before you to the door of the inner house; but on either side was a wicker partition, and a door in it, by which you went first into a large room or storehouse, twenty feet wide, and about thirty feet long, and through that into another, not quite so long: so that in the outer circle were ten handsome rooms, six of which were only to be come at through the apartments of the inner tent, and served as closets or retiring rooms to the respective chambers of the inner circle; and four large warehouses, or barns, or what you please to call them, which went through one another, two on either hand of the passage that led through the outer door to the inner tent.

Such a piece of basket-work, I believe, was never seen in the world, nor a house or tent so neatly contrived, much less so built. In this bee-hive lived the three families, that is to say, Will Atkins and his companion; the third was killed, but his wife remained, with three children, for she was, it seems, big with child when he died; and the other two were not at all backward to give the widow her full share of everything, I mean as to the corn, milk, grapes, etc., and when they killed a kid, or found a turtle on the shore; so that they all lived well enough; though, it was true, they were not so industrious as the other two, as has been observed already.

One thing, however, cannot be omitted, viz., that, as for religion, I do not know that there was anything of that kind among them: they often, indeed, put one another in mind that there was a God, by the very common method of seamen, viz., swearing by his name; nor were their poor ignorant savage wives much better for having been married to Christians, as we must call them; for as they knew very little of God themselves, so they were utterly incapable of entering into any discourse with their wives about a God, or to talk anything to them concerning religion.

The utmost of all the improvement which I can say the wives had made from them was, that they had taught them to speak English pretty well; and most of their children, which were near twenty in all, were taught to speak English too, from their first learning to speak, though they at first spoke it in a very broken manner, like their mothers. There was none of these children above six years old when I came thither, for it was not much above seven years that they had fetched these five savage ladies over; but they had all been pretty fruitful, for they had all children, more or less; I think the cook's mate's wife was big of her sixth child; and the mothers were all a good sort of well-governed, quiet, laborious women, modest and decent, helpful to one another, mighty observant and subject to their masters (I cannot call them husbands), and wanted nothing but to be well instructed in the Christian religion, and to be legally married; both which were happily brought about afterwards by my means, or, at least, in consequence of my coming among them.

HAVING THUS GIVEN an account of the colony in general, and pretty much of my runagate English, I must say something of the Spaniards, who were the main body of the family, and in whose story there are some incidents also remarkable enough.

I had a great many discourses with them about their circumstances when they were among the savages. They told me readily that they had no instances to give of their application or ingenuity in that country; that they were a poor, miserable, dejected handful of people; that if means had been put into their hands, yet they had so abandoned themselves to despair, and so sunk under the weight of their misfortunes, that they thought of nothing but starving. One of them, a grave and sensible man, told me he was convinced they were in the wrong; that it was not the part of wise men to give themselves up to their misery, but always to take hold of the helps which reason offered, as well for present support as for future deliverance: he told me that grief was the most senseless insignificant passion in the world, for that it regarded only things past, which were generally impossible to be recalled, or to be remedied, but had no views of things to come, and had no share in anything that looked like deliverance, but rather added to the affliction than proposed a remedy; and upon this he repeated a Spanish proverb, which though I cannot repeat in just the same words that he spoke it in, yet I remember I made it into an English proverb of my own, thus:

> In trouble to be troubled,
> Is to have your trouble doubled.

He ran on then in remarks upon all the little improvements I had made in my solitude; my unwearied application, as he called it; and how I had made a condition which in its circumstances was at first much worse than theirs, a thousand times more happy than theirs was, even now when they were all together. He told me it was remarkable that Englishmen had a greater presence of mind, in their distress, than any people that he ever met with: that their unhappy nation and the Portuguese were the worst men in the world to struggle with misfortunes; for that their first step in dangers, after the common efforts were over, was to despair, lie down under it, and die, without rousing their thoughts up to proper remedies for escape.

I told him their case and mine differed exceedingly; that they were cast upon the shore without necessaries, without supply of food, or present sustenance till they could provide it; that, it was true, I had this disadvantage and discomfort, that I was alone; but then the supplies I had providentially thrown into my hands, by the unexpected driving of the ship on shore, was such a help as would have encouraged any creature in the world to have applied himself as I had done. Senhor, says the Spaniard, had we poor Spaniards been in your case, we should never have got half those things out of the ship, as you did: nay, says he, we should never have found means to have got a raft to carry them, or to have got the raft on shore without boat or sail; and how much less should we have done if any of us had been alone! Well, I desired him to abate his compliment, and go on with the history of their coming on shore, where they landed. He told me they unhappily landed at a place where there were people without provisions; whereas, had they had the common sense to have put off to sea again, and gone to another island a little farther, they had found provisions, though without people; there being an island that way, as they had been told, where there were provisions, though no people; that is to say, that the Spaniards of Trinidad had frequently been there, and had filled the island with goats and hogs at several times, where they had bred in such multitudes, and where turtle and seafowls were in such plenty, that they could have been in no want of flesh, though they had found no bread; whereas here, they were only sustained with a few roots and herbs, which they understood not, and which had no substance in them, and which the inhabitants gave them sparingly enough: and who could treat them no better, unless they would turn cannibals, and eat men's flesh, which was the great dainty of their country.

They gave me an account how many ways they strove to civilise the savages they were with, and to teach them rational customs in the ordinary way of living, but in vain; and how they retorted it upon them, as unjust, that they who came there for assistance and support, should attempt to set up for instructors of those that gave them food; intimating, it seems, that none should set up for the instructors of others but those who could live without them.

They gave me dismal accounts of the extremities they were driven to; how sometimes they were many days without any food at all, the island they were upon being inhabited by a sort of savages that lived more indolent, and for that reason were less supplied with the necessaries of life, than they had reason to believe others were in the same part of the world; and yet they found that these savages were less ravenous and voracious than those who had better supplies of food. Also they added, they could not but see with what demonstrations of wisdom and goodness the governing providence of God directs the events of things in the world; which, they said, appeared in their circumstances; for if, pressed by the hardships they were under, and the barrenness of the country where they were, they had searched after a better to live in, they had then been out of the way of the relief that happened to them by my means.

They then gave me an account how the savages whom they lived among expected them to go out with them into their wars; and, it was true, that as they had fire-arms with them, had they not had the disaster to lose their ammunition, they should have been serviceable not only to their friends, but have made themselves terrible both to friends and enemies; but being without powder and shot, and yet in a condition that they could not in reason deny to go out with their landlords to their wars, so when they came into the field of battle, they were in a worse condition than the savages themselves: for they had neither bows nor arrows, nor could they use those the savages gave them; so they could do nothing but stand still, and be wounded with arrows, till they came up to the teeth of their enemy; and then indeed, the three halberds they had were of use to them; and they would often drive a whole little army before them with those halberds, and sharpened sticks put into the muzzles of their muskets: but that, for all this, they were sometimes surrounded with multitudes, and in great danger from their arrows, till at last they found the way to make themselves large targets of wood, which they covered with skins of wild beasts, whose names they knew not, and these covered them from the arrows of the savages: yet, notwithstanding these, they were sometimes in great danger; and five of them were once knocked down together with the clubs of the savages, which was the time when one of them was taken prisoner, that is to say, the Spaniard whom I had relieved: that at first they thought he had been killed; but when they afterwards heard he was taken prisoner, they were under the greatest grief imaginable, and would willingly have all ventured their lives to have rescued him.

They told me that when they were so knocked down, the rest of their company rescued them, and stood over them fighting till they were come to themselves, all but him who they thought had been dead; and then they made their way with their halberds and pieces, standing close together in a line, through a body of above a thousand savages, beating down all that came in their way, got the victory over their enemies, but to their great sorrow, because it was with the loss of their friend, whom the other party, finding him alive, carried off, with some others, as I gave an account before.

They described most affectionately how they were surprised with joy at the return of their friend and companion in misery, who, they thought, had been devoured by wild beasts of the worst kind, viz., by wild men; and yet how more and more they were surprised with the account he gave them of his errand, and that there was a Christian in any place near, much more one that was able, and had humanity enough, to contribute to their deliverance.

They described how they were astonished at the sight of the relief I sent them, and at the appearance of loaves of bread, things they had not seen since their coming to that miserable place: how often they crossed it and blessed it as bread sent from Heaven; and what a reviving cordial it was to their spirits to taste it, as also the other things I had sent for their supply; and, after all, they would have told me something of the joy they were in at the sight of a boat and pilots, to carry them away to the person and place from whence all these new comforts came, but it was impossible to express it by words, for their excessive joy naturally driving them to unbecoming extravagancies, they had no way to describe them, but by telling me they bordered upon lunacy, having no way to give vent to their passions suitable to the sense that was upon them; that in some it worked one way, and in some another; and that some of them, through a surprise of joy, would burst into tears, others be stark mad, and others immediately faint. This discourse extremely affected me, and called to my mind Friday's ecstasy when he met his father, and the poor people's ecstasy when I took them up at sea after their ship was on fire; the joy of the mate of the ship when he found himself delivered in the place where he expected to perish; and my own joy, when, after twenty-eight years' captivity, I found a good ship ready to carry me to my own country. All these things made me more sensible of the relation of these poor men, and more affected with it.

Having thus given a view of the state of things as I found them, I must relate the heads of what I did for these people, and the condition in which I left them. It was their opinion, and mine, too, that they would be troubled no more with the savages, or, if they were, they would be able to cut them off, if they were twice as many as before; so they had no concern about that. Then I entered into a serious discourse with the Spaniard, whom I call governor, about their stay in the island; for as I was not come to carry any of them off, so it would not be just to carry off some and leave others, who, perhaps, would be unwilling to stay if their strength was diminished. On the other hand, I told them I came to establish them there, not to remove them: and then I let them know that I had brought with me relief of sundry kinds for them; that I had been at a great charge to supply them with all things necessary, as well for their convenience as their defence: and that I had such and such particular persons with me, as well to increase and recruit their number, as by the particular necessary employments which they were bred to, being artificers, to assist them in those things in which at present they were in want.

They were all together when I talked thus to them; and before I delivered to them the stores I had brought, I asked them, one by one, if they had entirely forgot and buried the first animosities that had been among them, and would shake hands with one another, and engage in a strict friendship and union of interest, that so there might be no more misunderstandings and jealousies.

Will Atkins, with abundance of frankness and good-humour, said, they had met with affliction enough to make them all sober, and enemies enough to make them all friends; that, for his part, he would live and die with them; and was so far from designing anything against the Spaniards, that he owned they had done nothing to him but what his own mad humour made necessary, and what he would have done, and perhaps worse, in their case; and that he would ask them pardon, if I desired it, for the foolish and brutish things he had done to them, and was very willing and desirous of living in terms of entire friendship and union with them, and would do anything that lay in his power to convince them of it: and as for going to England, he cared not if he did not go thither these twenty years.

The Spaniards said they had, indeed, at first disarmed and excluded Will Atkins and his two countrymen for their ill conduct, as they had let me know, and they appealed to me for the necessity they were under to do so; but that Will Atkins had behaved himself so bravely in the great fight they had with the savages, and on several occasions since, and had showed himself so faithful to, and concerned for, the general interest of them all, that they had forgotten all that was past, and thought he merited as much to be trusted with arms, and supplied with necessaries, as any of them: and they had testified their satisfaction in him, by committing the command to him, next to the governor himself; and as they had entire confidence in him, and all his countrymen, so they acknowledged they had merited that confidence by all the methods that honest men could merit to be valued and trusted; and they most heartily embraced the occasion of giving me this assurance, that they would never have any interest separate from one another.

Upon these frank and open declarations of friendship, we appointed the next day to dine all together; and, indeed, we made a splendid feast. I caused the ship's cook and his mate to come on shore and dress our dinner, and the old cook's mate we had on shore assisted. We brought on shore six pieces of good beef, and four pieces of pork, out of the ship's provision, with our punchbowl, and materials to fill it; and, in particular, I gave them ten bottles of French claret, and ten bottles of English beer: things that neither the Spaniards nor the English had tasted for many years, and which, it may be supposed, they were very glad of. The Spaniards added to our feast five whole kids, which the cooks roasted: and three of them were sent, covered up close, on board the ship to the seamen, that they might feast on fresh meat from on shore, as we did with their salt meat from on board.

After this feast, at which we were very innocently merry, I brought out my cargo of goods: wherein that there might be no dispute about dividing, I showed them that there was a sufficiency for them all, desiring that they might all take an equal quantity of the goods that were for wearing: that is to say, equal when made up. As, first, I distributed linen sufficient to make every one of them four shirts, and, at the Spaniard's request, afterwards made them up six: these were exceedingly comfortable to them, having been what, as I may say, they had long since forgot the use of, or what it was to wear them. I allotted the English thin stuffs, which I mentioned before, to make every one a light coat like a frock, which I judged fittest for the heat of the season, cool and loose; and ordered that whenever they decayed they should make more, as they thought fit: the like for pumps, shoes, stockings, hats, etc.

I cannot express what pleasure, what satisfaction, sat upon the countenances of all these poor men, when they saw the care I had taken of them, and how well I had furnished them. They told me I was a father to them; and that having such a correspondent as I was in so remote a part of the world, it would make them forget that they were left in a desolate place; and they all voluntarily engaged to me not to leave the place without my consent.

Then I presented to them the people I had brought with me, particularly the tailor, the smith, and the two carpenters, all of them most necessary people; but, above all, my general artificer, than whom they could not name anything that was more useful to them: and the tailor, to show his concern for them, went to work immediately, and, with my leave, made them every one a shirt, the first thing he did; and, which was still more, he taught the women not only how to sew and stitch, and use the needle, but made them assist to make the shirts for their husbands, and for all the rest.

As to the carpenters, I scarce need mention how useful they were; for they took to pieces all my clumsy, unhandy things, and made them clever convenient tables, stools, bedsteads, cupboards, lockers, shelves, and everything they wanted of that kind. But, to let them see how nature made artificers at first, I carried the carpenters to see Will Atkins's basket-house, as I called it: and they both owned they never saw an instance of such natural ingenuity before, nor anything so regular and so handily built, at least of its kind: and one of them, when he saw it, after musing a good while, turning about to me, I am sure, says he, that man has no need of us; you need do nothing but give him tools.

Then I brought them out all my store of tools, and gave every man a digging-spade, a shovel, and a rake, for we had no harrows or ploughs; and to every separate place a pick-axe, a crow, a broad axe, and a saw; always appointing, that as often as any were broken or worn out, they should be supplied, without grudging, out of the general stores that I left behind. Nails, staples, hinges, hammers, chisels, knives, scissors, and all sorts of iron-work, they had without tale, as they required: for no man would take more than he wanted, and he must be a fool that would waste or spoil them on any account whatever; and, for the use of the smith, I left two tons of unwrought iron for a supply.

My magazine of powder and arms which I brought them was such, even to profusion, that they could not but rejoice at them: for now they could march as I used to do, with a musket upon each shoulder, if there was occasion; and were able to fight a thousand savages, if they had but some little advantages of situation, which also they could not miss, if they had occasion.

I carried on shore with me the young man whose mother was starved to death, and the maid also; she was a sober, well-educated, religious young woman, and behaved so inoffensively, that every one gave her a good word; she had, indeed, an unhappy life with us, there being no woman in the ship but herself, but she bore it with patience. After a while, seeing things so well ordered, and in so fine a way of thriving upon my island, and considering that they had neither business nor acquaintance in the East Indies, or reason for taking so long a voyage; I say, considering all this, both of them came to me, and desired I would give them leave to remain on the island, and be entered among my family, as they called it. I agreed to this readily; and they had a little plot of ground allotted to them, where they had three tents or houses set up, surrounded with a basket-work, pallisadoed like Atkins's, adjoining to his plantation. Their tents were contrived so that they had each of them a room apart to lodge in, and a middle tent, like a great storehouse, to lay their goods in, and to eat and drink in. And now the other two Englishmen removed their habitation to the same place; and so the island was divided into three colonies, and no more, viz., the Spaniards, with old Friday, and the first servants, at my old habitation under the hill, which was, in a word, the capital city; and where they had so enlarged and extended their works, as well under as on the outside of the hill, that they lived, though perfectly concealed, yet full at large. Never was there such a little city in a wood, and so hid, in any part of the world: for I verily believe a thousand men might have ranged the island a month, and, if they had not known there was such a thing, and looked on purpose for it, they would not have found it; for the trees stood so thick and so close, and grew so fast-woven one into another, that nothing but cutting them down first could discover the place, except the only two narrow entrances where they went in and out could be found, which was not very easy: one of them was close down at the water's edge, on the side of the creek, and it was afterwards above two hundred yards to the place; and the other was up a ladder at twice, as I have already formally described it; and they had also a large wood thick-planted on the top of the hill, containing above an acre, which grew apace, and concealed the place from all discovery there, with only one narrow place between two trees, not easily to be discovered, to enter on that side.

The other colony was that of Will Atkins, where there were four families of Englishmen, I mean those I had left there, with their wives and children; three savages that were slaves; the widow and the children of the Englishman that was killed; the young man and the maid; and, by the way, we made a wife of her before we went away. There was also the two carpenters and the tailor, whom I brought with me for them; also the smith, who was a very necessary man to them, especially as a gunsmith, to take care of their arms; and my other man, whom I called Jack-of-all-trades, who was in himself as good almost as twenty men; for he was not only a very ingenious fellow, but a very merry fellow; and before I went away we married him to the honest maid that came with the youth in the ship I mentioned before.

And now I speak of marrying, it brings me naturally to say something of the French ecclesiastic that I had brought with me out of the ship's crew whom I took up at sea. It is true, this man was a Roman, and perhaps it may give offence to some hereafter, if I leave anything extraordinary upon record of a man whom, before I begin, I must (to set him out in just colours) represent in terms very much to his disadvantage, in the account of Protestants: as, first, that he was a Papist; secondly, a Popish priest; and thirdly, a French Popish priest. But justice demands of me to give him a due character; and I must say, he was a grave, sober, pious, and most religious person; exact in his life, extensive in his charity, and exemplary in almost everything he did. What then can any one say against being very sensible of the value of such a man, notwithstanding his profession? though it may be my opinion, perhaps, as well as the opinion of others who shall read this, that he was mistaken.

The first hour that I began to converse with him after he had agreed to go with me to the East Indies, I found reason to delight exceedingly in his conversation; and he first began with me about religion in the most obliging manner imaginable. Sir, says he, you have not only under God (and at that he crossed his breast) saved my life, but you have admitted me to go this voyage in your ship, and by your obliging civility have taken me into your family, giving me an opportunity of free conversation. Now, sir, you see by my habit what my profession is, and I guess by your nation what yours is; I may think it is my duty, and doubtless it is so, to use my utmost endeavours, on all occasions, to bring all the souls I can to the knowledge of the truth, and to embrace the Catholic doctrine; but as I am here under your permission, and in your family, I am bound, in justice to your kindness, as well as in decency and good manners, to be under your government; and therefore I shall not, without your leave, enter into any debate on the points of religion in which we may not agree, further than you shall give me leave.

I told him his carriage was so modest, that I could not but acknowledge it; that it was true, we were such people as they called heretics, but that he was not the first Catholic I had conversed with without falling into inconveniences, or carrying the questions to any height in debate; that he should not find himself the worse used for being of a different opinion from us; and if we did not converse without any dislike on either side, it should be his fault, not ours.

He replied, that he thought all our conversation might be easily separated from disputes; that it was not his business to cap principles with every man he conversed with; and that he rather desired me to converse with him as a gentleman than as a religionist; and that, if I would give him leave at any time to discourse upon religious subjects, he would readily comply with it, and that he did not doubt but I would allow him also to defend his own opinions as well as he could; but that, without my leave, he would not break in upon me with any such thing. He told me further, that he would not cease to do all that became him, in his office as priest as well as a private Christian, to procure the good of the ship, and the safety of all that was in her; and though, perhaps, we would not join with him, and he could not pray with us, he hoped he might pray for us, which he would do upon all occasions. In this manner we conversed; and, as he was of the most obliging, gentleman-like behaviour, so he was, if I may be allowed to say so, a man of good sense, and, as I believe, of great learning.

He gave me a most diverting account of his life, and of the many extraordinary events of it; of many adventures which had befallen him in the few years that he had been abroad in the world; and particularly this was very remarkable, viz., that in the voyage he was now engaged in, he had the misfortune to be five times shipped and unshipped, and never to go to the place whither any of the ships he was in were at first designed. That his first intent was to have gone to Martinico, and that he went on board a ship bound thither at St. Malo; but, being forced into Lisbon by bad weather, the ship received some damage by running aground in the mouth of the river Tagus, and was obliged to unload her cargo there; but finding a Portuguese ship there bound to the Madeiras, and ready to sail, and supposing he should easily meet with a vessel there bound to Martinico, he went on board, in order to sail to the Madeiras; but the master of the Portuguese ship, being but an indifferent mariner, had been out of his reckoning, and they drove to Fayal; where, however, he happened to find a very good market for his cargo, which was corn, and therefore resolved not to go to the Madeiras, but to load salt at the isle of May, and to go away to Newfoundland. He had no remedy in this exigence but to go with the ship, and had a pretty good voyage as far as the Banks (so they call the place where they catch the fish); where, meeting with a French ship bound from France to Quebec, in the river of Canada, and from thence to Martinico, to carry provisions, he thought he should have an opportunity to complete his first design; but when he came to Quebec the master of the ship died, and the vessel proceeded no farther: so the next voyage he shipped himself for France, in the ship that was burned when we took them up at sea; and then shipped with us for the East Indies, as I have already said. Thus he had been disappointed in five voyages, all, as I may call it, in one voyage, besides what I shall have occasion to mention further of the same person.

But I shall not make digression into other men's stories, which have no relation to my own: I return to what concerns our affairs on the island.

H E CAME to me one morning, for he lodged among us all the while we were upon the island, and it happened to be just when I was going to visit the Englishmen's colony, at the farthest part of the island; I say, he came to me, and told me with a very grave countenance, that he had for two or three days desired an opportunity of some discourse with me, which he hoped would not be displeasing to me, because he thought it might in some measure correspond with my general design, which was, the prosperity of my new colony, and perhaps might put it, at least more than he thought it was, in the way of God's blessing.

I looked a little surprised at the last part of his discourse, and turning a little short, How, sir, said I, can it be said that we are not in the way of God's blessing, after such visible assistances and wonderful deliverances as we have seen here, and of which I have given you a large account?— If you had pleased, sir, said he, with a world of modesty, and yet with great readiness, to have heard me, you would have found no room to be displeased, much less to think so hard of me, that I should suggest that you have not had wonderful assistances and deliverances; and I hope, on your behalf, that you are in the way of God's blessing, as your design is exceeding good, and will prosper: but, sir, though it were more so than is even possible to you, yet there may be some among you that are not equally right in their actions; and you know, that in the story of the children of Israel, one Achan in the camp removed God's blessing from them, and turned his hand so against them, that six-and-thirty of them, though not concerned in the crime, were the objects of divine vengeance, and bore the weight of that punishment.

I was sensibly touched with his discourse, and told him his inference was so just, and the whole design seemed so sincere, and was really so religious in its own nature, that I was very sorry I had interrupted him, and begged him to go on: and in the mean time, because it seemed that what we had both to say might take up some time, I told him I was going to the Englishmen's plantations, and asked him to go with me, and we might discourse of it by the way. He told me he would the more willingly wait on me thither, because there partly the thing was acted which he desired to speak to me about; so we walked on, and I pressed him to be free and plain with me in what he had to say.

Why then, sir, says he, be pleased to give me leave to lay down a few propositions, as the foundation to what I have to say, that we may not differ in the general principles, though we may be of some differing opinions in the practice of particulars. First, sir, though we differ in some of the doctrinal articles of religion, and it is very unhappy it is so, especially in the case before us, as I shall show afterwards, yet there are some general principles in which we both agree, viz., that there is a God; and that this God having given us some stated general rules for our service and obedience, we ought not willingly and knowingly to offend him, either by neglecting to do what he has commanded, or by doing what he has expressly forbidden; and let our different religions be what they will, this general principle is readily owned by all, that the blessing of God does not ordinarily follow presumptuous sinning against his command; and every good Christian will be affectionately concerned to prevent any that are under his care living in a total neglect of God and his commands. It is not your men being Protestants, whatever my opinion may be of such, that discharges me from being concerned for their souls, and from endeavouring, if it lies before me, that they should live in as little distance from enmity with their Maker as possible, especially if you give me leave to meddle so far in your circuit.

I could not yet imagine what he aimed at, and told him I granted all he had said, and thanked him that he would so far concern himself for us; and begged he would explain the particulars of what he had observed, that, like Joshua, to take his own parable, I might put away the accursed thing from us.

Why then, sir, says he, I will take the liberty you give me; and there are three things, which, if I am right, must stand in the way of God's blessing upon your endeavours here, and which I should rejoice, for your sake, and their own, to see removed: and, sir, I promise myself that you will fully agree with me in them all, as soon as I name them; especially because I shall convince you that every one of them may, with great ease, and very much to your satisfaction, be remedied. First, sir, says he, you have here four Englishmen, who have fetched women from among the savages, and have taken them as their wives, and have had many children by them all, and yet are not married to them after any stated, legal manner, as the laws of God and man require; and therefore are yet, in the sense of both, no less than fornicators, if not living in adultery. To this, sir, I know you will object that there was no clergyman or priest of any kind, or of any profession, to perform the ceremony; nor any pen and ink, or paper, to write down a contract of marriage, and have it signed between them: and I know also, sir, what the Spanish governor has told you, I mean, of the agreement that he obliged them to make when they took those women, viz., that they should choose them out by consent, and keep separately to them, which, by the way, is nothing of a marriage, no agreement with the women, as wives, but only an agreement among themselves, to keep them from quarrelling. But, sir, the essence of the sacrament of matrimony (so he called it, being a Roman) consists not only in the mutual consent of the parties to take one another as man and wife, but in the formal and legal obligation that there is in the contract, to compel the man and woman, at all times to own and acknowledge each other; obliging the man to abstain from all other women, to engage in no other contract while these subsist, and, on all occasions, as ability allows, to provide honestly for them and their children; and to oblige the women to the same, or like conditions, *mutatis mutandis*, on their side. Now, sir, says he, those men may when they please or when occasion presents, abandon these women, disown their children, leave them to perish, and take other women, and marry them while these are living: and here he added, with some warmth, How, sir, is God honoured in this unlawful liberty? and how shall a blessing succeed your endeavours in this place, however good in themselves, and however sincere in your design, while these men, who at present are your subjects, under your absolute government and dominion, are allowed by you to live in open adultery?

I confess I was struck with the thing itself, but much more with the convincing arguments he supported it with; for it was certainly true, that though they had no clergyman upon the spot, yet a formal contract on both sides, made before witnesses and confirmed by any token which they had all agreed to be bound by, though it had been but breaking a stick between them, engaging the men to own these women for their wives upon all occasions, and never to abandon them or their children, and the women to the same with their husbands, had been an effectual lawful marriage in the sight of God; and it was a great neglect that it was not done. But I thought to have got off my young priest by telling him that all that part was done when I was not here; and they had lived so many years with them now, that if it was adultery, it was past remedy; they could do nothing in it now.

Sir, says he, asking your pardon for such freedom, you are right in this, that, it being done in your absence, you could not be charged with that part of the crime; but, I beseech you, flatter not yourself that you are not therefore under an obligation to do your utmost now to put an end to it. How can you think but that, let the time past lie on whom it will, all the guilt, for the future, will lie entirely upon you? because it is certainly in your power now to put an end to it, and in nobody's power but yours.

I was so dull still, that I did not take him right; but I imagined that, by putting an end to it, he meant that I should part them, and not suffer them to live together any longer; and I said to him I could not do that, by any means, for that it would put the whole island into confusion. He seemed surprised that I should so far mistake him. No, sir, says he, I do not mean that you should now separate them, but legally and effectually

marry them now; and as, sir, my way of marrying them may not be easy
to reconcile them to, though it will be effectual, even by your own laws,
so your way may be as well before God, and as valid among men; I
mean, by a written contract signed by both man and woman, and by all
the witnesses present, which all the laws of Europe would decree to be
valid.

I was amazed to see so much true piety, and so much sincerity of zeal,
besides the unusual impartiality in his discourse as to his own party or
church, and such true warmth for preserving the people that he had no
knowledge of or relation to; I say, for preserving them from transgress-
ing the laws of God, the like of which I had indeed not met with anywhere: but, recollecting what he had said of marrying them by a written
contract, which I knew he would stand to, I returned it back upon him,
and told him, I granted all that he had said to be just, and on his part
very kind; that I would discourse with the men upon the point now,
when I came to them; and I knew no reason why they should scruple to
let him marry them all, which I knew well enough would be granted to
be as authentic and valid in England as if they were married by one of
our own clergymen. What was afterwards done in this matter I shall
speak of by itself.

I then pressed him to tell me what was the second complaint which
he had to make, acknowledging that I was very much his debtor for the
first, and thanked him heartily for it. He told me he would use the same
freedom and plainness in the second, and hoped I would take it as well;
and this was, that notwithstanding these English subjects of mine, as he
called them, had lived with those women for almost seven years, had
taught them to speak English, and even to read it, and that they were,
as he perceived, women of tolerable understanding, and capable of instruction, yet they had not, to this hour, taught them anything of the
Christian religion, no, not so much as to know that there was a God,
or a worship, or in what manner God was to be served; or that their
own idolatry, and worshipping they knew not whom, was false and
absurd. This, he said, was an unaccountable neglect, and what God
would certainly call them to account for, and perhaps, at last, take the
work out of their hands—he spoke this very affectionately and warmly.
I am persuaded, says he, had those men lived in the savage country
whence their wives came, the savages would have taken more pains to
have brought them to be idolaters, and to worship the devil, than any of
these men, so far as I can see, have taken with them to teach them the
knowledge of the true God. Now, sir, said he, though I do not acknowledge your religion, or you mine, yet we would be glad to see the devil's
servants, and the subjects of his kingdom, taught to know the general
principles of the Christian religion: that they might, at least, hear of
God, and a Redeemer, and of the resurrection, and of a future state,—
things which we all believe; they would have, at least, been so much

nearer coming into the bosom of the true church than they are now, in the public profession of idolatry and devil-worship.

I could hold no longer; I took him in my arms, and embraced him with an excess of passion. How far, said I to him, have I been from understanding the most essential part of a Christian? viz., to love the interest of the Christian church, and the good of other men's souls: I scarce have known what belongs to the being of a Christian.—O, sir, do not say so, replied he; this thing is not your fault.—No, said I; but why did I never lay it to heart as well as you?—It is not too late yet, said he; be not too forward to condemn yourself.—But what can be done now? said I; you see I am going away.—Will you give me leave to talk with these poor men about it?—Yes, with all my heart, said I; and will oblige them to give heed to what you say too.—As to that, said he, we must leave them to the mercy of Christ; but it is your business to assist them, encourage them, and instruct them; and if you give me leave, and God his blessing, I do not doubt but the poor ignorant souls shall be brought home to the great circle of Christianity, if not into the particular faith we all embrace, and that even while you stay here. Upon this I said, I shall not only give you leave, but give you a thousand thanks for it. What followed on this account I shall mention also again in its place.

I now pressed him for the third article in which we were to blame. Why, really, says he, it is of the same nature; and I will proceed, asking your leave, with the same plainness as before; it is about your poor savages, who are, as I may say, your conquered subjects. It is a maxim, sir, that is, or ought to be, received among all Christians, of what church or pretended church soever, viz., the Christian knowledge ought to be propagated by all possible means, and upon all possible occasions. It is on this principle that our church sends missionaries into Persia, India, China; and that our clergy, even of the superior sort, willingly engage in the most hazardous voyages, and the most dangerous residence among murderers and barbarians, to teach them the knowledge of the true God, and to bring them over to embrace the Christian faith. Now, sir, you have such an opportunity here to have six- or seven-and-thirty poor savages brought over from idolatry to the knowledge of God, their Maker and Redeemer, that I wonder how you can pass such an occasion of doing good, which is really worth the expense of a man's whole life.

I was now struck dumb, indeed, and had not one word to say. I had here a spirit of true Christian zeal for God and religion before me, let his particular principles be of what kind soever: as for me, I had not so much as entertained a thought of this in my heart before, and I believe I should not have thought of it; for I looked upon these savages as slaves, and people whom, had we any work for them to do, we would have used as such, or would have been glad to have transported them to any other part of the world: for our business was to get rid of them; and we would all have been satisfied if they had been sent to any country, so they had never seen their own. But to the case;—I say, I was confounded at his discourse, and knew not what answer to make him.

He looked earnestly at me, seeing me in some disorder—Sir, says he, I shall be very sorry if what I have said gives you any offence.—No, no, said I, I am offended with nobody but myself; but I am perfectly confounded, not only to think that I should never take any notice of this before, but with reflecting what notice I am able to take of it now. You know, sir, said I, what circumstances I am in; I am bound to the East Indies in a ship freighted by merchants, and to whom it would be an insufferable piece of injustice to detain their ship here, the men lying all this while at victuals and wages on the owners' account. It is true, I agreed to be allowed twelve days here, and if I stay more, I must pay three pounds sterling *per diem* demurrage; nor can I stay upon demurrage above eight days more, and I have been here thirteen already; so that I am perfectly unable to engage in this work, unless I would suffer myself to be left behind here again; in which case, if this single ship should miscarry in any part of her voyage, I should be just in the same condition that I was left in here, at first, and from which I have been so wonderfully delivered. He owned the case was very hard upon me, as to my voyage; but laid it home upon my conscience, whether the blessing of saving thirty-seven souls was not worth venturing all I had in the world for. I was not so sensible of that as he was. I returned upon him thus: Why, sir, it is a valuable thing, indeed, to be an instrument in God's hand to convert thirty-seven heathens to the knowledge of Christ; but as you are an ecclesiastic, and are given over to the work, so that it seems so naturally to fall into the way of your profession, how is it then that you do not rather offer yourself to undertake it, than press me to do it?

Upon this he faced about just before me, as he walked along, and putting me to a full stop, made me a very low bow. I most heartily thank God and you, sir, said he, for giving me so evident a call to so blessed a work; and if you think yourself discharged from it, and desire me to undertake it, I will most readily do it, and think it a happy reward for all the hazards and difficulties of such a broken, disappointed voyage as I have met with, that I am dropped at last into so glorious a work.

I discovered a kind of rapture in his face while he spoke this to me; his eyes sparkled like fire, his face glowed, and his colour came and went, as if he had been falling into fits; in a word, he was fired with the joy of being embarked in such a work. I paused a considerable while before I could tell what to say to him; for I was really surprised to find a man of such sincerity and zeal, and carried out in his zeal beyond the ordinary rate of men, not of his profession only, but even of any profession whatsoever. But after I had considered it awhile, I asked him seriously if he was in earnest, and that he would venture, on the single consideration of an attempt on those poor people, to be locked up in an unplanted island for perhaps his life, and at last might not know whether he should be able to do them good or not?

He turned short upon me, and asked me what I called a venture? Pray, sir, said he, what do you think I consented to go in your ship to the East Indies for?—Nay, said I, that I know not, unless it was to preach to the Indians.—Doubtless it was, said he; and do you think, if I can convert these thirty-seven men to the faith of Jesus Christ, it is not worth my time, though I should never be fetched off the island again? Nay, is it not infinitely of more worth to save so many souls than my life is, or the life of twenty more of the same profession? Yes, sir, says he, I would give Christ and the blessed Virgin thanks all my days, if I could be made the least happy instrument of saving the souls of those poor men, though I were never to set my foot off this island, or see my native country any more. But since you will honour me with putting me into this work, for which I will pray for you all the days of my life, I have one humble petition to you besides.—What is that? said I.—Why, says he, it is, that you will leave your man Friday with me, to be my interpreter to them, and to assist me; for without some help I cannot speak to them, or they to me.

I was sensibly touched at his requesting Friday, because I could not think of parting with him, and that for many reasons: he had been the companion of my travels; he was not only faithful to me, but sincerely affectionate to the last degree; and I had resolved to do something considerable for him if he outlived me, as it was probable he would. Then I knew that as I had bred Friday up to be a Protestant, it would quite confound him to bring him to embrace another profession; and he would never, while his eyes were open, believe that his old master was a heretic, and would be damned; and this might, in the end, ruin the poor fellow's principles, and so turn him back again to his first idolatry. However, a sudden thought relieved me in this strait, and it was this: I told him I could not say that I was willing to part with Friday on any account whatever, though a work that to him was of more value than his life, ought to be of much more value than the keeping or parting with a servant. But, on the other hand, I was persuaded that Friday would by no means agree to part with me; and I could not force him to it without his consent, without manifest injustice; because I had promised I would never put him away, and he had promised and engaged to me that he would never leave me unless I put him away.

He seemed very much concerned at it, for he had no rational access to these poor people, seeing he did not understand one word of their language, nor they one word of his. To remove this difficulty, I told him Friday's father had learned Spanish, which I found he also understood, and he should serve him as an interpreter. So he was much better satisfied, and nothing could persuade him but he would stay and endeavour to convert them; but Providence gave another very happy turn to all this.

I come back now to the first part of his objections. When we came to the Englishmen, I sent for them all together, and after some account given them of what I had done for them, viz., what necessary things I had provided for them, and how they were distributed, which they were very sensible of, and very thankful for, I began to talk to them of the very scandalous life they led, and gave them a full account of the notice the clergyman had taken of it; and arguing how unchristian and irreligious a life it was, I first asked them if they were married men or bachelors? They soon explained their conditions to me, and showed that two of them were widowers, and the other three were single men or bachelors. I asked them with what conscience they could take those women, and lie with them as they had done, call them their wives, and have so many children by them, and not be lawfully married to them?

They all gave me the answer I expected, viz., that there was nobody to marry them; that they agreed before the governor to keep them as their wives, and to maintain them and own them as their wives; and they thought, as things stood with them, they were as legally married as if they had been married by a parson, and with all the formalities in the world.

I told them that no doubt they were married in the sight of God, and were bound in conscience to keep them as their wives; but that the laws of men being otherwise, they might desert the poor women and children hereafter; and that their wives being poor desolate women, friendless and moneyless, would have no way to help themselves. I therefore told them that, unless I was assured of their honest intent, I could do nothing for them, but would take care that what I did should be for the women and children without them; and that, unless they would give me some assurances that they would marry the women, I could not think it was convenient they should continue together as man and wife; for it was both scandalous to men and offensive to God, who they could not think would bless them if they went on thus.

All this went on as I expected; and they told me, especially Will Atkins, who now seemed to speak for the rest, that they loved their wives as well as if they had been born in their own native country, and would not leave them upon any account whatever: and they did verily believe their wives were as virtuous and as modest, and did, to the utmost of their skill, as much for them and for their children, as any women could possibly do; and they would not part with them on any account: and Will Atkins, for his own particular, added, that if any man would take him away, and offer to carry him home to England, and make him captain of the best man-of-war in the navy, he would not go with him, if he might not carry his wife and children with him; and if there was a clergyman in the ship, he would be married to her now with all his heart.

This was just as I would have it: the priest was not with me at that moment, but was not far off; so, to try him further, I told him I had a clergyman with me, and, if he was sincere, I would have him married next morning, and bade him consider of it, and talk with the rest. He said, as for himself, he need not consider of it at all, for he was very ready to do it, and was glad I had a minister with me, and he believed they would be all willing also. I then told him that my friend, the minister, was a Frenchman, and could not speak English, but I would act the clerk between them. He never so much as asked me whether he was a Papist or Protestant, which was indeed what I was afraid of; so we parted: I went back to my clergyman, and Will Atkins went in to talk with his companions. I desired the French gentleman not to say anything to them till the business was thorough ripe: and I told him what answer the men had given me.

Before I went from their quarter, they all came to me, and told me they had been considering what I had said; that they were glad to hear I had a clergyman in my company, and they were very willing to give me the satisfaction I desired, and to be formally married as soon as I pleased; for they were far from desiring to part with their wives, and that they meant nothing but what was very honest when they chose them. So I appointed them to meet me the next morning, and, in the mean time, they should let their wives know the meaning of the marriage law; and that it was not only to prevent any scandal, but also to oblige them that they should not forsake them, whatever might happen.

The women were easily made sensible of the meaning of the thing, and were very well satisfied with it, as indeed they had reason to be: so they failed not to attend all together at my apartment next morning, where I brought out my clergyman; and though he had not on a minister's gown, after the manner of England, or the habit of a priest, after the manner of France, yet having a black vest, something like a cassock, with a sash round it, he did not look very unlike a minister; and as for his language, I was his interpreter. But the seriousness of his behaviour to them, and the scruples he made of marrying the women because they were not baptised and professed Christians, gave them an exceeding reverence for his person: and there was no need, after that, to inquire whether he was a clergyman or not. Indeed, I was afraid his scruples would have been carried so far, as that he would not have married them at all; nay, notwithstanding all I was able to say to him, he resisted me, though modestly, yet very steadily: and at last refused absolutely to marry them, unless he had first talked with the men and the women too; and though I at first was a little backward to it, yet at last I agreed to it with a good will, perceiving the sincerity of his design.

When he came to them, he let them know that I had acquainted him with their circumstances, and with the present design; that he was very willing to perform that part of his function, and marry them, as I had desired; but that, before he could do it, he must take the liberty to talk with them. He told them, that in the sight of all indifferent men, and in the sense of the laws of society, they had lived all this while in open fornication; and that it was true, that nothing but the consenting to marry, or effectually separating them from one another, could now put an end to it; but there was a difficulty in it too, with respect to the laws of Christian matrimony, which he was not fully satisfied about, viz., that of marrying one that is a professed Christian to a savage, an idolater and a heathen, one that is not baptised; and yet that he did not see that there was time left to endeavour to persuade the women to be baptised, or to profess the name of Christ, whom they had, he doubted, heard nothing of, and without which they could not be baptised. He told them he doubted they were but indifferent Christians themselves; that they had but little knowledge of God or of his ways, and therefore he could not expect that they had said much to their wives on that head yet; but that, unless they would promise him to use their endeavours with their wives to persuade them to become Christians, and would, as well as they could, instruct them in the knowledge and belief of God that made them, and to worship Jesus Christ that redeemed them, he could not marry them; for he would have no hand in joining Christians with savages; nor was it consistent with the principles of the Christian religion, and was indeed expressly forbidden in God's law.

They heard all this very attentively, and I delivered it very faithfully to them from his mouth, as near his own words as I could; only sometimes adding something of my own, to convince them how just it was, and how I was of his mind: and I always very faithfully distinguished between what I said from myself, and what were the clergyman's words. They told me it was very true what the gentleman said, that they were very indifferent Christians themselves, and that they had never talked to their wives about religion. Lord, sir, says Will Atkins, how should we teach them religion? why, we know nothing ourselves; and besides, sir, said he, should we talk to them of God and Jesus Christ, and heaven and hell, it would make them laugh at us, and ask us what we believe ourselves. And if we should tell them that we believe all the things we speak of to them, such as of good people going to heaven, and wicked people to the devil, they would ask us where we intend to go ourselves, that believe all this, and are such wicked fellows as we indeed are. Why, sir, 'tis enough to give them a surfeit of religion at first hearing; folks must have some religion themselves before they pretend to teach other people. —Will Atkins, said I to him, though I am afraid that what you say has too much truth in it, yet can you not tell your wife that she is in the wrong; that there is a God, and a religion better than her own; that her gods are idols; that they can neither hear nor speak; that there is a great Being that made all things, and that can destroy all that he has made; that he rewards the good and punishes the bad; and that we are to be judged by him at last for all we do here? You are not so ignorant but even nature itself will teach you that all this is true; and I am satisfied you know it all to be true, and believe it yourself.—That is true, sir, said Atkins; but with what face can I say anything to my wife of all this, when she will tell me immediately it cannot be true?—Not true! said I; what do you mean by that?—Why, sir, said he, she will tell me it cannot be true that this God I shall tell her of can be just, or can punish or reward, since I am not punished and sent to the devil, that have been such a wicked creature as she knows I have been, even to her, and to everybody else; and that I should be suffered to live, that have been always acting so contrary to what I must tell her is good, and to what I ought to have done.—Why, truly, Atkins, said I, I am afraid thou speakest too much truth; and with that I informed the clergyman of what Atkins had said, for he was impatient to know. O, said the priest, tell him there is one thing will make him the best minister in the world to his wife, and that is, repentance; for none teach repentance like true penitents. He wants nothing but to repent, and then he will be so much the better qualified to instruct his wife; he will then be able to tell her that there is not only a God, and that he is the just rewarder of good and evil, but that he is a merciful Being, and with infinite goodness and long-suffering forbears to punish these that offend; waiting to be gracious, and willing not the death of a sinner, but rather that he should return and live: that oftentimes he suffers wicked men to go a long time, and even reserves damnation to the general day of retribution: that it is a clear evidence of God and of a future state, that righteous men receive not their reward, or wicked men their punishment, till they come into another world; and this will lead him to teach his wife the doctrine of the resurrection and of the last judgment. Let him but repent for himself, he will be an excellent preacher of repentance to his wife.

I repeated all this to Atkins, who looked very serious all the while, and who, we could easily perceive, was more than ordinarily affected with it: when, being eager, and hardly suffering me to make an end— I know all this, master, says he, and a great deal more; but I have not the impudence to talk thus to my wife, when God and my conscience know, and my wife will be an undeniable evidence against me, that I have lived as if I had never heard of a God or a future state, or anything about it; and to talk of my repenting, alas! (and with that he fetched a deep sigh, and I could see that the tears stood in his eyes) 'tis past all that with me. Past it, Atkins? said I; what dost thou mean by that?—I know well enough what I mean, says he; I mean 'tis too late, and that is too true.

I told the clergyman, word for word, what he said: the poor zealous priest,—I must call him so, for, be his opinion what it will, he had certainly a most singular affection for the good of other men's souls, and it would be hard to think he had not the like for his own—I say, this affectionate man could not refrain from tears; but, recovering himself, said to me, Ask him but one question: Is he easy that it is too late; or is he troubled, and wishes it were not so? I put the question fairly to Atkins; and he answered, with a great deal of passion, How could any man be easy in a condition that must certainly end in eternal destruction? that he was far from being easy; but that, on the contrary, he believed it would, one time or other, ruin him. What do you mean by that? said I. Why, he said, he believed he should one time or other cut his throat, to put an end to the terror of it.

The clergyman shook his head with great concern in his face, when I told him all this; but turning quick to me upon it, says, If that be his case, we may assure him it is not too late; Christ will give him repentance. But pray, says he, explain this to him; that as no man is saved but by Christ, and the merit of his passion procuring divine mercy for him, how can it be too late for any man to receive mercy? Does he think he is able to sin beyond the power or reach of divine mercy? Pray tell him, there may be a time when provoked mercy will no longer strive, and when God may refuse to hear, but that it is never too late for men to ask mercy; and we, that are Christ's servants, are commanded to preach mercy at all times, in the name of Jesus Christ, to all those that sincerely repent: so that it is never too late to repent.

I told Atkins all this, and he heard me with great earnestness; but it seemed as if he turned off the discourse to the rest, for he said to me, he would go and have some talk with his wife; so he went out awhile, and we talked to the rest. I perceived they were all stupidly ignorant as to matters of religion, as much as I was when I went rambling away from my father; and yet there were none of them backward to hear what had been said: and all of them seriously promised that they would talk with their wives about it, and do their endeavours to persuade them to turn Christians.

The clergyman smiled upon me when I reported what answer they gave, but said nothing a good while; but at last, shaking his head, We that are Christ's servants, says he, can go no further than to exhort and instruct; and when men comply, submit to the reproof, and promise what we ask, 'tis all we can do; we are bound to accept their good words; but, believe me, sir, said he, whatever you may have known of the life of that man you call Will Atkins, I believe he is the only sincere convert among them: I take that man to be a true penitent: I will not despair of the rest; but that man is apparently struck with the sense of his past life, and I doubt not, when he comes to talk of religion to his wife, he will talk himself effectually into it; for attempting to teach others is sometimes the best way of teaching ourselves. I know a man, who, having nothing but a summary notion of religion himself, and being wicked and profligate to the last degree in his life, made a thorough reformation in himself by labouring to convert a Jew. If that poor Atkins begins but once to talk seriously of Jesus Christ to his wife, my life for it, he talks himself into a thorough convert, makes himself a penitent; and who knows what may follow?

Upon this discourse, however, and their promising, as above, to endeavour to persuade their wives to embrace Christianity, he married the other two couples; but Will Atkins and his wife were not yet come in. After this, my clergyman waiting awhile, was curious to know where Atkins was gone: and turning to me, said, I entreat you, sir, let us walk out of your labyrinth here, and look; I dare say we shall find this poor man somewhere or other talking seriously to his wife, and teaching her already something of religion. I began to be of the same mind; so we went out together, and I carried him a way which none knew but myself, and where the trees were so very thick that it was not easy to see through the thicket of leaves, and far harder to see in than to see out; when coming to the edge of the wood, I saw Atkins and his tawny wife sitting under the shade of a bush, very eager in discourse; I stopped short till my clergyman came up to me, and then having showed him where they were, we stood and looked very steadily at them a good while. We observed him very earnest with her, pointing up to the sun, and to every quarter of the heavens, and then down to the earth, then out to the sea, then to himself, then to her, to the woods, to the trees. Now, says the clergyman, you see my words are made good, the man preaches to her; mark him now, he is telling her that our God has made him and her, and the heavens, the earth, the sea, the woods, the trees, etc.—I believe he is, said I. Immediately we perceived Will Atkins start upon his feet, fall down on his knees, and lift up both his hands. We supposed he said something, but could not hear him; it was too far for that. He did not continue kneeling half a minute, but comes and sits down by his wife, and talks to her again; we perceived then the woman very attentive, but whether she said anything to him, we could not tell. While the poor fellow was upon his knees, I could see the tears run plentifully down my clergyman's cheeks, and I could hardly forbear myself; but it was a great affliction to us both that we were not near enough to hear anything that passed between them. Well, however, we could come no nearer, for fear of disturbing them; so we resolved to see an end to this piece of still conversation, and it spoke loud enough to us without the help of voice. He sat down again, as I have said, close by her, and talked again earnestly to her, and two or three times we could see him embrace her most passionately; another time we saw him take out his handkerchief and wipe her eyes, and then kiss her again, with a kind of transport very unusual; and after several of these things, we saw him on a sudden jump up again, and lend her his hand to help her up, when immediately leading her by the hand a step or two, they both kneeled down together, and continued so about two minutes.

My friend could bear it no longer, but cries out aloud, St. Paul! St. Paul! behold he prayeth. I was afraid Atkins would hear him, therefore

I entreated him to withhold himself awhile, that we might see an end of the scene, which to me, I must confess, was the most affecting that ever I saw in my life. Well, he strove with himself for a while, but was in such raptures to think that the poor heathen woman was become a Christian, that he was not able to contain himself; he wept several times, then throwing up his hands and crossing his breast, said over several things ejaculatory, and by way of giving God thanks for so miraculous a testimony of the success of our endeavours; some he spoke softly, and I could not well hear others; some in Latin, some in French; then two or three times the tears would interrupt him, that he could not speak at all; but I begged that he would contain himself, and let us more narrowly and fully observe what was before us, which he did for a time, the scene not being near ended yet; for after the poor man and his wife were risen again from their knees, we observed he stood talking still eagerly to her, and we observed her motion, that she was greatly affected with what he said, by her frequently lifting up her hands, laying her hand to her breast, and such other postures as express the greatest seriousness and attention: this continued about half a quarter of an hour, and then they walked away; so we could see no more of them in that situation. I took this interval to talk with my clergyman; and first, I was glad to see the particulars we had both been witnesses to, that, though I was hard enough of belief in such cases, yet that I began to think it was all very sincere here, both in the man and his wife, however ignorant they might both be, and I hoped such a beginning would yet have a more happy end: And who knows, said I, but these two may in time, by instruction and example, work upon some of the others?—Some of them? said he, turning quick upon me; ay, upon all of them: depend upon it, if those two savages, for he has been but little better, as you relate it, should embrace Jesus Christ, they will never leave it till they work upon all the rest; for true religion is naturally communicative, and he that is once made a Christian will never leave a pagan behind him, if he can help it. I owned it was a most Christian principle to think so, and a testimony of true zeal, as well as a generous heart, in him. But, my friend, said I, will you give me leave to start one difficulty here? I cannot tell how to object the least thing against that affectionate concern which you show for the turning the poor people from their paganism to the Christian religion: but how does this comfort you while these people are, in your account, out of the pale of the Catholic church, without which you believe there is no salvation? so that you esteem these but heretics, and for other reasons as effectually lost as the pagans themselves.

To this he answered, with abundance of candour, thus: Sir, I am a Catholic of the Roman church, and a priest of the order of St. Benedict, and I embrace all the principles of the Roman faith: but yet, if you will believe me, and that I do not speak in compliment to you, or in respect to my circumstances and your civilities; I say, nevertheless, I do not look upon you who call yourselves reformed, without some charity: I dare not say (though I know it is our opinion in general) that you cannot be saved; I will by no means limit the mercy of Christ so far as to think that he cannot receive you into the bosom of his church, in a manner to us unperceivable; and I hope you have the same charity for us; I pray daily for your being all restored to Christ's church, by whatsoever method he, who is all-wise, is pleased to direct. In the mean time, sure you will allow it consists with me, as a Roman, to distinguish far between a Protestant and a pagan; between one that calls on Jesus Christ, though in a way which I do not think is according to the true faith, and a savage or a barbarian, that knows no God, no Christ, no Redeemer; and if you are not within the pale of the Catholic church, we hope you are nearer being restored to it than those who know nothing of God or of his church: and I rejoice, therefore, when I see this poor man, who, you say, has been a profligate, and almost a murderer, kneel down and pray to Jesus Christ, as we suppose he did, though not fully enlightened; believing that God, from whom every such work proceeds, will sensibly touch his heart, and bring him to the further knowledge of that truth in his own time: and if God shall influence this poor man to convert and instruct the ignorant savage, his wife, I can never believe that he shall be cast away himself. And have I not reason then to rejoice the nearer any are brought to the knowledge of Christ, though they may not be brought quite home into the bosom of the Catholic church just at the time when I may desire it, leaving it to the goodness of Christ to perfect his work in his own time, and in his own way? Certainly, I would rejoice if all the savages in America were brought, like this poor woman, to pray to God, though they were all to be Protestants at first, rather than they should continue pagans or heathens; firmly believing, that he that had bestowed the first light to them would farther illuminate them with a beam of his heavenly grace, and bring them into the pale of his church, when he should see good.

I WAS ASTONISHED at the sincerity and temper of this pious papist, as much as I was oppressed by the power of his reasoning; and it presently occurred to my thoughts, that if such a temper were universal, we might all be Catholic Christians, whatever church or particular profession we joined in; that a spirit of charity would soon work us all up into right principles; and as he thought that the like charity would make us all Catholics, so I told him I believed had all the members of his church the like moderation, they would soon all be Protestants.—And there we left that part; for we never disputed at all.

However, I talked to him another way, and taking him by the hand, My friend, says I, I wish all the clergy of the Romish church were blest with such moderation, and had an equal share of your charity. I am entirely of your opinion; but I must tell you, that if you should preach such doctrine in Spain or Italy, they would put you into the Inquisition.— It may be so, said he; I know not what they would do in Spain or Italy; but I will not say they would be the better Christians for that severity; for I am sure there is no heresy in abounding with charity.

As Will Atkins and his wife were gone, our business there was over, so we went back our own way; and when we came back, we found them waiting to be called in: observing this, I asked my clergyman if we should discover to him that we had seen him under the bush or not; and it was his opinion we should not, but that we should talk to him first, and hear what he would say to us; so we called him in alone, nobody being in the place but ourselves, and I began with him thus:

Will Atkins, said I, prithee what education had you? What was your father?

W. A. A better man than ever I shall be: Sir, my father was a clergyman.

R. C. What education did he give you?

W. A. He would have taught me well, sir; but I despised all education, instruction, or correction, like a beast as I was.

R. C. It is true, Solomon says, He that despises reproof is brutish.

W. A. Ay, sir, I was brutish indeed, for I murdered my father: for God's sake, sir, talk no more about that; sir, I murdered my poor father.

PR. Ha! a murderer!

Here the priest started (for I interpreted every word as he spoke) and looked pale: it seems he believed that Will had really killed his father.

R. C. No, no, sir, I do not understand him so: Will Atkins, explain yourself; you did not kill your father, did you, with your own hands?

W. A. No, sir, I did not cut his throat; but I cut the thread of all his comforts, and shortened his days: I broke his heart by the most ungrateful, unnatural return, for the most tender and affectionate treatment that father ever gave, or child could receive.

R. C. Well, I did not ask you about your father, to extort this confession: I pray God give you repentance for it, and forgive that and all your other sins; but I asked you because I see that though you have not much learning, yet you are not so ignorant as some are in things that are good; that you have known more of religion, a great deal, than you have practised.

W. A. Though you, sir, did not extort the confession that I make about my father, conscience does; and whenever we come to look back upon our lives, the sins against our indulgent parents are certainly the first that touch us; the wounds they make lie deepest, and the weight they leave will lie heaviest upon the mind, of all the sins we can commit.

R. C. You talk too feelingly and sensibly for me, Atkins; I cannot bear it.

W. A. You bear it, master! I dare say you know nothing of it.

R. C. Yes, Atkins; every shore, every hill, nay, I may say every tree in this island, is witness to the anguish of my soul for my ingratitude and bad usage of a good, tender father; a father much like yours, by your description: and I murdered my father as well as you, Will Atkins; but I think, for all that, my repentance is short of yours too, by a great deal.

I would have said more, if I could have restrained my passions; but I thought this poor man's repentance was so much sincerer than mine, that I was going to leave off the discourse and retire; for I was surprised with what he had said, and thought that instead of my going about to teach and instruct him this man was made a teacher and instructor to me in a most surprising and unexpected manner.

I laid all this before the young clergyman, who was greatly affected with it, and said to me, Did I not say, sir, that when this man was converted he would preach to us all? I tell you, sir, if this one man be made a true penitent, here will be no need of me; he will make Christians of all in the island.—But having a little composed myself, I renewed my discourse with Will Atkins. But, Will, said I, how comes the sense of this matter to touch you just now?

W. A. Sir, you have set me about a work that has struck a dart through my very soul; I have been talking about God and religion to my wife, in order, as you directed me, to make a Christian of her, and she has preached such a sermon to me as I shall never forget while I live.

R. C. No, no, it is not your wife has preached to you; but when you were moving religious arguments to her, conscience has flung them back upon you.

W. A. Ay, sir, with such force as is not to be resisted.

R. C. Pray, Will, let us know what passed between you and your wife; for I know something of it already.

W. A. Sir, it is impossible to give you a full account of it; I am too full to hold it, and yet have no tongue to express it; but let her have said what she will, and though I cannot give you an account of it, this I can tell you, that I have resolved to amend and reform my life.

R. C. But tell us some of it: how did you begin, Will? For this has been an extraordinary case, that is certain. She has preached a sermon, indeed, if she has wrought this upon you.

W. A. Why, I first told her of the nature of our laws about marriage, and what the reasons were that men and women were obliged to enter into such compacts, as it was neither in the power of one nor other to break; that otherwise order and justice could not be maintained, and men would run from their wives, and abandon their children, mix confusedly with one another, and neither families be kept entire, nor inheritances be settled by legal descent.

R. C. You talk like a civilian, Will. Could you make her understand what you meant by inheritance and families? They know no such things among the savages, but marry anyhow, without regard to relation, consanguinity, or family; brother and sister, nay, as I have been told, even the father and the daughter, and the son and the mother.

W. A. I believe, sir, you are misinformed, and my wife assures me of the contrary, and that they abhor it; perhaps, for any further relations, they may not be so exact as we are; but she tells me they never touch one another in the near relationship you speak of.

R. C. Well, what did she say to what you told her?

W. A. She said she liked it very well, and it was much better than in her country.

R. C. But did you tell her what marriage was?

W. A. Ay, ay; there began our dialogue. I asked her if she would be married to me our way. She asked me what way that was. I told her marriage was appointed by God; and here we had a strange talk together, indeed, as ever man and wife had, I believe.

N. B. This dialogue between Will Atkins and his wife I took down in writing, just after he had told it me, which was as follows:

WIFE. Appointed by God! Why, have you a God in your country?

W. A. Yes, my dear, God is in every country.

WIFE. No your God in my country; my country have the great old Benamuckee God.

W. A. Child, I am very unfit to show you who God is: God is in heaven, and made the heaven and the earth, the sea, and all that in them is.

WIFE. No makee de earth; no you God makee all earth: no makee my country.

Will Atkins laughed a little at her expression of God not making her country.

WIFE. No laugh; why laugh me? This nothing to laugh.

He was justly reproved by his wife, for she was more serious than he at first.

W. A. That's true indeed; I will not laugh any more, my dear.

WIFE. Why you say you God makee all?

W. A. Yes, child, our God made the whole world, and you and me, and all things; for he is the only true God, and there is no God but him; he lives for ever in heaven.

WIFE. Why you no tell me long ago?

W. A. That's true indeed; but I have been a wicked wretch, and have not only forgotten to acquaint thee with anything before, but have lived without God in the world myself.

WIFE. What? Have you a great God in your country, you no know him? No say O to him? No do good thing for him? That no possible.

W. A. It is true; though, for all that, we live as if there was no God in heaven, or that he had no power on earth.

WIFE. But why God let you do so? Why he no makee you good live?

W. A. It is all our own fault.

WIFE. But you say me he is great, much great, have much great power, can makee kill when he will, why he no makee kill when you no serve him, no say O to him, no be good mans?

W. A. That is true, he might strike me dead; and I ought to expect it, for I have been a wicked wretch, that is true; but God is merciful, and does not deal with us as we deserve.

WIFE. But then do you not tell God thankee for that too?

W. A. No, indeed, I have not thanked God for his mercy, any more than I have feared God for his power.

WIFE. Then you God no God; me no think believe he be such one, great much power, strong: no makee kill you though you make him so much angry.

W. A. What, will my wicked life hinder you from believing in God? What a dreadful creature am I! and what a sad truth it is, that the horrid lives of Christians hinder the conversion of heathens!

WIFE. How me think you have great much God up there (she points up to heaven) and yet no do well, no do good thing? Can he tell? Sure he no tell what you do?

W. A. Yes, yes, he knows and sees all things; he hears us speak, sees what we do, knows what we think, though we do not speak.

WIFE. What! he no hear you curse, swear, speak de great damn?

W. A. Yes, yes, hears it all.

WIFE. Where be then the much great power strong?

W. A. He is merciful, that is all we can say for it; and this proves him to be the true God; he is God, and not man, and therefore we are not consumed.

Here Will Atkins told us he was struck with horror, to think how he could tell his wife so clearly that God sees, and hears, and knows the secret thoughts of the heart, and all that we do, and yet that he had dared to do all the vile things he had done.

WIFE. Merciful! What you call that?

W. A. He is our father and maker, and he pities and spares us.

WIFE. So then he never makee kill, never angry when you do wicked; then he no good himself, or no great able.

W. A. Yes, yes, my dear, he is infinitely good and infinitely great, and able to punish too; and sometimes, to show his justice and vengeance, he lets fly his anger to destroy sinners and make examples; many are cut off in their sins.

WIFE. But no makee kill you yet; then he tell you, may be, that he no makee you kill: so you makee de bargain with him, you do bad thing, he no be angry at you when he be angry at other mans.

W. A. No, indeed; my sins are all presumptions upon his goodness; and he would be infinitely just if he destroyed me, as he has done other men.

WIFE. Well, and yet no kill, no makee you dead; what you say to him for that? You no tell him thankee for all that too?

W. A. I am an unthankful, ungrateful dog, that is true.

WIFE. Why he no makee you much good better? you say he makee you.

W. A. He made me, as he made all the world: it is I have deformed myself and abused his goodness, and made myself an abominable wretch.

WIFE. I wish you makee God know me; I no makee him angry, I no do bad wicked thing.

Here Will Atkins said his heart sunk within him, to hear a poor untaught creature desire to be taught to know God, and he such a wicked wretch that he could not say one word to her about God, but what the reproach of his own carriage would make most irrational to her to believe; nay, that already she had told him that she could not believe in God, because he, that was so wicked, was not destroyed.

W. A. My dear, you mean, you wish I could teach you to know God, not God to know you; for he knows you already, and every thought in your heart.

WIFE. Why then he know what I say to you now; he know me wish to know him; how shall he know who makee me?

W. A. Poor creature, he must teach thee, I cannot teach thee; I will pray to him to teach thee to know him, and forgive me, that am unworthy to teach thee.

The poor fellow was in such an agony at her desiring him to make her know God, and her wishing to know him, that he said he fell down on his knees before her, and prayed to God to enlighten her mind with the saving knowledge of Jesus Christ, and to pardon his sins, and accept of his being the unworthy instrument of instructing her in the principles of religion; after which he sat down by her again, and their dialogue went on.—This was the time when we saw him kneel down, and hold up his hands.

WIFE. What you put down the knee for? What you hold up the hand for? What you say? Who you speak to? What is all that?

W. A. My dear, I bow my knees in token of my submission to him that made me; I said O to him, as you call it; and as your old men do to their idol Benamuckee; that is, I prayed to him.

WIFE. What you say O to him for?

W. A. I prayed to him to open your eyes, and your understanding, that you may know him, and be accepted by him.

WIFE. Can he do that too?

W. A. Yes, he can; he can do all things.

WIFE. But now he hear what you say?

W. A. Yes; he has bid us pray to him, and promised to hear us.

WIFE. Bid you pray? When he bid you? How he bid you? What, you hear him speak?

W. A. No, we do not hear him speak; but he has revealed himself in many ways to us.

Here he was at a great loss to make her understand that God has revealed himself to us by his word, and what his word was; but at last he told it her thus:

W. A. God has spoken to some good men in former days, even from heaven, by plain words; and God has inspired good men by his Spirit; and they have written all his laws down in a book.

WIFE. Me no understand that; where is my book?

W. A. Alas! my poor creature, I have not this book; but I hope I shall one time or other get it for you, and help you to read it.

Here he embraced her with great affection; but with inexpressible grief that he had not a Bible.

WIFE. But how you makee me know that God teachee them to write that book?

W. A. By the same rule that we know him to be God.

WIFE. What rule? What way you know him?

W. A. Because he teaches and commands nothing but what is good, righteous, and holy, and tends to make us perfectly good, as well as perfectly happy; and because he forbids, and commands us to avoid, all that is wicked, that is evil in itself, or evil in its consequence.

WIFE. That me would understand, that me fain see; if he teachee all good thing, he makee all good thing, he give all thing, he hear me when I say O to him, as you do just now; he makee me good, if I wish to be good; he spare me, no makee kill me, when I no be good: all this you say he do, yet he be great God: me take, think, believe him to be great God; me say O to him with you, my dear.

Here the poor man could forbear no longer, but raised her up, made her kneel by him, and he prayed to God aloud to instruct her in the knowledge of himself, by his Spirit; and that by some good providence, if possible, she might some time or other come to a Bible, that she might read the word of God, and be taught by it to know him.—This was the time that we saw him lift her up by the hand, and saw him kneel down by her, as above.

They had several other discourses, it seems, after this, too long to be

set down here; and particularly she made him promise, that since he confessed his own life had been a wicked abominable course of provocations
against God, that he would reform it, and not make God angry any
more; lest he should make him dead, as he called it, and then she would
be left alone, and never be taught to know this God better; and lest he
should be miserable, as he had told her wicked men would be, after
death.

This was a strange account, and very affecting to us both, but particularly to the young clergyman; he was indeed wonderfully surprised
with it, but under the greatest affliction imaginable that he could not
talk to her, that he could not speak English, to make her understand
him; and as she spoke but very broken English, he could not understand
her; however, he turned himself to me, and told me that he believed that
there must be more to do with this woman than to marry her. I did not
understand him at first, but at length he explained himself, viz., that she
ought to be baptised. I agreed with him in that part readily, and was for
going about it presently. No, no; hold, sir, said he; though I would have
her be baptised by all means, yet I must observe that Will Atkins, her
husband, has indeed brought her, in a wonderful manner, to be willing
to embrace a religious life, and has given her just ideas of the being of a
God; of his power, justice, and mercy: yet I desire to know of him if he
has said anything to her of Jesus Christ, and of the salvation of sinners;
of the nature of faith in him, and redemption by him; of the Holy Spirit,
the resurrection, the last judgment, and a future state.

I called Will Atkins again, and asked him; but the poor fellow fell
immediately into tears, and told us he had said something to her of all
those things, but that he was himself so wicked a creature, and his conscience so reproached him with his horrid ungodly life, that he trembled
at the apprehensions that her knowledge of him should lessen the attention she should give to those things, and make her rather contemn religion than receive it; but he was assured, he said, that her mind was so
disposed to receive due impressions of all those things, and that if I
would but discourse with her, she would make it appear to my satisfaction that my labour would not be lost upon her.

Accordingly, I called her in, and placing myself as interpreter between
my religious priest and the woman, I entreated him to begin with her;
but sure such a sermon was never preached by a popish priest in these
latter ages of the world: and as I told him, I thought he had all the zeal,
all the knowledge, all the sincerity of a Christian, without the error of a
Roman Catholic; and that I took him to be such a clergyman as the
Roman bishops were, before the church of Rome assumed spiritual
sovereignty over the consciences of men. In a word, he brought the poor
woman to embrace the knowledge of Christ, and of redemption by him,
not with wonder and astonishment only, as she did the first notions of a

God, but with joy and faith; with an affection, and a surprising degree of understanding, scarce to be imagined, much less to be expressed; and, at her own request, she was baptised.

When he was preparing to baptise her, I entreated him that he would perform that office with some caution, that the man might not perceive he was of the Roman church, if possible, because of other ill consequences which might attend a difference among us in that very religion which we were instructing the other in. He told me that as he had no consecrated chapel, nor proper things for the office, I should see he would do it in a manner that I should not know by it that he was a Roman Catholic himself, if I had not known it before; and so he did; for saying only some words over to himself in Latin, which I could not understand, he poured a whole dishful of water upon the woman's head, pronouncing in French very loud, "Mary," (which was the name her husband desired me to give her, for I was her godfather,) "I baptise thee in the name of the Father, and of the Son, and of the Holy Ghost": so that none could know anything by it what religion he was of. He gave the benediction afterwards in Latin, but either Will Atkins did not know but it was French, or else did not take notice of it at that time.

As soon as this was over, we married them; and after the marriage was over, he turned to Will Atkins, and in a very affectionate manner exhorted him, not only to persevere in that good disposition he was in, but to support the convictions that were upon him by a resolution to reform his life; told him it was in vain to say he repented if he did not forsake his crimes: represented to him how God had honoured him with being the instrument of bringing his wife to the knowledge of the Christian religion, and that he should be careful he did not dishonour the grace of God; and that if he did, he would see the heathen a better Christian than himself; the savage converted, and the instrument cast away. He said a great many good things to them both; and then recommending them to God's goodness, gave them the benediction again, I repeating everything to them in English; and thus ended the ceremony. I think it was the most pleasant and agreeable day to me that ever I passed in my whole life.

But my clergyman had not done yet; his thoughts hung continually upon the conversion of the thirty-seven savages, and fain he would have stayed upon the island to have undertaken it; but I convinced him, first, that his undertaking was impracticable in itself; and, secondly, that perhaps I would put it into a way of being done in his absence to his satisfaction; of which by and by.

Having thus brought the affairs of the island to a narrow compass, I was preparing to go on board the ship, when the young man I had taken out of the famished ship's company came to me, and told me he understood I had a clergyman with me, and that I had caused the Englishmen to be married to the savages; that he had a match, too, which he desired might be finished before I went, between two Christians, which he hoped would not be disagreeable to me.

I knew this must be the young woman who was his mother's servant, for there was no other Christian woman on the island; so I began to persuade him not to do anything of that kind rashly, or because he found himself in this solitary circumstance. I represented to him that he had some considerable substance in the world, and good friends, as I understood by himself, and the maid also; that the maid was not only poor, and a servant, but was unequal to him, she being six or seven-and-twenty years old, and he not being seventeen or eighteen; that he might very probably, with my assistance, make a remove from this wilderness, and come into his own country again; and that then it would be a thousand to one but he would repent his choice, and the dislike of that circumstance might be disadvantageous to both. I was going to say more, but he interrupted me, smiling, and told me, with a great deal of modesty, that I mistook in my guesses, that he had nothing of that kind in his thoughts; and he was very glad to hear that I had an intent of putting them in a way to see their own country again; and nothing should have put him upon staying there, but that the voyage I was going was so exceeding long and hazardous, and would carry him quite out of the reach of all his friends; that he had nothing to desire of me, but that I would settle him in some little property in the island where he was, give him a servant or two, and some few necessaries, and he would settle himself here like a planter, waiting the good time when, if ever I returned to England, I would redeem them; and hoped I would not be unmindful of him when I came to England; that he would give me some letters to his friends in London, to let them know how good I had been to him, and in what part of the world, and what circumstances I had left him in; and he promised me that whenever I redeemed him, the plantation, and all improvements he had made upon it, let the value be what it would, should be wholly mine.

His discourse was prettily delivered, considering his youth, and was the more agreeable to me, because he told me positively the match was not for himself. I gave him all possible assurances that if I lived to come safe to England, I would deliver his letters, and do his business effectually; and that he might depend I should never forget the circumstances I had left him in: but still I was impatient to know who was the person to be married: upon which he told me it was my Jack-of-all-trades and his maid Susan. I was most agreeably surprised when he named the match; for indeed I thought it very suitable. The character of that man I have given already; and as for the maid, she was a very honest, modest, sober, and religious young woman; had a very good share of sense, was agreeable enough in her person, spoke very handsomely, and to the purpose, always with decency and good manners, and neither too backward to speak, when requisite, nor impertinently forward, when it was not her business: very handy and housewifely, and an excellent manager; fit, indeed, to have been governess to the whole island, and she knew very well how to behave in every respect.

The match being proposed in this manner, we married them the same day; and as I was father at the altar, as I may say, and gave her away, so I gave her a portion; for I appointed her and her husband a handsome large space of ground for their plantation; and, indeed, this match, and the proposal the young gentleman made to give him a small property in the island, put me upon parcelling it out amongst them, that they might not quarrel afterwards about their situation.

This sharing out the land to them I left to Will Atkins, who was now grown a sober, grave, managing fellow, perfectly reformed, exceedingly pious and religious, and as far as I may be allowed to speak positively in such a case, I verily believe he is a true penitent. He divided things so justly, and so much to every one's satisfaction, that they only desired one general writing under my hand for the whole, which I caused to be drawn up, and signed and sealed to them, setting out the bounds and situation of every man's plantation, and testifying that I gave them thereby severally a right to the whole possession and inheritance of the respective plantations or farms, with their improvements, to them and their heirs, reserving all the rest of the island as my own property, and a certain rent for every particular plantation after eleven years, if I, or any one from me, or in my name, came to demand it, producing an attested copy of the same writing.

As to the government and laws among them, I told them I was not capable of giving them better rules than they were able to give themselves; only I made them promise me to live in love and good neighbourhood with one another; and so I prepared to leave them.

One thing I must not omit, and that is, that being now settled in a kind of commonwealth among themselves, and having much business in hand, it was but odd to have seven-and-thirty Indians live in a nook of the island, independent, and, indeed, unemployed: for, excepting the providing themselves food, which they had difficulty enough to do sometimes, they had no manner of business or property to manage. I proposed, therefore, to the governor Spaniard that he should go to them, with Friday's father, and propose to them to remove, and either plant for themselves, or take them into their several families as servants, to be maintained for their labour, but without being absolute slaves; for I would not admit them to make them slaves by force, by any means; because they had their liberty given them by capitulation, as it were articles of surrender, which they ought not to break.

They most willingly embraced the proposal, and came all very cheerfully along with him: so we allotted them land, and plantations, which three or four accepted of, but all the rest chose to be employed as servants in the several families we had settled; and thus my colony was in a manner settled, as follows:—The Spaniards possessed my original habitation, which was the capital city, and extended their plantations all along the side of the brook, which made the creek that I have so often described, as far as my bower; and as they increased their culture, it went always eastward. The English lived in the north-east part, where Will Atkins and his comrades began, and came on southward and south-west, towards the back part of the Spaniards; and every plantation had a great addition of land to take in, if they found occasion, so that they need not jostle one another for want of room. All the east end of the island was left uninhabited, that if any of the savages should come on shore there only for their usual customary barbarities, they might come and go; if they disturbed nobody, nobody would disturb them; and no doubt but they were often ashore, and went away again, for I never heard that the planters were ever attacked or disturbed any more.

It now came into my thoughts that I had hinted to my friend the clergyman that the work of converting the savages might perhaps be set on foot in his absence to his satisfaction, and told him that now I thought it was put in a fair way; for the savages being thus divided among the Christians, if they would but every one of them do their part with those which came under their hands, I hoped it might have a very good effect.

He agreed presently in that, if they did their part. But how, says he, shall we obtain that of them? I told him we would call them all together, and leave it in charge with them, or go to them, one by one, which he thought best; so we divided it, he to speak to the Spaniards, who were all Papists, and I to the English, who were all Protestants; and we recommended it earnestly to them, and made them promise that they would never make any distinction of Papist or Protestant in their exhorting the savages to turn Christians, but teach them the general knowledge of the true God, and of their Saviour Jesus Christ; and they likewise promised us that they would never have any differences or disputes one with another about religion.

When I came to Will Atkins's house (I may call it so, for such a house, or such a piece of basket-work, I believe, was not standing in the world again), there I found the young woman I have mentioned above, and Will Atkins's wife, were become intimates; and this prudent, religious young woman had perfected the work Will Atkins had begun: and though it was not above four days after what I had related, yet the new-baptised savage woman was made such a Christian as I have seldom heard of in all my observation or conversation in the world.

It came next into my mind, in the morning before I went to them, that amongst all the needful things I had to leave with them, I had not left them a Bible, in which I showed myself less considering for them than my good friend the widow was for me, when she sent me the cargo of a hundred pounds from Lisbon, where she packed up three Bibles and a prayer-book. However, the good woman's charity had a greater extent than ever she imagined, for they were reserved for the comfort and instruction of those that made much better use of them than I had done.

I took one of the Bibles in my pocket, and when I came to Will Atkins's tent, or house, and found the young woman and Atkins's baptised wife had been discoursing of religion together, for Will Atkins told it me with a great deal of joy, I asked if they were together now, and he said yes; so I went into the house, and he with me, and we found them together very earnest in discourse. O sir, says Will Atkins, when God has sinners to reconcile to himself, and aliens to bring home, he never wants a messenger; my wife has got a new instructor; I knew I was as unworthy as I was incapable of that work; that young woman has been sent hither from heaven; she is enough to convert a whole island of savages. The young woman blushed, and rose up to go away, but I desired her to sit still; I told her she had a good work upon her hands, and I hoped God would bless her in it.

We talked a little, and I did not perceive they had any book among them, though I did not ask: but I put my hand into my pocket, and pulled out my Bible; Here, says I to Atkins, I have brought you an assistant that perhaps you had not before. The man was so confounded that he was not able to speak for some time; but recovering himself, he takes it with both his hands, and turning to his wife, Here, my dear, says he, did I not tell you our God, though he lives above, could hear what we said? Here's the book I prayed for when you and I kneeled down under the bush; now God has heard us, and sent it. When he had said so, the man fell into such transports of passionate joy, that between the joy of having it, and giving God thanks for it, the tears ran down his face like a child that was crying.

The woman was surprised, and was like to have run into a mistake that none of us were aware of, for she firmly believed God had sent the book upon her husband's petition. It is true, that providentially it was so, and might be taken so in a consequent sense; but I believe it would have been no difficult matter, at that time, to have persuaded the poor woman to have believed that an express messenger came from heaven on purpose to bring that individual book; but it was too serious a matter to suffer any delusion to take place; so I turned to the young woman, and told her we did not desire to impose upon the new convert, in her first and more ignorant understanding of things, and begged her to explain to her that God may be very properly said to answer our petitions when, in the course of his providence, such things are in a particular manner brought to pass as we petitioned for; but we did not expect returns from Heaven in a miraculous and particular manner, and it is our mercy that it is not so.

This the young woman did afterwards effectually, so that there was, I assure you, no priestcraft used here; and I should have thought it one of the most unjustifiable frauds in the world to have had it so. But the surprise of joy upon Will Atkins is really not to be expressed; and there, we may be sure, was no delusion. Sure no man was ever more thankful in the world for anything of its kind than he was for the Bible; nor, I believe, never any man was glad of a Bible from a better principle; and though he had been a most profligate creature, headstrong, furious, and desperately wicked, yet this man is a standing rule to us all for the well instructing children, viz., that parents should never give over to teach and instruct, nor ever despair of the success of their endeavours, let the children be ever so refractory, or, to appearance, insensible of instruction; for, if ever God, in his providence, touches the conscience of such, the force of their education returns upon them, and the early instruction of parents is not lost, though it may have been many years laid asleep, but, some time or other, they may find the benefit of it. Thus it was with this poor man: however ignorant he was of religion and Christian knowledge, he found he had some to do with now more ignorant than himself, and that the least part of the instruction of his good father that now came to his mind was of use to him.

Among the rest it occurred to him, he said, how his father used to insist so much on the inexpressible value of the Bible, the privilege and blessing of it to nations, families, and persons: but he never entertained the least notion of the worth of it till now, when being to talk to heathens, savages, and barbarians, he wanted the help of the written oracle for his assistance.

The young woman was glad of it also for the present occasion, though she had one, and so had the youth, on board our ship, among their goods, which were not yet brought on shore. And now having said so many things of this young woman, I cannot omit telling one story more of her and myself, which has something in it very informing and remarkable.

I have related to what extremity the poor young woman was reduced, how her mistress was starved to death, and died on board that unhappy ship we met at sea, and how the whole ship's company was reduced to the last extremity. The gentlewoman and her son, and this maid, were first hardly used, as to provisions, and at last totally neglected and starved; that is to say, brought to the last extremity of hunger.—One day, being discoursing with her on the extremities they suffered, I asked her if she could describe, by what she had felt, what it was to starve, and how it appeared? She told me she believed she could, and she told her tale very distinctly, thus:

First, sir, said she, we had for some days fared exceeding hard, and suffered very great hunger: but at last we were wholly without food of any kind, except sugar, and a little wine and water. The first day, after I had received no food at all, I found myself, towards evening, first empty and sick at the stomach, and nearer night much inclined to yawning and sleep. I laid down on a couch in the great cabin to sleep, and slept about three hours, and awaked a little refreshed, having taken a glass of wine when I lay down: after being about three hours awake, it being about five o'clock in the morning, I found myself empty, and my stomach sickish, and lay down again, but could not sleep at all, being very faint and ill; and thus I continued all the second day, with a strange variety, first hungry, then sick again, with retchings to vomit. The second night, being obliged to go to bed again without any food, more than a draught of fresh water, and being asleep, I dreamed I was at Barbadoes, and that the market was mightily stocked with provisions; that I bought some for my mistress, and went and dined very heartily. I thought my stomach was as full after this as it would have been after a good dinner; but when I awaked, I was exceedingly sunk in my spirits to find myself in the extremity of famine. The last glass of wine we had I drank, and put sugar in it, because of its having some spirit to supply nourishment; but there being no substance in the stomach for the digesting office to work upon, I found the only effect of the wine was, to raise disagreeable fumes from the stomach into the head: and I lay, as they told me, stupid and senseless, as one drunk, for some time. The third day, in the morning, after a night of strange, confused, and inconsistent dreams, and rather dozing than sleeping, I awaked ravenous and furious with hunger; and I question, had not my understanding returned and conquered it, whether, if I had been a mother, and had had a little child with me, its life would have been safe or not. This lasted about three hours; during which time I was twice raging mad as any creature in Bedlam, as my young master told me, and as he can now inform you.

In one of these fits of lunacy or distraction I fell down, and struck my face against the corner of a pallet bed, in which my mistress lay, and, with the blow, the blood gushed out of my nose; and the cabin-boy bringing me a little basin, I sat down and bled into it a great deal; and as the blood came from me, I came to myself, and the violence of the flame or fever I was in abated, and so did the ravenous part of the hunger. Then I grew sick, and retched to vomit, but could not, for I had nothing in my stomach to bring up. After I had bled some time, I swooned, and they all believed I was dead; but I came to myself soon after, and then had a most dreadful pain in my stomach, not to be described, not like the colic, but a gnawing, eager pain for food; and towards the night it went off, with a kind of earnest wishing or longing for food, something like, as I suppose, the longing of a woman with child. I took another draught of water, with sugar in it; but my stomach loathed the sugar, and brought it all up again: then I took a draught of water without sugar, and all stayed with me; and I laid me down upon the bed, praying me most heartily that it would please God to take me away; and composing my mind in hopes of it, I slumbered awhile, and then waking, thought myself dying, being light with vapours from an empty stomach;

I recommended my soul then to God, and earnestly wished that somebody would throw me into the sea.

All this while my mistress lay by me, just, as I thought, expiring, but bore it with much more patience than I; gave the last bit of bread she had left to her child, my young master, who would not have taken it, but she obliged him to eat it; and I believed it saved his life.

Towards the morning I slept again; and when I awoke, I fell into a violent passion of crying, and after that had a second fit of violent hunger: I got up ravenous, and in a most dreadful condition; had my mistress been dead, as much as I loved her, I am certain I should have eaten a piece of her flesh with as much relish, and as unconcerned, as ever I did eat the flesh of any creature appointed for food; and once or twice I was going to bite my own arm: at last I saw the basin in which was the blood I had bled at my nose the day before: I ran to it, and swallowed it with such haste, and such a greedy appetite, as if I wondered nobody had taken it before, and afraid it should be taken from me now. After it was down, though the thoughts of it filled me with horror, yet it checked the fit of hunger, and I took another draught of water, and was composed and refreshed for some hours after. This was the fourth day; and thus I held it till towards night; when, within the compass of three hours, I had all the several circumstances over again, one after another, viz., sick, sleepy, eagerly hungry, pain in the stomach, then ravenous again, then sick, then lunatic, then crying, then ravenous again, and so every quarter of an hour; and my strength wasted exceedingly; at night I laid me down, having no comfort but in the hope that I should die before morning.

All this night I had no sleep; but the hunger was now turned into a disease: and I had a terrible colic and griping, by wind, instead of food, having found its way into the bowels; and in this condition I lay till morning, when I was surprised with the cries and lamentations of my young master, who called out to me that his mother was dead: I lifted myself up a little, for I had not strength to rise, but found she was not dead, though she was able to give very little signs of life.

I had then such convulsions in my stomach, for want of some sustenance, that I cannot describe; with such frequent throes and pangs of appetite, that nothing but the tortures of death can imitate; and in this condition I was when I heard the seamen above cry out, A sail! a sail! and halloo and jump about as if they were distracted.

I was not able to get off from the bed, and my mistress much less; and my young master was so sick, that I thought he had been expiring; so we could not open the cabin door or get any account what it was that occasioned such confusion; nor had we any conversation with the ship's company for two days, they having told us that they had not a mouthful of anything to eat in the ship; and this they told us afterwards, they thought we had been dead. It was this dreadful condition we were in when you were sent to save our lives; and how you found us, sir, you know as well as I, and better too.

This was her own relation, and is such a distinct account of starving to death, as I confess, I never met with, and was exceeding entertaining to me. I am the rather apt to believe it to be a true account, because the youth gave me an account of a good part of it; though, I must own, not so distinct and so feeling as the maid: and the rather, because it seems his mother fed him at the price of her own life; but the poor maid, though her constitution being stronger than that of her mistress, who was in years, and a weakly woman too, she might struggle harder with it: I say, the poor maid might be supposed to feel the extremity something sooner than her mistress, who might be allowed to keep the last bit something longer than she parted with any to relieve the maid. No question, as the case is here related, if our ship, or some other, had not providentially met them, a few days more would have ended all their lives, unless they had prevented it by eating one another; and that even, as their case stood, would have served them but a little while, they being five hundred leagues from any land, or any possibility of relief, other than in the miraculous manner it happened: but this is by the way: I return to my disposition of things among the people.

And, first, it is to be observed here, that for many reasons I did not think fit to let them know anything of the sloop I had framed, and which I thought of setting up among them; for I found, at least at my first coming, such seeds of divisions among them, that I saw plainly, had I set up the sloop, and left it among them, they would, upon every light disgust, have separated, and gone away from one another, or perhaps have turned pirates, and so made the island a den of thieves, instead of a plantation of sober and religious people, as I intended it; nor did I leave the two pieces of brass cannon that I had on board, or the two quarter-deck guns that my nephew took extraordinary, for the same reason: I thought it was enough to qualify them for a defensive war against any that should invade them, but not to set them up for an offensive war, or to go abroad to attack others; which, in the end, would only bring ruin and destruction upon them: I reserved the sloop, therefore, and the guns, for their service another way, as I shall observe in its place.

Having now done with the island, I left them all in good circumstances and in a flourishing condition, and went on board my ship again the 6th of May, having been about twenty-five days among them; and as they were all resolved to stay upon the island till I came to remove them, I promised to send them further relief from the Brazils, if I could possibly find an opportunity; and, particularly, I promised to send them some cattle, such as sheep, hogs, and cows; as the two cows and calves which I brought from England, we had been obliged, by the length of our voyage, to kill them at sea, for want of hay to feed them.

THE NEXT DAY, giving them a salute of five guns at parting, we set sail, and arrived at the bay of All Saints, in the Brazils, in about twenty-two days, meeting nothing remarkable in our passage but this: that about three days after we had sailed, being becalmed, and the current setting strong to the E.N.E., running, as it were, into a bay or gulf on the land side, we were driven something out of our course, and once or twice our men cried out, Land to the eastward; but whether it was the continent or islands we could not tell by any means. But the third day, towards evening, the sea smooth, and the weather calm, we saw the sea, as it were, covered towards the land with something very black; not being able to discover what it was, till after some time, our chief mate, going up to the main-shrouds a little way, and looking at them with a perspective, cried out it was an army. I could not imagine what he meant by an army, and thwarted him a little hastily. Nay, sir, says he, don't be angry, for 'tis an army, and a fleet too; for I believe there are a thousand canoes, and you may see them paddle along, for they are coming towards us apace.

I was a little surprised, then, indeed, and so was my nephew the captain; for he had heard such terrible stories of them in the island, and having never been in those seas before, that he could not tell what to think of it, but said, two or three times, we should all be devoured. I must confess, considering we were becalmed, and the current set strong towards the shore, I liked it the worse; however, I bade them not be afraid, but bring the ship to an anchor as soon as we came so near to know that we must engage them.

The weather continued calm, and they came on apace towards us; so I gave order to come to an anchor, and furl all our sails: as for the savages, I told them they had nothing to fear but fire, and therefore they should get their boats out, and fasten them, one close by the head, and the other by the stern, and man them both well, and wait the issue in that posture: this I did, that the men in the boats might be ready with sheets and buckets to put out any fire these savages would endeavour to fix to the outside of the ship.

In this posture we lay by for them, and in a little while they came up with us; but never was such a horrid sight seen by Christians: though my mate was much mistaken in his calculation of their number, yet when they came up we reckoned about a hundred and twenty-six; some of them had sixteen or seventeen men in them, some more, and the least six or seven.

When they came nearer to us, they seemed to be struck with wonder and astonishment, as at a sight which doubtless they had never seen before; nor could they, at first, as we afterwards understood, know what to make of us; they came boldly up, however, very near to us, and seemed to go about to row round us; but we called to our men in the boats not to let them come too near them. This very order brought us to an engagement with them, without our designing it: for five or six of the large canoes came so near our long-boat that our men beckoned with their hands to keep them back, which they understood very well, and went back, but at their retreat about fifty arrows came on board us from those boats, and one of our men in the long-boat was very much wounded. However, I called to them not to fire by any means; but we handed down some deal boards into the boat, and the carpenter presently set up a kind of fence, like waste boards, to cover them from the arrows of the savages, if they should shoot again.

About half an hour afterwards they all came up in a body astern of us, and so near, as that we could easily discern what they were, though we could not tell their design; and I easily found they were some of my old friends, the same sort of savages that I had been used to engage with; and in a short time more they rowed a little farther out to sea, till they came directly broadside with us, and then rowed down straight upon us, till they came so near that they could hear us speak: upon this I ordered all my men to keep close, lest they should shoot any more arrows, and made all our guns ready; but being so near as to be within hearing, I made Friday go out upon the deck, and call out aloud to them in his language, to know what they meant; which accordingly he did. Whether they understood him or not, that I knew not; but as soon as he had called to them, six of them, who were in the foremost or nighest boat to us, turned their canoes from us, and stooping down, showed us their naked forms, accompanied with many indecent jestures and extravagancies: whether this was a defiance or challenge we know not, or whether it was done in mere contempt, or as a signal to the rest; but immediately Friday cried out they were going to shoot, and, unhappily for him, poor fellow, they let fly about three hundred of their arrows, and, to my inexpressible grief, killed poor Friday, no other man being in their sight. The poor fellow was shot with no less than three arrows, and about three more fell very near him; such unlucky marksmen they were!

I was so enraged at the loss of my old trusty servant and companion, that I immediately ordered five guns to be loaded with small shot, and four with great, and gave them such a broadside as they had never heard in their lives before, to be sure. They were not above half a cable length off when we fired; and our gunners took their aim so well that three or four of their canoes were overset, as we had reason to believe, by one shot only.

The ill manners of turning up their bare backsides to us gave us no great offence; neither did I know for certain whether that which would pass for the greatest contempt among us might be understood so by them or not; therefore, in return, I had only resolved to have fired four of five guns at them with powder only, which I knew would frighten them sufficiently: but when they shot at us directly, with all the fury they were capable of, and especially as they had killed my poor Friday, whom I so entirely loved and valued, and who, indeed, so well deserved it, I thought myself not only justifiable before God and man, but would have been very glad if I could have overset every canoe there, and drowned every one of them.

I can neither tell how many we killed, nor how many we wounded, at this broadside, but sure such a fright and hurry never was seen among such a multitude; there were thirteen or fourteen of their canoes split and overset in all, and the men all set a swimming: the rest, frightened out of their wits, scoured away as fast as they could, taking but little care to save those whose boats were split or spoiled with our shot; so I suppose that many of them were lost; and our men took up one poor fellow swimming for his life, above an hour after they were all gone.

The small shot from our cannon must needs kill and wound a great many; but, in short, we never knew anything how it went with them, for they fled so fast, that in three hours, or thereabouts, we could not see above three or four straggling canoes, nor did we ever see the rest any more; for a breeze of wind springing up the same evening, we weighed, and set sail for the Brazils.

We had a prisoner, indeed, but the creature was so sullen that he would neither eat nor speak, and we all fancied he would starve himself to death: but I took a way to cure him; for I made them take him and turn him into the long-boat, and make him believe they would toss him into the sea again, and so leave him where they found him, if he would not speak: nor would that do, but they really did throw him into the sea, and came away from him, and then he followed them, for he swam like a cork, and called to them, in his tongue, though they knew not one word of what he said: however, at last they took him in again, and then he began to be more tractable; nor did I ever design they should drown him.

We were now under sail again; but I was the most disconsolate creature alive for want of my man Friday, and would have been very glad to have gone back to the island to have taken one of the rest from there for my occasion; but it could not be; so we went on. We had one prisoner, as I have said, and it was a long time before we could make him understand anything; but, in time, our men taught him some English, and he began to be a little tractable. Afterwards, we inquired what country he came from, but could make nothing of what he said; for his speech was so odd, all gutturals, and he spoke in the throat in such a hollow, odd manner, that we could never form a word after him; and we were all of opinion that they might speak that language as well if they were gagged as otherwise; nor could we perceive that they had any occasion either for teeth, tongue, lips, or palate, but formed their words just as a hunting horn forms a tune, with an open throat. He told us, however, some time after, when we had taught him to speak a little English, that they were going with their kings to fight a great battle. When he said kings, we asked him how many kings? He said they were five nation (we could not make him understand the plural *s*), and that they all joined to go against two nation. We asked him what made them come up to us? He said, "To makee te great wonder look." Here it is to be observed, that all those natives, as also those of Africa, when they learn English, always add two *e*'s at the end of the words where we use one; and they place the accent upon them, as makee, takee, and the like; and we could not break them of it; nay I could hardly make Friday leave it off, though at last he did.

And now I name the poor fellow once more, I must take my last leave of him: Poor honest Friday! We buried him with all the decency and solemnity possible, by putting him into a coffin, and throwing him into the sea; and I caused them to fire eleven guns for him: and so ended the life of the most grateful, faithful, honest, and most affectionate servant, that man ever had.

We went now away with a fair wind for Brazil; and in about twelve days' time we made land, in the latitude of five degrees south of the line, being the north-easternmost land of all that part of America. We kept on S. by E. in sight of the shore four days, when we made Cape St. Augustine, and in three days came to an anchor off the Bay of All Saints, the old place of my deliverance, from whence came both my good and evil fate.

Never ship came to this port that had less business than I had, and yet it was with great difficulty that we were admitted to hold the least correspondence on shore; not my partner himself, who was alive, and made a great figure among them, not my two merchant trustees, not the fame of my wonderful preservation in the island, could obtain me that favour; but my partner remembering that I had given five hundred moidores to the priory of the monastery of the Augustines, and two hundred and seventy-two to the poor, went to the monastery, and obliged the prior that then was, to go to the governor, and get leave for me personally, with the captain and one more, besides eight seamen, to come on shore, and no more; and this upon condition absolutely capitulated for, that we should not offer to land any goods out of the ship, or to carry any person away without license. They were so strict with us as to landing and goods, that it was with extreme difficulty that I got on shore three bales of English goods, such as fine broad-cloths, stuffs, and some linen, which I had brought for a present to my partner.

He was a very generous, open-hearted man; though, like me, he came from little at first; and though he knew not that I had the least design of giving him anything, he sent me on board a present of fresh provisions, wine, and sweetmeats, worth above thirty moidores, including some tobacco, and three or four fine medals of gold: but I was even with him in my present, which, as I have said, consisted of fine broad-cloth, English stuffs, lace, and fine hollands: also I delivered him about the value of one hundred pounds sterling, in the same goods, for other uses; and I obliged him to set up the sloop, which I had brought with me from England, as I have said, for the use of my colony, in order to send the refreshments I intended to my plantation.

Accordingly, he got hands, and finished the sloop in a very few days, for she was already framed; and I gave the master of her such instructions as that he could not miss the place; nor did he miss them, as I had an account from my partner afterwards. I got him soon loaded with the small cargo I sent them; and one of our seamen, that had been on shore with me there, offered to go with the sloop and settle there, upon my letter to the governor Spaniard to allot him a sufficient quantity of land for a plantation, and giving him some clothes and tools for his planting work, which he said he understood, having been an old planter at Maryland, and a buccaneer into the bargain. I encouraged the fellow by granting all he desired; and, as an addition, I gave him the savage whom we had taken prisoner of war to be his slave, and ordered the governor Spaniard to give him his share of everything he wanted with the rest.

When we came to fit this man out, my old partner told me there was a certain very honest fellow, a Brazil planter of his acquaintance, who had fallen into the displeasure of the church, I know not what the matter is with him, says he, but on my conscience I think he is a heretic in his heart, and he has been obliged to conceal himself for fear of the Inquisition; that he would be very glad of such an opportunity to make his escape, with his wife, and two daughters; and if I would let them go to my island, and allot them a plantation, he would give them a small stock to begin with; for the officers of the Inquisition had seized all his effects and estate, and he had nothing left but a little household stuff, and two slaves: and, adds he, though I hate his principles, yet I would not have him fall into their hands, for he will be assuredly burned alive if he does.

I granted this presently, and joined my Englishman with them; and we concealed the man, and his wife and daughters, on board our ship, till the sloop put out to go to sea; and then, having put all their goods on board some time before, we put them on board the sloop after she was got out of the bay.

Our seaman was mightily pleased with this new partner; and their stocks, indeed, were much alike rich in tools, in preparations, and a farm; but nothing to begin with, except as above: however, they carried over with them, which was worth all the rest, some materials for planting sugarcanes, with some plants of canes, which he, I mean the Portugal man, understood very well.

Among the rest of the supplies sent to my tenants in the island, I sent them by the sloop three milch cows and five calves, about twenty-two hogs among them, three sows big with pig, two mares, and a stone-horse. For my Spaniards, according to my promise, I engaged three Portugal women to go, and recommended it to them to marry them, and use them kindly. I could have procured more women, but I remembered that the poor prosecuted man had two daughters, and that there were but five of the Spaniards that wanted; the rest had wives of their own, though in another country.

All this cargo arrived safe, and, as you may readily suppose, was very welcome to my old inhabitants, who were now, with this addition, between sixty and seventy people, besides little children, of which there were a great many. I found letters at London from them all, by way of Lisbon, when I came back to England, of which I shall also take some notice immediately.

I have now done with the island, and all manner of discourse about it; and whoever reads the rest of my memorandums would do well to turn his thoughts entirely from it, and expect to read of the follies of an old man, not warned by his own harms, much less by those of other men, to beware of the like; not cooled by almost forty years' miseries and disappointments; not satisfied with prosperity beyond expectation, nor made cautious by afflictions and distress beyond imitation.

I had no more business to go to the East Indies than a man at full liberty has to go to the turnkey at Newgate, and desire him to lock him up among the prisoners there, and starve him. Had I taken a small vessel from England, and gone directly to the island; had I loaded her, as I did the other vessel, with all the necessaries for the plantation, and for my people; taken a patent from the government here to have secured my property, in subjection only to that of England; had I carried over cannon and ammunition, servants, and people to plant, and taken possession of the place, fortified and strengthened it in the name of England, and increased it with people, as I might easily have done; had I then settled myself there, and sent the ship back laden with good rice, as I might also have done in six months' time, and ordered my friends to have fitted her out again for our supply; had I done this, and stayed there myself, I had at least acted like a man of common sense; but I was possessed with a wandering spirit, and scorned all advantages: I pleased myself with being the patron of the people I placed there, and doing for them in a kind of haughty, majestic way, like an old patriarchal monarch, providing for them as if I had been father of the whole family, as well as of the plantation: but I never so much as pretended to plant in the name of any government or nation, or to acknowledge any prince, or to call my people subjects to any one nation more than another: nay, I never so much as gave the place a name, but left it, as I found it, belonging to nobody, and the people under no discipline or government but my own; who, though I had influence over them as a father and benefactor, had no authority or power to act or command one way or other, further than voluntary consent moved them to comply: yet even this, had I stayed there, would have done well enough; but as I rambled from them, and came there no more, the last letters I had from any of them were by my partner's means, who afterwards sent another sloop to the place, and who sent me word, though I had not the letter till I got to London, several years after it was written, that they went on but poorly, were malcontent with their long stay there; that Will Atkins was dead; that five of the Spaniards were come away; and though they had not been much molested by the savages, yet they had had some skirmishes with them; and that they begged of him to write to me to think of the promise I had made to fetch them away, that they might see their country again before they died.

But I was gone a wildgoose chase, indeed! and they that will have any more of me must be content to follow me into a new variety of follies, hardships, and wild adventures, wherein the justice of Providence may be duly observed; and we may see how easily Heaven can gorge us with our own desires, make the strongest of our wishes be our affliction, and punish us most severely with those very things which we think it would be our utmost happiness to be allowed in. Whether I had business or no business, away I went: it is no time now to enlarge upon the reason or absurdity of my own conduct, but to come to the history; I was embarked for the voyage, and the voyage I went.

I shall only add a word or two concerning my honest popish clergyman: for let their opinion of us, and all other heretics in general, as they call us, be as uncharitable as it may, I verily believe this man was very sincere, and wished the good of all men: yet I believe he was upon the reserve in many of his expressions to prevent giving me offence; for I scarce heard him once call on the blessed Virgin, or mention St. Jago or his guardian angel, though so common with the rest of them: however, I say, I had not the least doubt of his sincerity and pious intentions on his own part; and I am firmly of opinion, if the rest of the popish missionaries were like him, they would strive to visit even the poor Tartars, and Laplanders, where they had nothing to give them, as well as covet to flock to India, Persia, China, etc., the most wealthy of the heathen countries; for if they expected to bring no gains to their church by it, it may well be admired how they came to admit the Chinese Confucius into the calendar of Christian saints. But this by the by.

A ship being ready to sail for Lisbon, my pious priest asked me leave to go thither; being still, as he observed, bound never to finish any voyage he began. How happy had it been for me if I had gone with him! But it was too late now: all things Heaven appoints for the best: had I gone with him, I had never had so many things to be thankful for, and the reader had never heard of the second part of the travels and adventures of Robinson Crusoe: so I must here leave exclaiming at myself, and go on with my voyage. From the Brazils we made directly over the Atlantic Sea to the Cape of Good Hope, and had a tolerable good voyage, our course generally south-east, now and then a storm, and some contrary winds, but my disasters at sea were at an end; my future rubs and cross events were to befall me on shore, that it might appear the land was as well prepared to be our scourge as the sea.

Our ship was on a trading voyage, and had a supercargo on board, who was to direct all her motions after she arrived at the Cape, only being limited to a certain number of days for stay, by charter-party, at the several ports she was to go. This was none of my business, neither did I meddle with it; my nephew, the captain, and the supercargo, adjusting all those things between them as they thought fit.

WE STAYED at the Cape no longer than was needful to take in fresh water, but made the best of our way for the coast of Coromandel. We were indeed informed that a French man-of-war of fifty guns, and two large merchant ships, were gone for the Indies; and as I knew we were at war with France, I had some apprehensions of them; but they went their own way, and we heard no more of them.

I shall not pester the reader with a tedious description of places, journals of our voyages, variations of the compass, latitudes, trade-winds, etc.; it is enough to name the ports and places which we touched at, and what occurred to us upon our passing from one to another. We touched first at the island of Madagascar, where, though the people are fierce and treacherous, and very well armed with lances and bows, which they use with inconceivable dexterity, yet we fared very well with them a while; they treated us very civilly; and, for some trifles which we gave them, such as knives, scissors, etc., they brought us eleven good fat bullocks of a middling size, which we took in, partly for fresh provisions for our present spending, and the rest to salt for the ship's use.

We were obliged to stay here some time after we had furnished ourselves with provisions; and I, who was always too curious to look into every nook of the world wherever I came, was for going on shore as often as I could. It was on the east side of the island that we went on shore one evening; and the people, who, by the way, are very numerous, came thronging about us, and stood gazing at us at a distance; but as we had traded freely with them, and had been kindly used, we thought ourselves in no danger; but when we saw the people, we cut three boughs out of a tree, and stuck them up at a distance from us; which, it seems, is a mark in that country, not only of truce and friendship, but when it is accepted, the other side sets up three poles or boughs, which is a signal that they accept the truce too; but then this is a known condition of the truce, that you are not to pass beyond their three poles, towards them, nor they to come past your three poles, or boughs, towards you; so that you are perfectly secure within the three poles, and all the space between your poles and theirs is allowed like a market for free converse, traffic, and commerce. When you go there, you must not carry your weapons with you; and if they come into that space, they stick up their javelins and lances all at the first poles, and come on unarmed: but if any violence is offered them, and the truce thereby broken, away they run to the poles, and lay hold of their weapons, and the truce is at an end.

It happened one evening when we went on shore, that a greater number of the people came down than usual, but all very friendly and civil; and they brought several kinds of provisions, for which we satisfied them with such toys as we had; their women, also, brought us milk and roots, and several things very acceptable to us, and all was quiet; and we made us a little tent or hut of some boughs of trees, and lay on shore all night.

I know not what was the occasion, but I was not so well satisfied to lie on shore as the rest; and the boat riding at an anchor about a stone's cast from the land, with two men in her to take care of her, I made one of them come on shore; and getting some boughs of trees to cover us also in the boat, I spread the sail on the bottom of the boat, and lay under the cover of the branches of the trees all night in the boat.

About two o'clock in the morning we heard one of our men make a terrible noise on the shore, calling out, for God's sake, to bring the boat in, and come and help them, for they were all like to be murdered; at the same time I heard the fire of five muskets, which was the number of the guns they had, and that three times over; for, it seems, the natives here were not so easily frightened with guns as the savages were in America, where I had to do with them. All this while I knew not what was the matter, but rousing immediately from sleep with the noise, I caused the boat to be thrust in, and resolved, with three fusees we had on board, to land and assist our men.

We got the boat soon to the shore, but our men were in too much haste; for being come to the shore, they plunged into the water, to get to the boat with all the expedition they could, being pursued by between three and four hundred men. Our men were but nine in all, and only five of them had fusees with them; the rest had pistols and swords, indeed, but they were of small use to them.

We took up seven of our men, and with difficulty enough too, three of them being very ill wounded; and that which was still worse was, that while we stood in the boat to take our men in, we were in as much danger as they were in on shore; for they poured their arrows in upon us so thick, that we were glad to barricade the side of the boat up with benches, and two or three loose boards, which, to our great satisfaction, we had by mere accident in the boat. And yet, had it been daylight, they are, it seems, such exact marksmen, that if they could have seen but the least part of any of us, they would have been sure of us. We had, by the light of the moon, a little sight of them, as they stood pelting us from the shore with darts and arrows; and having got ready our fire-arms, we gave them a volley, that we could hear, by the cries of some of them, had wounded several: however, they stood thus in battle array on the shore till break of day, which we suppose was that they might see the better to take their aim at us.

In this condition we lay, and could not tell how to weigh our anchor or set up our sail, because we must needs stand up in the boat, and they were sure to hit us as we were to hit a bird in a tree with small shot. We made signals of distress to the ship, which, though she rode a league off, yet my nephew, the captain, hearing our firing, and by glasses perceiving the posture we lay in, and that we fired towards the shore, pretty well understood us; and weighing anchor with all speed, he stood as near the shore as he durst with the ship, and then sent another boat, with ten hands in her, to assist us; but we called to them not to come too near, telling them what condition we were in; however they stood in near to us, and one of the men taking the end of a tow-line in his hand, and keeping one boat between him and the enemy, so that they could not perfectly see him, swam on board us, and made fast the line to the boat; upon which we slipped out a little cable, and leaving our anchor behind they towed us out of the reach of the arrows; we all the while lying close behind the barricado we had made.

As soon as we were got from between the ship and the shore, that we could lay her side to the shore, she ran along just by them, and poured in a broadside among them loaded with pieces of iron and lead, small bullets, and such stuff, besides the great shot, which made a terrible havoc among them.

When we were got on board and out of danger, we had time to examine into the occasion of this fray; and, indeed, our supercargo, who had been often in those parts, put me upon it; for he said he was sure the inhabitants would not have touched us after we had made a truce, if we had not done something to provoke them to it. At length it came out that an old woman who had come to sell us some milk, had brought it within our poles, and a young woman with her, who also brought some roots or herbs; and while the old woman (whether she was mother to the young woman or no they could not tell) was selling us the milk, one of our men offered some rudeness to the wench that was with her, at which the old woman made a great noise; however, the seaman would not quit his prize, but carried her out of the old woman's sight among the trees, it being almost dark: the old woman went away without her, and, as we may suppose, made an outcry among the people she came from, who, upon notice, raised this great army upon us in three or four hours; and it was great odds but we had all been destroyed.

One of our men was killed with a lance thrown at him just at the beginning of the attack, as he sallied out of the tent they had made: the rest came off free, all but the fellow who was the occasion of all the mischief, who paid dear enough for his black mistress, for we could not hear what became of him for a great while. We lay upon the shore two days after, though the wind presented, and made signals for him, and made our boat sail up shore and down shore several leagues, but in vain, so we were obliged to give him over; and if he alone had suffered for it, the loss had been less.

I could not satisfy myself, however, without venturing on shore once more, to try if I could learn anything of him or them: it was the third night after the action that I had a great mind to learn, if I could by any means, what mischief we had done, and how the game stood on the Indians' side. I was careful to do it in the dark, lest we should be attacked again; but I ought, indeed, to have been sure that the men I went with had been under my command, before I engaged in a thing so hazardous and mischievous, as I was brought into by it without design.

We took twenty as stout fellows with us as any in the ship, besides the supercargo and myself, and we landed two hours before midnight, at the same place where the Indians stood drawn up in the evening before: I landed here, because my design, as I have said, was chiefly to see if they had quitted the field, and if they had left any marks behind them of the mischief we had done them; and I thought if we could surprise one or two of them, perhaps we might get our man again, by way of exchange.

We landed without any noise, and divided our men into two bodies, whereof the boatswain commanded one, and I the other. We neither saw nor heard anybody stir when we landed; and we marched up, one body at a distance from the other, to the place; but at first could see nothing, it being very dark; till by and by our boatswain, who led the first party, stumbled and fell over a dead body. This made them halt awhile; for knowing by the circumstances that they were at the place where the Indians had stood, they waited for my coming up there. We concluded to halt till the moon began to rise, which we knew would be in less than an hour, when we could easily discern the havoc we had made among them. We told thirty-two bodies upon the ground, whereof two were not quite dead; some had an arm, and some a leg shot off, and one his hand; those that were wounded, we suppose, they had carried away.

When we had made, as I thought, a full discovery of all we could come to the knowledge of, I was resolved for going on board; but the boatswain and his party sent me word that they were resolved to make a visit to the Indian town, where these dogs, as they called them, dwelt, and asked me to go along with them; and if they could find them, as they still fancied they should, they did not doubt of getting a good booty; and it might be they might find Tom Jeffry there: that was the man's name we had lost.

Had they sent to ask my leave to go, I knew well enough what answer to have given them: for I should have commanded them instantly on board, knowing it was not a hazard fit for us to run, who had a ship, and ship-loading in our charge, and a voyage to make which depended very much upon the lives of the men; but as they sent me word they were resolved to go, and only asked me and my company to go along with them, I positively refused it, and rose up, for I was sitting on the ground, in order to go to the boat. One or two of the men began to importune me to go; and when I refused, began to grumble, and say that they were not under my command, and they would go. Come, Jack, says one of the men, will you go with me? I'll go for one. Jack said he would,—and then another,—and, in a word, they all left me but one, whom I persuaded to stay, and a boy left in the boat. So the supercargo and I, with the third man, went back to the boat, where we told them we should stay for them, and take care to take in as many of them as should be left; for I told them it was a mad thing they were going about, and supposed most of them would run the fate of Tom Jeffry.

They told me, like seamen, they would warrant it they would come off again, and they would take care, etc.; so away they went. I entreated them to consider the ship and the voyage, that their lives were not their own, and that they were intrusted with the voyage, in some measure; that if they miscarried, the ship might be lost for want of their help, and that they could not answer for it to God or man. But I might as well have talked to the mainmast of the ship; they were mad upon their journey, only they gave me good words, and begged I would not be angry; that they did not doubt but they would be back again in about an hour at furthest; for the Indian town, they said, was not above a half a mile off, though they found it above two miles before they got to it.

Well, they all went away; and though the attempt was desperate, and such as none but madmen would have gone about, yet, to give them their due, they went about it as warily as boldly: they were gallantly armed, for they had every man a fusee or musket, a bayonet, and a pistol; some of them had broad cutlasses, some of them had hangers, and the boatswain and two more had poleaxes; besides all which they had among them thirteen hand-grenadoes: bolder fellows, and better provided, never went about any wicked work in the world.

When they went out, their chief desire was plunder, and they were in mighty hopes of finding gold there; but a circumstance, which none of them were aware of, set them on fire with revenge, and made devils of them all. When they came to the few Indian houses which they thought had been the town, which was not above half a mile off, they were under a great disappointment, for there were not above twelve or thirteen houses; and where the town was, or how big, they knew not. They consulted, therefore, what to do, and were some time before they could resolve; for if they fell upon these, they must cut all their throats, and it was ten to one but some of them might escape, it being in the night, though the moon was up; and if one escaped, he would run and raise all the town, so they should have a whole army upon them: again, on the other hand, if they went away and left these untouched, for the people were all asleep, they could not tell which way to look for the town: however, the last was the best advice; so they resolved to leave them, and look for the town as well as they could. They went on a little way, and found a cow tied to a tree; this, they presently concluded, would be a good guide to them; for, they said, the cow certainly belonged to the town before them, or to the town behind them; and if they untied her, they should see which way she went: if she went back, they had nothing to say to her; but, if she went forward, they would follow her: so they cut the cord, which was made of twisted flags, and the cow went on before them, directly to the town; which, as they reported, consisted of above two hundred houses or huts, and in some of these they found several families living together.

Here they found all in silence, as profoundly secure as sleep could make them; and, first, they called another council, to consider what they had to do; and, in a word, they resolved to divide themselves into three bodies, and so set three houses on fire in three parts of the town; and as the men came out, to seize them and bind them (if any resisted, they need not be asked what to do then), and so to search the rest of the houses for plunder: but they resolved to march silently first through the town, and see what dimensions it was of, and if they might venture upon it or no.

They did so, and desperately resolved that they would venture upon them: but while they were animating one another to the work, three of them, who were a little before the rest, called out aloud to them, and told them that they had found Tom Jeffry: they all ran up to the place, where they found the poor fellow hanging up naked by one arm, and his throat cut. There was an Indian house just by the tree, where they found sixteen or seventeen of the principal Indians, who had been concerned in the fray with us before, and two or three of them wounded with our shot; and our men found they were awake, and talking one to another in that house, but knew not their number.

The sight of their poor mangled comrade so enraged them, as before, that they swore to one another they would be revenged, and that not an Indian that came into their hands should have any quarter; and to work they went immediately, and yet not so madly as might be expected from the rage and fury they were in. Their first care was to get something that would soon take fire, but, after a little search, they found that would be to no purpose; for most of the houses were low, and thatched with flags and rushes, of which the country is full: so they presently made some wild-fire, as we call it, by wetting a little powder in the palms of their hands; and in a quarter of an hour they set the town on fire in four or five places, and particularly that house where the Indians were not gone to bed.

As soon as the fire began to blaze, the poor frightened creatures began to rush out to save their lives, but met with their fate in the attempt; and especially at the door, where they drove them back, the boatswain himself killing one or two with his poleaxe; the house being large, and many in it, he did not care to go in, but called for a hand-grenado, and threw it among them, which at first frightened them, but, when it burst, made such havoc among them, that they cried out in a hideous manner. In short, most of the Indians who were in the open part of the house were killed or hurt with the grenado, except two or three who pressed to the door, which the boatswain and two more kept, with their bayonets on the muzzles of their pieces, and despatched all that came in their way: but there was another apartment in the house, where the prince or king, or whatever he was, and several others were; and these were kept in till the house, which was by this time all a light flame, fell in upon them, and they were smothered together.

All this while they fired not a gun, because they would not waken the people faster than they could master them; but the fire began to waken them fast enough, and our fellows were glad to keep a little together in bodies; for the fire grew so raging, all the houses being made of light combustible stuff, that they could hardly bear the street between them; and their business was to follow the fire, for the surer execution; as fast as the fire either forced the people out of those houses which were burning, or frightened them out of others, our people were ready at their doors to knock them on the head, still calling and hallooing one to another to remember Tom Jeffry.

While this was doing, I must confess I was very uneasy, and especially when I saw the flames of the town, which, it being night, seemed to be just by me. My nephew, the captain, who was roused by his men, seeing such a fire was very uneasy, not knowing what the matter was, or what danger I was in, especially hearing the guns too, for by this time they began to use their fire-arms; a thousand thoughts oppressed his mind concerning me and the supercargo, what would become of us; and, at last, though he could ill spare any more men, yet not knowing what exigence we might be in, he takes another boat, and with thirteen men and himself comes on shore to me.

He was surprised to see me and the supercargo in the boat, with no more than two men; and though he was glad that we were well, yet he was in the same impatience with us to know what was doing; for the noise continued, and the flame increased; in short, it was next to an impossibility for any man in the world to restrain his curiosity to know what had happened, or his concern for the safety of the men: in a word, the captain told me he would go and help his men, let what would come. I argued with him, as I did before with the men, the safety of the ship, the danger of the voyage, the interest of the owners and merchants, etc., and told him I and the two men would go, and only see if we could at a distance learn what was like to be the event, and come back and tell him. It was all one to talk to my nephew, as it was to talk to the rest before; he would go, he said; and he only wished he had left but ten men in the ship; for he could not think of having his men lost for want of help; he had rather lose the ship, the voyage, and his life and all; and away he went.

I was no more able to stay behind now than I was to persuade them not to go: so, in short, the captain ordered two men to row back the pinnace, and fetch twelve men more, leaving the long-boat at an anchor; and that when they came back, six men should keep the two boats, and six more come after us: so that he left only sixteen men in the ship; for the whole ship's company consisted of sixty-five men, whereof two were lost in the late quarrel which brought this mischief on.

Being now on the march, you may be sure we felt little of the ground we trod on; and being guided by the fire, we kept no path, but went directly to the place of the flame. If the noise of the guns was surprising to us before, the cries of the poor people were now quite of another nature, and filled us with horror. I must confess I was never at the sacking a city, or at the taking a town by storm. I had heard of Oliver Cromwell taking Drogheda, in Ireland, and killing man, woman, and child; and I had read of Count Tilly sacking the city of Magdeburg, and cutting the throats of twenty-two thousand of all sexes; but I never had an idea of the thing itself before, nor is it possible to describe it, or the horror that was upon our minds at hearing it. However, we went on, and at length came to the town, though there was no entering the streets of it for the fire. The first object we met with was the ruins of a hut or house, or rather the ashes of it, for the house was consumed; and just before it, plain enough to be seen by the light of the fire, lay four men and three women killed, and, as we thought, one or two more lay in the heap among the fire; in short, there were such instances of rage altogether barbarous, and of a fury something beyond what was human, that we thought it impossible our men could be guilty of it; or if they were the authors of it, we thought they ought to be every one of them put to the worst of deaths. But this was not all: we saw the fire increased forward, and the cry went on just as the fire went on; so that we were in the utmost confusion. We advanced a little way farther; and, behold, to our astonishment, three naked women, and crying in a most dreadful manner, came flying as if they had wings, and after them sixteen or seventeen men, natives, in the same terror and consternation, with three of our English butchers in the rear; who, when they could not overtake them, fired in among them, and one that was killed by their shot fell down in our sight. When the rest saw us, believing us to be their enemies, and that we would murder them as well as those that pursued them, they set up a most dreadful shriek, especially the women, and two of them fell down, as if already dead, with the fright.

My very soul shrunk within me, and my blood ran chill in my veins, when I saw this; and I believe, had the three English sailors that pursued them come on, I had made our men kill them all: however, we took some ways to let the poor flying creatures know that we would not hurt them; and immediately they came up to us, and kneeling down with their hands lifted up, made piteous lamentation to us to save them, which we let them know we would; whereupon they crept all together in a huddle close behind us, as for protection. I left my men drawn up together, and charging them to hurt nobody, but, if possible, to get at some of our people, and see what devil it was possessed them, and what they intended to do, and to command them off; assuring them that if they stayed till daylight, they would have a hundred thousand men about their ears: I say, I left them, and went among those flying people, taking only two of our men with me; and there was indeed a piteous spectacle among them; some of them had their feet terribly burned, with trampling and running through the fire, others their hands burned; one of the women had fallen down in the fire, and was very much burned before she could get out again; and two or three of the men had cuts in their backs and thighs, from our men pursuing; and another was shot through the body, and died while I was there.

I would fain have learned what the occasion of all this was, but I could not understand one word they said; though, by signs, I perceived some of them knew not what was the occasion themselves. I was so terrified, in my thoughts, at this outrageous attempt, that I could not stay there, but went back to my own men, and resolved to go into the middle of the town, through the fire, or whatever might be in the way, and put an end to it, cost what it would: accordingly, as I came back to my men, I told them my resolution, and commanded them to follow me; when at the very moment came four of our men, with the boatswain at their head, roving over heaps of bodies they had killed, all covered with blood and dust, as if they wanted more people to massacre, when our men hallooed to them as loud as they could halloo; and with much ado one of them made them hear, so that they knew who we were, and came up to us.

As soon as the boatswain saw us, he set up a halloo like a shout of triumph, for having, as he thought, more help come; and without waiting to hear me, Captain, says he, noble captain! I am glad you are come; we are not half done yet: villainous hell-hound dogs! I'll kill as many of them as poor Tom has hairs upon his head: we have sworn to spare none of them; we'll root out the very nation of them from the earth; and thus he ran on, out of breath too with action, and would not give us leave to speak a word.

At last, raising my voice, that I might silence him a little, Barbarous dog! said I, what are you doing? I won't have one creature touched more, upon pain of death: I charge you upon your life, to stop your hands, and stand still here, or you are a dead man this minute.—Why, sir, says he, do you know what you do, or what they have done? If you want a reason for what we have done, come hither; and with that he showed me the poor fellow hanging, with his throat cut.

I confess I was urged then myself, and at another time would have been forward enough; but I thought they had carried their rage too far, and remembered Jacob's words to his sons Simeon and Levi—"Cursed be their anger, for it was fierce; and their wrath, for it was cruel." But I had now a new task upon my hands; for when the men I carried with me saw the sight, as I had done, I had as much to do to restrain them as I should have had with the others; nay, my nephew himself fell in with them, and told me, in their hearing, that he was only concerned for fear of the men being overpowered; and as to the people, he thought not one of them ought to live; for they had all glutted themselves with the murder of the poor man, and that they ought to be used like murderers: upon these words, away ran eight of my men, with the boatswain and his crew, to complete their bloody work; and I, seeing it quite out of my power to restrain them, came away pensive and sad; for I could not bear the sight, much less the horrible noise and cries of the poor wretches that fell into their hands.

I got nobody to come back with me but the supercargo and two men, and with these walked back to the boat. It was a very great piece of folly in me, I confess, to venture back as it were alone; for as it began now to be almost day and the alarm had run over the country, there stood about forty men, armed with lances and bows, at the little place where the twelve or thirteen houses stood mentioned before; but by accident I missed the place, and came directly to the sea-side; and by the time I got to the sea-side it was broad day; immediately I took the pinnace and went on board, and sent her back to assist the men in what might happen.

I observed about the time that I came to the boat's side, that the fire was pretty well out, and the noise abated: but in about half an hour after

I got on board I heard a volley of our men's fire-arms, and saw a great smoke; this, as I understood afterwards, was our men falling upon the men who, as I said, stood at the few houses on the way, of whom they killed sixteen or seventeen, and set all the houses on fire, but did not meddle with the women or children.

By the time the men got to the shore again with the pinnace, our men began to appear; they came dropping in, not in two bodies as they went, but straggling here and there in such a manner, that a small force of resolute men might have cut them all off. But the dread of them was upon the whole country; and the men were surprised, and so frightened, that I believe a hundred of them would have fled at the sight of but five of our men; nor in all this terrible action was there a man that made any considerable defence; they were so surprised with the terror of the fire and the sudden attack of our men in the dark, that they knew not which way to turn themselves; for if they fled one way they were met by one party; if back again, by another; so that they were everywhere knocked down: nor did any of our men receive the least hurt, except one that sprained his foot, and another that had one of his hands burned.

I was very angry with my nephew, the captain, and, indeed, with all the men, in my mind, but with him in particular, as well for his acting so out of his duty, as commander of the ship, and having the charge of the voyage upon him, as in his prompting, rather than cooling the rage of his blind men, in so bloody and cruel an enterprise. My nephew answered me very respectfully, but told me that when he saw the body of the poor seaman whom they had murdered in so cruel and barbarous a manner, he was not master of himself, neither could he govern his passion: he owned he should not have done so, as he was commander of the ship; but as he was a man, and nature moved him, he could not bear it. As for the rest of the men, they were not subject to me at all, and they knew it well enough; so they took no notice of my dislike.

The next day we set sail, so we never heard any more of it. Our men differed in the account of the number they had killed; but according to the best of their accounts, put all together, they killed or destroyed about one hundred and fifty people, men, women and children, and left not a house standing in the town. As for the poor fellow Tom Jeffry, as he was quite dead (for his throat was so cut that his head was half off), it would do no service to bring him away; so they only took him down from the tree, where he was hanging by one hand.

However just our men thought this action, I was against them in it, and I always after that time told them God would blast the voyage; for I looked upon all the blood they shed that night to be murder in them; for though it is true that they had killed Tom Jeffry, yet Jeffry was the aggressor, had broken the truce, and had violated or debauched a young woman of theirs, who came down to them innocently, and on the faith of the public capitulation.

The boatswain defended this quarrel when we were afterwards on board. He said it was true that we seemed to break the truce, but really had not; and that the war was begun the night before by the natives themselves, who had shot at us, and killed one of our men without any just provocation; so that as we were in a capacity to fight them now, we might also be in a capacity to do ourselves justice upon them in an extraordinary manner; that though the poor man had taken a little liberty with the wench, he ought not to have been murdered, and that in such a villainous manner; and that they did nothing but what was just, and what the laws of God allowed to be done to murderers.

One would think this should have been enough to have warned us against going on shore amongst heathens and barbarians: but it is impossible to make mankind wise but at their own expense; and their experience seems to be always of most use to them when it is dearest bought.

We were now bound to the gulf of Persia, and from thence to the coast of Coromandel, only to touch at Surat; but the chief of the supercargo's design lay at the bay of Bengal; where if he missed his business outward-bound, he was to go up to China, and return to the coast as he came home.

The first disaster that befell us was in the gulf of Persia, where five of our men venturing on shore on the Arabian side of the gulf, were surrounded by the Arabians, and either all killed or carried away into slavery: the rest of the boat's crew were not able to rescue them, and had but just time to get off their boat. I began to upbraid them with the just retribution of Heaven in this case; but the boatswain very warmly told me, he thought I went farther in my censures than I could show any warrant for in Scripture; and referred to Luke xiii. 4, where our Saviour intimates that those men on whom the tower of Siloam fell were not sinners above all the Galileans; but that which put me to silence in the case was, that not one of these five men who were now lost were of those who went on shore to the massacre of Madagascar, so I always called it, though our men could not bear to hear the word *massacre* with any patience.

But my frequent preaching to them on the subject had worse consequences than I expected; and the boatswain who had been the head of the attempt, came up boldly to me one time, and told me he found that I brought that affair continually upon the stage: that I made unjust reflections upon it, and had used the men very ill on that account, and himself in particular; that I was but a passenger, and had no command in the ship, or concern in the voyage, they were not obliged to bear it; that they did not know but I might have some ill design in my head, and perhaps to call them to an account for it when they came to England; and that, therefore, unless I would resolve to have done with it, and also not to concern myself any further with him, or any of his affairs, he would leave the ship; for he did not think it was safe to sail with me among them.

I heard him patiently enough till he had done, and then told him, that I confessed I had all along opposed the massacre of Madagascar, and that I had, on all occasions, spoken my mind freely about it, though not more upon him than any of the rest; that as to having no command in the ship, that was true: nor did I exercise any authority, only took the liberty of speaking my mind in things which publicly concerned us all; and what concern I had in the voyage was none of his business; that I was a considerable owner in the ship; in that claim, I had conceived I had a right to speak even further than I had done, and would not be accountable to him or any one else; and began to be a little warm with him. He made but little reply to me at that time, and I thought the affair had been over. We were at this time in the road at Bengal; and being willing to see the place, I went on shore with the supercargo, in the ship's boat to divert myself; and towards evening was preparing to go on board, when one of the men came to me, and told me he would not have me trouble myself to come down to the boat, for they had orders not to carry me on board any more. Any one may guess what a surprise I was in at so insolent a message; and I asked the man who bade him deliver that message to me? He told me the cockswain. I said no more to the fellow, but bade him let them know he had delivered his message, and that I had given him no answer to it.

I immediately went and found out the supercargo, and told him the story; adding, which I presently foresaw, that there would be a mutiny in the ship; and entreated him to go immediately on board the ship in an Indian boat, and acquaint the captain of it. But I might have spared this intelligence, for before I had spoken to him on shore the matter was effected on board. The boatswain, the gunner, the carpenter, and all the inferior officers, as soon as I was gone off in the boat, came up, and desired to speak with the captain; and there the boatswain, making a long harangue, and repeating all he had said to me, told the captain, in a few words, that I was now gone peaceably on shore, they were loath to use any violence with me, which, if I had not gone on shore, they would otherwise have done, to oblige me to have gone; they therefore thought fit to tell him, that as they shipped themselves to serve in the ship, under his command, they would perform it well and faithfully; but if I would not quit the ship, or the captain oblige me to quit it, they would all leave the ship, and sail no farther with him; and at that world *all*, he turned his face towards the mainmast, which was, it seems, the signal agreed on between them, at which all the seamen, being got together there, cried out, *One and all! one and all!*

My nephew, the captain, was a man of spirit, and of great presence of mind; and though he was surprised, you may be sure at the thing, yet he told them calmly that he would consider of the matter; but that he could do nothing in it till he had spoken to me about it. He used some arguments with them to show them the unreasonableness and injustice of the thing: but it was all in vain; they swore and shook hands round before his face, that they would all go on shore, unless he would engage to them not to suffer me to come any more on board the ship.

This was a hard article upon him, who knew his obligation to me, and did not know how I might take it: so he began to talk smartly to them; told them that I was a very considerable owner of the ship, and that, in justice, he could not put me out of my own house; that this was the next door to serving me as the famous pirate Kidd had done, who made a mutiny in the ship, set the captain on shore on an uninhabited island, and ran away with the ship; that let them go into what ship they would, if ever they came to England again it would cost them very dear; that the ship was mine, and that he could not put me out of it; and that he would rather lose the ship and the voyage too than disoblige me so much; so they might do as they pleased: however, he would go on shore and talk with me, and invited the boatswain to go with him, and perhaps they might accommodate the matter with me. But they all rejected the proposal and said they would have nothing to do with me any more; and if I came on board, they would all go on shore. Well, said the captain, if you are all of this mind, let me go on shore and talk with him. So away he came to me with this account, a little after the message had been brought to me from the cockswain.

I was very glad to see my nephew, I must confess; for I was not without apprehensions that they would confine him by violence, set sail, and run away with the ship; and then I had been stripped naked in a remote country, having nothing to help myself: in short I had been in a worse case than when I was alone in the island. But they had not come to that length, it seems, to my satisfaction; and when my nephew told me what they had said to him, and how they had sworn and shook hands that they would one and all leave the ship if I was suffered to come on board, I told him he should not be concerned at it at all, for I would stay on shore: I only desired he would take care and send me all my necessary things on shore, and leave me a sufficient sum of money, and I would find my way to England as well as I could.

This was a heavy piece of news to my nephew, but there was no way to help it but to comply; so, in short, he went on board the ship again, and satisfied the men that his uncle had yielded to their importunity, and had sent for his goods from on board the ship; so that the matter was over in a few hours, the men returned to their duty, and I began to consider what course I should steer.

I WAS now alone in the most remote part of the world, as I think I may call it, for I was near three thousand leagues by sea farther off from England than I was at my island; only, it is true, I might travel here by land over the great Mogul's country to Surat, might go from thence to Bassora by sea, up the gulf to Persia, and take the way of the caravans, over the Desert of Arabia, to Aleppo and Scanderoon; from thence by sea again to Italy, and so overland into France; and this put together might at least be a full diameter of the globe, or more.

I had another way before me, which was to wait for some English ships, which were coming to Bengal from Achin, on the island of Sumatra, and get passage on board them for England. But as I came hither without any concern with the English East India Company, so it would be difficult to go from hence without their license, unless with great favour of the captains of the ships, or the Company's factors, and to both I was an utter stranger.

Here I had the mortification to see the ship set sail without me; a treatment I think a man in my circumstances scarce ever met with, except when pirates running away with the ship, and setting those that would not agree with their villainy on shore. Indeed, this was next door to it, both ways; however, my nephew left me two servants, or rather one companion and one servant; the first was clerk to the purser, whom he engaged to go with me, and the other was his own servant. I took me also a good lodging in the house of an Englishwoman, where several merchants lodged, some French, two Italians, or rather Jews, and one Englishman; here I was handsomely enough entertained: and that I might not be said to run rashly upon anything, I stayed here above nine months considering what course to take, and how to manage myself. I had some English goods with me of value, and a considerable sum of money; my nephew furnishing me with a thousand pieces-of-eight, and a letter of credit for more, if I had occasion, that I might not be straitened, whatever might happen.

I quickly disposed of my goods to advantage, and, as I originally intended, I bought here some very good diamonds, which, of all other things, were the most proper for me, in my present circumstances; because I could always carry my whole estate about me.

After a long stay here, and many proposals made for my return to England, none falling out to my mind, the English merchant who lodged with me, and whom I had contracted an intimate acquaintance with, came to me one morning. Countryman, says he, I have a project to communicate to you, which, as it suits with my thoughts, may, for aught I know, suit with yours also, when you shall have thoroughly considered it. Here we are posted, you by accident, and I by my own choice, in a part of the world very remote from our own country; but it is in a country where, by us who understand trade and business, a great deal of money is to be got. If you will put one thousand pounds to my one thousand pounds, we will hire a ship here, the first we can get to our minds; you shall be captain, I'll be merchant, and we'll go a trading voyage to China: for what should we stand still for? The whole world is in motion, rolling round and round; all the creatures of God, heavenly bodies and earthly, are busy and diligent: why should we be idle? There are no drones in the world but men; why should we be of that number?

I liked this proposal very well, and the more because it seemed to be expressed with so much good will, and in so friendly a manner. I will not say but that I might, by my loose unhinged circumstances, be the fitter to embrace a proposal for trade, or indeed anything else; whereas, otherwise, trade was none of my element. However, I might perhaps say with some truth, that if trade was not my element, rambling was, and no proposal for seeing any part of the world which I had never seen before could possibly come amiss to me.

It was, however, some time before we could get a ship to our minds, and when we had got a vessel, it was not easy to get English sailors; that is to say, so many as were necessary to govern the voyage and manage the sailors which we should pick up there. After some time we got a mate, a boatswain, and a gunner, English; a Dutch carpenter, and three foremastmen. With these we found we could do well enough, having Indian seamen, such as they were, to make up.

There are so many travellers who have written the history of their voyages and travels this way, that it would be very little diversion to anybody to give a long account of the places we went to, and the people who inhabit there: these things I leave to others, and refer the reader to those journals and travels of Englishmen of which many I find are published and more promised every day; it is enough for me to tell you that we made this voyage to Achin, in the island of Sumatra, and from thence to Siam, where we exchanged some of our wares for opium and some arrack; the first a commodity which bears a great price among the Chinese, and which, at that time, was much wanted there. In a word, we went up to Suskan, made a very great voyage, were eight months out, and returned to Bengal; and I was very well satisfied with my adventure. I observe that our people in England often admire how officers which the Company send into India, and the merchants which generally stay there, get such very great estates as they do, and sometimes come home worth sixty or seventy thousand pounds at a time; but it is no wonder, or at least we shall see so much further into it, when we consider the innumerable ports and places where they have a free commerce, that it will be none; and much less will it be so when we consider that at those places and ports where the English ships come, there is such great and constant demands for the growth of all other countries, that there is a certain vent for the returns, as well as a market abroad for the goods carried out.

In short, we made a very good voyage, and I got so much money by my first adventure, and such an insight into the method of getting more, that had I been twenty years younger, I should have been tempted to have stayed here, and sought no further for making any fortune: but what was all this to a man upwards of threescore, that was rich enough, and came abroad more in obedience to a restless desire of seeing the world than a covetous desire of gaining by it? And, indeed, I think it is with great justice I now call it restless desire, for it was so. When I was at home, I was restless to go abroad; and when I was abroad, I was restless to be at home. I say, what was this gain to me? I was rich enough already, nor had I any uneasy desires about getting more money; and therefore the profit of the voyage to me was of no great force for the prompting me forward to further undertakings; hence I thought that by this voyage I had made no progress at all, because I was come back, as I might call it, to the place from whence I came, as to home: whereas my eye, which, like that which Solomon speaks of, was never satisfied with seeing, was still desirous of wandering and seeing more. I was come into a part of the world which I was never in before, and that part, in particular, which I had heard much of, and was resolved to see as much of it as I could; and then I thought I might say I had seen all the world that was worth seeing.

But my fellow traveller and I had different notions: I do not name this to insist on my own, for I acknowledge his were the most just, and the most suited to the end of a merchant's life; who, when he is abroad upon adventures, it is his wisdom to stick to that, as the best thing for him, which he is like to get the most money by. My new friend kept himself to the nature of the thing, and would have been content to have gone like a carrier's horse, always to the same inn, backward and forward, provided he could, as he called it, find his account in it. On the other hand, mine was the notion of a mad rambling boy, that never cares to see a thing twice over. But this was not all; I had a kind of impatience upon me to be nearer home, and yet the most unsettled resolution imaginable which way to go. In the interval of these consultations, my friend, who was always upon the search for business, proposed another voyage to me among the Spice Islands, and to bring home a loading of cloves from the Manillas, or thereabouts; places, indeed, where the Dutch trade, but islands belonging partly to the Spaniards; though we went not so far, but to some other, where they have not the whole power, as they have at Batavia, Ceylon, etc.

We were not long in preparing for this voyage; the chief difficulty was in bringing me to come into it: however, at last, nothing else offering, and finding that really stirring about and trading, the profit being so great, and, as I may say, certain, had more pleasure in it, and had more satisfaction to my mind, than sitting still, which, to me especially, was the unhappiest part of my life, I resolved on this voyage too, which we made very successfully, touching at Borneo, and several islands whose names I do not remember, and came home in about five months. We sold our spice, which was chiefly cloves and some nutmegs, to the Persian merchants, who carried them away to the gulf; and making near five of one, we really got a great deal of money.

My friend, when we made up this account, smiled at me: Well, now, said he, with a sort of agreeable insult upon my indolent temper, is not this better than walking about here, like a man of nothing to do, and spending our time in staring at the nonsense and ignorance of the Pagans?—Why, truly, says I, my friend, I think it is, and I begin to be a convert to the principles of merchandising; but I must tell you, said I, by the way, you do not know what I am doing; for if I once conquer my backwardness, and embark heartily, as old as I am, I shall harass you up and down the world till I tire you; for I shall pursue it so eagerly, I shall never let you lie still.

But, to be short with my speculations, a little while after this there came in a Dutch ship from Batavia: she was a coaster, not an European trader, of about two hundred tons burthen; the men, as they pretended, having been so sickly, that the captain had not hands enough to go to sea with, he lay by at Bengal; and having, it seems, got money enough, or being willing, for other reasons, to go for Europe, he gave public notice he would sell his ship. This came to my ears before my new partner heard of it, and I had a great mind to buy it; so I went to him, and told him of it. He considered a while, for he was no rash man neither; but musing some time, he replied, She is a little too big; but, however, we will have her. Accordingly, we bought the ship, and agreeing with the master, we paid for her, and took possession. When we had done so, we resolved to entertain the men, if we could, to join them with those we had, for the pursuing our business; but on a sudden, they having received, not their wages, but their share of the money, as we afterwards learned, not one of them was to be found; we inquired much about them, and at length were told that they were all gone together by land to Agra, the great city of the Mogul's residence, and from thence to travel to Surat, and go by sea to the gulf of Persia.

Nothing had so much troubled me a good while as that I should miss the opportunity of going with them; for such a ramble, I thought, and in such company as would both have guarded and diverted me, would have suited mightily with my great design: and I should have both seen the world and gone homewards too; but I was much better satisfied a few days after, when I came to know what sort of fellows they were; for, in short, their history was, that this man they called captain was the gunner only, not the commander; that they had been a trading voyage, in which they had been attacked on shore by some of the Malays, who had killed the captain and three of his men; and that after the captain was killed, these men, eleven in number, had resolved to run away with the ship, which they did, and brought her to Bengal, leaving the mate and five men more on shore; of whom hereafter.

Well, let them get the ship how they would, we came honestly by her, as we thought, though we did not, I confess, examine into things so exactly as we ought; for we never inquired anything of the seamen, who would certainly have faltered in their account, contradicted one another, and perhaps contradicted themselves; or one how or other we should have had reason to have suspected them: but the man showed us a bill of sale for the ship, to one Emanuel Clostershoven, or some such name, for I suppose it was all a forgery, and called himself by that name, and we could not contradict him; and withal, having no suspicion of the thing, we went through with our bargain.

We picked up some more English sailors here after this, and some Dutch; and now we resolved for a second voyage to the south-east for cloves, etc.: that is to say, among the Philippine and Molucca isles; and, in short, not to fill up this part of my story with trifles, when what is to come is so remarkable, I spent from first to last, six years in this country, trading from port to port, backward and forward, and with very good success, and was now the last year with my new partner, going in the ship above mentioned, on a voyage to China, but designing first to Siam, to buy rice.

In this voyage, being by contrary winds obliged to beat up and down a great while in the straits of Malacca, and among the islands, we were no sooner got clear of those difficult seas than we found our ship had sprung a leak, and we were not able, by all our industry, to find out where it was. This forced us to make some port; and my partner, who knew the country better than I did, directed the captain to put into the river of Cambodia; for I had made the English mate, one Mr. Thompson, captain, not being willing to take the charge of the ship upon myself. This river lies on the north side of the great bay or gulf which goes up to Siam. While we were here, and going often on shore for refreshment, there comes to me one day an Englishman, and he was, it seems, a gunner's-mate on board an English East India ship which rode in the same river, at or near the city of Cambodia; what brought him hither we knew not; but he comes to me, and speaking English, Sir, says he, you are a stranger to me, and I to you, but I have something to tell you that very nearly concerns you.

I looked steadfastly at him a good while, and thought at first I had known him, but I did not: If it very nearly concerns me, said I, and not yourself, what moves you to tell it to me?—I am moved, says he, by the imminent danger you are in, and for aught I see, you have no knowledge of it.—I know no danger I am in, says I, but that my ship is leaky, and I cannot find it out; but I intend to lay her aground to-morrow, to see if I can find it.—But, sir, says he, leaky or not leaky, find it or not find it, you will be wiser than to lay your ship on shore to-morrow, when you hear what I have to say to you: do you know, sir, said he, the town of Cambodia lies about fifteen leagues up this river? and there are two large English ships about five leagues on this side, and three Dutch.—Well, said I, and what is that to me?—Why, sir, said he, is it for a man that is upon such adventures as you are, to come into a port and not examine first what ships there are there, and whether he is able to deal with them? I suppose you do not think you are a match for them? I was amused very much at his discourse, but not amazed at it, for I could not conceive what he meant; and I turned short upon him, and said, Sir, I wish you would explain yourself; I cannot imagine what reason I have to be afraid of any of the Company's ships, or Dutch ships; I am no interloper; what can they have to say to me? He looked like a man half angry and half pleased, and pausing awhile, but smiling, Well, sir, says he, if you think yourself secure, you must take your chance; I am sorry your fate should blind you against good advice: but assure yourself, if you do not put to sea immediately, you will the very next tide be attacked by five long-boats full of men, and perhaps, if you are taken, you will be hanged for a pirate, and the particulars be examined afterwards. I thought, sir, added he, I should have met with a better reception than this, for doing you a piece of service of such importance.—I can never be ungrateful, said I, for any service, or to any man that offers me any kindness: but it is past my comprehension what they should have such a design upon me for: however, since you say there is no time to be lost, and that there is some villainous design on hand against me, I will go on board this minute, and put to sea immediately, if my men can stop the leak, or if we can swim without stopping it: but, sir, said I, shall I go away ignorant of the cause of all this? Can you give me no further light into it?—I can tell you but part of the story, sir, says he; but I have a Dutch seaman here with me, and I believe I could persuade him to tell you the rest; but there is scarce time for it: but the short of the story is this, the first part of which, I suppose, you know well enough, viz., that you were with this ship at Sumatra; that there your captain was murdered by the Malays, with three of his men; and that you or some of those that were on board with you, ran away with the ship, and are since turned pirates. This is the sum of the story, and you will all be seized as pirates, I can assure you, and executed with very little ceremony; for you know merchant ships show but little law to pirates, if they get them into their power.—Now you speak plain English, said I, and I thank you; and though I know nothing that we have done like what you talk of, for I am sure we came honestly and fairly by the ship; yet seeing such a work is doing, as you say, and that you seem to mean honestly, I will be upon my guard.—Nay, sir, says he, do not talk about being upon your guard; the best defence is, to be out of the danger; if you have any regard for your life, and the lives of all your men, put to sea, without fail, at high water; and as you have a whole tide before you, you will be gone too far out before they can come down; for they will come away at high water, and as they have twenty miles to come, you will get near two hours of them by the difference of the tide, not reckoning the length of the way; besides, as they are only boats, and not ships, they will not venture to follow you far out to sea, especially if it blows.—Well, said I, you have been very kind in this; what shall I do for you to make you amends? Sir, says he, you may not be willing to make me any amends, because you may not be convinced of the truth of it: I will make an offer to you; I have nineteen months' pay due to me on board the ship ——, which I came out of England in; and the Dutchman that is with me had seven months' pay due to him; if you will make good our pay to us, we will go along with you: if you find nothing more in it, we will desire no more; but if we do convince you that we have saved your lives, and the ship, and the lives of all the men in her, we will leave the rest to you.

I consented to this readily, and went immediately on board, and the two men with me. As soon as I came to the ship's side, my partner, who was on board, came out on the quarter-deck, and called to me, with a great deal of joy, O ho! O ho! we have stopped the leak! we have stopped the leak!—Say you so! said I, thank God; but weigh anchor then immediately.—Weigh! says he: what do you mean by that? What is the matter?—Ask no questions, said I; but all hands to work, and weigh without losing a minute. He was surprised, but, however, he called the captain, and he immediately ordered the anchor to be got up: and though the tide was not quite down, yet a little land breeze blowing, we stood out to sea. Then I called him into the cabin, and told him the story; and we called in the men, and they told us the rest of it: but as it took up a great deal of time before we had done a seaman comes to the cabin door, and called out to us that the captain bade him tell us we were chased. Chased! says I; by what?—By five sloops, or boats, says the fellow, full of men.—Very well, said I; then it is apparent there is something in it. In the next place I ordered all our men to be called up, and told them there was a design to seize the ship, and to take us for pirates, and asked them if they would stand by us, and by one another: the men answered cheerfully, one and all, that they would live and die with us. Then I asked the captain what way he thought best for us to manage a fight with them; for resist them I was resolved we would, and that to the last drop. He said readily that the way was to keep them off with our great shot as long as we could, and then fire at them with our small arms, to keep them from boarding us; but when neither of these would do any longer, we should retire to our close quarters; perhaps they had not materials to break open our bulk-heads, or get in upon us.

The gunner had, in the mean time, orders to bring two guns to bear fore and aft, out of the steerage, to clear the deck, and load them with musket bullets and small pieces of old iron, and what came next to hand; and thus we made ready for fight: but all this while we kept out to sea, with wind enough, and could see the boats at a distance, being five large long-boats, following us with all the sail they could make.

Two of those boats (which by our glasses we could see were English) outsailed the rest, were near two leagues ahead of them, and gained upon us considerably, so that we found they would come up with us; upon which we fired a gun without ball, to intimate that they should bring to; and we put out a flag of truce, as a signal for parley; but they came crowding after us, till they came within shot, when we took in our white flag, they having made no answer to it, and hung out a red flag, and fired at them with shot. Notwithstanding this, they came on till they were near enough to call to them with a speaking-trumpet which we had on board; so we called to them, and bade them keep off, at their peril.

It was all one; they crowded after us, and endeavoured to come under our stern, so as to board us on our quarter; upon which, seeing they were resolute for mischief, and depended upon the strength that followed them, I ordered to bring the ship to, so that they lay upon our broadside; when immediately we fired five guns at them, one of which had been levelled so true as to carry away the stern of the hindermost boat, and bringing them to the necessity of taking down their sail, and running all to the head of the boat to keep her from sinking; so she lay by, and had enough of it; but seeing the foremost boat crowd on after us, we made ready to fire at her in particular. While this was doing, one of the three boats, that was behind, being forwarder than the other two, made up to the boat which we had disabled, to relieve her, and we could see her take out the men; we called again to the foremost boat, and offered a truce, to parley again, and to know what her business was with us; but had no answer, only she crowded close under our stern. Upon this our gunner, who was a very dexterous fellow, run out his two chase guns, and fired again at her, but the shot missing, the men in the boat shouted, waved their caps, and came on; but the gunner, getting quickly ready again, fired among them a second time, one shot of which, though it missed the boat itself, yet fell in among the men, and we could easily see had done a great deal of mischief among them; but we took no notice of that, wore the ship again, and brought our quarter to bear upon them, and firing three guns more, we found the boat was almost split to pieces; in particular, her rudder and a piece of her stern was shot quite away; so they handed her sail immediately, and were in great disorder. But to complete their misfortune, our gunner let fly two guns at them again: where he hit them we could not tell, but we found the boat was sinking, and some of the men already in the water: upon this I immediately manned out our pinnace, which we had kept close by our side, with orders to pick up some of the men, if they could, and save them from drowning, and immediately come on board the ship with them, because we saw the rest of the boats began to come up. Our men in the pinnace followed their orders, and took up three men, one of whom was just drowning, and it was a good while before we could recover him. As soon as they were on board, we crowded all the sail we could make, and stood farther out to sea; and we found that when the other three boats came up to the first, they gave over their chase.

Being thus delivered from a danger, which, though I knew not the reason of it, yet seemed to be much greater than I apprehended, I resolved that we should change our course, and not let any one know whither we were going: so we stood out to sea·eastward, quite out of the course of all European ships, whether they were bound to China or anywhere else within the commerce of the European nations.

When we were at sea, we began to consult with the two seamen, and inquire what the meaning of all this should be; and the Dutchman let us into the secret at once, telling us that the fellow that sold us the ship, as we said, was no more than a thief that had run away with her. Then he told us how the captain, whose name too he told us, though I do not remember it now, was treacherously murdered by the natives on the coast of Malacca, with three of his men; and that he, this Dutchman, and four more, got into the woods, where they wandered about a great while, till at length he, in particular, in a miraculous manner, made his escape, and swam off to a Dutch ship, which, sailing near the shore in its way from China, had sent their boat on shore for fresh water; that he durst not come to that part of the shore where the boat was, but made shift in the night to take the water farther off, and swimming a great while, at last the ship's boat took him up.

He then told us that he went to Batavia, where two of the seamen belonging to the ship arrived, having deserted the rest in their travels, and gave an account that the fellow who had run away with the ship sold her at Bengal to a set of pirates, which were gone a cruising in her; and that they had already taken an English ship and two Dutch ships very richly laden.

This latter part was found to concern us directly, though we knew it to be false; yet as my partner said very justly, if we had fallen into their hands, and they had had such a prepossession against us beforehand, it had been in vain for us to have defended ourselves, or to hope for any good quarter at their hands; and especially considering that our accusers had been our judges, and that we could have expected nothing from them but what rage would have dictated, and an ungoverned passion have executed: and therefore it was his opinion we should go directly back to Bengal, from whence we came, without putting in at any port whatever; because there we could give a good account of ourselves, could prove where we were when the ship put in, of whom we bought her, and the like; and which was more than all the rest, if we were put upon the necessity of bringing it before the proper judges, we should be sure to have some justice, and not to be hanged first and judged afterwards.

I was some time of my partner's opinion; but after a little more serious thinking, I told him I thought it was a very great hazard for us to attempt returning to Bengal, for that we were on the wrong side of the Straits of Malacca, and that if the alarm was given, we should be sure to be waylaid on every side, as well by the Dutch of Batavia as the English elsewhere; that if we should be taken, as it were, running away, we should even condemn ourselves, and there would want no more evidence to destroy us. I also asked the English sailor's opinion, who said he was of my mind, and that we should certainly be taken. This danger a little startled my partner, and all the ship's company, and we immediately resolved to go away to the coast of Tonquin, and so on to the coast of China; and pursuing the first design as to trade, find some way or other to dispose of the ship, and come back in some of the vessels of the country, such as we could get. This was approved of as the best method for our security; and accordingly we steered away N.N.E., keeping above fifty leagues off from the usual course to the eastward. This, however, put us to some inconvenience; for, first, the winds, when we came to that distance from the shore, seemed to be more steadily against us, blowing almost trade, as we call it, from the E. and E.N.E., so that we were a long while upon our voyage, and we were but ill provided with victuals for so long a run; and, which was still worse, there was some danger that those English and Dutch ships, whose boats pursued us, whereof some were bound that way, might be got in before us, and if not, some other ship bound to China might have information of us from them, and pursue us with the same vigour.

I must confess, I was now very uneasy, and thought myself, including the late escape from the long-boats, to have been in the most dangerous condition that ever I was through my past life; for whatever ill circumstances I had been in, I was never pursued for a thief before: nor had I ever done anything that merited the name of dishonest or fraudulent, much less thievish; I had chiefly been my own enemy, or, as I may rightly say, I had been nobody's enemy but my own; but now I was embarrassed in the worst condition imaginable; for though I was perfectly innocent, I was in no condition to make that innocence appear; and if I had been taken, it had been under a supposed guilt of the worst kind. This made me very anxious to make an escape, though which way to do it I knew not, or what port or place we could go to. My partner seeing me thus dejected, though he was the most concerned at first, began to encourage me, and describing to me the several ports of that coast, told me he would put in on the coast of Cochin China, or the Bay of Tonquin, intending to go afterwards to Macao, a town once in possession of the Portuguese, and where still a great many European families resided; and particularly the missionary priests usually went thither, in order to their going forward to China.

Hither then we resolved to go; and accordingly, though after a tedious and irregular course, and very much straitened for provisions, we came within sight of the coast very early in the morning; and upon reflection on the past circumstances we were in, and the danger if we had not escaped, we resolved to put into a small river, which, however, had depth enough of water for us, and to see if we could, either overland or by the ship's pinnace, come to know what ships were in any port thereabouts. This happy step was, indeed, our deliverance; for though we did not immediately see any European ships in the bay of Tonquin, yet the next morning there came into the bay two Dutch ships; and the third, without any colours spread out, but which we believed to be a Dutchman, passed by at about two leagues' distance, steering for the coast of China: and in the afternoon went by two English ships steering the same course; and thus we thought we saw ourselves beset with enemies both one way and the other. The place we were in was wild and barbarous; the people thieves, even by occupation or profession; and though, it is true, we had not much to seek of them, and, except getting a few provisions, cared not how little we had to do with them, yet it was with much difficulty that we kept ourselves from being insulted by them, several ways. We were in a small river of this country, within a few leagues of its utmost limits northward; and by our boat we coasted north-east, to the point of land which opens the great bay of Tonquin; and it was in this beating up along the shore that we discovered we were surrounded with enemies. The people we were among were the most barbarous of all the inhabitants of the coast, having no correspondence with any other nation, and dealing only in fish and oil, and such gross commodities; and it may be particularly seen that they are the most barbarous of any of the inhabitants. Among other customs, they have this one, viz., that if any vessel has the misfortune to be shipwrecked upon their coast, they presently make the men all prisoners or slaves; and it was not long before we found a piece of their kindness this way, on the occasion following.

I have observed above, that our ship sprung a leak at sea, and that we could not find it out; and it happened that, as I have said, it was stopped unexpectedly in the happy minute of our being to be seized by the Dutch and English ships in the bay of Siam; yet as we did not find the ship so perfectly tight and sound as we desired, we resolved, while we were at this place, to lay her on shore, and take out what heavy things we had on board, and clean her bottom: and, if possible, to find out where the leaks were. Accordingly, having lightened the ship, and brought all our guns and other moveables to one side, we tried to bring her down, that we might come at her bottom; but, on second thoughts, we did not care to lay her on dry ground, neither could we find a proper place for it.

The inhabitants, who had never been acquainted with such a sight, came wandering down the shore to look at us; and seeing the ship lie down on one side in such a manner, and heeling in towards the shore, and not seeing our men, who were at work on her bottom with stages, and with their boats, on the off-side, they presently concluded that the ship was cast away, and lay so fast on the ground. On this supposition, they all came about us in two or three hours' time, with ten or twelve large boats, having some of them eight, some ten men in a boat, intending, no doubt, to have come on board and plundered the ship; and if they had found us there, to have carried us away for slaves to their king, or whatever they call him, for we knew nothing of their governor.

When they came up to the ship and began to row round her, they discovered us all hard at work on the outside of the ship's bottom and side, washing, and graving, and stopping, as every seafaring man knows how. They stood for a while gazing at us, and we who were a little surprised, could not imagine what their design was; but being willing to be sure, we took this opportunity to get some of us into the ship, and others to hand down arms and ammunition to those that were at work to defend themselves with, if there should be occasion; and it was no more than need: for in less than a quarter of an hour's consultation, they agreed, it seems, that the ship was really a wreck; and that we were all at work endeavouring to save her, or to save our lives by the help of our boats; and when we handed our arms into the boats, they concluded, by that motion, that we were endeavouring to save some of our goods; upon this they took it for granted we all belonged to them, and away they came directly upon our men, as if it had been in a line of battle.

Our men, seeing so many of them, began to be frightened, for we lay but in an ill posture to fight, and cried out to us to know what they should do. I immediately called to the men that worked upon the stages, to slip them down, and get up the side into the ship; and bade those in the boat to row round, and come on board; and those few of us who were on board worked with all the strength and hands we had, to bring the ship to rights; but, however, neither the men upon the stages nor those in the boats could do as they were ordered, before the Cochin Chinese were upon them; and two of their boats boarded our long-boat, and began to lay hold on the men as their prisoners.

The first man they laid hold on was an English seaman, a stout, strong fellow, who, having a musket in his hand, never offered to fire it, but laid it down in the boat, like a fool, as I thought; but he understood his business better than I could teach him, for he grappled the pagan, and dragged him by main force out of their boat into ours, where taking him by the ears, he beat his head so against the boat's gunnel, that the fellow died in his hands; and, in the mean time, a Dutchman, who stood next, took up the musket, and with the butt-end of it so laid about him, that he knocked down five of them who attempted to enter the boat. But this was doing little towards resisting thirty or forty men, who fearless, because ignorant of their danger, began to throw themselves into the longboat, where we had but five men in all to defend it; but the following incident, which deserved our laughter, gave our men a complete victory.

Our carpenter being prepared to grave the outside of the ship, as well as to pay the seams where he had calked her to stop the leaks, had got two kettles just let down into the boat, one filled with boiling pitch, and the other with rosin, tallow, and oil, and such stuff as the shipwrights use for that work; and the man that attended the carpenter had a great iron ladle in his hand, with which he supplied the men that were at work with the hot stuff: two of the enemy's men entered the boat just where this fellow stood, being in the foresheets; he immediately saluted them with a ladleful of the stuff, boiling hot, which so burned and scalded them, being half naked, that they roared out like bulls, and enraged with the fire, leaped both into the sea. The carpenter saw it, and cried out, Well done, Jack! give them some more of it: and stepping forward himself, takes one of the mops, and dipping it in the pitch-pot, he and his man threw it among them so plentifully, that, in short, of all the men in the three boats there was not one that escaped being scalded and burned with it, in a most frightful, pitiful manner, and made such a howling and crying, that I never heard a worse noise; for it is worth observing, that though pain naturally makes all people cry out, yet every nation has a particular way of exclamation, and makes noises as different from one another as their speech. I cannot give the noise those creatures made a better name than howling, nor a name more proper to the tone of it; for I never heard anything more like the noise of the wolves, which, as I have said, I heard howl in the forest on the frontiers of Languedoc.

I was never better pleased with a victory in my life; not only as it was a perfect surprise to me, and that our danger was imminent before, but, as we got this victory without any bloodshed, except of that man the fellow killed with his naked hands, and which I was very much concerned at, for I was sick of killing such poor savage wretches, even though it was in my own defence, knowing they came on errands which they thought just and knew no better; and that though it may be a just thing, because necessary (for there is no necessary wickedness in nature), yet I thought it was a sad life, when we must be always obliged to be killing our fellow-creatures to preserve ourselves; and, indeed, I think so still, and I would even now suffer a great deal, rather than I would take away the life even of the worst person injuring me; and I believe all considering people who know the value of life would be of my opinion, if they entered seriously into the consideration of it.

But to return to my story;—All the while this was doing, my partner and I, who managed the rest of the men on board, had with great dexterity brought the ship almost to rights, and having got the guns into their places again, the gunner called to me to bid our boat get out of the way, for he would let fly among them. I called back again to him, and bid him not offer to fire, for the carpenter would do the work without him; but bid him heat another pitch-kettle, which our cook, who was on board, took care of: but the enemy was so terrified with what they had met with in their first attack, that they would not come on again; and some of them who were farthest off, seeing the ship swim, as it were upright, began, as we suppose, to see their mistake, and give over the enterprise, finding it was not as they expected. Thus we got clear of their merry fight, and having got some rice, and some roots and bread, with about sixteen hogs, on board, two days before, we resolved to stay here no longer, but go forward, whatever came of it; for we made no doubt but we should be surrounded the next day with rogues enough, perhaps more than our pitch-kettle would dispose of for us. We therefore got all our things on board the same evening, and the next morning were ready to sail: in the mean time, lying at anchor at some distance from the shore, we were not so much concerned, being now in a fighting posture, as well as in a sailing posture, if any enemy had presented. The next day, having finished our work within board, and finding our ship was perfectly healed of all her leaks, we set sail. We would have gone into the bay of Tonquin, for we wanted to inform ourselves of what was to be known concerning the Dutch ships that had been there; but we durst not stand in there, because we had seen several ships go in, as we supposed, but a little before; so we kept on N.E. towards the island of Formosa, as much afraid of being seen by a Dutch or English merchant ship, as a Dutch or English merchant ship in the Mediterranean is of an Algerine man-of-war.

When we were thus got to sea, we kept on N.E. as if we would go to the Manillas or the Philippine islands, and this we did that we might not fall into the way of any of the European ships; and then we steered north, till we came to the latitude of 22 deg. 30 min., by which means we made the island of Formosa directly, where we came to an anchor, in order to get water and fresh provisions, which the people there, who were very courteous and civil in their manners, supplied us with willingly, and dealt very fairly and punctually with us in all their agreements and bargains, which is what we did not find among other people, and may be owing to the remains of Christianity which was once planted here by a Dutch missionary of Protestants, and is a testimony of what I have often observed, viz., that the Christian religion always civilises the people and reforms their manners, where it is received, whether it works saving effects upon them or no.

From thence we sailed still north, keeping the coast of China at an equal distance, till we knew we were beyond all the ports of China where our European ships usually come; being resolved, if possible, not to fall into any of their hands, especially in this country; where, as our circumstances were, we could not fail of being entirely ruined.

Being now come to the latitude of thirty degrees, we resolved to put into the first trading port we should come at; and standing in for the shore, a boat came off two leagues to us, with an old Portuguese pilot on board, who knowing us to be an European ship, came to offer his service, which, indeed, we were glad of, and took him on board; upon which, without asking us whither we would go, he dismissed the boat he came in, and sent it back.

I thought it was now so much in our choice to make the old man carry us whither we would, that I began to talk to him about carrying us to the gulf of Nanquin, which is the most northern part of the coast of China. The old man said he knew the gulf of Nanquin very well, but smiling, asked us what we would do there? I told him we would sell our cargo, and purchase China wares, calicoes, raw silks, tea, wrought silks, etc., and so would return by the same course we came. He told us our best port had been to have put in at Macao, where we could not have failed of a market for our opium to our satisfaction, and might for our money have purchased all sorts of China goods as cheap as we could at Nanquin.

Not being able to put the old man out of his talk, of which he was very opinionated or conceited, I told him we were gentlemen as well as merchants, and that we had a mind to go and see the great city of Peking, and the famous court of the monarch of China. Why then, says the old man, you should go to Ningpo, where, by the river which runs into the sea there, you may go up within five leagues of the great canal. This canal is a navigable stream, which goes through the heart of that vast empire of China, crosses all the rivers, passes some considerable hills by the help of sluices and gates, and goes up to the city of Peking, being in length near two hundred and seventy leagues.

Well, said I, Senhor Portuguese, but that is not our business now; the great question is, if you can carry us up to the city of Nanquin, from whence we can travel to Peking afterwards? He said he could do so very well, and that there was a great Dutch ship gone up that way just before. This gave me a little shock, for a Dutch ship was now our terror, and we had much rather have met the devil, at least if he had not come in too frightful a figure; and we depended upon it that a Dutch ship would be our destruction, for we were in no condition to fight them; all the ships they trade with into those parts being of great burden, and of much greater force than we were.

The old man found me a little confused, and under some concern, when he named a Dutch ship; and said to me, Sir, you need be under no apprehensions of the Dutch; I suppose they are not now at war with your nation!—No, said I, that's true; but I know not what liberties men may take when they are out of the reach of the laws of their own country.

—Why, says he, you are no pirates; what need you fear? They will not meddle with peaceable merchants, sure.

If I had any blood in my body that did not fly up into my face at that word, it was hindered by some stop in the vessels appointed by nature to circulate it, for it put me into the greatest disorder and confusion imaginable; nor was it possible for me to conceal it so, but the old man easily perceived it.

Sir, says he, I find you are in some disorder in your thoughts at my talk; pray be pleased to go which way you think fit, and, depend upon it, I'll do you all the service I can.—Why, senhor, said I, it is true, I am a little unsettled in my resolution at this time, whither to go in particular; and I am something more so for what you said about pirates. I hope there are no pirates in these seas; we are but in an ill condition to meet with them, for you see we have but a small force, and are but very weakly manned.—O, sir, says he, don't be concerned, I do not know that there have been any pirates in these seas these fifteen years, except one, which was seen, as I hear, in the bay of Siam, about a month since; but you may be assured she is gone to the southward; nor was she a ship of any great force, or fit for the work: she was not built for a privateer, but was run away with by a reprobate crew that was on board, after the captain and some of his men had been murdered by the Malayans, at or near the island of Sumatra.—What! said I, seeming to know nothing of the matter, did they murder the captain?—No, said he, I don't understand that they murdered him; but as they afterwards ran away with the ship, it is generally believed that they betrayed him into the hands of the Malayans, who did murder him; and perhaps they procured them to do it.—Why then, said I, they deserve death as if they had done it themselves.—Nay, says the old man, they do deserve it; and they will certainly have it, if they light upon any English or Dutch ship; for they have all agreed together, that if they meet that rogue they'll give him no quarter.—But, said I to him, you say the pirate is gone out of the seas; how can they meet with him then?—Why, that's true, says he, they do say so; but he was, as I tell you, in the bay of Siam, in the river Cambodia; and was discovered there by some Dutchmen who belonged to the ship, and who were left on shore when they ran away with her; and some English and Dutch traders being in the river, they were within a little of taking him: nay, said he, if the foremost boats had been well seconded by the rest, they had certainly taken him; but he, finding only two boats within reach of him, tacked about, and fired at those two, and disabled them before the others came up, and then standing off to sea, the others were not able to follow, and so he got away; but they have all so exact a description of the ship, that they will be sure to know her; and wherever they find her they have vowed to give no quarter either to the captain or seamen, but to hang them all up at the yard-arm.—What! said I, will they execute them right or wrong; hang them first, and judge them afterwards?—O sir, says the old pilot, there is no need to make a formal business of it with such rogues as those; let them tie them back to back, and set them a diving, 'tis no more than they deserve.

I knew I had my old man fast on board, and that he could do no harm, so that I turned short upon him: Well now, senhor, said I, this is the very reason why I would have you carry us up to Nanquin, and not put back to Macao, or to any other part of the country where the English or Dutch ships come; for be it known to you, senhor, those captains of the English and Dutch ships are a parcel of rash, proud, insolent fellows, that neither know what belongs to justice, nor how to behave themselves as the laws of God and nature direct; but being proud of their offices, and not understanding their power, they would act the murderers to punish robbers; would take upon them to insult men falsely accused, and determine them guilty without due inquiry: and perhaps I may live to bring some of them to account for it, when they may be taught how justice is to be executed; and that no man ought to be treated as a criminal till some evidence may be had of the crime, and that he is the man.

With this I told him that this was the very ship they attacked, and gave him a full account of the skirmish we had with their boats, and how foolishly and cowardly they behaved. I told him all the story of our buying the ship, and how the Dutchman served us. I told him the reasons I had to believe the story of killing the master by the Malayans was true, as also the running away with the ship; but it was all a fiction of their own to suggest that the men had turned pirates, and they ought to have been sure it was so before they had ventured to attack us by surprise, and oblige us to resist them; adding, that they would have the blood of those men, whom we killed there in just defence, to answer for.

The old man was amazed at this relation, and told us we were very much in the right to go away to the north; and that if he might advise us, it should be to sell the ship in China, which we might very well do, and buy or build another in the country; and, said he, though you will not get so good a ship, yet you may get one able enough to carry you and all your goods back to Bengal, or anywhere else. I told him I would take his advice when I came to any port where I could find a ship for my turn, or get any customer to buy this. He replied, I should meet with customers enough for the ship at Nanquin, and that a Chinese junk would serve me very well to go back again; and that he would procure me people both to buy one and sell the other. Well but, senhor, said I, as you say they know the ship so well, I may, perhaps, if I follow your measures, be instrumental to bring some honest innocent men into a terrible broil, and perhaps to be murdered in cold blood; for wherever they find the ship, they will prove the guilt upon the men, by proving this was the ship, and so innocent men may probably be overpowered and murdered.— Why, says the old man, I'll find out a way to prevent that also; for as I know all those commanders you speak of very well, and shall see them all as they pass by, I will be sure to set them to rights in the thing, and let them know that they had been so much in the wrong; that though the people who were on board at first might run away with the ship, yet it was not true that they had turned pirates; and that, in particular, these were not the men that first went off with the ship, but innocently bought her for the trade; and I am persuaded they will so far believe me, as at least to act more cautiously for the time to come.

While these things were passing between us, by way of discourse, we went forward directly for Nanquin, and in about thirteen days' sail came to an anchor at the south-west point of the great gulf of Nanquin; where, by the way, I came by accident to understand that two Dutch ships were gone the length before me, and that I should certainly fall into their hands. I consulted my partner again in this exigency, and he was as much at a loss as I was, and would very gladly have been safe on shore almost anywhere: however, I was not in such perplexity neither, but I asked the old pilot if there was no creek or harbour which I might put into and pursue my business with the Chinese privately, and be in no danger of the enemy. He told me, if I would sail to the southward about forty-two leagues, there was a little port called Quinchang, where the fathers of the mission usually landed from Macao, on their progress to teach the Christian religion to the Chinese, and where no European ships ever put in; and if I thought to put in there, I might consider what further course to take when I was on shore. He confessed, he said, it was not a place for merchants except that at some certain times they had a kind of a fair there, when the merchants from Japan came over thither to buy the Chinese merchandises.

We all agreed to go back to this place; the name of the port, as he called it, I may perhaps spell wrong, for I do not particularly remember it, having lost this, together with the names of many other places set down in a little pocket-book, which was spoiled by the water by an accident; but this I remember, that the Chinese or Japanese merchants we corresponded with called it by a different name from that which our Portuguese pilot gave it, and pronounced it as above, Quinchang.

As we were unanimous in our resolution to go to this place, we weighed the next day, having only gone twice on shore where we were to get fresh water; on both which occasions the people of the country were very civil to us, and brought us abundance of things to sell to us, I mean of provisions, plants, roots, tea, rice, and some fowls, but nothing without money.

We came to the other port (the wind being contrary) not till five days, but it was very much to our satisfaction; and I was joyful, and I may say thankful, when I set my foot on shore, resolving, and my partner too, that if it was possible to dispose of ourselves and effects any other way, though not every way to our satisfaction, we would never set one foot on board that unhappy vessel more; and, indeed, I must acknowledge, that of all the circumstances of life that ever I had any experience of, nothing makes mankind so completely miserable as that of being in constant fear. Well does the Scripture say, "the fear of man brings a snare"; it is a life of death, and the mind is so entirely oppressed by it, that it is capable of no relief.

Nor did it fail of its usual operations upon the fancy, by heightening every danger, representing the English and Dutch captains to be men incapable of hearing reason, or of distinguishing between honest men and rogues; or between a story calculated for our own turn, made out of nothing, on purpose to deceive, and a true genuine account of our whole voyage, progress, and design; for we might many ways have convinced any reasonable creature that we were not pirates; the goods we had on board, the course we steered, our frankly showing ourselves, and entering into such and such ports; and even our very manner, the force we had, the number of men, the few arms, little ammunition, short provisions; all these would have served to convince any men that we were no pirates. The opium and other goods we had on board would make it appear the ship had been at Bengal. The Dutchmen, who, it was said, had the names of all the men that were in the ship, might easily see that we were a mixture of English, Portuguese, and Indians, and but two Dutchmen on board. These, and many other particular circumstances, might have made it evident to the understanding of any commander, whose hands we might fall into, that we were no pirates. But fear, that blind, useless passion, worked another way, and threw us into the vapours; it bewildered our understandings, and set the imagination at work to form a thousand terrible things that perhaps might never happen. We first supposed, as indeed everybody else had related to us, that the seamen on board the English and Dutch ships, but especially the Dutch, were so enraged at the name of a pirate, and especially at our beating off their boats and escaping, that they would not give themselves leave to inquire whether we were pirates or no; but would execute us offhand, as we call it, without giving us any room for a defence. We reflected that there really was so much apparent evidence before them, that they would scarce inquire after any more; as, first, that the ship was certainly the same, and that some of the seamen among them knew her, and had been on board her; and, secondly, that when we had intelligence at the river of Cambodia that they were coming down to examine us, we fought their boats and fled; so that we made no doubt but they were as fully satisfied of our being pirates, as we were satisfied of the contrary; and, as I often said, I know not but I should have been apt to have taken those circumstances for evidence, if the tables were turned, and my case was theirs; and have made no scruple of cutting all the crew to pieces, without believing, or perhaps considering, what they might have to offer in their defence.

But let that be how it will, these were our apprehensions; and both my partner and I scarce slept a night without dreaming of halters and yard-arms, that is to say, gibbets; of fighting, and being taken; of killing, and being killed: and one night I was in such a fury in my dream, fancying the Dutchmen had boarded us, and I was knocking one of their seamen down, that I struck my doubled fist against the side of the cabin I lay in, with such a force, as wounded my hand grievously, broke my knuckles, and cut and bruised the flesh, so that it awaked me out of my sleep.

Another apprehension I had was, the cruel usage we might meet with from them if we fell into their hands: then the story of Amboyna came into my head, and how the Dutch might perhaps torture us, as they did our countrymen there, and make some of our men, by extremity of torture, confess those crimes they never were guilty of, or own themselves and all of us to be pirates, and so they would put us to death with a formal appearance of justice; and that they might be tempted to do this for the gain of our ship and cargo, which was worth four or five thousand pounds, put all together.

These things tormented me and my partner too, night and day; nor did we consider that the captains of ships have no authority to act thus; and if we had surrendered prisoners to them, they could not answer the destroying us, or torturing us, but would be accountable for it when they came to their own country; this, I say, gave me no satisfaction; for if they were to act thus with us, what advantage would it be to us that they should be called to an account for it? or if we were first to be murdered, what satisfaction would it be to us to have them punished when they came home?

I cannot refrain taking notice here what reflections I now had upon the vast variety of my particular circumstances; how hard I thought it was, that I, who had spent forty years in a life of continual difficulties, and was at last come, as it were, to the port or haven which all men drive at, viz., to have rest and plenty, should be a volunteer in new sorrows by my own unhappy choice; and that I, who had escaped so many dangers in my youth, should now come to be hanged in my old age, and in so remote a place, for a crime which I was not in the least inclined to, much less guilty of.

After these thoughts, something of religion would come in; and I would be considering that this seemed to me to be a disposition of immediate Providence, and I ought to look upon it and submit to it as such; that although I was innocent as to men, I was far from being innocent as to my Maker; and I ought to look in and examine what other crimes in my life were most obvious to me, and for which Providence might justly inflict this punishment as retribution; and that I ought to submit to this, just as I would to a shipwreck, if it had pleased God to have brought such a disaster upon me.

In its turn, natural courage would sometimes take its place, and then I would be talking myself up to vigorous resolutions; that I would not be taken to be barbarously used by a parcel of merciless wretches in cold blood; that it were much better to have fallen into the hands of the savages, though I was sure they would feast upon me when they had taken me, than those who would perhaps glut their rage upon me by inhuman tortures and barbarities; that in the case of the savages I always resolved to die fighting to the last gasp, and why should I not do so now, seeing it was much more dreadful, to me at least, to think of falling into these men's hands, than ever it was to think of being eaten by men? for the savages, give them their due, would not eat a man till he was killed and dead, but that these men had many arts beyond the cruelty of deatl.. Whenever these thoughts prevailed, I was sure to put myself into a kind of fever with the agitation of a supposed fight; my blood would boil, and my eyes sparkle, as if I were engaged, and I always resolved to take no quarter at their hands; but, even at last, if I could resist no longer, I would blow up the ship and all that was in her, and leave them but little booty to boast of.

The greater weight the anxieties and perplexities of these things were to our thoughts while we were at sea, the greater was our satisfaction when we saw ourselves on shore; and my partner told me he dreamed he had a very heavy load upon his back, which he was to carry up a hill, and found that he was not able to stand longer under it; but that the Portuguese pilot came and took it off his back, and the hill disappeared, the ground before him appearing all smooth and plain: and truly it was so; they were all like men who had a load taken off their backs. For my part, I had a weight taken off from my heart that it was not able any longer to bear; and, as I said above, we resolved to go no more to sea in that ship. When we came on shore, the old pilot, who was now our friend, got us a lodging and a warehouse for our goods, which, by the way, was much the same; it was a little house, or hut, with a larger house adjoining to it, all built with canes, and palisadoed round with large canes, to keep out pilfering thieves, of which, it seems, there were not a few in that country; however, the magistrates allowed us a little guard, and we had a soldier with a kind of halberd, or half-pike, who stood sentinel at our door; to whom we allowed a pint of rice, and a little piece of money about the value of threepence, per day, so that our goods were kept very safe.

The fair, or mart, usually kept in this place, had been over some time; however, we found that there were three or four junks in the river, and two Japaners, I mean ships from Japan, with goods which they had bought in China, and were not gone away, having some Japanese merchants on shore.

The first thing our old Portuguese pilot did for us was, to get us acquainted with three missionary Romish priests who were in town, and who had been there some time converting the people to Christianity; but we thought they made but poor work of it, and made them but sorry

Christians when they had done: however, that was none of our business. One of these was a Frenchman, whom they called Father Simon; another was a Portuguese, and the third, a Genoese: but Father Simon was courteous, easy in his manner, and very agreeable company; the other two were more reserved, seemed rigid and austere, and applied seriously to the work they came about, viz., to talk with, and insinuate themselves among, the inhabitants, wherever they had opportunity. We often ate and drank with those men; and though, I must confess, the conversion, as they call it, of the Chinese to Christianity is so far from the true conversion required to bring heathen people to the faith of Christ, that it seems to amount to little more than letting them know the name of Christ, and say some prayers to the Virgin Mary and her Son, in a tongue which they understand not, and to cross themselves, and the like; yet it must be confessed that the religionists, whom we call missionaries, have a firm belief that these people will be saved, and that they are the instruments of it; and, on this account, they undergo not only the fatigue of the voyage, and the hazards of living in such places, but oftentimes death itself, with the most violent tortures, for the sake of this work.

But to return to my story. This French priest, Father Simon, was appointed, it seems, by order of the chief of the mission, to go up to Peking, the royal seat of the Chinese emperor, and waited only for another priest, who was ordered to come to him from Macao, to go along with him; and we scarce ever met together but he was inviting me to go that journey; telling me how he would show me all the glorious things of that mighty empire, and, among the rest, the greatest city in the world; a city, said he, that your London and our Paris put together, cannot be equal to. This was the city of Peking, which, I confess, is very great, and infinitely full of people; but as I looked on those things with different eyes from other men, so I shall give my opinion of them in a few words, when I come in course of my travels to speak more particularly of them.

But, first, I come to my friar or missionary. Dining with him one day, and being very merry together, I showed some little inclination to go with him; and he pressed me and my partner very hard, and with a great many persuasions, to consent. Why, Father Simon, says my partner, should you desire our company so much? you know we are heretics, and you do not love us, nor cannot keep us company with any pleasure.—O, says he, you may perhaps be good Catholics in time; my business here is to convert heathens, and who knows but I may convert you too?—Very well, Father, said I, so you will preach to us all the way?—I will not be troublesome to you, says he; our religion does not divest us of good manners: besides, we are here like countrymen; and so we are, compared to the place we are in; and if you are Huguenots, and I a Catholic, we may all be Christians at last; at least, we are all gentlemen, and we may converse so, without being uneasy to one another. I liked this part of his discourse very well, and it began to put me in mind of my priest that I had left in the Brazils; but this Father Simon did not come up to his character by a great deal; for though Father Simon had no appearance of a criminal levity in him neither, yet he had not that fund of Christian zeal, strict piety, and sincere affection to religion, that my other good ecclesiastic had.

But to leave him a little, though he never left us, nor soliciting us to go with him; we had something else before us at first, for we had all this while our ship and our merchandise to dispose of, and we began to be very doubtful what we should do, for we were now in a place of very little business; and once I was about to venture to sail for the river of Kilam, and the city of Nanquin: but Providence seemed now more visibly, as I thought, than ever, to concern itself in our affairs; and I was encouraged, from this very time, to think I should one way or other get out of this entangled circumstance, and be brought home to my own country again, though I had not the least view of the manner. Providence, I say, began here to clear up our way a little; and the first thing that offered was, that our old Portuguese pilot brought a Japan merchant to us, who inquired what goods we had; and, in the first place, he bought all our opium, and gave us a very good price for it, paying us in gold by weight, some in small pieces of their own coin, and some in small wedges, of about ten or eleven ounces each. While we were dealing with him for our opium, it came into my head that he might perhaps deal for the ship too, and I ordered the interpreter to propose it to him: he shrugged up his shoulders at it, when it was first proposed to him; but in a few days after he came to me, with one of the missionary priests for his interpreter, and told me he had a proposal to make to me, which was this: he had bought a great quantity of goods of us, when he had no thoughts of proposals made to him of buying the ship; and that, therefore, he had not money enough to pay for the ship: but if I would let the same men who were in the ship navigate her, he would hire the ship to go to Japan; and would send them from thence to the Philippine islands with another loading, which he would pay the freight of before they went from Japan, and at their return he would buy the ship. I began to listen to his proposal, and so eager did my head still run upon rambling, that I could not but begin to entertain a notion of going myself with him, and so to sail from the Philippine islands away to the South Seas: accordingly I asked the Japanese merchant if he would not hire us to the Philippine islands, and discharge us there. He said, No, he could not do that, for then he could not have the return of his cargo; but he would discharge us in Japan, at the ship's return. Well, still I was for taking him at that proposal, and going myself; but my partner, wiser than myself, persuaded me from it, representing the dangers, as well of the seas as of the Japanese, who are a false, cruel, and treacherous people; likewise those of the Spaniards at the Philippines, more false, cruel, and treacherous than they.

But to bring this long turn of our affairs to a conclusion; the first thing we had to do was, to consult with the captain of the ship, and with his men, and know if they were willing to go to Japan: and while I was doing this, the young man whom my nephew had left with me as my companion for my travels came to me, and told me that he thought that voyage promised very fair, and that there was a great prospect of advantage, and he would be very glad if I undertook it; but that if I would not, and would give him leave, he would go as a merchant, or how I pleased to order him; that if ever he came to England, and I was there and alive, he would render me a faithful account of his success, which should be as much mine as I pleased. I was really loath to part with him; but considering the prospect of advantage, which was really considerable, and that he was a young fellow as likely to do well in it as any I knew, I inclined to let him go; but I told him I would consult my partner, and give him an answer the next day. My partner and I discoursed about it, and my partner made a most generous offer: You know it has been an unlucky ship, said he, and we both resolve not to go to sea in it again: if your steward (so he called my man) will venture the voyage, I will leave my share of the vessel to him, and let him make the best of it; and if we live to meet in England, and he meets with success abroad, he shall account for one half of the profits of the ship's freight to us; the other shall be his own.

If my partner, who was no way concerned with my young man, made him such an offer, I could no less than offer him the same: and all the ship's company being willing to go with him, we made over half the ship to him in property, and took a writing from him, obliging him to account for the other; and away he went to Japan. The Japan merchant proved a very punctual, honest man to him: protected him at Japan, and got him a license to come on shore, which the Europeans in general have not lately obtained; paid him his freight very punctually; sent him to the Philippines, loaded with Japan and China wares, and a supercargo of their own, who, trafficking with the Spaniard, brought back European goods again, and a great quantity of cloves and other spices; and there he was not only paid his freight very well, and at a very good price, but not being willing to sell the ship then, the merchant furnished him with goods on his own account; and with some money, and some spices of his own which he brought with him, he went back to the Manillas to the Spaniards, where he sold his cargo very well. Here, having got a good acquaintance at Manilla, he got his ship made a free ship; and the governor of Manilla hired him to go to Acapulco in America, on the coast of Mexico, and gave him a license to land there, and to travel to Mexico, and to pass in any Spanish ship to Europe with all his men. He made the voyage to Acapulco very happily, and there he sold his ship; and having there also obtained allowance to travel by land to Porto Bello, he found means, somehow or other, to get to Jamaica, with all his treasure; and about eight years after came to England exceeding rich, of which I shall take notice in its place: in the mean time, I return to our particular affairs.

Being now to part with the ship and ship's company, it came before us, of course, to consider what recompense we should give to the two men that gave us such timely notice of the design against us in the river Cambodia. The truth was, they had done us a very considerable service, and deserved well at our hands; though, by the way, they were a couple of rogues too: for as they believed the story of our being pirates, and that we had really run away with the ship, they came down to us not only to betray the design that was formed against us, but to go to sea with us as pirates; and one of them confessed afterwards that nothing else but the hopes of going a roguing brought him to do it: however, the service they did us was not the less; and therefore, as I had promised to be grateful to them, I first ordered the money to be paid them which they said was due to them on board their respective ships; over and above that, I gave each of them a small sum of money in gold, which contented them very well; then I made the Englishman gunner in the ship, the gunner being now made second mate and purser; the Dutchman I made boatswain: so they were both very well pleased, and proved very serviceable, being both able seamen, and very stout fellows.

We were now on shore in China: if I thought myself banished and remote from my own country at Bengal, where I had many ways to get home for my money, what could I think of myself now, when I was got about a thousand leagues farther off from home, and perfectly destitute of all manner of prospect of return? All we had for it was this, that in about four months' time there was to be another fair at the place where we were, and then we might be able to purchase all sorts of the manufactures of the country, and withal might possibly find some Chinese junks or vessels from Tonquin, that would be to be sold, and would carry us and our goods whither we pleased. This I liked very well, and resolved to wait; besides, as our particular persons were not obnoxious, so if any English or Dutch ships came thither, perhaps we might have an opportunity to load our goods, and get passage to some other place in India, nearer home. Upon these hopes we resolved to continue here; but, to divert ourselves, we took two or three journeys into the country. First, we went ten days' journey, to the city of Nanquin, a city well worth seeing, indeed; they say it has a million of people in it: it is regularly built, the streets all exactly straight, and cross one another in direct lines, which gives the figure of it great advantage. But when I come to compare the miserable people of these countries with ours, their fabrics, their manner of living, their government, their wealth, and their glory, as some call it, I must confess that I scarcely think it worth my while to mention them here. It is very observable, that we wonder at the grandeur, the riches, the pomp, the ceremonies, the government, the manufac-

turers, the commerce, and conduct of these people; not that it is to be
wondered at, or, indeed, in the least to be regarded, but because having a
true notion of the barbarity of those countries, the rudeness and the ignorance that prevails there, we do not expect to find any such thing so far
off. Otherwise, what are their buildings to the palaces and royal buildings of Europe? What their trade to the universal commerce of England,
Holland, France, and Spain? What are their cities to ours, for wealth,
strength, gaiety of apparel, rich furniture, and infinite variety? What are
their ports, supplied with a few junks and barks, to our navigation, our
merchant fleets, our large and powerful navies? Our city of London has
more trade than half their mighty empire: one English, Dutch, or French
man-of-war of eighty guns, would be able to fight almost all the shipping belonging to China: but the greatness of their wealth, their trade,
the power of their government, and the strength of their armies, may be
a little surprising to us; because, as I have said, considering them as a
barbarous nation of pagans, little better than savages, we did not expect
such things among them. And this, indeed, is the advantage with which
all their greatness and power is represented to us; otherwise, it is in itself
nothing at all: for what I have said of their ships may be said of their
armies and troops: all the forces of their empire, though they were to
bring two millions of men into the field together, would be able to do
nothing but ruin the country, and starve themselves, if they were to besiege a strong town in Flanders, or to fight a disciplined army. One good
line of German cuirassiers, or of French cavalry, might withstand all the
horse of China: a million of their foot could not stand before one em-
battled body of our infantry, posted so as not to be surrounded, though
they were not to be one to twenty in number: nay, I do not boast if I say
that thirty thousand German or English foot, and ten thousand horse,
well managed, could defeat all the forces of China. And so of our fortified towns, and of the art of our engineers in assaulting and defending
towns: there is not a fortified town in China could hold out one month
against the batteries and attacks of an European army; and, at the same
time, all the armies of China could never take such a town as Dunkirk,
provided it was not starved—no, not in a ten years' siege. They have
fire-arms, it is true, but they are awkward and uncertain in their going
off: and their powder has but little strength. Their armies are badly disciplined, and want skill to attack, or temper to retreat; and, therefore, I
must confess, it seemed strange to me, when I came home, and heard our
people say such fine things of the power, glory, magnificence, and trade
of the Chinese; because, as far as I saw, they appeared to be a contemptible herd or crowd of ignorant sordid slaves, subjected to a government
qualified only to rule such a people: and were not its distance inconceiv-
ably great from Muscovy, and the Muscovite empire in a manner as
rude, impotent, and ill governed as they, the Czar of Muscovy might
with ease drive them all out of their country, and conquer them in one

campaign: and had the Czar (who is now a growing prince) fallen this way, instead of attacking the warlike Swedes, and equally improved himself in the art of war, as they say he has done; and if none of the powers of Europe had envied or interrupted him, he might by this time have been emperor of China, instead of being beaten by the king of Sweden at Narva, when the latter was not one to six in number. As their strength and their grandeur, so their navigation, commerce, and husbandry are very imperfect, compared to the same things in Europe; also in their knowledge, their learning, and in their skill in the sciences, they are either very awkward or defective, though they have globes and spheres, and a smattering of the mathematics, and think they know more than all the world besides; but they know little of the motions of the heavenly bodies; and so grossly and absurdly ignorant are their common people, that when the sun is eclipsed, they think a great dragon has assaulted it, and is going to run away with it; and they fall a clattering with all the drums and kettles in the country, to fright the monster away, just as we do to hive a swarm of bees.

As this is the only excursion of the kind which I have made in all the accounts I have given of my travels, I shall make no more such: it is none of my business, nor any part of my design; but to give an account of my own adventures through a life of inimitable wanderings, and a long variety of changes, which, perhaps, few that come after me will have heard the like of: I shall therefore say very little of all the mighty places, desert countries, and numerous people I have yet to pass through, more than relates to my own story, and which my concern among them will make necessary.

I WAS now, as near as I can compute, in the heart of China, about thirty degrees north of the line, for we were returned from Nanquin: I had, indeed, a mind to see the city of Peking, which I had heard so much of, and Father Simon importuned me daily to do it. At length his time of going away being set, and the other missionary who was to go with him being arrived from Macao, it was necessary that we should resolve either to go or not; so I referred it wholly to my partner, and left it wholly to his choice, who at length resolved it in the affirmative; and we prepared for our journey. We set out with very good advantage as to finding the way, for we got leave to travel in the retinue of one of their Mandarins, a kind of viceroy or principal magistrate in the province where they reside, and who take great state upon them, travelling with great attendance, and with great homage from the people, who are sometimes greatly impoverished by them, being obliged to furnish provisions for them and all their attendants in their journeys. That which I particularly observed, as to our travelling with his baggage, was this, that though we received sufficient provisions both for ourselves and our horses from the country, as belonging to the Mandarin, yet we were obliged to pay for everything we had after the market price of the country, and the Mandarin's steward collected it duly from us; so that our travelling in the retinue of the Mandarin, though it was a very great kindness to us, was not such a mighty favour in him, but was a great advantage to him, considering there were about thirty other people travelled in the same manner besides us, under the protection of his retinue; for the country furnished all the provisions for nothing to him, and yet he took our money for them.

We were twenty-five days travelling to Peking, through a country infinitely populous, but I think badly cultivated; the husbandry, the economy, and the way of living miserable, though they boast so much of the industry of the people: I say miserable, if compared with our own, but not so to these poor wretches, who know no other. The pride of the people is infinitely great, and exceeded by nothing but their poverty, in some parts, which adds to that which I call their misery; and I must needs think the naked savages of America live much more happily than the poorest sort of these, because as they have nothing, so they desire nothing: whereas these are proud and insolent, and in the main are in many parts mere beggars and drudges; their ostentation is inexpressible; and, if they can, they love to keep multitudes of servants or slaves, which is to the last degree ridiculous, as well as the contempt of all the world but themselves.

I must confess, I travelled more pleasantly afterwards in the deserts and vast wildernesses of Grand Tartary than here; and yet the roads here are well paved and well kept, and very convenient for travellers; but nothing was more awkward to me than to see such a haughty, imperious, insolent people, in the midst of the grossest simplicity and ignorance; and my friend Father Simon and I used to be very merry upon these occasions, to see the beggarly pride of these people. For example, coming by the house of a country gentleman, as Father Simon called him, about ten leagues off the city of Nanquin, we had first of all the honour to ride with the master of the house about two miles; the state he rode in was a perfect Don Quixotism, being a mixture of pomp and poverty. His habit was very proper for a scaramouch, or merry-andrew, being a dirty calico, with hanging sleeves, tassels, and cuts and slashes almost on every side: it covered a taffety vest, as greasy as a butcher's, and which testified that his honour must be a most exquisite sloven. His horse was but a poor, starved, hobbling creature, and he had two slaves follow him on foot to drive the poor creature along; he had a whip in his hand, and he belaboured the beast as fast about the head as his slaves did about the tail; and thus he rode by us, with about ten or twelve servants, going from the city to his country seat, about half a league before us. We travelled on gently, but this figure of a gentleman rode away before us; and as we stopped at a village about an hour to refresh us, when we came by the country seat of this great man, we saw him in a little place before his door, eating his repast. It was a kind of a garden, but he was very easy to be seen; and we were given to understand that the more we looked at him the better he would be pleased. He sat under a tree, something like the palmetto, which effectually shaded him over the head, and on the south side; but under the tree was also placed a large umbrella, which made that part look well enough. He sat lolling back in a great elbow-chair, being a heavy corpulent man, and had his meat brought him by two women slaves; he had two more, one of which fed the squire with a spoon, and the other held the dish with one hand, and scraped off what he let fall upon his worship's beard and taffety vest with the other; while the great fat brute thought it below him to employ his own hands in any of those familiar offices, which kings and monarchs would rather do than be troubled with the clumsy fingers of their servants.

I took this time to think what pains men's pride put them to, and how troublesome a haughty temper, thus ill managed, must be to a man of common sense; and leaving the poor wretch to please himself with our looking at him, as if we admired his pomp, though we really pitied and contemned him, we pursued our journey; only Father Simon had the curiosity to stay to inform himself what dainties the country justice had to feed on in all his state, which he had the honour to taste of, and which was, I think, a mess of boiled rice, with a great piece of garlic in it, and a little bag filled with green pepper, and another plant which they have there, something like our ginger, but smelling like musk, and tasting like mustard; all this was put together, and a small piece of lean mutton boiled in it, and this was his worship's repast; four or five servants more attended at a distance, who, we supposed, were to eat of the same after their master.

As for our Mandarin with whom we travelled, he was respected as a king, surrounded always with his gentlemen, and attended in all his appearances with such pomp, that I saw little of him but at a distance; but this I observed, that there was not a horse in his retinue but that our carrier's pack-horses in England seemed to me to look much better; though it was hard to judge rightly, for they were so covered with equipage, mantles, trappings, etc., that we could scarce see anything but their feet and the heads as they went along.

I was now light-hearted, and all my trouble and perplexity that I have given an account of being over, I had no anxious thought about me, which made this journey the pleasanter to me; nor had I any ill accident attend me, only in passing or fording a small river my horse fell, and made me free of the country, as they call it, that is to say, threw me in; the place was not deep, but it wetted me all over. I mention it, because it spoiled my pocket-book, wherein I had set down the names of several people and places which I had occasion to remember, and which, not taking due care of, the leaves rotted, and the words were never after to be read, to my great loss as to the names of some places I touched at in this journey.

At length we arrived at Peking: I had nobody with me but the youth whom my nephew the captain had given me to attend me as a servant, and who proved very trusty and diligent; and my partner had nobody with him, but one servant, who was a kinsman. As for the Portuguese pilot, he being desirous to see the court, we bore his charges for his company, and to use him as an interpreter, for he understood the language of the country, and spoke good French, and a little English; and, indeed, this old man was a most useful implement to us everywhere: for we had not been above a week at Peking, when he came laughing, Ah, Senhor Inglese, says he, I have something to tell you will make your heart glad! —My heart glad! says I; what can that be? I don't know anything in this country can either give me joy or grief, to any great degree.—Yes, yes, said the old man, in broken English, make you glad, me sorry.—Why, said I, will it make you sorry?—Because, said he, you have brought me here twenty-five days' journey, and will leave me to go back alone, and which way shall I get to my port afterwards without a ship, without a horse, without *pecune:* so he called money, being his broken Latin, of which he had abundance to make us merry with. In short, he told us there was a great caravan of Muscovite and Polish merchants in the city, preparing to set out on their journey by land to Muscovy, within four or five weeks, and he was sure we would take the opportunity to go with them, and leave him behind to go back alone.

I confess I was greatly surprised with this good news, and had scarce power to speak to him for some time; but at last I turned to him, How do you know this? said I. Are you sure it is true?—Yes, says he: I met this morning in the street an old acquaintance of mine, an Armenian, who is among them: he came last from Astracan, and was designing to go to Tonquin, where I formerly knew him, but has altered his mind, and is now resolved to go with the caravan to Moscow, and so down the river Wolga to Astracan.—Well, senhor, says I, do not be uneasy about being left to go back alone; if this be a method for my return to England, it shall be your fault if you go back to Macao at all. We then went to consult together what was to be done; and I asked my partner what he thought of the pilot's news, and whether it would suit with his affairs. He told me he would do just as I would; for he had settled all his affairs so well at Bengal, and left his effects in such good hands, that as we had made a good voyage here, if he could vest it in China silks, wrought and raw, such as might be worth the carriage, he would be content to go to England, and then make his voyage back to Bengal by the Company's ships.

Having resolved upon this, we agreed that if our Portuguese pilot would go with us, we would bear his charges to Moscow, or to England, if he pleased; nor, indeed, were we to be esteemed over generous in that neither, if we had not rewarded him farther, the service he had done us being really worth more than that: for he had not only been a pilot to us at sea, but he had been like a broker for us on shore; and his procuring for us the Japan merchant was some hundreds of pounds in our pockets. So we consulted together about it, and being willing to gratify him, which was but doing him justice, and very willing also to have him with us besides, for he was a most necessary man on all occasions, we agreed to give him a quantity of coined gold, which, as I compute it, came to about one hundred and seventy-five pounds sterling, between us, and to bear all his charges, both for himself and horse, except only a horse to carry his goods. Having settled this between ourselves, we called him to let him know what we had resolved. I told him he had complained of our being to let him go back alone, and I was now to tell him we were resolved he should not go back at all; that as we had resolved to go to Europe with the caravan, we resolved also he should go with us; and that we called him to know his mind. He shook his head, and said, it was a long journey, and he had no *pecune* to carry him thither, or to subsist himself when he came there. We told him we believed it was so, and therefore we had resolved to do something for him that should let him see how sensible we were of the service he had done us, and also how agreeable he was to us: and then I told him what we had resolved to give him here, which he might lay out as we would do our own; and that as for his charges, if he would go with us we would set him safe on shore (life and casualties excepted) either in Muscovy or England, which he would at our own charge, except only the carriage of his goods. He received the proposal like a man transported, and told us he would go with us over the whole world; and so we all prepared for our journey. However, as it was with us, so it was with the other merchants: they had many things to do; and instead of being ready in five weeks, it was four months and some days before all things were got together.

It was the beginning of February, our style, when we set out from Peking. My partner and the old pilot had gone express back to the port where we had first put in, to dispose of some goods which we had left there; and I, with a Chinese merchant whom I had some knowledge of at Nanquin, and who came to Peking on his own affairs, went to Nanquin, where I bought ninety pieces of fine damasks, with about two hundred pieces of other very fine silks of several sorts, some mixed with gold, and had all these brought to Peking against my partner's return; besides this, we bought a very large quantity of raw silk, and some other goods, our cargo amounting, in these goods only, to about three thousand five hundred pounds sterling; which, together with tea, and some fine calicoes, and three camels' loads of nutmegs and cloves, loaded in all eighteen camels for our share, besides those we rode upon; which, with two or three spare horses, and two horses loaded with provisions, made us, in short, twenty-six camels and horses in our retinue.

The company was very great, and, as near as I can remember, made between three and four hundred horse, and upwards of one hundred and twenty men, very well armed, and provided for all events: for as the Eastern caravans are subject to be attacked by the Arabs, so are these by the Tartars; but they are not altogether so dangerous as the Arabs, nor so barbarous, when they prevail.

The company consisted of people of several nations; but there were above sixty of them merchants or inhabitants of Moscow, though of them some were Livonians: and to our particular satisfaction, five of them were Scots, who appeared also to be men of great experience in business, and of very good substance.

When we had travelled one day's journey, the guides, who were five in number, called all the gentlemen and merchants, that is to say, all the passengers except the servants, to a great council as they called it. At this council every one deposited a certain quantity of money to a common stock, for the necessary expense of buying forage on the way, where it was not otherwise to be had, and for satisfying the guides, getting horses, and the like: and here they constituted the journey, as they called it, viz., they named captains and officers to draw us all up, and give the word of command, in case of an attack, and give every one their turn of command; nor was this forming us into order any more than what we found needful upon the way, as shall be observed.

The road on all sides of the country is very populous, and is full of potters and earth-makers, that is to say, people that temper the earth for the China-ware; and as I was coming along, our Portugal pilot, who had always something or other to say to make us merry, came sneering to me, and told me he would show me the greatest rarity in all the country, and that I should have this to say of China, after all the ill-humoured things I had said of it, that I had seen one thing which was not to be seen in all the world beside. I was very importunate to know what it was: at last he told me it was a gentleman's house built with China-ware. Well, says I, are not the materials of their buildings the product of their own country, and so it is all China-ware, is it not?—No, no, says he, I mean it is a house all made of China-ware, such as you call it in England, or, as it is called in our country, porcelain.—Well, says I, such a thing may be; how big is it? Can we carry it in a box upon a camel? If we can, we will buy it.—

Upon a camel! says the old pilot, holding up both his hands; why there is a family of thirty people lives in it.

I was then curious, indeed, to see it; and when I came to it, it was nothing but this: it was a timber house, or a house built, as they call it in England, with lath and plaster; but all this plastering was really China-ware, that is to say, it was plastered with the earth that makes China-ware. The outside, which the sun shone hot upon, was glazed, and looked very well, perfectly white, and painted with blue figures, as the large China-ware in England is painted, and hard as if it had been burned. As to the inside, all the walls instead of wainscot, were lined with hardened and painted tiles, like the little square tiles we call galley-tiles in England, all made of the finest China, and the figures exceeding fine, indeed, with extraordinary variety of colors, mixed with gold, many tiles making but one figure, but joined so artificially, the mortar being made of the same earth, that it was very hard to see where the tiles met. The floors of the rooms were of the same composition, and as hard as the earthen floors we have in use in several parts of England; as hard as stone, and smooth, but not burned and painted, except some smaller rooms, like closets, which were all as it were paved with the same tile: the ceiling, and all the plastering work in the whole house, were of the same earth; and, after all, the roof was covered with tiles of the same, but of a deep shining black. This was a China-ware house, indeed, truly and literally to be called so, and had I not been upon a journey, I could have stayed some days to see and examine the particulars of it. They told me there were fountains and fishponds in the garden, all paved on the bottom and sides with the same; and fine statues set up in rows on the walks, entirely formed of the porcelain earth, and burned whole.

As this is one of the singularities of China, so they may be allowed to excel in it; but I am very sure they excel in their accounts of it; for they told me such incredible things of their performance in crockery-ware, for such it is, that I care not to relate, as knowing it could not be true. They told me, in particular, of one workman that made a ship with all its tackle, and masts and sails, in earthen-ware, big enough to carry fifty men. If they had told me he launched it, and made a voyage to Japan in it, I might have said something to it, indeed; but as it was, I knew the whole of the story, which was, in short, asking pardon for the word, that the fellow lied: so I smiled, and said nothing to it.

This odd sight kept me two hours behind the caravan, for which the leader of it for the day fined me about the value of three shillings: and told me, if it had been three days' journey without the wall, as it was three days' within, he must have fined me four times as much, and made me ask pardon the next council day: I promised to be more orderly; and, indeed, I found afterwards the orders made for keeping all together were absolutely necessary for our common safety.

In two days more we passed the great China wall, made for a fortification against the Tartars: and a very great work it is, going over hills and mountains in a needless track, where the rocks are impassable, and the precipices such as no enemy could possibly enter, or indeed climb up, or where, if they did, no wall could hinder them. They tell us its length is near a thousand English miles, but that the country is five hundred in a straight measured line, which the wall bounds, without measuring the windings and turnings it takes: it is about four fathoms high, and as many thick in some places.

I stood still an hour, or thereabout, without trespassing our orders (for so long the caravan was in passing the gate), to look at it on every side, near and far off, I mean that was within my view; and the guide of our caravan, who had been extolling it for the wonder of the world, was mighty eager to hear my opinion of it. I told him it was a most excellent thing to keep out the Tartars; which he happened not to understand as I meant it, and so took it for a compliment; but the old pilot laughed: O, Senhor Inglese, says he, you speak in colours.—In colours! said I; what do you mean by that?—Why, you speak what looks white this way, and black that way: gay one way, and dull another. You tell him it is a good wall to keep out Tartars; you tell me by that it is good for nothing but to keep out Tartars. I understand you, Senhor Inglese; I understand you, but Senhor Chinese understood you his own way.—Well, says I, senhor, do you think it would stand out an army of our country people, with a good train of artillery, or our engineers, with two companies of miners? Would not they batter it down in ten days, that an army might enter a battalia; or blow it up in the air, foundation and all, that there should be no sign of it left? —Ay, ay, says he, I know that. The Chinese wanted mightily to know what I said, and I gave him leave to tell him a few days after, for we were then almost out of their country, and he was to leave us in a little time after this; but when he knew what I said, he was dumb all the rest of the way, and we heard no more of his fine story of the Chinese power and greatness while he stayed.

After we passed this mighty nothing, called a wall, something like the Picts' wall, so famous in Northumberland, built by the Romans, we began to find the country thinly inhabited, and the people rather confined to live in fortified towns and cities, as being subject to the inroads and depredations of the Tartars, who rob in great armies, and therefore are not to be resisted by the naked inhabitants of an open country. And here I began to find the necessity of keeping together in a caravan as we travelled, for we saw several troops of Tartars roving about; but when I came to see them distinctly, I wondered more that the Chinese empire should be conquered by such contemptible fellows; for they are a mere horde of wild fellows, keeping no order, and understanding no discipline or manner of fight. Their horses are poor lean creatures, taught nothing, and fit for nothing; and this we found the first day we saw them, which was after we entered the wilder part of the country. Our leader for the day gave leave for about sixteen of us to go a hunting, as they call it, and what was this but hunting of sheep: however, it may be called hunting too, for the creatures are the wildest and swiftest of foot that ever I saw of their kind; only they will not run a great way, and you are sure of sport when you begin the chase, for they appear generally thirty or forty in a flock, and, like true sheep, always keep together when they fly.

In pursuit of this odd sort of game, it was our hap to meet with about forty Tartars; whether they were hunting mutton as we were, or whether they looked for another kind of prey, we know not; but as soon as they saw us, one of them blew a kind of horn very loud, but with a barbarous sound that I had never heard before, and, by the way, never care to hear again: we all supposed this was to call their friends about them, and so it was; for in less than ten minutes a troop of forty or fifty more appeared at about a mile distance; but our work was over first, as it happened.

One of the Scots merchants of Moscow happened to be amongst us, and as soon as he heard the horn he told us that we had nothing to do but to charge them immediately, without loss of time; and drawing us up in a line, he asked if we were resolved. We told him we were ready to follow him; so he rode directly towards them. They stood gazing at us like a mere crowd, drawn up in no order, nor showing the face of any order at all; but as soon as they saw us advance, they let fly their arrows, which, however, missed us very happily: it seems they mistook not their aim, but their distance; for their arrows all fell a little short of us, but with so true an aim, that had we been about twenty yards nearer, we must have had several men wounded, if not killed.

Immediately we halted, and though it was at a great distance, we fired, and sent them leaden bullets for wooden arrows, following our shot full gallop, to fall in among them sword in hand, for so our bold Scot that led us directed. He was, indeed, but a merchant, but he behaved with such vigour and bravery on this occasion, and yet with such cool courage too, that I never saw any man in action fitter for command. As soon as we came up to them, we fired our pistols in their faces, and then drew; but they fled in the greatest confusion imaginable. The only stand any of them made was on our right, where three of them stood, and, by signs, called the rest to come back to them, having a kind of scimitar in their hands, and their bows hanging to their backs. Our brave commander, without asking anybody to follow him, gallops up close to them, and with his fusee knocks one of them off his horse, killed the second with his pistol, and the third ran away; and thus ended our fight: but we had this misfortune attending it, that all our mutton we had in chase got away. We had not a man killed or hurt; but as for the Tartars, there were about five of them killed; how many were wounded we knew not; but this we knew, that the other party were so frightened with the noise of our guns, that they made off, and never made any attempt upon us.

We were all this while in the Chinese dominions, and therefore the

Tartars were not so bold as afterwards: but in about five days we entered a vast, great, wild desert, which held us three days and nights' march; and we were obliged to carry our water with us in great leathern bottles, and to encamp all night, just as I have heard they do in the desert of Arabia.

I asked our guides whose dominion this was in; and they told me this was a kind of border, that might be called no man's land, being a part of Great Karakathay, or Grand Tartary; but, however, it was all reckoned as belonging to China, but, that there was no care taken here to preserve it from the inroads of thieves, and therefore it was reckoned the worst desert in the whole march, though we were to go over some much larger.

In passing this wilderness, which was at first very frightful to me, we saw, two or three times, little parties of the Tartars, but they seemed to be upon their own affairs, and to have no design upon us; and so, like the man who met the devil, if they had nothing to say to us, we had nothing to say to them; we let them go. Once, however, a party of them came so near as to stand and gaze at us; whether it was to consider if they should attack us or not, we knew not; but when we were passed at some distance by them, we made a rear guard of forty men, and stood ready for them, letting the caravan pass half a mile or thereabouts before us: but after a while they marched off; only we found they saluted us with five arrows at their parting, one of which wounded a horse, so that it disabled him, and we left him, poor creature, in great need of a good farrier: they might shoot more arrows, which might fall short of us, but we saw no more arrows or Tartars that time.

We travelled near a month after this, the ways not being so good as at first, though still in the dominions of the emperor of China, but lay for the most part in villages, some of which were fortified, because of the incursions of the Tartars. When we were come to one of these towns (it was about two days and a half journey before we were to come to the city of Naum), I wanted to buy a camel, of which there are plenty to be sold all the way upon that road, and horses also, such as they are, because so many caravans coming that way, they are often wanted. The person that I spoke to get me a camel, would have gone and fetched one for me; but I, like a fool, must be officious, and go myself along with him: the place was about two miles out of the village, where it seems they kept the camels and horses feeding under a guard.

I walked it on foot, with my old pilot and a Chinese, being very desirous of a little variety. When we came to the place, it was a low marshy ground, walled round with a stone wall, piled up dry, without mortar or earth among it, like a park, with a little guard of Chinese soldiers at the door. Having bought a camel, and agreed for the price, I came away, and the Chinese man that went with me led the camel, when on a sudden came up five Tartars on horseback; two of them seized the fellow and took the camel from him, while the other three stepped up to me and my old pilot, seeing us, as it were, unarmed, for I had no weapon about me but my sword, which could but ill defend me against three horsemen. The first that came up stopped short upon my drawing my sword, for they are arrant cowards; but a second coming upon my left, gave me a blow on the head, which I never felt till afterwards, and wondered, when I came to myself, what was the matter, and where I was, for he laid me flat on the ground; but my never-failing old pilot, the Portuguese (so Providence, unlooked for, directs deliverances from dangers which to us are unforeseen), had a pistol in his pocket, which I knew nothing of, nor the Tartars neither; if they had, I suppose they would not have attacked us; but cowards are always boldest when there is no danger. The old man seeing me down, with a bold heart stepped up to the fellow that had struck me, and laying hold of his arm with one hand, and pulling him down by main force a little towards him with the other, shot him in the head, and laid him dead upon the spot. He then immediately stepped up to him who had stopped us, as I said, and before he could come forward again, made a blow at him with a scimitar which he always wore, but missing the man, cut his horse in the side of his head, cut one of the ears off, by the root, and a great slice down by the side of his face. The poor beast, enraged with the wound, was no more to be governed by his rider, though the fellow sat well enough too, but away he flew, and carried him quite out of the pilot's reach and at some distance, rising upon his hind legs, threw down the Tartar, and fell upon him.

In this interval, the poor Chinese came in who had lost the camel, but he had no weapon; however, seeing the Tartar down, and his horse fallen upon him, away he runs to him, and seizing upon an ugly ill-favoured weapon he had by his side, something like a pole-axe but not a pole-axe neither, he wrenched it from him, and made shift to knock his Tartarian brains out with it. But my old man had the third Tartar to deal with still; and seeing he did not fly, as he expected, nor come on to fight him, as he apprehended, but stood stock-still, the old man stood still too, and fell to work with his tackle, to charge his pistol again; but as soon as the Tartar saw the pistol, away he scoured, and left my pilot, my champion I called him afterward, a complete victory.

By this time I was a little recovered; for I thought when I first began to wake, that I had been in a sweet sleep; but, as I said above, I wondered where I was, how I came upon the ground, and what was the matter. But a few moments after, as sense returned, I felt pain, though I did not know where; so I clapped my hand to my head, and took it away bloody: then I felt my head ache; and then, in a moment, memory returned, and everything was present to me again. I jumped upon my feet instantly, and got hold of my sword, but no enemies in view: I found a Tartar lie dead, and his horse standing very quietly by him; and, looking further, I saw my champion and deliverer, who had been to see what the Chinese had done, coming back with his hanger in his hand: the old man, seeing me on my feet, came running to me, and embraced me with a great deal of joy, being afraid before that I had been killed; and seeing me bloody, would see how I was hurt: but it was not much, only what we call a broken head; neither did I afterwards find any great inconvenience from the blow, for it was well again in two or three days.

We made no great gain, however, by this victory, for we lost a camel and gained a horse; but that which was remarkable, when we came back to the village, the man demanded to be paid for the camel; I disputed it, and it was brought to a hearing before the Chinese judge of the place. To give him his due, he acted with a great deal of prudence and impartiality; and, having heard both sides, he gravely asked the Chinese man that went with me to buy the camel, whose servant he was? I am no servant, says he, but went with the stranger.—At whose request? says the justice. At the stranger's request, says he. Why, then, says the justice, you were the stranger's servant for the time; and the camel being delivered to his servant, it was delivered to him, and he must pay for it.

I confess the thing was so clear, that I had not a word to say: but, admiring to see such just reasoning upon the consequence, and an accurate stating of the case, I paid willingly for the camel, and sent for another; but, you may observe, I did not go to fetch it myself any more, for I had had enough of that.

The city of Naum is a frontier of the Chinese empire: they call it fortified, and so it is, as fortifications go there; for this I will venture to affirm, that all the Tartars in Karakathay, which, I believe, are some millions, could not batter down the walls with their bows and arrows; but to call it strong, if it were attacked with cannon, would be to make those who understand it laugh at you.

We wanted, as I have said, above two days' journey of this city, when messengers were sent express to every part of the road to tell all travellers and caravans to halt till they had a guard sent for them; for that an unusual body of Tartars, making ten thousand in all, had appeared in the way, about thirty miles beyond the city.

This was very bad news to travellers; however, it was carefully done of the governor, and we were very glad to hear we should have a guard. Accordingly two days after, we had two hundred soldiers sent us from a garrison of the Chinese, on our left, and three hundred more from the city of Naum, and with these we advanced boldly, the three hundred soldiers from Naum marched in our front, the two hundred in our rear, and our men on each side of our camels, with our baggage, and the whole caravan in the centre: in this order, and well prepared for battle, we thought ourselves a match for the whole ten thousand Mogul Tartars, if they had appeared; but the next day, when they did appear, it was quite another thing.

It was early in the morning, when, marching from a well situated little town, called Changu, we had a river to pass, which we were obliged to ferry; and, had the Tartars had any intelligence, then had been the time to have attacked us, when the caravan being over, the rear guard was behind, but they did not appear there. About three hours after, when we were entered upon a desert of about sixteen miles over, behold, by a cloud of dust they raised, we saw an enemy was at hand; and they were at hand, indeed, for they came on upon the spur.

The Chinese, our guard on the front, who had talked so big the day before, began to stagger; and the soldiers frequently looked behind them, which is a certain sign in a soldier that he is just ready to run away. My old pilot was of my mind; and, being near me, called out, Senhor Inglese, says he, those fellows must be encouraged, or they will ruin us all; for if the Tartars come on, they will never stand it.—I am of your mind, said I; but what must be done?—Done! says he, let fifty of our men advance, and flank them on each wing, and encourage them; and they will fight like brave fellows in brave company: but, without this, they will every man turn his back. Immediately I rode up to our leader, and told him, who was exactly of our mind: and accordingly fifty of us marched to the right wing, and fifty to the left, and the rest made a line of rescue; and so we marched, leaving the last two hundred men to make a body by themselves, and to guard the camels; only that, if need were, they should send a hundred men to assist the last fifty.

In a word, the Tartars came on, and an innumerable company they were: how many we could not tell, but ten thousand, we thought, was the least: a party of them came on first and viewed our posture, traversing the ground in the front of our line; and, as we found them within gun-shot, our leader ordered the two wings to advance swiftly, and give them a salvo on each wing with their shot, which was done; but they went off, and I suppose back, to give an account of the reception they were likely to meet with; and, indeed, that salute cloyed their stomachs, for they immediately halted, stood awhile to consider of it, and wheeling off to the left, they gave over their design, and said no more to us for that time; which was very agreeable to our circumstances, which were but very indifferent for a battle with such a number.

Two days after we came to the city of Naun, or Naum; we thanked the governor for his care of us, and collected to the value of a hundred crowns, or thereabouts, which he gave to the soldiers sent to guard us; and here we rested one day. This is a garrison, indeed, and there were nine hundred soldiers kept here; but the reason of it was, that formerly the Muscovite frontiers lay nearer to them than they now do, the Muscovites having abandoned that part of the country, which lies from this city west for about two hundred miles, as desolate and unfit for use; and more especially being so very remote, and so difficult to send troops thither for its defence: for we had yet above two thousand miles to Muscovy, properly so called.

After this we passed several great rivers, and two dreadful deserts;

one of which we were sixteen days passing over; and which, as I said, was to be called no man's land; and, on the 13th of April, we came to the frontiers of the Muscovite dominions. I think the first town, or fortress, whichever it may be called, that belonged to the Czar of Muscovy, was called Arguna, being on the west side of the river Arguna.

I could not but discover an infinite satisfaction that I was so soon arrived in, as I called it, a Christian country, or, at least in a country governed by Christians: for though the Muscovites do, in my opinion, but just deserve the name of Christians, yet such they pretend to be, and are very devout in their way. It would certainly occur to any man who travels the world as I have done, and who had any power of reflection, what a blessing it is to be brought into the world where the name of God and a Redeemer is known, adored and worshipped; and not where the people, given up by Heaven to strong delusions, worship the devil, and prostrate themselves to stocks and stones; worship monsters, elements, horrid-shaped animals, and statues or images of monsters. Not a town or city we passed through but had their pagodas, their idols, and their temples, and ignorant people worshipping even the works of their own hands. Now we came where, at least, a face of the Christian worship appeared; where the knee was bowed to Jesus; and whether ignorantly or not, yet the Christian religion was owned, and the name of the true God was called upon and adored, and it made my soul rejoice to see it. I saluted the brave Scots merchant I mentioned above with my first acknowledgment of this; and taking him by the hand, I said to him, Blessed be God, we are once again among Christians. He smiled, and answered, Do not rejoice too soon, countryman; these Muscovites are but an odd sort of Christians; and but for the name of it, you may see very little of the substance for some months farther of our journey. Well, says I, but still it is better than paganism and worshipping of devils.—Why, I will tell you, says he, except the Russian soldier in the garrisons, and a few of the inhabitants of the cities upon the road, all the rest of this country, for above a thousand miles farther, is inhabited by the worst and most ignorant of pagans: and so, indeed, we found it.

W E WERE now launched into the greatest piece of solid earth, if I under-
stand anything of the surface of the globe, that is to be found in any part
of the world; we had, at least, twelve thousand miles to the sea, eastward; two thousand to the bottom of the Baltic sea, westward; and
above three thousand, if we left that sea and went on west, to the British
and French channels; we had full five thousand miles to the Indian or
Persian sea, south; and about eight hundred to the Frozen sea, north.
Nay, if some people may be believed, there might be no sea, north-east,
till we came round the pole, and consequently into the north-west, and
so had a continent of land into America, the Lord knows where; though
I could give some reasons why I believed that to be a mistake.
    As we entered into the Muscovite dominions a good while before we
came to any considerable towns, we had nothing to observe there but
this: first, that all the rivers run to the east: as I understood by the chart,
which some in our caravan had with them, it was plain all those rivers
ran into the great river Yamour, or Amour; which river, by the natural
course of it, must run into the East sea, or Chinese Ocean. The story they
tell us, that the mouth of this river is choked up with bulrushes of a monstrous growth, viz., three feet about, and twenty or thirty feet high, I
must be allowed to say, I believe nothing of it; but, as its navigation is of
no use, because there is no trade that way, the Tartars, to whom it alone
belongs, dealing in nothing but cattle, so nobody, that ever I heard of,
has been curious enough either to go down to the mouth of it in boats,
or come up from the mouth of it in ships, as far as I can find: but this is
certain, that this river running east, in the latitude of about fifty degrees, carries a vast concourse of rivers along with it, and finds an ocean
to empty itself in that latitude: so we are sure of sea there.
    Some leagues to the north of this river there are several considerable
rivers, whose streams run as due north as the Yamour runs east, and
these are all found to join their waters with the great river Tartarus,
named so from the northernmost nations of the Mogul Tartars; who, as
the Chinese say, were the first Tartars in the world; and who, as our
geographers allege, are the Gog and Magog mentioned in sacred story.
These rivers running all northward, as well as all the other rivers I am

yet to speak of, make it evident that the northern ocean bounds the land also on that side; so that it does not seem rational in the least to think that the land can extend itself to join with America on that side, or that there is not a communication between the northern and eastern ocean: but of this I shall say no more; it was my observation at that time, and therefore I take notice of it in this place.

We now advanced from the river Arguna by easy and moderate journeys, and were very visibly obliged to the care the Czar of Muscovy has taken to have cities and towns built in as many places as it is possible to place them, where his soldiers keep garrison, something like the stationary soldiers placed by the Romans in the remotest countries of their empire; some of which that I had read of were placed in Britain, for the security of commerce, and for the lodging travellers; and thus it was here: for wherever we came, though at these towns and stations the garrisons and governors were Russian and professed Christians, yet the inhabitants were mere pagans; sacrificing to idols, and worshipping the sun, moon, and stars, or all the host of heaven; and not only so, but were, of all the heathens and pagans that ever I met with, the most barbarous, except only that they did not eat men's flesh, as our savages of America did.

Some instances of this we met within the country between Arguna, where we enter the Muscovite dominions, and a city of Tartars and Russians together, called Nertzinskoi, in which is continued desert or forest, which cost us twenty days to travel over. In a village, near the last of these places, I had the curiosity to go and see their way of living, which is most brutish and insufferable; they had, I suppose, a great sacrifice that day; for there stood out, upon an old stump of a tree, an idol made of wood, frightful as the devil; at least, as anything we can think of to represent the devil can be made: it had a head not so much as resembling any creature that the world ever saw; ears as big as goats' horns, and as high; eyes as big as a crown piece; a nose like a crooked ram's horn, and a mouth extended four-cornered, like that of a lion, with horrible teeth, hooked like a parrot's under-bill: it was dressed up in the filthiest manner that you could suppose: its upper garment was of sheep-skins, with the wool outward; a great Tartar bonnet on the head, with two horns growing through it: it was about eight feet high, yet had no feet nor legs, nor any other proportion of parts.

This scarecrow was set up at the outer side of the village; and, when I came near to it, there were sixteen or seventeen creatures, whether men or women I could not tell, for they made no distinction by their habits, all lying flat upon the ground round this formidable block of shapeless wood: I saw no motion among them any more than if they had been all logs of wood, like the idol, and at first I really thought they had been so; but, when I came a little nearer, they started up upon their feet, and raised a howling cry, as if it had been so many deep-mouthed hounds, and walked away, as if they were displeased at our disturbing them. A little way off from the idol, and at the door of a tent or hut, made all of sheep-skins and cow-skins dried, stood three butchers,—I thought they were such: when I came nearer to them, I found they had long knives in their hands; and in the middle of the tent appeared three sheep killed, and one young bullock or steer. These, it seems, were sacrifices to that senseless log of an idol; the three men were priests belonging to it, and the seventeen prostrated wretches were the people who brought the offering, and were making their prayers to that stock.

I confess, I was more moved at their stupidity and brutish worship of a hobgoblin than ever I was at anything in my life; to see God's most glorious and best creature, to whom he had granted so many advantages, even by creation above the rest of the works of his hands, vested with a reasonable soul, and that soul adorned with faculties and capacities adapted both to honour his Maker, and be honoured by him, sunk and degenerated to a degree so very stupid as to prostrate itself to a frightful nothing, a mere imaginary object, dressed up by themselves, and made terrible to themselves by their own contrivance, adorned only with clouts and rags; and that this should be the effect of mere ignorance, wrought up into hellish devotion by the devil himself; who, envying to his Maker the homage and adoration of his creatures, had deluded them into such sordid and brutish things as one would think should shock nature itself!

But what signified all the astonishment and reflection of thoughts: thus it was, and I saw it before my eyes, and there was no room to wonder at it, or think it impossible: all my admiration turned to rage, and I rode up to the image or monster, call it what you will, and with my sword made a stroke at the bonnet that was on its head, and cut it in two; and one of our men that was with me took hold of the sheep-skin that covered it, and pulled at it; when, behold, a most hideous outcry and howling ran through the village, and two or three hundred people came about my ears, so that I was glad to scour for it, for we saw some had bows and arrows; but I resolved from that moment to visit them again.

Our caravan rested three nights at the town, which was about four miles off, in order to provide some horses which they wanted, several of the horses having been lamed and jaded with the badness of the way, and the long march over the last desert; so we had some leisure here to put my design in execution. I communicated my design to the Scots merchant of Moscow, of whose courage I had sufficient testimony: I told him what I had seen, and with what indignation I had since thought that human nature could be so degenerate; I told him, if I could get but four or five men well armed, to go with me, I was resolved to go and destroy that vile, abominable idol, and let them see that it had no power to help itself; and consequently could not be an object of worship, or to be prayed to, much less help them that offered sacrifices to it.

He laughed at me:—says he, Your zeal may be good, but what do

you propose to yourself by it?—Propose! said I; to vindicate the honour
of God, which is insulted by this devil-worship.—But how will it vindicate the honour of God, said he, while the people will not be able to
know what you mean by it, unless you could speak to them, and tell
them so? And then they will fight you, and beat you too, I'll assure you;
for they are desperate fellows, and that especially in defence of their
idolatry.—Can we not, said I, do it in the night, and then leave them the
reasons and the causes in writing in their own language?—Writing! said
he; why, there is not a man in five nations of them that knows anything
of a letter, or how to read a word any way.—Wretched ignorance! said
I to him: however, I have a great mind to do it; perhaps nature may
draw inferences from it to them, to let them see how brutish they are to
worship such horrid things.—Look you, sir, said he, if your zeal prompts
you to it so warmly, you must do it; but, in the next place, I would have
you consider, these wild nations of people are subjected by force to the
Czar of Muscovy's dominion, and you do this, it is ten to one but they
will come by thousands to the governor of Nertzinskoi, and demand
satisfaction; and if he cannot give them satisfaction, it is ten to one but
they revolt; and it will occasion a new war with all the Tartars in the
country.

This, I confess, put new thoughts into my head for awhile, but I
harped upon the same string still; and all that day I was uneasy to put
my project in execution. Towards the evening the Scots merchant met
me by accident in our walk about the town, and desired to speak with
me: I believe, said he, I have put you off your good design; I have been
a little concerned about it since: for I abhor idolatry as much as you can
do.—Truly, said I, you have put it off a little, as to the execution of it,
but you have not put it out of my thoughts; and I believe I shall do it
before I quit this place, though I were to be delivered up to them for
satisfaction.—No, no, said he, God forbid they should deliver you up to
such a crew of monsters! They shall not do that neither; that would be
murdering you indeed.—Why, said I, how would they use me?—Use
you! said he, I'll tell you how they served a poor Russian, who affronted
them in their worship, just as you did, and whom they took prisoner,
after they had lamed him with an arrow, that he could not run away:
they took him and stripped him stark-naked, and set him upon the top
of the idol-monster, and stood all round him, and shot as many arrows
into him as would stick over his whole body, and then they burnt him,
and all the arrows sticking in him, as a sacrifice to the idol.—And was
this the same idol? said I. Yes, said he, the very same.—Well, said I, I will
tell you a story. So I related the story of our men at Madagascar, and
how they burnt and sacked the village there, and killed man, woman,
and child, for their murdering one of our men, just as it is related before;
and I added, that I thought we ought to do so to this village.

He listened very attentively to the story; but when I talked of doing so to that village, he said, You mistake very much; it was not this village, it was almost a hundred miles from this place; but it was the same idol, for they carry him about in procession all over the country.— Well, said I, then that idol ought to be punished for it; and it shall, said I, if I live this night out.

In a word, finding me resolute, he liked the design, and told me I should not go alone, but he would go with me, but he would go first and bring a stout fellow, one of his countrymen, to go also with us: and one, said he, as famous for his zeal as you can desire any one to be against such devilish things as these. In a word, he brought me his comrade, a Scotsman, whom he called Captain Richardson; and gave him a full account of what I had seen, and also what I intended; and he told me readily, he would go with me if it cost him his life. So we agreed to go, only we three. I had, indeed, proposed it to my partner, but he declined it. He said, he was ready to assist me to the utmost, and upon all occasions, for my defence; but this was an adventure quite out of his way: so, I say, we resolved upon our work, only we three and my man-servant, and to put it in execution that night about midnight, with all the secrecy imaginable.

However, upon second thoughts, we were willing to delay it till the next night, because, the caravan being to set forward in the morning, we supposed the governor could not pretend to give them any satisfaction upon us when we were out of his power. The Scots merchant, as steady in his resolution for the enterprise as bold in executing, brought me a Tartar's robe or gown of sheep-skins, and a bonnet, with a bow and arrows, and had provided the same for himself and his countryman, that the people, if they saw us, should not determine who we were.

All the first night we spent in mixing up some combustible matter with aqua vitæ, gunpowder, and such other materials as we could get; and, having a good quantity of tar in a little pot, about an hour after night we set out upon our expedition.

We came to the place about eleven o'clock at night, and found that the people had not the least jealousy of danger attending their idol. The night was cloudy; yet the moon gave us light enough to see that the idol stood just in the same posture and place that it did before. The people seemed to be all at their rest; only, that in the great hut, or tent, as we called it, where we saw the three priests whom we mistook for butchers, we saw a light, and going up close to the door, we heard people talking as if there were five or six of them; we concluded, therefore, that if we set wildfire to the idol, these men would come out immediately, and run up to the place to rescue it from the destruction that we intended for it; and what to do with them we knew not. Once we thought of carrying it away and setting fire to it at a distance, but when we came to handle it, we found it too bulky for our carriage; so we were at a loss again. The second Scotsman was for setting fire to the tent or hut, and knocking the creatures that were there on the head, when they came out; but I could not join with that; I was against killing them, if it were possible to avoid it. Well, then, said the Scots merchant, I will tell you what we will do: we will try to make them prisoners, tie their hands, and make them stand and see their idol destroyed.

As it happened, we had twine or packthread enough about us, which we used to tie our firelocks all together with: so we resolved to attack these people first, and with as little noise as we could. The first thing we did, we knocked at the door, when, one of the priests coming to it, we immediately seized upon him, stopped his mouth, and tied his hands behind him, and led him to the idol, where we gagged him that he might not make a noise, tied his feet also together, and left him on the ground.

Two of us then waited at the door, expecting that another would come out, to see what the matter was: but we waited so long till the third man came back to us; and then nobody coming out, we knocked again gently, and immediately out came two more, and we served them just in the same manner, but were obliged to go all with them, and lay them down by the idol some distance from one another; when, going back, we found two more were come out to the door, and a third stood behind them within the door. We seized the two, and immediately tied them, when the third stepping back, and crying out, my Scots merchant went in after him; taking out a composition we had made, that would only smoke and stink, he set fire to it and threw it in among them: by that time the other Scotsman and my man, taking charge of the two men already bound, and tied together also by the arm, led them away to the idol, and left them there to see if their idol would relieve them, making haste back to us.

When the furze we had thrown in had filled the hut with so much smoke that they were almost suffocated, we then threw in a small leather bag of another kind, which flamed like a candle, and following it in, we found there were but four people, and, as we supposed, had been about some of their diabolical sacrifices. They appeared, in short, frightened to death, at least so as to sit trembling and stupid, and not able to speak neither, for the smoke.

In a word, we took them, bound them as we had done the others, and all without any noise. I should have said we brought them out of the house, or hut, first; for indeed we were not able to bear the smoke any more than they were. When we had done this, we carried them all together to the idol: when we came there we fell to work with him; and first we daubed him all over, and his robes also, with tar, and such other stuff as we had, which was tallow mixed with brimstone: then we stopped his eyes and ears and mouth full of gunpowder; then we wrapped up a great piece of wildfire in his bonnet; and then sticking all the combustibles we had brought with us upon him, we looked about to see if we could find anything else to help to burn him; when my Scotsman remembered that by the tent, or hut, where the men were, there lay a heap of dry forage, whether straw or rushes I do not remember; away he and the other Scotsman ran and fetched their arms full of that. When we had done this, we took all our prisoners, and brought them, having untied their feet and ungagged their mouths, and made them stand up, and set them before their monstrous idol, and then set fire to the whole.

We stayed by it a quarter of an hour, or thereabouts, till the powder in the eyes and mouth and ears of the idol blew up, and, as we could perceive, had split and deformed the shape of it: and, in a word, till we saw it burned into a mere block or log of wood; and setting dry forage to it, we found it would be soon quite consumed; so we began to think of going away: but the Scotsman said, No, we must not go, for these poor deluded wretches will all throw themselves into the fire, and burn themselves with the idol. So we resolved to stay till the forage was burnt down too, and then came away and left them.

After the feat was performed, we appeared in the morning among our fellow travellers, exceeding busy in getting ready for our journey; nor could any man suggest that we had been anywhere but in our beds, as travellers might be supposed to be, to fit themselves for the fatigues of the day's journey.

But the affair did not end so: the next day came a great number of the country people to the town gates, and in a most outrageous manner demanded satisfaction of the Russian governor for the insulting their priests, and burning their Cham Chi-Thaungu. The people of Nertzinskoi were at first in a great consternation, for they said the Tartars were already no less than thirty thousand strong. The Russian governor sent out messengers to appease them, and gave them all the good words imaginable; assuring them that he knew nothing of it, and that there had not a soul in his garrison been abroad, so that it could not be from anybody there; but if they could let him know who did it, they should be exemplarily punished. They returned haughtily, that all the country reverenced the great Cham Chi-Thaungu, who dwelt in the sun, and no mortal would have dared to offer violence to his image but some Christian miscreant; and they therefore resolved to denounce war against him and all the Russians, who, they said, were miscreants and Christians.

The governor, still patient, and unwilling to make a breach, or to have any cause of war alleged to be given by him, the Czar having strictly charged them to treat the conquered country with gentleness and civility, gave them still all the good words he could. At last he told them there was a caravan gone towards Russia that morning, and perhaps it was some of them who had done them this injury; and that if they would be satisfied with that, he would send after them to inquire into it. This seemed to appease them a little; and accordingly the governor sent after us, and gave us a particular account how the thing was; intimating withal, that if any in our caravan had done it, they should make their escape; but that, whether we had done it or no, we should make all the haste forward that was possible; and that, in the mean time, he would keep them in play as long as he could.

This was very friendly in the governor: however, when it came to the caravan, there was nobody knew anything of the matter; and as for us that were guilty, we were least of all suspected. However, the captain of the caravan for the time took the hint that the governor gave us, and we travelled two days and two nights without any considerable stop, and then we lay at a village called Plothus: nor did we make any long stop here, but hastened on towards Jarawena, another of the Czar of Muscovy's colonies, and where we expected we should be safe. But upon the second day's march from Plothus, by the clouds of dust behind us at a great distance, some of our people began to be sensible we were pursued. We had entered a great desert, and had passed by a great lake called Schaks Oser, when we perceived a very great body of horse appear on the other side of the lake, to the north, we travelling west. We observed they went away west, as we did, but had supposed we would have taken that side of the lake, whereas we very happily took the south side; and in two days more they disappeared again: for they, believing we were still before them, pushed on till they came to the river Udda, a very great river when it passes farther north, but when we came to it we found it narrow and fordable.

The third day, they had either found their mistake, or had intelligence of us, and came pouring in upon us towards the dusk of the evening. We had, to our great satisfaction, just pitched upon a place for our camp, which was very convenient for the night; for as we were upon a desert, though but at the beginning of it, that was above five hundred miles over, we had no towns to lodge at, and, indeed, expected none but the city Jarawena, which we had yet two days' march to: the desert, however, had some few woods in it on this side, and little rivers, which ran all into the great river Udda; it was in a narrow strait, between little but very thick woods, that we pitched our little camp for that night, expecting to be attacked before morning.

Nobody knew but ourselves what we were pursued for: but as it was usual for the Mogul Tartars to go about in troops in that desert, so the caravans always fortify themselves every night against them, as against armies of robbers; and it was therefore no new thing to be pursued.

But we had this night, of all the nights of our travels, a most advantageous camp; for we lay between two woods, with a little rivulet running just before our front, so that we could not be surrounded, or attacked any way but in our front or rear. We took care also to make our front as strong as we could, by placing our packs, with our camels and horses, all in a line on the inside of the river, and felling some trees in our rear.

In this posture we encamped for the night; but the enemy was upon us before we had finished our situation. They did not come on us like thieves, as we expected, but sent three messengers to us, to demand the men to be delivered to them that had abused their priests, and burned their god Cham Chi-Thaungu with fire, that they might burn them with fire; and upon this, they said, they would go away, and do us no further harm, otherwise they would destroy us all. Our men looked very blank at this message, and began to stare at one another, to see who looked with the most guilt in their faces; but, nobody was the word; nobody did it. The leader of the caravan sent word he was well assured that it was not done by any of our camp; that we were peaceable merchants, travelling on our business; that we had done no harm to them or to any one else; and that, therefore, they must look farther for their enemies who had injured them, for we were not the people; so desired them not to disturb us, for, if they did, we should defend ourselves.

They were far from being satisfied with this for an answer; and a great crowd of them came running down in the morning by break of day, to our camp; but seeing us in such an unaccountable situation, they durst come no farther than the brook in our front, where they stood, and showed us such a number that indeed terrified us very much: for those that spoke least of them spoke of ten thousand. Here they stood and looked at us awhile, and then setting up a great howl, they let fly a crowd of arrows among us; but we were well enough fortified for that, for we sheltered under our baggage, and I do not remember that one of us was hurt.

Some time after this, we saw them move a little to our right, and expected them on the rear; when a cunning fellow, a Cossack of Jarawena, in the pay of the Muscovites, calling to the leader of the caravan, said to him, I'll go send all these people away to Siheilka: this was a city four or five days' journey at least to the right, and rather behind us. So he takes his bow and arrows, and getting on horseback, he rides away from our rear directly, as it were back to Nertzinskoi; after this, he takes a great circuit about, and comes directly on the army of the Tartars, as if he had been sent express to tell them a long story, that the people who had burned the Cham Chi-Thaungu were gone to Siheilka, with a caravan of miscreants, as he called them, that is to say, Christians; and that they had resolved to burn the god Schal-Isar, belonging to the Tongueses.

As this fellow was himself a mere Tartar, and perfectly spoke their language, he counterfeited so well, that they all took it from him, and away they drove in a most violent hurry to Siheilka, which, it seems, was five days' journey to the north; and in less than three hours they were entirely out of our sight, and we never heard any more of them, nor whether they went to Siheilka or no. So we passed away safely on to Jarawena, where there was a garrison of Muscovites, and there we rested five days, the caravan being exceedingly fatigued with the last day's hard march, and with want of rest in the night.

From this city we had a frightful desert, which held us twenty-three days' march. We furnished ourselves with some tents here, for the better accommodating ourselves in the night; and the leader of the caravan procured sixteen carriages, or waggons of the country, for carrying our water or provisions; and these carriages were our defence, every night, round our little camp; so that had the Tartars appeared, unless they had been very numerous indeed, they would not have been able to hurt us.

We may well be supposed to want rest again after this long journey: for in this desert we neither saw house nor tree, and scarce a bush; though we saw abundance of the sable-hunters, who are all Tartars of the Mogul Tartary, of which this country is a part; and they frequently attack small caravans, but we saw no numbers of them together.

After we had passed this desert, we came into a country pretty well inhabited; that is to say, we found our towns and castles, settled by the Czar of Muscovy, with garrisons of stationary soldiers, to protect the caravans, and defend the country against the Tartars, who would otherwise make it very dangerous travelling; and his czarish majesty has given such strict orders for the well guarding the caravans and merchants, that if there are any Tartars heard of in the country, detachments of the garrisons are always sent to see the travellers safe from station to station. And thus the governor of Adinskoy, whom I had an opportunity to make a visit to, by means of the Scots merchant, who was acquainted with him, offered us a guard of fifty men, if we thought there was any danger, to the next station.

I thought, long before this, that as we came nearer to Europe we should find the country better inhabited, and the people more civilised; but I found myself mistaken in both: for we had yet the nation of the Tongueses to pass through, where we saw the same tokens of paganism and barbarity as before; only as they were conquered by the Muscovites, they were not so dangerous; but for rudeness of manners and idolatry, no people in the world ever went beyond them: they are clothed all in skins of beasts, and their houses are built of the same; you know not a man from a woman, neither by the ruggedness of their countenances nor their clothes; and in the winter, when the ground is covered with snow, they live underground in vaults, which have cavities going from one to another.

If the Tartars had their Cham Chi-Thaungu for a whole village or country, these had idols in every hut and every cave; besides, they worship the stars, the sun, the water, the snow, and, in a word, everything they do not understand, and they understand but very little; so that every element, every uncommon thing, sets them a sacrificing. I met with nothing peculiar to myself in all this country, which I reckon was, from the desert I spoke of last, at least four hundred miles, half of it being another desert, which took us up twelve days' severe travelling, without house or tree; and we were obliged again to carry our own provisions, as well water as bread. After we were out of this desert, and had travelled two days, we came to Janezay, a Muscovite city or station on the great river Janezay (Yemsey), which, they told us there, parted Europe from Asia.

Here I observed ignorance and paganism still prevailed, except in the Muscovite garrisons; all the country between the river Oby and the river Janezay is as entirely pagan, and the people as barbarous, as the remotest of the Tartars; nay, as any nation, for aught I know, in Asia or America. I also found, which I observed to the Muscovite governors whom I had an opportunity to converse with, that the poor pagans are not much wiser, or near Christianity, for being under the Muscovite government; which they acknowledged was true enough: but that, as they said, was none of their business; that if the Czar expected to convert his Siberian, Tonguese, or Tartar subjects, it should be done by sending clergymen among them, not soldiers: and, they added, with more sincerity than I expected, that they found it was not so much the concern of their monarch to make the people Christians as it was to make them subjects.

From this river to the great river Oby, we crossed a wild uncultivated country, barren of people and good management; otherwise it is in itself a most pleasant, fruitful, and agreeable country. What inhabitants we found in it are all pagans, except such as are sent among them from Russia: for this is the country, I mean on both sides the river Oby, whither the Muscovite criminals that are not put to death are banished, and from whence it is next to impossible they should ever come away.

I have nothing to say of my particular affairs till I came to Tobolski, the capital city of Siberia, where I continued some time on the following occasion.

We had now been almost seven months on our journey, and winter began to come on apace; whereupon my partner and I called a council about our particular affairs, in which we found it proper, as we were bound for England, and not for Moscow, to consider how to dispose of ourselves. They told us of sledges and reindeer to carry us over the snow in the winter time; and, indeed, they have such things that it would be incredible to relate the particulars of, by which means the Russians travel more in the winter than they can in summer, as in these sledges they are able to run night and day; the snow being frozen, is one universal covering to nature, by which the hills, vales, rivers, and lakes are all smooth and hard as a stone, and they run upon the surface, without any regard to what is underneath.

But I had no occasion to push at a winter journey of this kind; I was bound to England, not to Moscow, and my route lay two ways: either I must go on as the caravan went, till I came to Jaroslaw, and then go off west for Narva, and the gulf of Finland, and so to Dantzic, where I might possibly sell my China cargo to good advantage; or I must leave the caravan at a little town on the Dwina, from whence I had but six days by water to Archangel, and from thence might be sure of shipping either to England, Holland, or Hamburgh.

Now, to go any of these journeys in the winter would have been preposterous: for as to Dantzic, the Baltic would have been frozen up, and I could not get passage; and to go by land in those countries was far less safe than among the Mogul Tartars: likewise, to go to Archangel in October, all the ships would be gone from thence, and even the merchants who dwell there in summer retire south to Moscow in the winter, when the ships are gone; so that I could have nothing but extremity of cold to encounter, with a scarcity of provisions, and must lie in an empty town all the winter: so that, upon the whole, I thought it much my better way to let the caravan go, and make provision to winter where I was, at Tobolski, in Siberia, in the latitude of about sixty degrees, where I was sure of three things to wear out a cold winter with, viz., plenty of provisions, such as the country afforded, a warm house, with fuel enough, and excellent company.

I was now in a quite different climate from my beloved island, where I never felt cold, except when I had my ague; on the contrary, I had much to do to bear any clothes on my back, and never made any fire but without doors, which was necessary for dressing my food, etc. Now I made me three good vests, with large robes or gowns over them, to hang down to the feet, and button close to the wrists; and all these lined with furs, to make them sufficiently warm.

As to a warm house, I must confess I greatly disliked our way in England of making fires in every room in the house in open chimneys, which, when the fire was out, always kept the air in the room cold as the climate; but taking an apartment in a good house in the town, I ordered a chimney to be built like a furnace, in the centre of six several rooms, like a stove; the funnel to carry the smoke went up one way, the door to come at the fire went in another, and all the rooms were kept equally warm, but no fire seen, just as they heat the bagnios in England. By this means, we had always the same climate in all the rooms, and an equal heat was preserved; and how cold soever it was without, it was always warm within: and yet we saw no fire, nor were ever incommoded with smoke.

The most wonderful thing of all was, that it should be possible to meet with good company here, in a country so barbarous as that of the most northerly parts of Europe, near the frozen ocean, within but a very few degrees of Nova Zembla. But this being the country where the state criminals of Muscovy, as I observed before, are all banished, this city was full of noblemen, gentlemen, soldiers, and courtiers of Muscovy. Here was the famous prince Gallitzen, the old general Robostiski, and several other persons of note, and some ladies. By means of my Scots merchant, whom, nevertheless, I parted with here, I made an acquaintance with several of these gentlemen; and from these, in the long winter nights in which I stayed here, I received several very agreeable visits.

It was talking one night with Prince ——, one of the banished ministers of state belonging to the Czar of Muscovy, that the discourse of my particular case began. He had been telling me abundance of fine things of the greatness, the magnificence, the dominions, and the absolute power of the emperor of the Russians: I interrupted him, and told him I was a greater and more powerful prince than even the Czar of Muscovy was, though my dominions were not so large, or my people so many. The Russian grandee looked a little surprised, and fixing his eyes steadily upon me, began to wonder what I meant. I told him his wonder would cease when I had explained myself. First, I told him I had absolute disposal of the lives and fortunes of all my subjects; that, notwithstanding my absolute power, I had not one person disaffected to my government, or to my person, in all my dominions. He shook his head at that, and said, There, indeed, I outdid the Czar of Muscovy. I told him that all the lands in my kingdom were my own, and all my subjects were not only my tenants, but tenants at will; that they would all fight for me to the last drop; and that never tyrant, for such I acknowledged myself to be, was ever so universally beloved, and yet so horribly feared by his subjects.

After amusing him with these riddles in government for a while, I opened the case, and told him the story at large of my living in the island; and how I managed both myself and the people that were under me, just as I have since minuted it down. They were exceedingly taken with the story, and especially the prince, who told me with a sigh, that the true greatness of life was to be masters of ourselves; that he would not have exchanged such a state of life as mine to be Czar of Muscovy; and that he found more felicity in the retirement he seemed to be banished to there, than ever he found in the highest authority he enjoyed in the court of his master the Czar; that the height of human wisdom was to bring our tempers down to our circumstances, and to make a calm within, under the weight of the greatest storms without. When he came first hither, he said he used to tear the hair from his head, and the clothes from his back, as others had done before him; but a little time and consideration had made him look into himself, as well as round him, to things without: that he found the mind of man, if it was but once brought to reflect upon the state of universal life, and how little this world was concerned in its true felicity, was perfectly capable of making a felicity for itself, fully satisfying to itself, and suitable to its own best ends and desires, with but very little assistance from the world: the air to breathe in, food to sustain life, clothes for warmth, and liberty for exercise, in order to health, completed, in his opinion, all that the world could do for us; and though the greatness, the authority, the riches, and the pleasures which some enjoyed in the world, had much in them that was agreeable to us, yet all those things chiefly gratified the coarsest of our affections, such as our ambition, our particular pride, avarice, vanity, and sensuality; all which, being the mere product of the worst part of man, were in themselves crimes, and had in them the seeds of all manner of crimes; but neither were related to, nor concerned with, any of those virtues that constituted us wise men, or of those graces that distinguished us as Christians; that being now deprived of all the fancied felicity which he enjoyed in the full exercise of all those vices, he said he was at leisure to look upon the dark side of them, where he found all manner of deformity, and was now convinced that virtue only makes a man truly wise, rich, and great, and preserves him in the way to a superior happiness in a future state; and in this, he said, they were more happy in their banishment than all their enemies were, who had the full possession of all the wealth and power they had left behind them. Nor, sir, says he, do I bring my mind to this politically, by the necessity of my circumstances, which some call miserable; but, if I know anything of myself, I would not now go back, though the Czar my master should call me, and reinstate me in all my former grandeur; I say, I would no more go back to it than I believe my soul, when it shall be delivered from this prison of the body, and has had a taste of the glorious state beyond life, would come back to the gaol of flesh and blood it is now enclosed in, and leave heaven, to deal in the dirt and crime of human affairs.

He spoke this with so much warmth in his temper, so much earnestness and motion of his spirits, that it was evident it was the true sense of his soul; there was no room to doubt his sincerity. I told him I once thought myself a kind of monarch in my old station, of which I had given him an account; but that I thought he was not only a monarch, but a great conqueror; for that he that has got a victory over his own exorbitant desires, and the absolute dominion over himself, whose reason entirely governs his will, is certainly greater than he that conquers a city. But, my lord, said I, shall I take the liberty to ask you a question?—With all my heart, says he. If the door of your liberty was opened, said I, would you not take hold of it to deliver you from this exile?—Hold, said he, your question is subtle, and requires some serious, just distinctions, to give it a sincere answer; and I will give it you from the bottom of my heart. Nothing that I know of in this world, would move me to deliver myself from this state of banishment, except these two; first, the enjoyment of my relations; and, secondly, a little warmer climate: but I protest to you that to go back to the pomp of the court, the glory, the power, the hurry of a minister of state; the wealth, the gaiety, and the pleasures of a courtier; if my master should send me word this moment that he restores to me all he banished me from, I protest, if I know myself at all, I would not leave this wilderness, these deserts, and these frozen lakes, for the palace at Moscow.—But, my lord, said I, perhaps you not only are banished from the pleasures of the court, and from the power, authority, and wealth you enjoyed before, but you may be absent too from some of the conveniences of life; your estate, perhaps, confiscated, and your effects plundered; and the supplies left you here may not be suitable to the ordinary demands of life.—Ay, says he, that is as you suppose me to be a lord, or a prince, etc.; so, indeed, I am; but you are now to consider me only as a man, a human creature, not at all distinguished from another; and so I can suffer no want, unless I should be visited with sickness and distempers. However, to put the question out of dispute, you see our manner: we are, in this place, five persons of rank; we live perfectly retired, as suited to a state of banishment; we have something rescued from the shipwreck of our fortunes, which keeps us from the mere necessity of hunting for food; but the poor soldiers, who are here without that help, live in as much plenty as we, who go into the woods and catch sables and foxes: the labouring of a month will maintain them a year; and, as the way of living is not expensive, so it is not hard to get sufficient to ourselves. So that objection is out of doors.

I have not room to give a full account of the most agreeable conversation I had with this truly great man; in all which he showed that his mind was so inspired with a superior knowledge of things, so supported by religion, as well as by a vast share of wisdom, that his contempt of the world was really as much as he had expressed, and that he was always the same to the last, as will appear in the story I am going to tell.

I had been here eight months, and a dark, dreadful winter I thought it; the cold so intense that I could not so much as look abroad without being wrapped in furs, and a mask of fur before my face, or rather a hood, with only a hole for breath, and two for sight: the little daylight we had was, as we reckoned, for three months, not above five hours a day, and six at most; only that snow lying on the ground continually and the weather clear, it was never quite dark. Our horses were kept, or rather starved, underground, and as for our servants, whom we hired here to look after ourselves and horses, we had, every now and then, their fingers and toes to thaw and take care of, lest they should mortify and fall off.

It is true, within doors we were warm, the houses being close, the walls thick, the lights small, and the glass all double. Our food was chiefly the flesh of deer, dried and cured in the season; bread good enough, but baked as biscuits; dried fish of several sorts, and some flesh of mutton and of the buffaloes, which is pretty good meat. All the stores of provisions for the winter are laid up in the summer, and well cured: our drink was water, mixed with aqua vitæ instead of brandy; and for a treat, mead instead of wine, which, however, they have excellent good. The hunters, who venture abroad all weathers, frequently brought us in fine venison, and sometimes bear's flesh, but we did not much care for the last. We had a good stock of tea, with which we treated our friends, as above, and we lived very cheerfully and well, all things considered.

It was now March, the days grown considerably longer, and the weather at least tolerable; so the other travellers began to prepare sledges to carry them over the snow, and to get things ready to be going: but my measures being fixed, as I have said, for Archangel, and not for Muscovy or the Baltic, I made no motion; knowing very well that the ships from the south do not set out for that part of the world till May or June, and that if I was there by the beginning of August, it would be as soon as any ships would be ready to go away; and therefore I made no haste to be gone, as others did: in a word, I saw a great many people, nay, all the travellers, go away before me. It seems, every year they go from thence to Muscovy for trade, viz., to carry furs, and buy necessaries, which they bring back with them to furnish their shops: also others went on the same errand to Archangel; but then they all being to come back again, above eight hundred miles, went all out before me.

In the month of May I began to make all ready to pack up; and, as I was doing this, it occurred to me that, seeing all these people were banished by the Czar of Muscovy to Siberia, and yet, when they came there, were left at liberty to go whither they would, why they did not then go away to any part of the world, wherever they thought fit; and I began to examine what should hinder them from making such an attempt. But my wonder was over when I entered upon that subject with the person I have mentioned, who answered me thus: Consider, first, sir, said he, the place where we are; and, secondly, the condition we are in; especially the generality of the people who are banished hither. We are surrounded with stronger things than bars or bolts: on the north side an unnavigable ocean, where ship never sailed, and boat never swam; every other way, we have above a thousand miles to pass through the Czar's own dominions, and by ways utterly impassable, except by the roads made by the government, and through the towns garrisoned by his troops; so that we could neither pass undiscovered by the road, nor subsist any other way: so that it is in vain to attempt it.

I was silenced, indeed, at once, and found that they were in a prison every jot as secure as if they had been locked up in the castle at Moscow: however, it came into my thoughts that I might certainly be made an instrument to procure the escape of this excellent person; and that, whatever hazard I ran, I would certainly try if I could carry him off. Upon this I took an occasion, one evening, to tell him my thoughts. I represented to him that it was very easy for me to carry him away, there being no guard over him in the country; and as I was not going to Moscow, but to Archangel, and that I went in the retinue of a caravan, by which I was not obliged to lie in the stationary towns in the desert, but could encamp every night where I would, we might easily pass uninterrupted to Archangel, where I would immediately secure him on board

an English ship, and carry him safe along with me; and as to his subsistence, and other particulars, it should be my care, till he could better
supply himself.

He heard me very attentively, and looked earnestly on me all the while
I spoke; nay, I could see in his very face that what I said put his spirits
into an exceeding ferment: his colour frequently changed, his eyes looked
red, and his heart fluttered, that it might be even perceived in his countenance; nor could he immediately answer me when I had done, and as it
were hesitated what he would say to it: but after he had paused a little,
he embraced me, and said, How unhappy are we, unguarded creatures
as we are, that even our greatest acts of friendship are made snares unto
us, and we are made tempters of one another! My dear friend, said he,
your offer is so sincere, has such kindness in it, is so disinterested in itself,
and is so calculated for my advantage, that I must have very little knowledge of the world if I did not both wonder at it, and acknowledge the
obligation I have upon me to you for it. But did you believe I was sincere
in what I have often said to you of my contempt of the world? Did you
believe I spoke my very soul to you, and that I had really obtained that
degree of felicity here that had placed me above all that the world could
give me? Did you believe I was sincere when I told you I would not go
back, if I was recalled even to be all that I once was in the court, with
the favour of the Czar my master? Did you believe me, my friend, to be
an honest man; or did you believe me to be a boasting hypocrite? Here
he stopped, as if he would hear what I would say; but, indeed, I soon
after perceived that he stopped because his spirits were in motion, his
great heart was full of struggles, and he could not go on. I was, I confess,
astonished at the thing as well as at the man, and I used some arguments
with him to urge him to set himself free; that he ought to look upon this
as a door opened by Heaven for his deliverance, and a summons by
Providence who has the care and disposition of all events, to do himself
good, and to render himself useful in the world.

He had by this time recovered himself: How do you know, sir, says he,
warmly, but that, instead of a summons from Heaven, it may be a feint
of another instrument; representing in alluring colours to me the show
of felicity as a deliverance, which may in itself be my snare, and tend
directly to my ruin? Here I am free from the temptation of returning to
my former miserable greatness; there I am not sure but that all the seeds
of pride, ambition, avarice, and luxury, which I know remain in nature,
may revive and take root, and, in a word, again overwhelm me; and then
the happy prisoner, whom you see now master of his soul's liberty, shall
be the miserable slave of his own senses, in the full of all personal liberty.
Dear sir, let me remain in this blessed confinement, banished from the
crimes of life, rather than purchase a show of freedom at the expense of
the liberty of my reason, and at the future happiness which I now have
in my view, but shall then, I fear, quickly lose sight of: for I am but

flesh; a man, a mere man; have passions and affections as likely to pos-
sess and overthrow me as any man: O be not my friend and tempter
both together!

If I was surprised before, I was quite dumb now, and stood silent,
looking at him, and, indeed, admiring what I saw. The struggle in his
soul was so great, that though the weather was extremely cold, it put him
into a most violent sweat, and I found he wanted to give vent to his mind;
so I said a word or two, that I would leave him to consider of it, and
wait on him again, and then I withdrew to my own apartment.

About two hours after, I heard somebody at or near the door of my
room, and I was going to open the door, but he had opened it and came
in. My dear friend, says he, you had almost overset me, but I am recovered. Do not take it ill that I do not close with your offer; I assure
you it is not for want of sense or the kindness of it in you; and I came to
make the most sincere acknowledgment of it to you; but I hope I have
got the victory over myself.—My lord, said I, I hope you are fully satisfied that you do not resist the call of Heaven.—Sir, said he, if it had been
from Heaven, the same power would have influenced me to have accepted it: but I hope, and am fully satisfied, that it is from Heaven that I
declined it; and I have infinite satisfaction in the parting, that you shall
leave me an honest man still, though not a free man.

I had nothing to do but to acquiesce, and make professions to him of
my having no end in it but a sincere desire to serve him. He embraced me
very passionately, and assured me he was sensible of that, and should
always acknowledge it; and with that he offered me a very fine present of
sables, too much, indeed, for me to accept from a man in his circumstance, and I would have avoided them, but he would not be refused.

The next morning I sent my servant to his lordship with a small present of tea, and two pieces of China damask, and four little wedges of
Japan gold, which did not all weigh above six ounces or thereabout, but
were far short of the value of his sables, which, when I came to England,
I found worth near two hundred pounds. He accepted the tea, and one
piece of the damask, and one of the pieces of gold, which had a fine
stamp upon it, of the Japan coinage, which I found he took for the rarity
of it, but would not take any more; and he sent word by my servant that
he desired to speak with me.

When I came to him, he told me I knew what had passed between us,
and hoped I would not move him any more in that affair; but that, since
I had made such a generous offer to him, he asked me if I had kindness
enough to offer the same to another person that he would name to me, in
whom he had a great share of concern. I told him that I could not say
I inclined to do so much for any but himself, for whom I had a particular
value, and should have been glad to have been the instrument of his deliverance; however, if he would please to name the person to me, I would
give him my answer. He told me it was his only son: who, though I had

not seen him, yet he was in the same condition with himself, and above two hundred miles from him, on the other side the Oby; but that, if I consented, he would send for him.

I made no hesitation, but told him I would do it. I made some ceremony in letting him understand that it was wholly on his account; and that seeing I could not prevail on him, I would show my respect to him by my concern for his son: but these things are too tedious to repeat here. He sent away the next day for his son; and in about twenty days he came back with the messenger, bringing six or seven horses loaded with very rich furs, and which, in the whole, amounted to a very great value. His servants brought the horses into the town, but left the young lord at a distance till night, when he came incognito into our apartment, and his father presented him to me, and, in short, we concerted the manner of our travelling, and everything proper for the journey.

I had bought a considerable quantity of sables, black fox-skins, fine ermines, and such other furs as are very rich, in that city, in exchange for some of the goods I had brought from China: in particular for the cloves and nutmegs, of which I sold the greatest part here, and the rest afterward at Archangel, for a much better price than I could have got at London; and my partner, who was sensible of the profit, and whose business more particularly than mine was merchandise, was mightily pleased with our stay, on account of the traffick we made here.

It was the beginning of June when I left this remote place, a city, I believe little heard of in the world; and indeed, it is so far out of the road of commerce, that I know not how it should be much talked of. We were now reduced to a very small caravan, having only thirty-two horses and camels in all, and all of them passed for mine, though my new guest was proprietor of eleven of them; it was most natural also that I should take more servants with me than I had before; and the young lord passed for my steward; what great man I passed for myself I know not, neither did it concern me to inquire. We had here the worst and the largest desert to pass over that we met with in our whole journey: I call it worst, because the way was very deep in some places, and very uneven in others; the best we had to say for it was, that we thought we had no troops of Tartars or robbers to fear, and that they never came on this side the river Oby, or at least but very seldom; but we found it otherwise.

My young lord had a faithful Muscovite, or rather a Siberian servant, who was perfectly acquainted with the country, and led us by private roads, so that we avoided coming into the principal towns and cities upon the great road, such as Tumen, Soloy Kamskoi, and several others; because the Muscovite garrisons which are kept there are very curious and strict in their observation upon travellers, and searching lest any of the banished persons of note should make their escape that way into Muscovy; but by this means, as we were kept out of the cities, so our whole journey was a desert, and we were obliged to encamp and lie in our tents, when we might have had very good accommodation in the cities on the way: this the young lord was so sensible of, that he would not allow us to lie abroad when we came to several cities on the way, but lay abroad himself, with his servant, in the woods, and met us always at the appointed places.

We were just entered Europe, having passed the river Kama, which in these parts is the boundary between Europe and Asia, and the first city on the European side was called Soloy Kamskoi, which is as much as to say, the great city on the river Kama; and here we thought to see some evident alteration in the people; but we were mistaken: for as we had a vast desert to pass, which is near seven hundred miles long in some places, but not above two hundred miles over where we passed it, so, till we came past that horrible place, we found very little difference between that country and the Mogul Tartary: the people are mostly pagans, and little better than the savages of America; their houses and towns full of idols, and their way of living wholly barbarous, except in the cities, as above, and the villages near them, where they are Christians, as they call themselves, of the Greek church; but have their religion mingled with so many relics of superstition, that it is scarce to be known in some places from mere sorcery and witchcraft.

In passing this forest, I thought, indeed, we must (after all our dangers were to our imagination escaped, as before) have been plundered and robbed, and perhaps murdered, by a troop of thieves: of what country they were I am yet at a loss to know, but they were all on horseback, carried bows and arrows, and were at first about forty-five in number: they came so near to us as to be within two musket shots, and asking no questions, surrounded us with their horses, and looked very earnestly upon us twice: at length they placed themselves just in our way; upon which we drew up in a little line, before our camels, being not above sixteen men in all; and being drawn up thus, we halted, and sent out the Siberian servant, who attended his lord, to see who they were: his master was the more willing to let him go because he was not a little apprehensive that they were a Siberian troop sent out after him. The man came up near them with a flag of truce, and called to them; but though he spoke several of their languages, or dialects of languages rather, he could not understand a word they said: however, after some signs to him not to come nearer to them, at his peril, the fellow came back no wiser than he went; only that by their dress, he said, he believed them to be some Tartars of Kalmuck, or of the Circassian hordes, and that there must be more of them upon the great desert, though he had never heard that any of them were seen so far north before.

About an hour after, they again made a motion to attack us, and rode round our little wood to see where they might break in; but finding us always ready to face them, they went off again; and we resolved not to stir for that night.

This was small comfort to us; however, we had no remedy: there was on our left hand, at about a quarter of a mile distance, a little grove, and very near the road; I immediately resolved we should advance to those trees, and fortify ourselves as well as we could there; for, first, I considered that the trees would in a great measure cover us from their arrows; and, in the next place, they could not come to charge us in a body: it was, indeed, my old Portuguese pilot who proposed it, and who had this excellency attending him, that he was always readiest and most apt to direct and encourage us in cases of the most danger. We advanced immediately, with what speed we could, and gained that little wood; the Tartars, or thieves, for we knew not what to call them, keeping their stand, and not attempting to hinder us. When we came thither, we found to our great satisfaction, that it was a swampy piece of ground, and on the one side a very great spring of water, which running out in a little brook, was a little farther joined by another of the like size; and was, in short, the source of a considerable river called afterwards the Wirtska: the trees which grew about this spring were not above two hundred, but very large, and stood pretty thick, so that as soon as we got in we saw ourselves perfectly safe from the enemy, unless they attacked us on foot.

While we stayed here waiting the motion of the enemy some hours, without perceiving they made any movement, our Portuguese, with some help, cut several arms of trees half off, and laid them hanging across from one tree to another, and in a manner fenced us in. About two hours before night, they came down directly upon us; and though we had not perceived it, we found they had been joined by some more of the same, so that they were near fourscore horse; whereof, however, we fancied some were women. They came on till they were within half shot of our little wood, when we fired one musket without ball, and called to them in the Russian tongue to know what they wanted, and bade them keep off; but they came on with a double fury up to the woodside, not imagining we were so barricaded that they could not easily break in. Our old pilot was our captain, as well as our engineer, and desired us not to fire upon them till they came within pistol-shot, that we might be sure to kill; and that when we did fire, we should be sure to take good aim: we bade him give the word of command, which he delayed so long, that they were some of them within two pikes' length of us when we let fly. We aimed so true that we killed fourteen of them, and wounded several others, as also several of their horses; for we had all of us loaded our pieces with two or three bullets at least.

They were terribly surprised with our fire, and retreated immediately about one hundred rods from us, in which time we loaded our pieces again, and seeing them keep that distance, we sallied out, and catched four or five of their horses, whose riders we supposed were killed: and coming up to the dead, we judged they were Tartars, but knew not how they came to make an excursion of such an unusual length.

We slept little, you may be sure, but spent the most part of the night in strengthening our situation, and barricading the entrances into the wood, and keeping a strict watch. We waited for daylight, and when it came, it gave us a very unwelcome discovery, indeed; for the enemy, who we thought were discouraged with the reception they met with, were now greatly increased, and had set up eleven or twelve huts or tents, as if they were resolved to besiege us: and this little camp they had pitched upon the open plain, about three quarters of a mile from us. We were, indeed, surprised at this discovery; and now, I confess, I gave myself over for lost, and all that I had; the loss of my effects did not lie so near me, though very considerable, as the thoughts of falling into the hands of such barbarians, at the latter end of my journey, after so many difficulties and hazards as I had gone through, and even in sight of our port, where we expected safety and deliverance. As to my partner, he was raging, and declared that to lose his goods would be his ruin, and that he would rather die than be starved; and he was for fighting to the last drop.

The young lord, as gallant as ever flesh showed itself, was for fighting to the last also; and my old pilot was of the opinion that we were able to resist them all in the situation we were then in; and thus we spent the day in debates of what we should do; but towards evening we found that the number of our enemies still increased, and we did not know but by the morning they might be a still greater number; so I began to inquire of those people we had brought from Tobolski, if there were no private ways, by which we might avoid them in the night, and perhaps retreat to some town, or get help to guard us over the desert. The Siberian, who was servant to the young lord, told us, if we designed to avoid them, and not fight, he would engage to carry us off in the night, to a way that went north, towards the river Petrou, by which he made no question but we might get away, and the Tartars never the wiser; but, he said, his lord had told him he would not retreat, but would rather choose to fight. I told him he mistook his lord; for that he was too wise a man to love fighting for the sake of it; and that I knew his lord was brave enough, by what he had showed already; but that his lord knew better than to desire seventeen or eighteen men to fight five hundred, unless an unavoidable necessity forced them to it; and that, if he thought it possible for us to escape in the night, we had nothing else to do but to attempt it. He answered, if his lordship gave him such orders he would lose his life if he did not perform it: we soon brought his lord to give that order, though privately, and we immediately prepared for the putting it in practice.

And, first, as soon as it began to be dark, we kindled a fire in our little camp, which we kept burning, and prepared so as to make it burn all night, that the Tartars might conclude we were still there; but as soon as it was dark, and we could see the stars (for our guide would not stir before), having all our horses and camels ready loaded, we followed our new guide, who I soon found steered himself by the north star.

After we had travelled two hours very hard, it began to be lighter still; not that it was quite dark all night, but the moon began to rise, so that, in short, it was rather lighter than we wished it to be; but by six o'clock the next morning we were got above thirty miles, having almost spoiled our horses. Here we found a Russian village, named Kermazinskoy, where we rested, and heard nothing of the Kalmuck Tartars that day. About two hours before night we set out again, and travelled till eight the next morning, though not quite so hard as before; and about seven o'clock we passed a little river, called Kirtza, and came to a good large town inhabited by Russians, called Gzomoys: there we heard that several troops of Kalmucks had been abroad upon the desert, but that we were now completely out of danger of them, which was to our great satisfaction. Here we were obliged to get some fresh horses; and having need enough of rest, we stayed five days; and my partner and I agreed to give the honest Siberian who brought us thither the value of ten pistoles.

In five days more we came to Veuslima, upon the river Wirtzogda, and running into the Dwina: we were there, very happily, near the end of our travels by land, that river being navigable, in seven days' passage, to Archangel. From hence we came to Lawrenskoy the 3d of July; and providing ourselves with two luggage boats, and a barge for our own convenience, we embarked the 7th and arrived all safe at Archangel the 18th, having been a year, five months, and three days on the journey, including our stay of eight months at Tobolski. We were obliged to stay at this place six weeks for the arrival of the ships, and must have tarried longer, had not a Hamburgher come in above a month sooner than any of the English ships: when, after some consideration that the city of Hamburgh might happen to be as good a market for our goods as London, we all took freight with him; and, having put our goods on board, it was most natural for me to put my steward on board to take care of them: by which means my young lord had a sufficient opportunity to conceal himself, never coming on shore again all the time we stayed there; and this he did that he might not be seen in the city, where some of the Moscow merchants would certainly have seen and discovered him.

We then set sail from Archangel the 20th of August, the same year; and after no extraordinary bad voyage, arrived safe in the Elbe the 18th of September. Here my partner and I found a very good sale for our goods, as well those of China as the sables, etc., of Siberia; and dividing the produce, my share amounted to three thousand four hundred and seventy-five pounds seventeen shillings and threepence, including about six hundred pounds' worth of diamonds which I purchased at Bengal.

Here the young lord took his leave of us, and went up the Elbe, in order to go to the court of Vienna, where he resolved to seek protection, and could correspond with those of his father's friends who were left alive. He did not part without testimonies of gratitude for the service I had done him, and sense of my kindness to the prince his father.

To conclude, having stayed near four months in Hamburgh, I came from thence by land to the Hague, where I embarked in the packet, and arrived in London the 10th of January, 1705, having been absent from England ten years and nine months. And here I resolved to prepare for a longer journey than all these, having lived a life of infinite variety seventy-two years, and learned sufficiently to know the value of retirement, and the blessing of ending our days in peace.

About the Author

Daniel Defoe was born Daniel Foe in London in 1660. Though his father intended him for the ministry, Defoe set up in the hosiery trade. He traveled widely and became particularly expert in economic theory. A staunch supporter of William of Orange (William III), Defoe wrote pamphlets in support of his regime, but ran afoul of William's successor, Queen Anne, with the publication of his satire *The Shortest Way with the Dissenters* (1702), which landed him in Newgate Prison. Upon his release in 1704 he founded *The Review*, an important early newspaper that expressed the views and aspirations of the rising English commercial class. Defoe then turned to writing fictional works which he passed off as histories. The first and most successful of these, *Robinson Crusoe*, was published when Defoe was nearly sixty. A period of tremendous creativity followed, producing *A Journal of the Plague Year*, *Moll Flanders*, and *Roxana* within the next four years. He continued writing political and economic treatises, as well as travel books, for the rest of his life—over 250 attributed works in all. Defoe died in London in 1731.